Diversity and Society

I dedicate this book to my mother, Mrs. Alize T. Healey.

Diversity and Society
Race, Ethnicity, and Gender

Joseph F. Healey
Christopher Newport University

PINE FORGE PRESS
An Imprint of Sage Publications, Inc.
Thousand Oaks • London • New Delhi

For information:

 Pine Forge Press
A Sage Publications Company
2455 Teller Road
Thousand Oaks, California 91320
www.pineforge.com

Sage Publications Ltd.
6 Bonhill Street
London EC2A 4PU
United Kingdom

Sage Publications India Pvt. Ltd.
B-42, Panchsheel Enclave
Post Box 4109
New Delhi 110 017 India

Printed in the United States of America

Library of Congress Cataloging-in-Publication Data

Healey, Joseph F., 1945-
Diversity and society: Race, ethnicity, and gender / Joseph F. Healey.
      p. cm.
Rev. ed. of: Race, ethnicity, gender, and class. 3rd. ed. 2003.
Includes bibliographical references and index.
ISBN 0-7619-8805-X (paper)
   1. Minorities—United States. 2. Ethnicity—United States. 3. Racism—United States.
4. Group identity—United States. 5. Social conflict—United States. 6. United States—Race
relations. 7. United States—Ethnic relations. 8. United States—Social conditions. I. Healey,
Joseph F., 1945- Race, ethnicity, gender, and class. II. Title.
E184.A1H415 2004b
305.8'00973—dc21

                               2003011979

This book is printed on acid-free paper.

04   05   06   10   9   8   7   6   5   4   3   2

Acquisitions Editor:	Jerry Westby
Editorial Assistant:	Vonessa Vondera
Production Editor:	Denise Santoyo
Copy Editor:	A. J. Sobczak
Proofreader:	Desiree Dreeuws
Typesetter:	C&M Digitals (P) Ltd.
Cover Designer:	Michelle Lee Kenny

Contents

PART III

Understanding Dominant-Minority Relations in the United States Today   95

Preface

Of all the challenges confronting the United States today, those relating to minority groups continue to be among the most urgent and the most daunting. Discrimination and racial inequality are part of our national heritage and—along with equality, freedom, and justice—prejudice and racism are among our oldest values. Minority group issues penetrate every aspect of society, and virtually every item on the national agenda—welfare and health care reform, crime and punishment, safety in the streets, the future of the family, even defense spending, foreign policy, and the war on terrorism and the invasion of Iraq—has some connection with dominant-minority relations.

These issues will not be resolved easily or quickly: They are deep-rooted and consequential, and relatively few Americans seem willing to see them clearly or discuss them candidly. As a society, we have little hope of resolving these dilemmas unless we confront them openly and honestly. They will not simply disappear, and they will not resolve themselves. This textbook contributes to the discussion by presenting information, raising questions, and probing issues. My intent is to help students improve their knowledge and understanding of the issues and clarify their thinking regarding matters of race and ethnicity.

This text has been written for undergraduate students—sociology majors and nonmajors alike. It makes minimal assumptions about knowledge of history or sociological concepts, and the material is presented in a way that students will find accessible and coherent. For example, a unified set of themes and concepts is used throughout the text. The analysis is consistent and continuous, even while examining multiple perspectives and various points of view. The bulk of the conceptual framework is introduced in the first four chapters. These concepts and analytical themes are then used in a series of case studies of minority groups in contemporary America and in an investigation of group relations in various societies around the globe. In the final chapter, main points and themes are summarized and reviewed, the analysis is brought to a conclusion, and some speculations are made regarding the future.

The analysis is in the tradition of conflict theory, but this text does not aspire to a full presentation of that tradition. Other perspectives are introduced and applied, but no attempt is made to give equal attention to all current sociological paradigms. The text does not try to explain everything, nor does it attempt to include all possible analytical points of view. Rather, the goals are

1. To present the sociology of minority group relations in a way that students will find understandable as well as intellectually challenging.

2. To deal with the issues and tell the stories behind the issues in a textbook that is both highly readable and a demonstration of the power and importance of thinking sociologically. In particular, this text stresses a macrosociological approach. That is, the text emphasizes the larger processes, structures, and institutions that shape societal life, while still giving some attention to the more psychological or "micro" concepts such as prejudice.

3. To explore the diversity of experiences within each minority group, particularly

in the experiences of minority group males and females. Gender differences are explored for each minority group, and, in about half of the chapters, gender issues are highlighted in a special section.

4. To present the material in a broadly comparative frame of reference. The various American minority groups are continually compared with each other, and cross-national comparisons are presented in special sections in about half the chapters and in Chapter 10.

5. To stress the innumerable ways in which American minority groups are inseparable from American society. The relative success of this society is due no less to the contributions of minority groups than to those of the dominant group. The nature of the minority group experience has changed as the larger society has changed, and to understand America's minority groups is to understand some elemental truths about America. To raise the issues of race and ethnicity is to ask what it means, and what it has meant, to be an American.

This text is an abridged and updated version of *Race, Ethnicity, Gender, and Class: The Sociology of Group Conflict and Change* (3rd edition), also published by Pine Forge Press. The larger volume contains a number of additional features, greater detail, and more explanation and examples (particularly of individual prejudice and discrimination). This volume retains the case study approach and, most important, the conceptual framework for the analysis of group relations that was developed in the larger text.

A companion volume including readings and other features is available for this text. The readings are organized in chapters that parallel this text and are drawn from a variety of sources and represent a wealth of viewpoints. They were selected and edited to maximize student interest. The companion volume also includes "current debates" on such topics as affirmative action and immigration and narratives written by people who have personally experienced (and sometimes triumphed over) racism and discrimination. These "personal narratives" give a human face to the concepts that are at the core of sociological analysis.

Acknowledgments

All textbooks, even those with a single author's name on the title page, are profoundly collaborative efforts. This book has been shaped by more than 30 years of teaching minority relations and by the thoughts and reactions of hundreds of students. My approach to this subject has grown from years of "field testing" ideas, concepts, theory, and research and constant monitoring of what seemed to help students make sense of the world they live in. I acknowledge and thank my students for their myriad contributions.

When I was a student, I had the great good fortune of learning from faculty members who were both accomplished scholars and exceptionally dedicated teachers. Each of them contributed to my interest in and commitment to sociology, but two stand out in my memory as mentors and intellectual role models: Professors Edwin H. Rhyne and Charles S. Green. Dr. Rhyne encouraged me as a young scholar and quite literally introduced me to the world of ideas and the life of the mind. Later in my career, Dr. Green showed me what it means to be a professional scholar, a sociologist, and a teacher. Their influence on my life was profound, and I thank them deeply.

I am no less indebted to my colleagues Dr. Robert Durel, Lea Pellett, Virginia Purtle, and Michael Lewis of Christopher Newport University. They have been unflagging in their support of this project, and I thank them for their academic, logistical, and intellectual assistance. I would also like to thank Lynn Maycroft for her invaluable support and assistance, and Stacy Stratton for her help. Jerry Westby provided guidance and support on many levels, and I thank him deeply for his many contributions.

This text has benefited in innumerable ways from the reactions and criticisms of a group of reviewers who proved remarkably insightful about the subject matter and about the challenges of college teaching. I can no longer even estimate the number of points in the process of writing and research where the comments of the reviewers led to significant improvements in scholarship and clarity, and to more meaningful treatments of the subject. The shortcomings that remain are, of course, my responsibility, but whatever quality this text has is a direct result of the insights and expertise of these reviewers. I thank the following:

Rick Baldoz, University of Hawaii, Manoa

Jan Fiola, Minnesota State University Moorhead

David Lopez, California State University, Northridge

Peggy Lovell, University of Pittsburgh

Gonzalo Santos, California State University, Bakersfield

Carol Ward, Brigham Young University

For permission to reprint the chapter opening photos, grateful acknowledgment is made to the publishers and copyright holders.

Chapter 1: Circle of children, Roland Charles/The Black Gallery

Chapter 2: Chinese post office, Hulton, Archive Photos

Chapter 3: Slave poster, Copyright © Topham/The Image Works

Chapter 4: Melting pot migrant labor, Dorothea Lange Collection/The Oakland Museum

Chapter 5: March on Washington, Copyright © Steven Schapiro/Stockphoto.com

Chapter 6: Shawl Dance, Sarah Dent/Shooting Back Foundation

Chapter 7: Interstate pedestrians, Don Bartletti/Copyright ©1997, *Los Angeles Times,* reprinted with permission.

Chapter 8: Young Japanese evacuee, National Archives

Chapter 9: Americanization class, Library of Congress

Chapter11: Little dreamers, Jeffrey/The Black Gallery

Part I

An Introduction to the Study of Minority Groups in the United States

The United States is a nation of groups as well as individuals. These groups vary along a number of dimensions, including size, wealth, education, race, culture, religion, and language. Some of these groups have been part of American society since colonial days, and others have formed in the past few years.

How should all these groups relate to one another? Who should be considered American? Should we preserve the multitude of cultural heritages and languages that currently exist and stress our diversity? Or should we encourage everyone to adopt Anglo-American culture and strive to become more similar and unified? Should we emphasize our similarities or celebrate our differences? Is it possible to do both?

Questions of unity and diversity are among the most pressing in the United States today. In this text, we analyze these and many other questions. Our goal is to develop a broader, more informed understanding of the past and present forces that have created and sustained the groups that compose U.S. society. Part I introduces many of the important questions, concepts, and themes that will be developed and explored in later chapters.

1

Diversity in the United States
Questions and Concepts

What does it mean to be an American? Is the United States splintering into separate racial and ethnic groups? Is there a limit to the amount of diversity our society can tolerate? Should the number of immigrants entering the United States be reduced? Should Spanish become an official second language? Should multiculturalism be a part of the public school curriculum? Should everyone celebrate Black History Month?

These kinds of questions are crucial, but they are not new. Our past is punctuated with debates—often passionate and frequently violent—about unity and diversity, and the continuing controversies suggest that these issues are far from settled. Indeed, virtually every question that arises in the public

forum has some implication for group relations, and the recent high levels of immigration have re-energized concern for the integrity of American culture and the primacy of the English language. Today, as in the past, some argue that our diversity is a great strength, the fuel that propels American energy and creativity. Others, now as before, see our differences as a liability that saps our strength and weakens our solidarity. Does our multiplicity lead us forward or hold us back? Should we emphasize our unity or celebrate our diversity?

Relationships between the larger society and the myriad American minority groups remain a primary issue—perhaps *the* primary issue—in American life. What kind of society are we becoming? What *should* it mean to be

American? In the past, opportunity and success have been far more available to white Anglo-Saxon Protestant males than to members of other groups. Most Americans, even the favored males, would agree that this definition of American is far too narrow, but how inclusive should the definition be? How wide can the limits be stretched before national unity is threatened? How narrow can they be before the desire to preserve our distinct heritages is unjustly and unnecessarily stifled?

THE INCREASING VARIETY OF AMERICAN MINORITY GROUPS

The issues raised in the introductory paragraphs are especially urgent because America is in a period of increasing diversity, largely because of high rates of immigration. Over the past three decades, the number of immigrants arriving in the United States has more than tripled, rising from less than 300,000 a year to almost one million (U.S. Bureau of the Census, 2002, p. 10). The current wave of immigrants includes groups from all over the globe. Can our society deal successfully with this diversity of cultures, languages, and races?

The concerns sparked by immigration are compounded by a variety of long-standing, unresolved minority issues and grievances. Charts and graphs presented in Chapters 5 through 9 show persistent gaps in income, poverty rates, and other measures of affluence and equality between minority groups and national norms. In many ways, the problems and concerns of African Americans, Native Americans, Hispanic Americans, and Asian Americans today are just as formidable as they were a generation ago.

As one way of gauging the dimensions of diversity, consider the five groups listed in Exhibit 1.1. Before examining the size and growth patterns of these groups, consider the labels used to identify them. Although commonly used, the labels are arbitrary. None of these groups has clear or unambiguous boundaries, and they do not divide the U.S. population into homogeneous subunits. Two people selected from within any one of these categories might be as different from each other as any two people selected from

different categories. The people included in each category may share some physical or cultural traits, but they will also vary by social class, religion, gender, and in thousands of other ways. For example, people classified as Asians and Pacific Islanders represent scores of different national and linguistic backgrounds (Japanese, Samoans, Vietnamese, Pakistanis, and so forth), and the category "Native Americans, Eskimos, Aleuts" includes people from hundreds of different tribes and reservations. The groups named in Exhibit 1.1 appear frequently in government reports and in the professional literature of the social sciences, and, for the sake of convenience, the labels will be used in this text. We need to recognize, however, that the names are arbitrary conventions that should never be mistaken for unchanging or "natural" divisions.

Turning to the Exhibit itself, the relative sizes of the groups are presented for 1980 and 2000, and group sizes are estimated for two future dates. The increasing diversity of U.S. society is reflected in the declining predominance of non-Hispanic whites from 1980 through the middle of the 21st century. As the proportional share of white Americans declines, other groups will grow in relative size. Asian and Pacific Islander populations are projected to increase dramatically over the next half century, more than doubling their proportion of the total population. Hispanic Americans will also double their relative size. They already have surpassed African Americans and became the largest U.S. minority group in 2001 (Schmitt, 2001). Finally, African Americans and Native Americans will increase in numbers but will remain at roughly their present proportional share of the population.

The projections into the future are only educated guesses, but they presage profound change for the United States. Within the next five decades, the total percentage of minority group Americans will increase from less than 30% to almost 50%. Our society will grow more diverse racially, culturally, and linguistically. The United States will become less white, less European, and more like the world as a whole. Some see these changes as threats to traditional white middle-class American

Exhibit 1.1   Groups in American Society (percentage of total population)

	Actual		*Projected*	
	1980	*2000*	*2025*	*2050*
Non-Hispanic whites	80	72	62	53
African Americans	12	12	13	13
Native Americans, Eskimos, Aleuts	<1	<1	<1	<1
Asians and Pacific Islanders	2	4	6	9
Hispanic Americans	6	12	18	24
Total population	226,546,000	275,130,000	337,815,000	403,687,000

SOURCE: U.S. Bureau of the Census (2003c, p. 19).

values and lifestyles. Others see them as an opportunity for the emergence of other equally attractive and legitimate value systems.

Also note that, even though the categories in Exhibit 1.1 are broad, they do not provide a place for the growing numbers of Americans who come from multiple races and/or cultures. Between 1980 and 2000, the number of "mixed" marriages (i.e., those uniting people of different racial backgrounds and those uniting Hispanics with non-Hispanics) doubled in number (from 1.5 million to 3.2 million) as well as in the percentage of all marriages (from 3.1% to 5.7%) (U.S. Bureau of the Census, 2002, p. 47). The children of these marriages represent a small but growing group in American society. According to the 2000 U.S. Census, about 6.4 million people (2.3% of the total population) classified themselves in two racial or ethnic groups, and another 450,000 people claimed membership in three or more groups (U.S. Bureau of the Census, 2001a.). Obviously, the number of "mixed" Americans will continue to grow as the number of "mixed" marriages increases, and this group will assume an increasingly prominent role in the daily life of society.

THE GOALS OF THIS TEXT

These first few paragraphs have raised a lot of questions. The purpose of this text is to help you develop some answers and some thoughtful, informed positions on these issues, guided by the formidable demographic trends identified in the previous section and by a careful consideration of the issues and grievances of American minority groups. You should be aware from the beginning that the questions addressed here are complex and that the answers we seek are not obvious or easy. Indeed, there is no guarantee that we as a society will be able or willing to resolve all the problems of intergroup relations in the United States. However, we will never make progress in this area unless we confront the issues honestly and with an accurate base of knowledge and understanding. Certainly, these issues will not resolve themselves or disappear if they are ignored.

In the course of our investigation, we will rely on sociology and other social sciences for concepts, theory, and information. Our primary emphasis will be macrosociological. This means that we will emphasize the larger social structures (institutions, social classes) and large-scale social processes (group competition, assimilation) as opposed to more micro-level phenomena such as individual prejudice. Chapters 1 and 2 introduce and define many of the ideas that will guide our investigation. Chapters 3 and 4 explore how relations between the dominant group and minority groups have evolved in American society, using African Americans as a primary case study. Chapters 5–9 apply the concepts and theories developed in the first four chapters to the present situation of the major U.S. minority groups. In Chapter 10, we consider group relations in a number of other societies, and in the final chapter we summarize the analysis, reach some conclusions, and speculate about the future of group relations in our society.

WHAT IS A MINORITY GROUP?

Before we can begin to sort out the issues, we need common definitions and a common vocabulary for discussion. We begin with the term *minority group*. Taken literally, the mathematical connotation of this term is a bit misleading because it implies that minority groups are small. In reality, a minority group can be quite large and can even be a numerical majority of the population. Women, for example, are sometimes considered to be a separate minority group, but they are a numerical majority of the U.S. population. In South Africa, as in many nations created by European colonization, whites are a numerical minority (less than 30% of the population), but despite recent changes, they remain the most powerful and affluent group.

Minority status has more to do with the distribution of resources and power than with simple numbers. The definition of minority group used in this book is based on Wagley and Harris (1958). According to this definition, a minority group has five characteristics:

- The members of the group experience a pattern of disadvantage or inequality.
- The members of the group share a visible trait or characteristic that differentiates them from other groups.
- The minority group is a self-conscious social unit.
- Membership in the group usually is determined at birth.
- Members tend to marry within the group.

The first two of these traits—inequality and visibility—are the most important and will occupy most of our attention in the material that follows.

Inequality

Stratification, or the unequal distribution of valued goods and services, is a basic feature of society. Every human society, except perhaps the simplest hunter-gatherer societies, is stratified to some degree; that is, the resources of the society are distributed so that some get more and others less. Societies are divided into horizontal layers (or strata), often called *social classes,* which differ from one another in the amount of valued goods and services they command. Many criteria (such as education, age, gender, and talent) may affect a person's social class position and his or her access to resources and opportunity. Minority group membership is one of these criteria, and it has had a powerful impact on the distribution of resources in the United States and many other societies.

Inequality—some pattern of disability and disadvantage—is the most important defining characteristic of a minority group. The nature of the disability and the degree of disadvantage can be highly variable, ranging from exploitation, slavery, and genocide at one extreme to such "slight" irritants as a lack of desks for left-handed students or a policy of racial exclusion at an expensive country club at the other extreme. (Note, however, that you might not agree that the irritant is slight if you are a left-handed student awkwardly taking notes at a right-handed desk or if you are a golf aficionado who happens to be African American.) Whatever its scope or severity, whether it extends to wealth, jobs, housing, political power, police protection, or health care, or opportunities for upward mobility, the pattern of disadvantage is the essence of minority group membership.

In this section, we briefly consider some theories about the nature and dimensions of stratification. Then, we focus on how minority group status relates to stratification. During this discussion, several key concepts and themes used throughout this book are identified.

Theoretical Perspectives

Sociology and the other social sciences have been concerned with stratification and human inequality since the formation of the discipline in the 19th century. An early and important contributor to our understanding of the nature and significance of social inequality was Karl Marx, the noted social philosopher. Half a century later, sociologist Max Weber, a central figure in the development of the discipline, critiqued and elaborated on Marx's view of social inequality. We will consider their views as well as those of Gerhard Lenski, a contemporary sociologist whose ideas about the influence of economic and technological development on social stratification have considerable relevance when comparing societies and understanding their evolution.

Karl Marx. Karl Marx is best known for writing *The Communist Manifesto* in 1848 (Marx & Engels, 1848/1967). He was also the primary architect of a political, economic, and social philosophy that has played a major role in world affairs for nearly 150 years. Marxism is more than just a form of communism; it is a complex theory of history and social change in which inequality is a central concept and concern.

Marx argued that the most important source of inequality in society was the system of economic production. More specifically, he focused on the *means of production,* or the materials, tools, resources, and organizations by which the society produces and distributes goods and services. In an agricultural society, the means of production include land, draft animals, and plows. In an industrial society, the means of production include factories, commercial enterprises, banks, and transportation systems such as railroads.

All societies include two main social classes that struggle over the means of production. One class owns or controls the means of production. In the case of an industrial society, Marx called this elite or ruling class capitalists or the *bourgeoisie.* The other class is the working class, or the *proletariat.* Marx believed that conflict between these classes was inevitable and that the ultimate result of this class struggle would be the victory of the working class, followed by the creation of a utopian society without exploitation, coercion, or inequality: in other words, a classless society.

Marxism has been extensively revised and updated since the 19th century. Still, modern social science owes a great deal to Marx's views on inequality and his insights on class struggle and social conflict. As you shall see, Marxism remains an important body of work and a rich source of insight into group relations in industrial society.

Max Weber. One of Marx's major critics was Max Weber, a German sociologist who did most of his work around the turn of the 20th century. Weber thought that Marx's view of inequality was too narrow. Whereas Marx saw social class as a matter of economic position or relationship to the means of production, Weber noted that inequality involved more dimensions than just the economic. Individuals could be members of the elite in some ways but not in others. For example, an aristocratic family that has fallen on hard financial times might belong to the elite in terms of family lineage but not in terms of wealth. Or, to use a more contemporary example, a major figure in the illegal drug trade could enjoy substantial wealth but be held in low esteem otherwise.

Weber expanded on Marx's view of inequality by identifying three separate stratification systems. First, there is economic inequality based on ownership or control of property, wealth, and income. This is similar to Marx's concept of class, and in fact, Weber used the term *class* to identify this form of inequality.

A second system of stratification revolves around differences in *prestige* between groups, or the amount of honor, esteem, or respect given to us by others. Class position is one factor that affects the amount of prestige enjoyed by a person. Other factors might include family lineage, athletic ability, and physical appearance. In the United States and other societies, prestige is affected by the groups to which people belong, and members of minority groups typically receive less prestige than members of the dominant group.

Weber's third stratification system is *power,* or the ability to influence others, have an impact on the decision-making processes of society, and pursue and protect one's self-interest and achieve one's goals. One source of power is a person's standing in politically active organizations, such as labor unions or pressure groups, which lobby state and federal legislatures. Some politically active groups have access to great wealth and can use their riches to promote their causes. Other groups may rely more on their size and their ability to mobilize large demonstrations to achieve their goals. Political groups and the people they represent vary in their ability to affect the political process and control decision making; that is, they vary in the amount of power they can mobilize.

Typically, these three dimensions of stratification go together: Wealthy, prestigious groups will be more powerful (more likely to achieve their goals or protect their self-interest) than low-income groups or groups with little prestige. It is important to realize, however, that the three dimensions are separate and that even groups that are impoverished or command little prestige have found ways to express their concerns and pursue their goals.

Gerhard Lenski. Gerhard Lenski is a contemporary sociologist who follows Weber and distinguishes between class (or property), prestige, and power. Lenski has expanded on Weber's ideas, however, by analyzing stratification in the context of societal evolution or the *level of development* of a society. He has argued that the nature of inequality (the degree of inequality or the specific criteria affecting a group's position) is closely related to *subsistence technology,* the means by which the society satisfies basic needs such as hunger and thirst. A preindustrial agricultural society relies on human and animal labor to generate the calories necessary to sustain life. Inequality in this type of society centers on control of land and labor because they are the most important means of production at that level of development.

In a modern industrial society, however, land ownership is not as crucial as ownership of manufacturing and commercial enterprises. At the industrial level of development, control of capital is more important than control of land, and the nature of inequality changes accordingly.

The United States has recently entered still another stage of development, often referred to as postindustrial society. In this type of society, economic growth is powered by developments in new technology, computer-related fields, information processing, and scientific research. It seems fairly safe to speculate that economic success at this next level of development will be closely related to familiarity with new technologies and education in general (Chirot, 1994, p. 88; see also Bell, 1973). Thus, as we shift to an information-based, high-tech, postindustrial society, the advantages conferred by higher levels of education will be magnified and groups that have less access to schooling will likely suffer an even greater handicap in the pursuit of resources, opportunities, and success.

Minority Group Status and Stratification

The theoretical perspectives we have just reviewed raise three important points about the connections between minority group status and stratification. First, as already noted, minority group status affects access to wealth and income, prestige, and power. A society in which minority groups systematically receive less of these valued goods is stratified, at least partly, by race and ethnicity. In the United States, minority group status has been and continues to be one of the most important and powerful determinants of life chances, health and wealth, and success. These patterns of inequality are documented and explored throughout this text, but even casual observation will reveal that minority groups control proportionately fewer resources and that minority group status and inequality are intimately and complexly intertwined.

Second, although social classes and minority groups are correlated, they are separate social realities. The degree to which one is dependent on the other varies from group to group and time to time. Also, each minority group is divided internally by systems of inequality based on class, status, or power, and in the same way, members of the same social class may be separated by ethnic or racial differences. Thus, some minority group members can be economically successful, wield great political power, or enjoy high prestige even while the majority of their group languishes in poverty and powerlessness.

The third point concerning the connections between stratification and minority groups brings us to group conflict, a central concern of this text. You will see repeatedly that minority-dominant group relationships are created by struggle over the control of valued goods and services. The dominant group constructs minority group structures (such as slavery) in order to control commodities such as land or labor, maintain its position in the stratification system, or eliminate a perceived threat to its well-being. Struggles over property, wealth, prestige, and power lie at the heart of every dominant-minority relationship. Karl Marx believed that all aspects of society and culture were shaped to benefit the elite or ruling class and sustain the economic system that underlies its privileged position. The treatment of minority groups throughout American history provides a good deal of evidence to support Marx's point.

Visibility

The second defining characteristic of a minority group is some *visible trait or characteristic* that sets members of the group apart and that the dominant group holds in low esteem. The trait can be cultural (language, religion, speech patterns, or dress styles), physical (skin color, stature, or facial features), or both. Groups that are defined primarily by their cultural characteristics are called *ethnic minority groups*. Examples of such groups are Irish Americans and Jewish Americans. Groups defined primarily by their physical characteristics are *racial minority groups*, such as African Americans and Native Americans. Note that these categories overlap. So-called ethnic groups may have (or may be thought to have) distinguishing physical characteristics (for

example, the stereotypical Irish red hair or Jewish nose), and racial groups commonly have (or are thought to have) cultural traits that differ from those of the dominant group (for example, differences in dialect, religious values, or cuisine).

These distinguishing traits set social boundaries and separate people into distinct groups. The traits are outward signs that identify minority group members and help to maintain the patterns of disadvantage. The dominant group has (or, at one time, had) sufficient power to create the distinction between groups and thus solidify a higher position for itself. The highly visible markers of group membership are crucial. Without them, it would be difficult or impossible to identify who was in which group, and the system of minority group oppression would soon collapse.

It is important to realize that the characteristics that mark the boundaries between groups usually are not significant in and of themselves. They reflect the outcomes of previous struggles between dominant and minority groups and are selected for their visibility and convenience. They are chosen as a result of a social process, not because they are important in any other sense. This point can be illustrated with the concepts of race and gender, the most socially visible marks of group membership in U.S. society.

Race

Race became a matter of concern in Western European history in relatively recent times. In the 1500s, during the Age of Discovery, Europeans first came into continuous contact with the peoples of Africa, Asia, and the Americas and became more aware of and curious about the physical differences between people. Europeans also conquered, colonized, and sometimes destroyed the peoples and cultures they encountered. From the beginning, the European awareness of the differences between the races was linked to notions of inferior and superior (conquered vs. conquering) peoples. For centuries, the European tradition has been to see race in this political and military context and to intermix biological realities with judgments about the relative merits of the various races.

Because of its particular origins in Western European thought, the concept of race has come to have both a biological and a social dimension. Biologically, a race is an isolated, inbreeding population with a distinctive genetic heritage (Harris, 1988, p. 8). Biological investigations of race have focused on the construction of systems of classification that (ideally) would provide a category for every race and every person. Some of these typologies are quite elaborate and include scores of races and subraces. For example, the Caucasian race is often subdivided into Nordics (blond, fair-skinned Northern Europeans), Mediterraneans (dark-haired Southern Europeans), and Alpines (those falling between the first two categories).

The major limitation of these taxonomies is that even the most elaborate fail to identify clear dividing lines between racial groups, primarily because of the ambiguous and indeterminate nature of race. Most racial traits run gradually from one extreme to the other. There is no clear or definite point, for example, at which "black" skin color stops and "white" skin color begins. Furthermore, the genes that determine the so-called racial characteristics (for example, skin color or hair texture) can occur in every possible combination. Skin color, for example, can be blended with other characteristics in an infinite variety of ways. A given individual might have a skin color that is associated with one race, the hair texture of a second, the nasal shape of a third, and so forth. Many individuals fit into more than one racial category or none at all. This ambiguity makes it impossible to establish racial categories that are not arbitrary, and the attempt to do so has been almost completely abandoned in the sciences.

Even though race is not regarded as an important biological characteristic, it is still an important social concept, and it continues to be seen as a significant way of differentiating among people. Race, along with gender, is one of the first things people notice about one another. In the United States, we tend to ignore the biological realities of multiple ancestry and ambiguous classification and to see people as belonging to one and only one racial group. Furthermore, we tend to see race as a simple, unambiguous matter of skin color. Let's examine the biology of this most prominent marker of racial membership.

Skin color is derived from melanin, a pigment that everyone, except albinos, has. The skin color associated with each "race" is a function of the amount of melanin in the skin, which, in turn, is thought to relate to climate and to the amount of sunlight characteristic of a given ecology. In areas with intense sunlight, at or near the equator, melanin acts as a screen and protects the skin against the ultraviolet (UV) rays of the sun that cause sunburn and, more significantly, skin cancer. Thus, higher levels of melanin and darker skin colors are found in peoples who are adapted to an equatorial ecology. In peoples adapted to areas with less intense sunlight, the amount of melanin is lower, and skin color is therefore lighter. The lower concentration of melanin may also be an adaptation to a particular ecology. It maximizes the synthesis of vitamin D, which is important for the absorption of calcium and protection against disorders such as rickets. Thus, the skin color of any group (the amount of melanin) balances the need for vitamin D and the need for protection from UV rays in a particular ecological setting. (For more information, see Harris, 1988, pp. 98–114; and for a different view, see Vigilant, 1997, pp. 49–62.)

From a scientific point of view, that's all there is to skin color: The most visible marker of minority group membership is a superficial and relatively unimportant biological trait. In the United States, race is more a social than a biological reality, and racial minority groups are creations of historical and social—not biological—processes (see Omi & Winant, 1986; Smedley, 1999). Who belongs to which racial group is largely a matter of social definition and tradition, not biology. Membership in ethnic minority groups is even more arbitrary and subjective than membership in racial groups because the former are distinguished by characteristics that are less visible (language, religion, or customs) and more changeable than skin color.

Gender

You have already seen that minority groups can be divided internally by social class and other factors. An additional source of differentiation is gender. Like race, gender has both a biological and a social component and can be a highly visible and convenient way of judging and sorting people. From birth, the biological differences between the sexes form the basis for different *gender roles,* or societal expectations about proper behavior, attitudes, and personality traits. In virtually all societies, including those at the advanced industrial stage, adult work roles tend to be separated by gender, and boys and girls are socialized differently in preparation for these adult roles. In hunter-gatherer societies, for example, boys train for the role of hunter, whereas girls learn the skills necessary for successful harvesting of vegetables, fruit, and other foodstuffs. In industrial societies, girls tend to learn nurturing skills that will help them take primary responsibility for the well-being of family and community members, and boys learn aggressiveness, which is considered necessary for their expected roles as leaders, combatants, and providers in a highly competitive society.

The exact makeup of gender roles and relationships varies across time and from society to society, but gender and inequality usually have been closely related, and men typically claim more property, prestige, and power. The societies of Western Europe and the United States, like most, have a strong tradition of *patriarchy,* or male dominance, throughout the social structure. In a patriarchal society, men have more control over the economy and more access to leadership roles in religion, politics, and other institutions. In these societies, women possess many characteristics of a minority group (namely, a pattern of disadvantage based on group membership marked by a physical stigma). Thus, women could be, and in many ways should be, treated as a separate minority group.

In this book, however, rather than discussing women as a separate group, I will explore the divergent experiences of men and women within each minority group. This approach will permit us to analyze the ways in which race, ethnicity, gender, and class combine, overlap, and crosscut each other to form a "matrix of domination" (Hill-Collins, 1991, pp. 225–227). We will consider how the interests and experiences of females of different groups and classes coincide with and diverge from each other and from those of the men in their groups. For example, on some issues, African American females might have interests identical to white females and opposed to African American males. On other issues, the constellations of interests might be reversed. As you shall see, the experience of minority group membership varies by gender, and the way in which gender is experienced is not the same for every group.

History generally has been and is written from the standpoint of the "winners," that is, those in power. The voices of minority groups generally have been repressed, ignored, forgotten, or trivialized. Much of the history of slavery in America, for instance, has been told from the viewpoint of the slave owners. Slaves were kept illiterate by law and had few mechanisms for recording their thoughts or experiences. A more balanced and accurate picture of slavery began to emerge only in the past few decades, when scholars began to dig beneath the written records and memoirs of the slave owners and reconstruct the experiences of African Americans from nonwritten materials such as oral traditions and the physical artifacts left by the slaves.

Similarly, our understanding of minority groups tends to be based on the experiences of the males of the group, and the experiences of the females are much less well-known and documented. If the voices of minority groups have been hushed, those of female minority group members have been virtually silenced. One of the important trends in contemporary scholarship is to adjust this skewed focus and systematically incorporate gender as a factor in the minority group experience (Espiritu, 1997; Zinn & Dill, 1994).

Other Minority Group Characteristics

A third characteristic of minority groups, in addition to inequality and visibility, is that they are *self-conscious social units,* aware of their differentiation from the dominant group and of their shared disabilities. This shared social status can provide the basis for strong intragroup bonds and a sense of solidarity, and it can lead to views of the world that are quite different from those of the dominant group and other minority groups. For example, public opinion polls frequently show vast differences between dominant and minority groups in their views of the seriousness and extent of discrimination in American society. One recent poll showed that twice as many blacks (65%) as whites (33%) agree that discrimination is the reason black Americans have "worse jobs, incomes, and housing than white people" (National Opinion Research Council [NORC], 2000 General Social Survey [GSS]). Also, a Gallup poll showed that more than twice as many whites (75%) as blacks (32%) believe that blacks and whites are treated the same way in their local communities (Gallup Organization, 2000). Similar disagreements surface constantly over national policy issues ranging from affirmative action to welfare reform (for an analysis of these differences, see Kinder & Winter, 2001).

These disparities between blacks and whites are particularly common when issues related to criminal justice and policing arise. Surveys show sizable differences between the groups in their perceptions of the fairness of the police and the court system, differences that have been reinforced by highly publicized instances of police violence against blacks such as the beating of Rodney King in Los Angeles, and the murder of Amadou Diallo in New York City (Bobo, 2001, p. 281). A number of other criminal justice issues divide the communities, including racial profiling, "driving while black," and support for capital punishment. These differences were dramatically revealed by the reactions of the two groups to the acquittal of former football star and celebrity O. J. Simpson on charges of murdering his ex-wife, Nicole Brown Simpson, and her friend, Ron Goldman. One survey showed that 85% of black Americans but only 32% of white Americans agreed with the jury's decision to acquit (Whitaker, 1995, pp. 30–34). Evidence such as this underscores the differing perceptions of the groups that constitute U.S. society and the conflicting interests and traditions that separate their realities.

A fourth characteristic of minority groups is that, in general, membership is an *ascribed status,* one that is acquired at birth. The trait that identifies minority group membership typically cannot be changed easily or at all, and minority group status usually is involuntary and for life.

Finally, minority group members tend to marry within their own groups. This pattern can be the result of voluntary choices made by members of the minority group, policies and customs enforced by the dominant group, or some combination of these forces. In fact, only a generation ago in America, interracial marriages were against the law in many states. The state laws against *miscegenation* were declared unconstitutional in the late 1960s by the U.S. Supreme Court (Bell, 1992).

Which Groups Are Minority Groups?

Our five-part definition is lengthy, but note how inclusive it is. Although it encompasses "traditional" minority groups such as African Americans and Native Americans, it also could be applied to other groups (with perhaps a little stretching). For instance, women arguably fit the first four criteria and can be analyzed with many of the same concepts and ideas that guide the analysis of other minority groups. Also, gay and lesbian Americans; Americans with disabilities; the left-handed; the aged; and very short, very tall, or very obese people could fit the definition of minority group without much difficulty. Although we shouldn't be whimsical or capricious about matters of definition, it is important to note that the analysis developed in this book can be applied more generally than you might realize at first and may lead to some fresh insights about a wide variety of groups and people.

FOCUS ON GENDER

THE BIOLOGICAL BASIS OF RACE AND GENDER

The huge majority of social scientists regard race as a triviality, a social construction formulated in certain historical circumstances (like the era of European colonialism) when it was needed to help justify the unequal treatment of minority groups. What about gender? Is it also a social creation designed by men to rationalize their higher status? Or do the commonly observed gender differences (e.g., men are more aggressive, women more nurturing) have a biological basis stronger and more controlling than that supposedly associated with race? Are men and women different because of nature (differences in biology and genetic inheritance) or because of nurture (differences in expectations and experience for boys and girls during childhood socialization)?

Needless to say, responses to these questions vary both in the scientific community and in society at large. On one hand, some people (including most sociologists) argue that gender roles are overwhelmingly learned and that the commonly observed gender differences in adults are the results of the fact that society puts boys and girls on different tracks of development from the moment of birth. Evidence for this point of view includes the malleable, open-ended nature of infants and the great range of behavioral and personality repertoires within each gender (e.g., some females are more aggressive than some males, and some males are more tender and nurturing than some females). Also, according to this view, the fact that "appropriate" behaviors for males and females vary from culture to culture and from time to time and are not fixed and permanent is taken as proof that there is no biological basis for gender roles.

On the other hand, some believe that the behavioral differences between males and females are "hardwired" in our genetic code just as surely and permanently as the differences in reproductive organs. Sociologist Steven Goldberg (1999), for example, argued that some gender characteristics are universal. He observed that males are more aggressive and that they control leadership positions and power structures in every society about which we have information. Goldberg believes that this is so because men are predisposed to pursue status and dominance over other pleasures and rewards of life—safety, wealth, leisure, and so forth—and that this tendency is the result of biology and genetic inheritance, not socialization or learning (1999, p. 54).

Still other scientists are pursuing a third approach that combines nature and nurture. In this view, genetic inheritance and socialization experiences work together in a variety of ways, some exquisitely subtle, to produce the commonly observed gender differences in adults. For example, sociologist Richard Udry (2000) reported the results of an investigation into the *combined* effects of biology and experience on the adult personalities of a sample of 351 women. He argued that one root of adult gender differences may lie in the biology of sex, specifically, the extent to which fetuses are exposed to the male hormone testosterone. Of course, male fetuses are exposed to much higher levels than females, and this prebirth experience, in Udry's view, is what makes males more responsive to postbirth learning experiences that stress aggression and toughness. Thus, the biology of sex may predispose or sensitize males and females in very different ways and prepare them for differential socialization experiences.

Udry's research goes beyond this general difference between the sexes and asks if women who had been exposed to different levels of testosterone in the womb have different personality characteristics as adults. He found that the women in the study who had higher levels of prenatal exposure to testosterone were more "masculine" in their behavior as adults and that this pattern persisted even for the women whose mothers had strongly encouraged them to become more feminine when they were children (Udry, 2000, p. 450). These and similar results led Udry to conclude that prenatal and postnatal experiences interact in complex ways to produce the differences that are seen as "typical" of men and women. Nature or biology seems to set limits and establish tendencies, but these potentials are then emphasized or minimized by nurture or experience, and it is the interaction between the two forces that produces the wide variation in, for example, aggressive or nurturing behaviors within the genders. Udry noted that these findings, if they are verified in future research, do not invalidate or refute explanations of gender differences that stress socialization or nurture. They do, however, require recognition that biology sets some (very broad?) limits on the effects of gender socialization.

If Udry (2000) and (especially) Goldberg (1999) are correct, then gender is not an arbitrary social construct, at least not in the same way as race. However, it is important to recognize that this debate about the possible biological bases for gender roles is far from over. The research is limited in many ways, and the evidence is open to a variety of interpretations. For example, Udry's sample was selected from a group of patients who happened to use a particular health care facility, and his results cannot be generalized to larger or more diverse populations. Furthermore, scientific objectivity is often an issue when researching questions that can be so emotionally charged. Prejudicial sentiments and the pervasive sexism of the surrounding society can tinge and color even the most carefully crafted research project.

Where does that leave us? Can the view that adult gender roles are entirely learned be sustained? Must social scientists at least admit the possibility of biological influences? How powerful are the genetic tendencies that may underlie gender role differences? Although these issues are not fully resolved, it seems that the strongest role that biology could play is to shape and predispose males and females to follow different patterns in their development. Gender, like race, becomes a social construction when it is treated as an unchanging, fixed difference and then used to deny opportunity and equality to women.

KEY CONCEPTS
IN DOMINANT-MINORITY
RELATIONS

To fully understand dominant-minority relations, we need to take account of two distinct levels of analysis and distinguish between two dimensions on each level. We need to distinguish between what is true for individuals (the psychological level of analysis) and what is true for groups or society as a whole (the sociological level of analysis). We also need to make a further distinction on both the individual and the group levels. At the individual level, there can be a difference between what people think and feel about other groups and how they actually behave toward members of that group. A person might express negative feelings about other groups in private but deal fairly with members of the group in face-to-face interactions. Groups and entire societies may display this same kind of inconsistency. A society may express support for equality in its official documents or formal codes of law, while simultaneously treating minority groups in unfair and destructive ways. An example of this kind of inconsistency is the

Exhibit 1.2   Four Concepts in Dominant-Minority Relations

	Level of Analysis	
Dimension	Individual	Group or Societal
Thinking/feeling	Prejudice	Ideological racism
Doing	Discrimination	Institutional discrimination

contrast between the commitment to equality stated in the Declaration of Independence ("All men are created equal") and the actual treatment of black slaves, Anglo-American women, and Native Americans at the time the document was written.

At the individual level, social scientists refer to the "thinking/feeling" part of this dichotomy as *prejudice* and the "doing" part as *discrimination*. At the group level, the term *ideological racism* describes the "thinking/ feeling" dimension and *institutional discrimination* describes the "doing" dimension. Exhibit 1.2 presents the differences among these four concepts. In the sections of the chapter below, we will devote most of our attention to the individual-level concepts, but in the chapters that follow, we emphasize the sociological level of analysis.

Prejudice

Prejudice is the tendency of an individual to think about other groups in negative ways, to attach negative emotions to those groups, and to prejudge individuals on the basis of their group membership. Individual prejudice has two aspects: the *cognitive*, or thinking, aspect and the *affective*, or feeling, part. A prejudiced person thinks about other groups in terms of *stereotypes*, generalizations that are thought to apply to all group members. Examples of familiar stereotypes include notions such as "women are emotional," "Jews are stingy," "blacks are lazy," "the Irish are drunks," and "Germans are authoritarian." A prejudiced person also experiences negative emotional responses to other groups, including contempt, disgust, arrogance, and hatred. People vary in their levels of prejudice, and levels of prejudice vary in the same person from one time to another and from one group to another. We can say that a person is prejudiced to the extent that he or she uses stereotypes in his or her thinking about other groups and/or has negative emotional reactions to other groups.

Generally, the two dimensions of prejudice are highly correlated with each other; however, they are distinct and separate, and they can vary independently. One person may think entirely in stereotypes but feel no particular negative emotional response to any group. Another person may feel a very strong aversion toward a group but be unable to articulate a clear or detailed stereotype of that group.

Causes of Prejudice

American social scientists of all disciplines have made prejudice a primary concern and have produced literally thousands of articles and books on the topic. They have approached the subject from a variety of theoretical perspectives and have asked a wide array of different questions. One firm conclusion that has emerged is that prejudice is not a single, unitary phenomenon. It has a variety of possible causes (some more psychological and individual, others more sociological and cultural) and can present itself in a variety of forms (some blatant and vicious, others subtle and indirect). No single theory has emerged that can explain prejudice in all its complexity. In keeping with the macrosociological approach of this text, we will focus primarily on the theories that stress the causes of prejudice that are related to culture, social structure, and group relationships.

Competition Between Groups and the Origins of Prejudice. Every form of prejudice—even the most ancient—started at some specific point in history. If we go back far enough in time, we can find a moment that predates anti-black prejudice, anti-Semitism, negative stereotypes about Native Americans or Hispanic Americans, or antipathy against Asian Americans. What sorts of conditions create prejudice?

The one common factor that seems to account for the origin of any specific prejudice is competition between groups: some episode in which one group successfully dominates, takes resources from, or eliminates a threat from some other group. The successful group becomes the dominant group, and the other group becomes the minority group. Why is group competition associated with the emergence of prejudice? Typically, prejudice is more a result of the competition than a cause. Its role is to help mobilize emotional energy for the contest, justify rejection and attack, and rationalize the structures of domination, like slavery or segregation, that result from the competition. Groups react to the competition and to the threat presented by the other group with antipathy and stereotypes about the "enemy" group: Prejudice emerges from the heat of the contest.

The relationship between prejudice and competition has been demonstrated in a variety of settings and situations ranging from labor strikes to international war to social psychology labs. In the chapters to come, we will examine the role of prejudice during the creation of slavery in North America, as a reaction to periods of high immigration, and as an accompaniment to myriad forms of group competition. Here, to illustrate our central point about competition and prejudice, we will examine a classic experiment from the sociological literature. The experiment was conducted in the 1950s at a summer camp for 11- and 12-year-old boys known as Robber's Cave.

The camp director, social psychologist Muzafer Sherif, divided the campers into two groups, the Rattlers and the Eagles (Sherif, Harvey, White, Hood, & Sherif, 1961). The groups lived in different cabins and were continually pitted against each other in a wide range of activities. Games, sports, and even housekeeping chores were set up on a competitive basis. The boys in each group began to express negative feelings (prejudice) against the other group. Competition and prejudicial feelings grew quite intense and were manifested in episodes of name-calling and raids on the "enemy" group.

Sherif attempted to reduce the harsh feelings he had created by bringing the campers together in various pleasant situations featuring food, movies, and other treats. But the rival groups only used these opportunities to express their enmity. Sherif then came up with some activities that required the members of the rival groups to work cooperatively with each other. For example, the researchers deliberately sabotaged some plumbing to create an emergency that required the efforts of everyone to resolve. As a result of these cooperative activities, intergroup "prejudice" was observed to decline, and, eventually, friendships were formed across groups.

In the Robber's Cave experiment, as in many actual group relationships, prejudice (negative feelings and stereotypes about other campers) arose to help mobilize feelings and to justify rejection and attacks, both verbal and physical, against the out-group. When group competition was reduced, the levels of prejudice abated and eventually disappeared, again demonstrating that prejudice is caused by competition, not the other way around.

Although the Robber's Cave experiment illustrates our central point, we must be cautious in generalizing from these results. The experiment was conducted in an artificial environment with young boys (all white) who had no previous acquaintance with each other and no history of grievances or animosity. Thus, these results may be only partially generalizable to group conflicts in the "real world." Nonetheless, Robber's Cave illustrates a fundamental connection between group competition and prejudice that we will observe repeatedly in the chapters to come. Competition and the desire to protect resources and status and to defend against threats from other groups are the primary motivations for the construction of traditions of prejudice and structures of inequality that benefit the dominant group.

Culture, Socialization, and the Persistence of Prejudice. Prejudice originates in group competition of some sort but often outlives the conditions of its creation. It can persist, full-blown and intense, long after the episode that sparked its creation has faded from memory. How does prejudice persist through time?

In his classic analysis of American race relations, *An American Dilemma* (1944/1962), Swedish economist Gunnar Myrdal proposed the idea that prejudice is perpetuated through time by a self-fulfilling prophecy or a *vicious cycle,* as illustrated in Exhibit 1.3. The dominant group uses its power to force the minority group into an inferior status, such as slavery, as shown in the diagram in area (1). Partly to motivate the construction of a system of racial stratification and partly to justify its existence, individual prejudice and racist belief systems are invented and accepted by the dominant group, as shown in area (2). Individual prejudices are reinforced by the everyday observation of the inferior status of the minority group. The fact that the minority group is in fact impoverished, enslaved, or otherwise exploited confirms and strengthens the attribution of inferiority. The belief in inferiority motivates further discrimination and unequal treatment, as shown in area (3) of the diagram, which reinforces the inferior status, which validates the prejudice and racism, which justifies further discrimination, and so on. Over not too many generations, a stable, internally reinforced system of racial inferiority becomes an integral, unremarkable, and (at least for the dominant group) accepted part of everyday life.

Culture is conservative, and, once created, prejudice will be sustained over time just like any set of attitudes, values, and beliefs. Future generations will learn prejudice in the same way and for the same reasons that they learn any other aspect of their culture. Thus, prejudice and racism come to us through our cultural heritage as a unified package of stereotypes, emotions, and ideas. We learn which groups are "good" and which are "bad" in the same way we learn table manners and religious beliefs (Pettigrew, 1958, 1971, p. 137; Simpson & Yinger, 1985, pp. 107, 108). When prejudice is part of the cultural heritage, individuals learn to think and feel negatively toward other groups as a routine part of socialization. Much of the prejudice expressed by Americans—and the people of many other societies—is the normal result of a typical socialization in families, communities, and societies that are, to some degree, racist. Given our long history of intense racial and ethnic exploitation, it is not surprising that Americans continue to manifest antipathy toward and stereotypical ideas about other groups.

The idea that prejudice is learned during socialization is reinforced by studies of the development of prejudice in children. Research shows that people are born without bias and have to be taught whom to like and dislike. Children become aware of group differences (e.g., black vs. white) at a very early age. By age 3 or younger, they recognize the significance and the permanence of racial groups and can accurately classify people on the basis of skin color and other cues (Brown, 1995, pp. 121–136; Katz, 1976, p. 126). Once the racial or group categories are mentally established, the child begins the process of learning the "proper" attitudes and stereotypes to associate with the various groups, and both affective and cognitive prejudice begin to grow at an early age.

It is important to note that children can acquire prejudice even when parents and other caregivers do not teach it overtly or directly. Adults control the socialization process and valuable resources (food, shelter, praise), and children are motivated to seek their approval and conform to their expectations (at least in the early years). There are strong pressures on the child to learn and internalize the perceptions of the older generation, and even a casual comment or an overheard remark can establish or reinforce negative beliefs or feelings about members of other groups (Ashmore & DelBoca, 1976).

Exhibit 1.3   Myrdal's Vicious Cycle

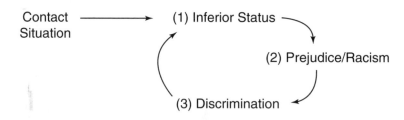

SOURCE: Based on Myrdal (1944/1962, pp. 25–28).

Children need not be directly instructed about presumed minority group characteristics; it is often said that racial attitudes are "caught and not taught."

A somewhat different line of research on the development of prejudice argues that children are actively engaged in their learning and that their levels of prejudice reflect their changing intellectual capabilities. Children as young as 5 to 6 months old can make some simple distinctions (e.g., by gender or race) between categories of people. The fact that this capability emerges so early in life suggests that it is not simply a response to adult teaching. "Adults use categories to simplify and make sense of their environment; apparently children do the same" (Brown, 1995, p. 126). Gross, simplistic distinctions between people may help very young children organize and understand the world around them. The need for such primitive categorizations may decline as the child becomes more experienced in life and more sophisticated in his or her thinking. Doyle and Aboud (1995), for example, found that prejudice was highest for younger children and actually decreased between kindergarten and the third grade. The decline was related to increased awareness of racial similarities (as well as differences) and diverse perspectives on race (see also Black-Gutman & Hickson, 1996; Brown, 1995, pp. 149–159; Powlishta, Serbin, Doyle, & White, 1994). Thus, changing levels of prejudice in children may reflect an interaction between the child's changing mental capacities and their environment rather than a simple or straightforward learning of racist cultural beliefs or values.

Further evidence for the cultural nature of prejudice is provided by research on the concept of social distance. _Social distance_ is related to prejudice but is not quite the same thing. Social distance is defined as the degree of intimacy which a person is willing to accept in his or her relations with members of other groups. The most intimate relationship would be close kinship, and the most distant relationship is exclusion from the country. The inventor of the social distance scale was Emory Bogardus (1933), who specified a total of seven degrees of social distance:

1. To close kinship by marriage
2. To my club as personal chums
3. To my street as neighbors
4. To employment in my occupation
5. To citizenship in my country
6. As visitors only to my country
7. Would exclude from my country

Research using social distance scales demonstrates that Americans rank other groups in similar ways across time and space. The consistency indicates a common frame of reference or set of perceptions, a continuity of vision possible only if perceptions have been standardized by socialization in a common culture.

Exhibit 1.4 presents some results of six administrations of the scale to samples of Americans from 1926 to 1993. The groups are listed by the rank order of their scores for 1926. The average scores for 1926 show that the sample expressed the least social distance against the English, the average score of 1.06 indicating virtually no sense of distance. The

Exhibit 1.4   Results of American Social Distance Rankings of Other Groups, 1926–1993

Rank	1926	Score	1946	Score	1956	Score	1966	Score	1977	Score	1993	Score
1	English	1.06	Am. whites	1.04	Am. whites	1.08	Am. whites	1.07	Am. whites	1.25	Irish	1.14
2	Am. whites	1.10	Canadians	1.11	Canadians	1.16	English	1.14	English	1.39	English	1.17
3	Canadians	1.13	English	1.13	English	1.23	Canadians	1.15	Canadians	1.42	Italians	1.19
4	Scots	1.13	Irish	1.24	French	1.47	French	1.36	French	1.58	French	1.20
5	Irish	1.30	Scots	1.26	Irish	1.56	Irish	1.40	Italians	1.65	Swedish	1.21
6	French	1.32	French	1.31	Swedish	1.57	Swedish	1.42	Swedish	1.68	Scots	1.22
7	Germans	1.46	Norwegians	1.35	Scots	1.60	Norwegians	1.50	Irish	1.69	Danish	1.23
8	Swedish	1.54	Dutch	1.37	Germans	1.61	Italians	1.51	Dutch	1.82	Norwegians	1.25
9	Dutch	1.56	Swedish	1.40	Dutch	1.63	Scots	1.53	Scots	1.83	Dutch	1.25
10	Norwegians	1.59	Germans	1.59	Norwegians	1.66	Germans	1.54	Native Am.	1.84	Germans	1.27
11	Spanish	1.72	Finns	1.63	Finns	1.80	Dutch	1.54	Germans	1.87	Spanish	1.29
12	Finns	1.83	Czechs	1.76	Italians	1.89	Finns	1.67	Norwegians	1.93	Poles	1.30
13	Russians	1.88	Russians	1.83	Poles	2.07	Greeks	1.82	Spanish	1.98	Russians	1.33
14	Italians	1.94	Poles	1.84	Spanish	2.08	Spanish	1.93	Finns	2.00	Greeks	1.38
15	Poles	2.01	Spanish	1.94	Greeks	2.09	Jews	1.97	Jews	2.01	Jews	1.42
16	Armenians	2.06	Italians	2.28	Jews	2.15	Poles	1.98	Greeks	2.02	Native Am.	1.44
17	Czechs	2.08	Armenians	2.29	Czechs	2.22	Czechs	2.02	African Am.	2.03	African Am.	1.55
18	Native Am.	2.38	Greeks	2.29	Armenians	2.33	Native Am.	2.12	Poles	2.11	Mexicans	1.56
19	Jews	2.39	Jews	2.32	Japanese Am.	2.34	Japanese Am.	2.14	Mexican Am.	2.17	Japanese	1.62
20	Greeks	2.47	Native Am.	2.45	Native Am.	2.35	Armenians	2.18	Japanese Am.	2.18	Chinese	1.68
21	Mexicans	2.69	Chinese	2.50	Filipinos	2.46	Filipinos	2.31	Armenians	2.20	Koreans	1.72
22	Japanese	2.80	Mexican Am.	2.52	Mexican Am.	2.51	Chinese	2.34	Czechs	2.23	Turks	1.77
23	Filipinos	3.00	Filipinos	2.76	Turks	2.52	Mexican Am.	2.37	Chinese	2.29	Hindu	1.95
24	African Am.	3.28	Mexicans	2.89	Russians	2.56	Russians	2.38	Filipinos	2.31	Arabs	2.21
25	Turks	3.30	Turks	2.89	Chinese	2.68	Japanese	2.41	Japanese	2.38		
26	Chinese	3.36	Japanese Am.	2.90	Japanese	2.41	Turks	2.48	Mexicans	2.40		
27	Koreans	3.60	Koreans	3.05	African Am.	2.74	Koreans	2.51	Indians	2.55		
28	Indians	3.91	Indians	3.43	Mexicans	2.79	Mexicans	2.56	Turks	2.55		
29			African Am.	3.60	Indians	2.80	African Am.	2.56	Russians	2.57		
30			Japanese	3.61	Koreans	2.83	Indians	2.62	Koreans	2.63		
Mean		2.14		2.12		2.08		1.92		1.93		1.43
Range		2.85		2.57		1.75		1.56		1.38		1.07

SOURCES: 1926–1977: Smith and Dempsey (1983, p. 588); 1993: Kleg and Yamamoto (1998).

NOTE: Am. whites = American whites, African Am. = African Americans (the term "Negroes" was used in the earlier studies), Japanese Am. = Japanese Americans, Mexican Am. = Mexican Americans, Native Am. = Native Americans (the term "Indians-American" was used before 1993).

greatest distance was expressed against Indians (from Asia), with a score of 3.91. On average, the sample would admit this group only to "employment in my occupation" and not to "my street as neighbors."

Note, first of all, the stability in the rankings. The *scores* generally decrease from decade to decade, indicating less social distance and presumably a decline in prejudice over the years. The *rankings* of the various groups, however, were roughly the same in 1993 as they were in 1926. If you pick a few groups and trace their positions across the decades, you will note that although some groups rise and fall over the nearly 70-year period, the overall ranking in the latest year is highly correlated with that in the earliest year. Considering the changes the society experienced between 1926 and 1993 (the Great Depression, World War II and the Korean War, the Cold War with the U.S.S.R., the Civil Rights movement, the resumption of large-scale immigration, etc.), this overall continuity in group rankings is remarkable.

Second, note the nature of the ranking: Groups with origins in Northern and Western Europe are ranked highest, followed by groups from Southern and Eastern Europe, with racial minorities near the bottom. These preferences reflect the relative status of these groups in the U.S. hierarchy of racial/ethnic groups. The rankings also reflect the relative amount of exploitation and prejudice directed at each group over the course of U.S. history.

Finally, note how the relative positions of some groups change with international and domestic relations. For example, both Japanese and Germans fell in the rankings after the end of World War II (1946). Comparing 1966 with 1946, Russians fell and the Japanese rose, reflecting changing patterns of alliance and enmity in the global system of societies. The dramatic rise of Native Americans and African Americans from 1966 to 1977 may reflect declining levels of overt prejudice in American society.

Although these patterns of social distance scores support the general point that prejudice is cultural, this body of research has some important limitations. The respondents generally were college students from a variety of campuses, not representative samples of the population, and the differences in scores from group to group sometimes were very small. Still, the stability of the patterns cannot be ignored: The top two or three groups are always Northern European, Poles and Jews are always ranked in the middle third of the groups, and Chinese and Japanese always fall in the bottom third. African Americans and Native Americans were also ranked toward the bottom until the most recent rankings.

The stability in the group rankings over the seven decades from the 1920s to the 1990s strongly suggests that Americans view the various groups through the same culturally shaped lens. A sense of social distance, a perception of some groups as "higher" or "better" than others, is part of the cultural package of intergroup prejudices we acquire from socialization into American society. The social distance patterns illustrate the power of culture to shape individual perceptions and preferences and attest to the fundamentally racist nature of American culture.

The Sociology of Prejudice

The sociological approach to prejudice stresses several points. Prejudice has its origins in competition between groups, and it is more a result of that competition than a cause. It is created at a certain time in history to help mobilize feelings and emotional energy for competition and to rationalize the consignment of a group to minority status. It then becomes a part of the cultural heritage and is passed on to later generations as part of their "taken for granted" world, where it helps to shape their perceptions and reinforce the very group inferiority that was its original cause.

Discrimination

At the individual level, discrimination is defined as the unequal treatment of a person or persons based on group membership. An example of discrimination is when an employer decides not to hire an individual because he or she is African American (or Puerto Rican, Jewish, Chinese, and so on). If the unequal treatment is based on the group membership of the individual, the act is discrimination.

One obvious and common cause of discrimination is prejudice. However, just as the cognitive and affective aspects of prejudice can be independent, discrimination and prejudice do not necessarily occur together. For example, the social situation surrounding the individual may encourage or discourage discrimination, regardless of the level of prejudice. Social situations in which prejudice is strongly approved and supported might evoke discrimination in otherwise unprejudiced individuals. In the southern United States during the height of segregation, or in South Africa during the period of state-sanctioned racial inequality, it was usual and customary for whites to treat blacks in discriminatory ways. Regardless of their actual level of prejudice, white people in these situations faced strong social pressure to conform to the commonly accepted patterns of racial superiority and participate in acts of discrimination.

On the other hand, situations in which there are strong norms of equal and fair treatment may stifle the tendency of even the most bigoted individual to discriminate. For example, if a community vigorously enforces antidiscrimination laws, even the most prejudiced merchant might refrain from treating minority group customers unequally. Highly prejudiced individuals may not discriminate so that they can "do business" (or, at least, avoid penalties or sanctions) in an environment in which discrimination is not tolerated or is too costly. Also, people normally subscribe to many different value systems, some of which may be mutually contradictory. Even people who are devout racists may also believe in and be guided by democratic, egalitarian values.

One of the earliest demonstrations of the difference between what people think and feel (prejudice) and what they actually do (discrimination) was provided by sociologist Robert LaPiere (1934). In the 1930s, he escorted a Chinese couple on a tour of the United States. At that time, Chinese and other Asians were the victims of widespread discrimination and exclusion, and anti-Chinese prejudice was quite high, as demonstrated by the scores in Exhibit 1.4. However, LaPiere and his companions dined in restaurants and stayed in hotels without incident for the entire trip and experienced discrimination only once. Six months later, LaPiere wrote to every establishment the group had patronized and inquired about reservations. He indicated that some of the party were Chinese and asked if that would be a problem. Of those establishments that replied (about half), 92% said that they would not serve Chinese and would be unable to accommodate the party.

Why the difference? On LaPiere's original visit, anti-Asian prejudice may well have been present but was not expressed to avoid making a scene. In a different situation—the more distant interaction of letters and correspondence—the restaurant and hotel staff may have allowed their prejudice to be expressed in open discrimination because the potential for embarrassment was much less.

To summarize, discrimination and prejudice tend to be found together, but they are not the same thing. Discrimination can be motivated by negative feelings and stereotypes, but it also can be a response to social pressures exerted by others.

Ideological Racism

The group or societal equivalent of individual prejudice is ideological racism, a belief system that asserts that a particular group is inferior. As I pointed out earlier, this form of prejudice is incorporated into a society's culture and passed on to individuals from generation to generation. However, as opposed to individual prejudice, ideological racism is a part of the cultural heritage and exists apart from the people who inhabit a society at a specific time (Andersen, 1993, p. 75; See & Wilson, 1988, p. 227). An example of ideological racism was the elaborate system of beliefs and ideas that attempted to justify slavery in the American South. The exploitation of slaves was "explained" in terms of the innate racial inferiority of blacks, and this cluster of beliefs was absorbed by each new generation of Southern whites during socialization.

This book analyzes ethnic as well as racial minority groups, but there is no widely used or convenient term for ideologies that attribute inferiority to groups based on cultural factors. Thus, we will take some liberties and use the term ideological racism to refer to belief systems focused on these nonracial traits—some forms of anti-Semitism, for example. The term *ideological sexism*—analogous to ideological racism but focused on gender differences—will be used when we analyze patterns of inequality between males and females.

I have already pointed out that people socialized into societies with strong racist ideologies will very likely absorb racist ideas and be highly prejudiced. At the same time, we need to remember that ideological racism and individual prejudice are different things with different causes and different locations in the society. Racism is not a prerequisite for prejudice; prejudice may exist even in the absence of an ideology of racism.

Institutional Discrimination

Our final concept, and a major concern in the chapters to come, is the societal equivalent of individual discrimination. *Institutional discrimination* refers to a pattern of unequal treatment based on group membership, a pattern built into the daily operations of society, whether or not it is consciously intended. This form of inequality can permeate public schools, the criminal justice system, and the political and economic institutions of a society. When these institutions and organizations operate so as to routinely put members of some groups at a disadvantage, institutional discrimination is present.

Institutional discrimination can be obvious and overt. For many years following the Civil War, African Americans in the South were prevented from voting by practices such as poll taxes and rigged literacy tests. For nearly a century, well into the 1960s, elections and elected offices in the South were limited to whites only. The purpose of this blatant pattern of institutional discrimination was widely understood by black and white Southerners alike: It existed to disenfranchise the black community and keep it politically powerless.

At other times, institutional discrimination may operate more subtly and without conscious intent. If public schools use aptitude tests that are biased in favor of the dominant group, decisions about who does and who does not take college preparatory courses may be made on racist grounds, even if everyone involved sincerely believes that they are merely applying objective criteria in a rational way. Whenever a decision-making process has unequal consequences for dominant and minority groups, institutional discrimination may be at work.

Note that although a particular discriminatory policy may be implemented and enforced by individuals, the policy is more appropriately thought of as an aspect of the operation of the institution as a whole. Election officials in the South during segregation did not have to be personally prejudiced themselves to implement these discriminatory policies, nor do public school administrators today.

A major thesis of this book is that the relative advantage of the dominant group is maintained from day to day by widespread institutional discrimination and ideological racism. Members of the dominant group who are socialized into communities with strong racist ideologies and a great deal of institutional discrimination are likely to be personally prejudiced and to routinely practice acts of individual discrimination. The respective positions of dominant and minority groups are preserved over time through the mutually reinforcing patterns of prejudice, racism, and discrimination on both individual and institutional levels.

MAIN POINTS

- The United States faces enormous problems with minority-dominant relationships. Even while many historic grievances of minority groups remain unresolved, society is rapidly becoming more diverse, culturally, linguistically, and racially.

- A minority group has five defining characteristics: a pattern of disadvantage, identification by some visible mark, awareness of its disadvantaged status, a membership determined at birth, and a tendency to marry within the group.

- A stratification system has three different dimensions (class, prestige, and power), and the nature of inequality in a society varies by its level of development. Minority groups and social class are correlated in numerous and complex ways.

- Race is a criterion widely used to identify minority group members. As a biological concept, race has been largely abandoned, but as a social category, race maintains a powerful influence on the way we think about one another.

- Minority groups are differentiated internally by social class, age, region of residence, and many other variables. In this book, I focus on gender as a source of variation within minority groups.

- Four crucial concepts for analyzing dominant-minority relations are prejudice, discrimination, ideological racism, and institutional discrimination.

QUESTIONS FOR REVIEW AND STUDY

1. What kind of society should the United States strive to become? In your view, does the increasing diversity of American society represent a threat or an opportunity? Should we acknowledge and celebrate our differences, or should we strive for more unity and conformity? What possible dangers and opportunities are inherent in increasing diversity?

2. What groups should be considered "minorities?" Using each of the five criteria included in the definition presented in this chapter, should gays and lesbians be considered a minority group? How about left-handed people or people who are very overweight?

3. What is a social construction? How do race and gender differ in this regard? What does it mean to say "Gender becomes a social construction—like race—when it is treated as an unchanging, fixed difference and then used to deny opportunity and equality to women?"

4. Define and explain each of the terms in Exhibit 1.2. Cite an example of each from your own experiences.

5. From a sociological point of view, what causes prejudice? What is the relationship between prejudice and competition? How is prejudice sustained through time? How does prejudice differ from discrimination?

6. How does "ideological racism" differ from prejudice? Which concept is more sociological? Why? How does institutional discrimination differ from discrimination? Which concept is more sociological? Why?

INTERNET RESEARCH PROJECT

A. Updating Data on Diversity

Update Exhibit 1.1, "Groups in American Society." Visit the Web site of the U.S. Census Bureau (www.census.gov) to get the latest estimates of the sizes of minority groups in the United States. Good places to begin the search for data include "Minority Links," "Statistical Abstract," and the list at "Subjects A to Z."

B. How Does the U.S. Government Define Race?

In this chapter, I stressed the point that race is at least as much a social construction as a biological reality. Does the federal government see race as a biological reality or a social convention? Search the Census Bureau Web site for information on the government's definition of race. How was a person's race defined in the 2000 Census? How does this differ from previous censuses? Who determines a person's race, the government or the person filling out the census form? Is this treatment of race based on a biological approach or a more arbitrary social perspective? Given the goals of the Census (e.g., to accurately count the number and types of people in the U.S. population), is this a reasonable approach to classifying race? Why or why not?

C. Test Your Individual Level of Racial Prejudice

Go to the site https://buster.cs.yale.edu/implicit/. Click on "Demonstration" and take the Race Implicit Attitudes Test. Be sure to explore the site and learn more about the test before signing off. What type of prejudice (personality-based, culture-based, or prejudice that results from group competition) does the IAT measure? Do you feel that the test produced valid results in your case?

FOR FURTHER READING

Allport, Gordon. 1954. *The Nature of Prejudice*. Reading, MA: Addison-Wesley.
The classic work on individual prejudice.

Feagin, Joseph. 2001. *Racist America*. New York: Routledge.
A passionate analysis of the pervasiveness of racism and anti-black prejudice in America.

Omi, Michael, & Winant, Howard. 1986. *Racial Formation in the United States from the 1960s to the 1980s*. New York: Routledge and Kegan Paul.
An adept analysis of the social and political uses of race.

Smedley, Audrey. 1993. *Race in North America: Origin and Evolution of a Worldview*. Boulder, CO: Westview.
An analysis of the origins of the American view of race.

Takaki, Ronald. 1993. *A Different Mirror: A History of Multicultural America*. Boston: Little, Brown.
A highly readable look at minority groups and cultural diversity in American life.

Zinn, Maxine Baca, & Dill, Bonnie Thornton. (Eds.). 1994. *Women of Color in U.S. Society*. Philadelphia: Temple University Press.
A wide-ranging collection of articles examining the intersecting forces of race, class, and gender in the United States.

2

Assimilation and Pluralism

This chapter continues to look at the ways in which ethnic and racial groups in the United States relate to one another. Two concepts, assimilation and pluralism, are at the core of the discussion. Each includes a variety of possible group relationships and pathways along which group relations might develop.

Assimilation is a process in which formerly distinct and separate groups come to share a common culture and merge together socially. As a society undergoes assimilation, differences among groups begin to decrease. *Pluralism,* on the other hand, exists when groups maintain their individual identities. In a pluralistic society, groups remain separate, and their cultural and social differences persist over time.

In some ways, assimilation and pluralism are contrary processes, but they are not mutually exclusive. They may occur together in a variety of combinations within a particular society or group. Some segments of a society may be assimilating, while others are maintaining (or even increasing) their differences. As we shall see in Chapters 5–9, virtually every minority group in the United States has, at any given time, some members who are assimilating and others who are preserving or reviving traditional cultures. Some Native Americans, for example, are pluralistic. They live on or near reservations, are strongly connected to their heritage, and speak their native languages. Other Native Americans are very much assimilated into the dominant society and live in urban areas, speak English only, and know relatively little about their traditional cultures. Both assimilation and pluralism are important forces in the everyday lives of Native Americans and most other minority groups.

In this chapter, I analyze assimilation and pluralism and consider theories in which they play central roles. The first two sections of the chapter explore theories and concepts that grew out of the sociological examination of the massive immigration from Europe to the United States between the 1820s and 1920s. A great deal of energy has been devoted to documenting, describing, and understanding the experiences of these immigrants and their descendants, and a rich and complex literature has been developed. We then briefly examine other possible group goals and, in the fourth section of the chapter, we examine a more contemporary theory developed in response to the experiences of recent (post-1965) immigrants to the United States. The newest arrivals differ in many ways from the earlier wave of European immigrants, and theories based on the experiences of the latter will not necessarily apply to the former. By the end of this chapter, you will be familiar with many of the concepts needed to understand the variety of possible minority-dominant group situations, the directions our society (and the groups within it) can take, and the relationships between concepts that will guide us throughout this text.

ASSIMILATION

We begin with assimilation because the emphasis in U.S. group relations historically has been on this goal rather than on pluralism. This section presents some of the most important sociological theories and concepts that have been used to describe and analyze assimilation in the United States.

Types of Assimilation

Assimilation is a general term for a process that can follow a number of different pathways. One form of assimilation is expressed in the metaphor of the "melting pot," a process in which different groups come together and contribute in roughly equal amounts to create a common culture and a new, unique society. Popular understandings of the American experience of assimilation often use the melting pot concept and stress the idea that diverse peoples came together to construct U.S. society and American culture. The melting pot metaphor sees assimilation as benign and egalitarian, a process that emphasizes sharing and inclusion.

Although it is a powerful image in our society, the melting pot is not an accurate description of how American assimilation actually proceeded (Abrahamson, 1980, pp. 152–154). Some groups—especially racial minority groups—have been largely excluded from the "melting" process. Furthermore, the melting pot brew has had a distinctly Anglocentric flavor: "For better or worse, the white Anglo-Saxon Protestant tradition was for two centuries—and in crucial respects still is—the dominant influence on American culture and society" (Schlesinger, 1992, p. 28).

Contrary to the melting pot image, assimilation in the United States generally has been a coercive and largely one-sided process better described by the terms *Americanization* or *Anglo-conformity*. Rather than an equal sharing of elements and a gradual blending of diverse peoples, assimilation in the United States was designed to maintain the predominance of the British-type institutional patterns created during the early years of American society. Under Anglo-conformity, immigrant and minority groups were expected to adapt to Anglo-American culture as quickly as possible.

Historically, Americanization has been a precondition for access to better jobs, education, and other opportunities. Assimilation has meant that minority groups have had to give up their traditions and adopt the traditions of Anglo-American culture. To be sure, many groups and individuals were (and continue to be) eager to conform to Anglo culture even if it meant losing much or all of their heritage. For other groups, Americanization created conflict, anxiety, demoralization, and resentment, reactions which we will examine later in this text.

The "Traditional" Perspective on Assimilation: Theories and Concepts

The conclusion that the melting pot is not an accurate description of American assimilation comes from research on the immigrants who came from Europe between the 1820s and the 1920s. The sociologists who studied these experiences developed a body of theories and concepts so rich and so well established that we can call it the *traditional* perspective on assimilation. As you will see, these scholars have made invaluable contributions, and their thinking is impressively complex and comprehensive. This does not mean, of course, that they have exhausted the possibilities or answered (or asked) all the questions. Theorists studying American pluralism and contemporary scholars studying more recent immigrants both have questioned many aspects of traditional assimilation theory and have made a number of important contributions of their own.

Robert Park

Many traditional theories of assimilation are grounded in the work of Robert Park. He was one of a group of scholars who had a major hand in establishing sociology as a discipline in the United States in the 1920s and 1930s. Park believed that intergroup relations go through a predictable set of phases that he called a "race relations cycle." When groups first come into contact (through immigration, conquest, etc.), relations are conflictual and competitive. Eventually, however, the process, or cycle, moves toward assimilation, or the "interpenetration and fusion" of groups (Park & Burgess, 1924, p. 735).

Park argued further that assimilation is inevitable in a democratic and industrial society. In a political system based on democracy, fairness, and impartial justice, all groups eventually will secure equal treatment under the law. In an industrial economy, people tend to be judged on rational grounds—that is, on the basis of their abilities and talents—and not by ethnicity or race. Park believed that as American society modernized, urbanized, and industrialized, the boundaries between ethnic and racial groups would gradually lose their importance. Those boundaries eventually would dissolve, and a more "rational" and unified society would emerge (see also Geschwender, 1978, pp. 19–32; Hirschman, 1983).

Social scientists have examined, analyzed, and criticized Park's conclusions for nearly 80 years. One frequently voiced criticism is that he did not specify a time frame for the completion of assimilation, and therefore his idea that assimilation is "inevitable" cannot be tested. Until the exact point in time when assimilation was complete, we would not know whether the theory was wrong or whether we just had not waited long enough.

An additional criticism of Park's theory is that he did not describe the nature of the assimilation process in much detail. How would assimilation proceed? How would everyday life change? Which aspects of the group would change first?

Milton Gordon

To clarify some of the issues left unresolved by Park, we turn to the works of sociologist Milton Gordon, who made a major contribution to theories of assimilation in his book *Assimilation in American Life* (1964). In it, he broke down the overall process of assimilation into seven subprocesses; we will focus on the first three. Before considering these phases of assimilation, we need to consider some new concepts and terms.

Gordon made a distinction between the cultural and the structural components of society. *Culture* encompasses all aspects of the way of life associated with a group of people. It includes language, religious beliefs, customs and rules of etiquette, and the values and ideas people use to organize their lives and interpret their existence. The *social structure*, or structural components of a society, includes networks of social relationships,

Exhibit 2.1   Gordon's Stages of Assimilation

Stage	Process
1. Acculturation (cultural assimilation)	The group learns the culture, language, and value systems of the dominant society.
2. Integration (structural assimilation)	
At the secondary level:	Members of the group enter the public institutions and organizations of the dominant society.
At the primary level:	Members of the group enter into the cliques, clubs, and friendship groups of the dominant society.
3. Intermarriage (marital assimilation)	Members of the group intermarry with members of the dominant group on a large-scale basis.

SOURCE: Adapted from Gordon (1964, p. 71). Adapted with permission.

groups, organizations, stratification systems, communities, and families. The social structure organizes the work of the society and connects individuals to one another and to the larger society.

It is common in sociology to separate the social structure into primary and secondary sectors. The *primary sector* includes interpersonal relationships that are intimate and personal, such as families and groups of friends. Groups in the primary sector are small. The *secondary sector* consists of groups and organizations that are more public, task oriented, and impersonal. Organizations in the secondary sector often are very large and include businesses, factories, schools and colleges, and bureaucracies.

With these distinctions in mind, we can examine Gordon's model of assimilation, also summarized in Exhibit 2.1. The first three stages, in order, are

1. *Cultural assimilation, or acculturation.* In this phase, members of the minority group learn the culture of the dominant group. Acculturation to the dominant Anglo-American culture might include learning the English language, changing eating habits, adopting new value systems, or altering the spelling of the family surname.

2. *Structural assimilation, or integration.* In the second stage of assimilation, the minority group enters the social structure of the larger society. Integration typically begins in the secondary sector and gradually moves into the primary sector. That is, before people can form friendships with members of other groups (integration into the primary sector), they must first become acquaintances. The initial contact between groups often occurs in public institutions such as schools and workplaces (integration into the secondary sector). Once a group has entered the institutions and public sectors of the larger society, according to Gordon, integration into the primary sector and the other stages of assimilation will follow (although not necessarily quickly). The greater their integration into the secondary sector, the more nearly equal the minority group will be to the dominant group in income, education, and occupational prestige. Measures of integration into the primary sector include the extent to which people have acquaintances, close friends, or neighbors from other groups.

3. *Marital assimilation,* or intermarriage. When integration into the primary sector becomes substantial, the basis for Gordon's third stage of assimilation is established. People are most likely to select spouses from

among their primary relations, and thus, in Gordon's view, primary structural integration typically precedes intermarriage.

Gordon argued that acculturation was a prerequisite for integration. Given the stress on Anglo-conformity, a member of an immigrant or minority group would not be able to compete for jobs or other opportunities in the secondary sector of the social structure until he or she had learned the dominant group's culture. Gordon also believed, however, that successful acculturation does not automatically ensure that a group will begin the integration phase. The dominant group may still exclude the minority group from its institutions and limit the opportunities available to the group. Gordon argued that "acculturation without integration" (or Americanization without equality) is a common situation in the United States for many minority groups, especially racial minority groups.

In Gordon's theory, movement from acculturation to integration is the crucial step in the assimilation process. Once that step is taken, all the other subprocesses will occur in due time. Gordon's idea that assimilation runs a certain course in a certain order echoes Park's conclusion regarding the inevitability of the process.

Forty years after Gordon published his analysis of assimilation, some of his conclusions have been called into question. For example, the individual subprocesses of assimilation that Gordon saw as linked in a certain order are often found to occur independently of one another (Yinger, 1985, p. 154). A group may integrate before acculturating or combine the subprocesses in other ways. In addition, many researchers no longer think of the process of assimilation as necessarily linear or one-way (Greeley, 1974). Groups (or segments thereof) may "reverse direction" and become less assimilated over time, revive their traditional cultures, relearn the old language, or revitalize ethnic organizations or associations.

Nonetheless, Gordon's overall model continues to guide our understanding of the process of assimilation, to the point that a large part of the research agenda for contemporary studies of immigrants consists of assessing the extent to which their experiences can be described in Gordon's terms (Alba & Nee, 1997). In fact, Gordon's model will provide a major organizational framework for the case studies presented in Chapters 5–9.

Human Capital Theory

Why did some European immigrant groups acculturate and integrate more rapidly than others? Although not a theory of assimilation per se, *human capital theory* offers one possible answer to this question. This theory explains status attainment—or the level of success achieved by an individual in society—as a direct result of educational levels, personal values and skills, and other individual characteristics and abilities. Education is seen as an investment in human capital, not unlike the investment a business might make in machinery or new technology. The greater the investment in a person's human capital, the higher the probability of success. Blau and Duncan (1967), in their pioneering statement of status attainment theory, found that even the relative advantage conferred by having a high-status father is largely mediated through education. In other words, high levels of affluence and occupational prestige are not so much a result of being born into a privileged status as they are the result of the superior education that affluence makes possible.

Human capital theory would explain upward mobility for immigrant groups in terms of the resources and cultural characteristics of the members of the group, especially their levels of education and familiarity with English. Success would be seen as a direct result of individual effort and the wise investment of personal resources. According to this theory, people or groups that do not achieve success haven't tried hard enough, haven't made the right kinds of educational investments, or have values or habits that limit their ability to compete.

More than most sociological theories, human capital theory is consistent with traditional American culture and values. Both tend to see success as an individual phenomenon, a reward for hard work, sustained effort, and good character. Both tend to assume that success is equally available to all and that the larger society is open and neutral in its distribution of rewards and opportunity. Both tend to see assimilation as a highly desirable, benign process that blends diverse peoples and cultures into a strong, unified whole. Thus, people or groups that resist Americanization or question its benefits are seen as threatening, illegitimate, or dangerous.

On one level, human capital theory is an important theory of success and upward mobility, and we will, on occasion, use the theory to analyze the experiences of minority and immigrant groups. On another level, the theory is so resonant with American "commonsensical" views of success and failure that we may tend to use it uncritically. A final judgment on the validity of the theory will be more appropriately made at the end of the text, but you should be aware of the major limitations of the theory from the beginning. First, as an explanation of minority group experience, human capital theory is not so much "wrong" as it is incomplete. In other words, and as we shall see, it doesn't take account of all the factors that affect mobility and assimilation. Second, the assumption that U.S. society is—or ever has been—equally open and fair to all groups is simply wrong. We will point out other strengths and the limits of this perspective as we move through the text.

Assimilation Patterns

In this section, we will explore the patterns of assimilation followed by European immigrants and their descendants. These patterns have been established by research conducted in the traditional perspective and are consistent with the model of assimilation developed by Gordon.

The Importance of Generations

People today—social scientists, politicians, and ordinary citizens—often fail to recognize the time and effort it takes for a group to become completely Americanized.

For most European immigrant groups, the process took generations, and it was the grandchildren or the great-grandchildren of the immigrants, not the immigrants themselves, who finally acculturated and integrated. Mass immigration from Europe ended in the 1920s, but the assimilation of European ethnic groups was not completed until well after World War II (and in some ways, it is still not complete).

Here's a rough summary of how assimilation proceeded for these European immigrants. The first generation, or the actual immigrants, settled in ethnic neighborhoods such as "Little Italy" and made only limited movement toward acculturation and integration. They focused their energies on the network of family and social relationships encompassed within their own groups. Of course, many of them—most often the men—had to leave the neighborhood for work and other reasons, and these excursions required some familiarity with the larger society. Some English had to be learned, and taking a job outside the neighborhood is, almost by definition, a form of integration. Nonetheless, the first generation lived and died largely within the context of the "old country," which had been re-created within the new.

The next generation, or the children of the immigrants, found themselves in a position of psychological or social marginality: They were partly ethnic and partly American but full members of neither group. They were born in America but in households and neighborhoods that were ethnic, not American. They learned the old language first and were socialized in the old ways. As they entered childhood, however, they entered the public schools, where they were socialized into the Anglo-American culture.

Very often, the world the second generation learned about at school conflicted with the world they inhabited at home. For many groups, the family values of the old country often expected children to subordinate their self-interests to the interests of their elders and of the family as a whole. For example, the selection of a marriage partner was heavily influenced by and subject to the approval

Exhibit 2.2   Some Comparisons Between Italians and WASPs

	WASPs[a]	First	Second	Third and Fourth
			Generation	
Percentage with some college	42.4	19.0	19.4	41.7
Average years of education	12.6	9.0	11.1	13.4
Percentage white collar	34.7	20.0	22.5	28.8
Percentage blue collar	37.9	65.0	53.9	39.0
Average occupational prestige	42.5	34.3	36.8	42.5
Percentage of "unmixed" Italian males marrying non-Italian females	—	21.9	51.4	67.3

SOURCE: Adapted from Alba (1985), Tables 5–3, 5–4, and 6–2. The data are originally from the NORC General Social Surveys, 1975–1980, and the Current Population Survey, 1979. Copyright © 1985 Richard D. Alba. Reprinted with permission.

a. WASPs were not separated by generation, and some of the differences between groups may be the result of factors such as age. That is, the older WASPs may have levels of education more comparable to first-generation Italian Americans than WASPs as a whole.

of parents, customs, and expectations that conflicted sharply with American ideas about individualism and romantic love. Differences of this sort often caused painful conflict between the ethnic first generation and their Americanized children.

As the second generation progressed toward adulthood, they tended to move out of the old neighborhoods. Their geographic mobility often was motivated by social mobility. They were much more acculturated than their parents, spoke English fluently, and enjoyed a wider range of occupational choices and opportunities. Discriminatory policies in education, housing, and the job market sometimes limited them, but they were upwardly mobile, and in their pursuit of jobs and careers, they left behind the ethnic subcommunity and many of the customs of their parents.

The members of the third generation, or the grandchildren of the immigrants, typically were born and raised in non-ethnic settings. English was their first (and often their only) language, and their values and perceptions were thoroughly American. Although family and kinship ties with grandparents and the old neighborhood often remained strong, ethnicity for this generation was a

relatively minor part of their daily realities and their self-images. Visits on weekends and holidays and family rituals revolving around the cycles of birth, marriage, and death might connect the third generation to the world of their ancestors, but in terms of their everyday lives, they were American, not ethnic.

The pattern of assimilation by generation is as follows:

- The first generation began the process and was at least slightly acculturated and integrated.
- The second generation was very acculturated and highly integrated (at least in the secondary sectors of the society).
- The third generation finished the acculturation process and enjoyed high levels of integration at both the secondary and the primary levels.

Exhibit 2.2 illustrates these patterns in terms of the structural assimilation of Italian Americans (see Chapter 9 for additional data on the assimilation of white ethnic groups). The educational and occupational characteristics of this group converge with those of white Anglo-Saxon Protestants (WASPs) as the generations change. For example, the percentage of Italian Americans with some college shows a gap of more than 20 points between the first and second generations and WASPs. Italians of the third and fourth generations, though, are virtually identical to WASPs on this measure of integration in the secondary sector. The other differences between Italians and WASPs shrink in a similar fashion from generation to generation.

The first five measures of educational and occupational attainment in Exhibit 2.2 illustrate the generational pattern of integration (structural assimilation). The last comparison measures marital assimilation, or intermarriage. It displays the percentage of males of *unmixed*, or 100% Italian heritage, who married females outside the Italian community. Once more, the tendency is for integration, now at the primary level, to increase across the generations. The huge majority of first-generation males married within their group (only 21.9% married non-Italians). By the third generation, 67.3% of the males were marrying non-Italians.

This generational pattern fits the experiences of groups other than European immigrants and their descendants. For example, Exhibit 2.3 illustrates some patterns of acculturation for Latino Americans today. By the third generation, only 1% speak "only or more Spanish" as the primary home language, and cultural values closely approximate those of the dominant group.

Of course, this model of step-by-step, linear assimilation by generation fits some groups better than others. For example, immigrants from Northern and Western Europe (except the Irish) generally were more similar, racially and culturally, to the dominant group and tended to be more educated and skilled. They experienced relatively easier acceptance and tended to complete the assimilation process in three generations or less. In contrast, immigrants from Ireland and from Southern and Eastern Europe were mostly uneducated, unskilled peasants who were more likely to join the huge army of industrial labor that manned American factories, mines, and mills. These groups were more likely to remain at the bottom of the American class structure for generations and to have risen to middle-class prosperity only in the recent past.

It's important to keep this generational pattern in mind when examining present-day immigration. It is common for newcomers to be criticized for their "slow" pace of assimilation, but their "progress" takes on a new aspect when viewed in the light of the time frame for assimilation followed by European immigrants. Especially with modern forms of transportation, immigration can be very fast. Assimilation, on the other hand, is by nature slow.

Immigration as a Collective Experience

Another noteworthy pattern in the immigration experience is the way that immigrant groups tended to follow "chains" established and maintained by their members. Some versions of the traditional assimilation perspective (especially human capital theory) treat immigration and status attainment as purely individual matters. To the contrary, scholars have demonstrated that immigration to the United States was in large measure a group phenomenon. Immigrant chains stretched across the oceans, and these chains were held together by the ties of kinship, language, religion, culture, and a sense of common peoplehood (Bodnar, 1985; Tilly, 1990). The networks supplied information, money for passage, family news, and job offers.

Here's how chain immigration worked. Someone from a village in, say, Poland, would make it to the United States. The successful immigrant would send word to the home village, perhaps by hiring a letter writer. Along with news and stories of his adventures, he would send his address. Within months, another immigrant from the village, perhaps a brother or other relative, would show up at the address of the original immigrant. After his months of experience in the new society, the original immigrant could lend assistance, provide a place to sleep, help with job hunting, and orient the newcomer to the area.

Before long, others from the village would arrive, in need of the same sort of introduction

Exhibit 2.3   Latino Acculturation

Language

	"What language do you usually speak at home?"		
	Only/More Spanish	*Both Equally*	*Only/More English*
First generation	73%	20%	6%
Second generation	17%	43%	40%
Third generation	1%	21%	78%

	"In what language are the TV programs you usually watch?"		
	Only/More Spanish	*Both Equally*	*Only/More English*
First generation	31%	42%	27%
Second generation	5%	26%	68%
Third generation	1%	11%	88%

Family Values

	"Is it better for children to live in their parents' home until they get married?"
	Yes
First generation	87%
Second generation	62%
Third generation	46%
Non-Latinos	42%

	"In general, the husband should have the final say in family matters."
	Yes
First generation	46%
Second generation	27%
Third generation	24%
Non-Latinos	26%

SOURCE: Godstein and Suro (2000). Used with permission.

NOTE: These results are from a telephone survey of about 2,400 Latinos and 2,000 non-Latino adults conducted in the summer of 1999. Projections to the population are accurate to within ± 2 percentage points.

to the mysteries of America. The compatriots would tend to settle close to one another, in the same building or on the same block. Soon, entire neighborhoods were filled with people from a certain village, province, or region. In these ethnic enclaves, the old language was spoken and the old ways were observed. Businesses were started, churches or synagogues were founded, families were begun, and mutual aid societies and other organizations were formed. There was safety in numbers as well as comfort and security in a familiar, if transplanted, set of traditions and customs.

As we saw earlier in this chapter, the immigrants often responded to U.S. society by attempting to re-create as much of their old world as possible. Partly to avoid the harsher forms of rejection and discrimination and partly to band together for solidarity and mutual support, immigrants created their own miniature social worlds within the bustling metropolises of the industrializing Northeast and the West Coast. These Little Italys, Little Warsaws, Little Irelands, Greektowns, Chinatowns, and Little Tokyos were safe havens that insulated the immigrants from the larger society and allowed them to establish bonds with one another, organize a group life, pursue their own group interests, and have some control over the pace of their adjustment to American culture. For some groups and in some areas, the ethnic subcommunity was a short-lived phenomenon. For others—especially Jewish immigrants—the neighborhood became the dominant structure of their lives, and the networks continued to function long after arrival in the United States.

Variations in Assimilation

Assimilation is a complex process that is never exactly the same for any two groups. Sociologists have paid particular attention to the way that religion, social class, and gender have shaped the overall patterns of European immigration in the late 1800s and early 1900s. They also have investigated the way that immigrants' reasons for coming to this country have affected the experiences of different groups.

Religion

A major differentiating factor in the experiences of European immigrant groups, recognized by Gordon and other students of American assimilation, was religion. Protestant, Catholic, and Jewish immigrants lived in different neighborhoods, occupied different niches in the workforce, formed separate networks of affiliation and groups, and chose their marriage partners from different pools of people.

One important study that documented the importance of religion for European immigrants and their descendants (and also reinforced the importance of generations) was conducted by sociologist Ruby Jo Kennedy (1944). She studied intermarriage patterns in New Haven, Connecticut, over a 70-year period ending in the 1940s and found that the immigrant generation chose marriage partners from a pool whose boundaries were marked by ethnicity *and* religion. For example, Irish Catholics married other Irish Catholics, Italian Catholics married Italian Catholics, Irish Protestants married Irish Protestants, and so forth across all the ethnic/religious divisions she studied.

As the children and grandchildren of the immigrants married, their pool of partners continued to be bounded by religion, but not so much by ethnicity. Thus, later generations of Irish Catholics continued to marry other Catholics but were less likely to marry other Irish. As assimilation proceeded, ethnic group boundaries faded (or "melted"), but religious boundaries did not. Kennedy described this phenomenon as a *triple melting pot*: a pattern of structural assimilation within each of the three religions (Kennedy, 1944, 1952).

Will Herberg (1960), another important scholar of American assimilation, also explored the connection between religion and ethnicity. He noted that the pressures of acculturation did not affect all aspects of ethnicity equally. European immigrants and their descendants were strongly encouraged to learn English, but they were not so pressured to change their religious beliefs. Very often, their religious faith was the strongest connection between later generations and their immigrant ancestors. The American tradition of religious tolerance allowed the descendants of the European immigrants to preserve this tie to their roots without being seen as "un-American." As a result, the Protestant, Catholic, and Jewish faiths came to occupy roughly equal degrees of legitimacy in American society.

Thus, for many descendants of European immigrants, religion became a vehicle through which their ethnicity could be expressed. For many members of this group, religion and ethnicity were fused, and ethnic traditions and identities came to have a religious expression. For countless millions, attendance at church or synagogue became not only a religious act but also a way of connecting with one's ancestors and a way of locating oneself in time and space, an aspect of identity that linked oneself, however tenuously, to the old country and to ancestors.

Social Class

Social class is a central feature of social structure, and not surprisingly, it affected the European immigrant groups in a number of ways. First, social class combined with religion to shape the social world of the descendants of the European immigrants. In fact, one of Gordon's (1964) most important conclusions was that U.S. society in the 1960s actually consisted of not three but four melting pots, one for each of the major ethnic/religious groups and one for black Americans; each of these was subdivided internally by social class. In his view, the most significant structural unit within American society was the *ethclass,* defined by the intersection of the religious/ethnic and social class boundaries (e.g. working-class Catholic, upper-class Protestant, etc.). Thus, people weren't "simply American" but tended to identify with, associate with, and choose their spouses from within their ethclass.

Second, social class also affected structural integration. The huge majority of the post-1880s European immigrants were working class, and because they "entered U.S. society at the bottom of the economic ladder, and . . . stayed close to that level for the next half century, ethnic history has been essentially working class history" (Morawska, 1990, p. 215; see also Bodnar, 1985). For generations, many groups of Eastern and Southern European immigrants acculturated not to middle-class American culture but to an urban, working-class, blue-collar set of lifestyles and values. Even today, ethnicity for many groups remains interconnected with social class factors, and a familiar stereotype of the white ethnic is the hard-hat construction worker.

Gender

Anyone who wants to learn about the experience of immigration will find a huge body of literature incorporating every imaginable discipline and genre. The great bulk of this material, however, concerns the immigrant experience in general or is focused specifically on male immigrants. The experiences of female immigrants have been much less recorded and, hence, are far less accessible. We are still learning how different male and female immigration experiences sometimes were.

Many immigrant women came from cultures with strong patriarchal traditions and had much less access than the men to leadership roles, education, and prestigious, high-paying occupations. As was the case with slave women, the voices of immigrant women have been muted. The research that has been done, however, documents the fact that immigrant women played multiple roles both during immigration and during the process of adjusting to U.S. society. As would be expected in patriarchal societies, the roles of wife and mother were central, but immigrant women were involved in other activities as well.

In general, male immigrants outnumbered female immigrants. It was common for the male members of a family to immigrate first and send for the women only after they had secured lodging, a job, and a certain level of stability. Women immigrants' experiences were quite varied, however, and in some cases, women were prominent among the "first wave" of immigrants. During the 19th century, for example, a high percentage of Irish immigrants were young single women. They came to America seeking jobs and often wound up employed in domestic work, a role that permitted them to live "respectably" in a family setting. In 1850, about 75% of all Irish immigrant women in New York City worked as servants, and most of the rest were employed in textile mills and factories. As late as 1920, 81% of employed Irish-born women in the United States worked as domestics. Factory work was the second most prevalent form of employment (Blessing, 1980; see also Steinberg, 1981).

Because the economic situation of immigrant families typically was precarious, it was common for women to be involved in wage labor. The type and location of the work varied from group to group. Whereas Irish women were concentrated in domestic work and factories and mills, these forms of employment were rare for Italian women. Italian culture had strong norms of patriarchy, and "one of the culture's strongest prohibitions was directed against contact between women and male strangers" (Alba, 1985, p. 53). Thus, acceptable work situations for Italian women were likely to involve tasks that could be performed at home: doing laundry, taking in boarders, and doing piecework for the garment industry. Italian women who worked outside the home were likely to find themselves in single-sex settings among other immigrant women. Thus, women immigrants from Italy tended to be far less acculturated and integrated than those from Ireland.

Eastern European Jewish women represent a third pattern of adjustment to America. They were part of a flow of refugees from religious persecution, and most came with their husbands and children in intact family units. According to Steinberg (1981), "Few were independent bread-winners, and when they did work, they usually found employment in the . . . garment industry. Often they worked in small shops as family members" (p. 161).

It was common for the women of immigrant groups to combine work and home. "Peasant women were accustomed to productive work within the family economy. . . . Placing their highest priority on family needs, women stayed home whenever possible, shifting roles quickly according to family necessity" (Evans, 1989, p. 131). More closely connected to home and family than the men were, immigrant women typically were less likely than the men to learn to read or speak English, or otherwise to acculturate, and were significantly more influential in preserving the heritage of their groups.

Younger, single, second-generation women tended to seek employment outside the home. They found opportunities in the industrial sector and in clerical and sales work, occupations that were quickly stereotyped as "women's work." Women were seen as working only to supplement the family treasury, and this assumption was used to justify a lower wage scale. Evans reports that in the late 1800s, "Whether in factories, offices, or private homes . . . women's wages were about half of those of men" (1989, p. 135). These patterns of discrimination motivated women, both immigrant and native born, to join the labor movement (Evans, 1989; Seller, 1987; Wertheimer, 1979).

On a positive note, Seller (1987) rejected the stereotype of immigrant women as subservient, unassimilated preservers of the "old ways" who were content to remain in the background and concluded that they played a central role in both acculturation and immigration:

Immigrant women built social, charitable, and educational institutions that spanned the neighborhood and the nation. They established day care centers, restaurants, hotels, employment agencies, and legal aid bureaus. They wrote novels, plays, and poetry. They campaigned for a variety of causes, from factory legislation to birth control, from cleaner streets to cleaner government. (p. 198)

Motivation for Immigration: Sojourning

Some versions of the traditional perspective and the "taken-for-granted" views of many Americans assume that assimilation is desirable and therefore desired. However, immigrant groups were highly variable in their interest in Americanization, a factor that greatly shaped their experiences.

Some groups were very committed to Americanization. Eastern European Jews, for example, came to America because of religious persecution and planned to make America their home from the beginning. They left their homeland in fear for their lives and had no plans and no possibility of returning. They intended to stay, for they had nowhere else to go. (The nation of Israel was not founded until 1948.) These immigrants committed themselves to learning English, becoming citizens, and familiarizing themselves with their new society as quickly as possible.

Other immigrants had no intention of becoming American citizens and therefore had little interest in Americanization. These *sojourners,* or "birds of passage," were oriented to the old country and intended to return once they had accumulated enough capital to be successful in their home villages or provinces. Because immigration records are not very detailed, it is difficult to assess the exact numbers of immigrants who returned to the old country (see Wyman, 1993). We do know, however, that a large percentage of Italian immigrants were sojourners. It is estimated that 3.8 million Italians landed in the United States between 1899 and 1924, and 2.1 million departed during the same interval (Nelli, 1980, p. 547).

PLURALISM

Sociologists and the public in general have become more interested in pluralism and ethnic diversity in the past few decades. Interest has been stimulated in part by the fact that the assimilation predicted by Park (and implicit in the conventional wisdom of many Americans) has not materialized. Perhaps we simply haven't waited long enough, but as the 21st century begins, distinctions among the racial minority groups in our society show few signs of disappearing, and the descendants of the European immigrants maintain a stubborn, if diminishing, interest in their ethnicity (see Chapter 9).

The increased interest in pluralism no doubt also has been stimulated by the increasing social and cultural diversity of U.S. society that is reflected in Exhibit 1.1. Controversies over issues such as "English-only" policies, bilingual education, and welfare rights for immigrants are common, often bitter, and sometimes violent. Many Americans feel that diversity or pluralism has now exceeded acceptable limits and that the unity of the nation is at risk.

Finally, interest in pluralism and ethnicity in general has been stimulated by developments around the globe. In recent years, several nation-states have disintegrated into smaller units based on language, culture, race, and ethnicity. Recent events in Afghanistan, Iraq, India, Eastern Europe, the former U.S.S.R., Yugoslavia, Canada, Rwanda, and other African nations, to mention just a few examples, have provided dramatic and often tragic evidence of the persistence of ethnic identities and enmities throughout decades or even centuries of submergence and suppression in larger national units.

In short, pluralism has become more prominent because domestic cultural diversity has increased and because ethnic groups, in the United States and elsewhere, have persisted as consequential forces in modern industrialized society. In contemporary debates, discussions of diversity and pluralism often are couched in the language of *multiculturalism,* a general term for a variety of programs and ideas that stress mutual respect for all groups and for the multiple heritages that shaped the United States. In the rest of this section, we discuss the nature of pluralism and present some of the relevant theoretical background for the continuing debate.

Types of Pluralism

We can distinguish various types of pluralism by using some of the concepts introduced in the discussion of assimilation. *Cultural pluralism* exists when groups have not acculturated and each maintains its own identity. The groups might speak different languages, practice different religions, and have different value systems. The groups are part of the same society and might even live in adjacent areas, but in some ways, they live in different worlds. Many Native Americans are culturally pluralistic, maintaining their traditional languages and cultures and living on isolated reservations. The Amish, a religious community sometimes called the Pennsylvania Dutch, are also a culturally pluralistic group. They are committed to a way of life organized around farming, and they maintain a culture and an institutional life that is separate from the dominant culture (see Hostetler, 1980;

Kephart & Zellner, 1994; Kraybill & Bowman, 2001).

A second type of pluralism, following Gordon's subprocesses, exists when a group has acculturated but not integrated. That is, the group has adopted the Anglo-American culture but does not have full and equal access to the institutions of the larger society. In this situation, called *structural pluralism,* cultural differences are minimal, but the groups occupy different locations in the social structure. The groups may speak with the same accent, eat the same food, pursue the same goals, and sub-scribe to the same values, but they also may maintain separate organizational systems, including different churches, clubs, schools, and neighborhoods. Under structural plural-ism, the various groups practice a common cul-ture but do so in different places and with minimal interaction across group boundaries. An example of structural pluralism can be found on any Sunday morning in the Christian churches of the United States. Not only are local parishes separated by denomination, but they are also often identified with specific ethnic groups or races. What happens in the various churches—the rituals, the expressions of faith, the statements of core values and beliefs—is similar and expresses a common, shared culture based on Christianity. Structurally, however, this common culture is expressed in separate buildings and by separate congregations. Gordon's conclusion that U.S. society consisted of four separate melting pots, or subsocieties—differentiated by race, ethnic-ity, religion, and class—illustrates one concep-tion of structural pluralism.

A third type of pluralism reverses the order of Gordon's first two phases: integration without acculturation. This situation is exem-plified by a group that has had some material success (measured by wealth or income, for example) but has not become Americanized (learned English, adopted American values and norms, etc.). Some immigrant groups have found niches in American society in which they can survive and, occasionally, prosper economically without acculturating.

Two different situations can be used to illustrate this pattern. An *enclave minority* establishes its own neighborhood and relies on a set of interconnected businesses, each of which usually is small in scope, for its eco-nomic survival. Some of these businesses serve the group, whereas others serve the larger society. The Cuban American community in South Florida and "Chinatowns" in many larger American cities are examples of ethnic enclaves. A similar pattern of adjustment, the *middleman minority,* also relies on small shops and retail firms, but the businesses are more dispersed throughout a large area rather than concentrated in a specific locale. Some Chinese American communities fit this second pattern, as do Korean American green gro-ceries and Indian American–owned motels (Portes & Manning, 1986).

The economic success of enclave and mid-dleman minorities is due in part to the strong ties of cooperation and mutual aid within their groups. The ties are based, in turn, on cultural bonds that would weaken if accultur-ation took place. In contrast with Gordon's idea that acculturation is a prerequisite to integration, whatever success these groups enjoy is due in part to the fact that they have *not* Americanized. At various times and places, Jewish, Chinese, Japanese, Korean, and Cuban Americans have formed enclaves or been middleman minorities (see Bonacich & Modell, 1980; Kitano & Daniels, 2001).

Each of these situations (enclave and mid-dleman minorities) can be considered either as a type of pluralism (emphasizing the absence of acculturation) or as a type of assimilation (emphasizing a high level of economic equal-ity). Keep in mind that assimilation and plu-ralism are not opposites but can occur in a variety of combinations.

Theoretical Perspectives on Pluralism

Many theoretical discussions of pluralism begin with a consideration of the work of Horace Kallen. In articles published in the magazine *The Nation* (1915a, 1915b), Kallen argued that people should not have to surren-der their culture and traditions to become full participants in American society. He rejected the Anglo-conformist, assimilationist model of his day and contended that the existence of separate ethnic groups, even with separate cultures, religions, and languages, was consistent with democracy and other core American values. In Gordon's terms, Kallen believed that integration and equality were possible without extensive acculturation and that American society could be a federation of diverse groups, a mosaic of harmonious and interdependent cultures and peoples (Kallen, 1915a, 1915b; see also Abrahamson, 1980; Gleason, 1980).

Indeed, distinctive ethnic groups persist in American society, a fact that contemporary scholars have tried to understand. Most of their work deals with white ethnic groups, the descendants of immigrants from Europe. The persistence of racial minority groups—with their more visible identifying characteristics and their long histories of rejection, exploitation, prejudice, and racism—is less difficult to explain.

In their influential study *Beyond the Melting Pot,* Glazer and Moynihan (1970) analyzed both ethnic and racial minority groups in New York City. They found that well into the 1960s, white ethnic groups retained a vital significance for their members despite massive acculturation over the decades. The groups changed form and function over time but remained important social entities, valued by their members and showing few signs of disappearing. White ethnic groups in New York City helped to shape the self-image of their members while providing a way to belong to the larger society. They linked members to one another through networks of mutual support and aid, and they served as a base of organization for political purposes and for relationships with other ethnic groups. Glazer and Moynihan concluded, "The point about the melting pot is that it did not happen" (p. 290).

In a study of ethnicity that relied heavily on public opinion polls given to large, representative samples of Americans, Greeley (1974) also found a great deal of evidence for the continuing existence and importance of white ethnic groups in American life. Greeley criticized the common assumption that differences between groups would diminish over time in a simple, straightforward process of homogenization to the Anglo-American norm. He concluded that the sense of ethnicity or the strength of a person's identification with his or her ethnic group can vary from time to time and take on new dimensions. For example, Greeley used the term *ethnogenesis* to describe a process in which new minority groups can be formed from combinations of a variety of traditions, including Anglo-American traditions. He noted that there is "a deliberate and self-conscious attempt to *create* a 'Spanish-speaking' ethnic group"; that "an American Indian group is *struggling to emerge*"; and that "in Chicago there is even an effort . . . to *create* an Appalachian white ethnic group" (Greeley, 1974, pp. 295–296, emphasis added). In all three examples, Greeley identified situations in which single, unified, self-conscious groups could emerge in the future, even though they did not exist at the time he was writing. Greeley concluded that "ethnicity is not a residual social force that is slowly and gradually disappearing; it is, rather, a dynamic, flexible social mechanism that can be called into being rather quickly and transformed and transmuted to meet changing situations and circumstances" (1974, p. 301; see also Alba, 1990).

A process parallel to ethnogenesis can also occur with racial minority groups. Just as new ethnic groupings can emerge by combining different traditions, so can new "racial" groups arise from intermarriage. As I noted in Chapter 1, people of mixed racial heritages have organized to promote their own interests. They desire recognition from governmental agencies and revisions of the racial choices available on official surveys and census forms. The multiple racial choices used in the 2000 Census reflect the desires of this emerging group in American society. Note that, contrary to the traditional perspective on assimilation, the development of a new mixed-race group (or groups) indicates that increasing rates of intermarriage can lead to *more* minority groups, not fewer. The creation of racially based minority groups independent of the traditional racial divisions based on skin color is also a striking illustration of the essentially social nature of race (see Chapter 1).

What social forces might cause ethnic or racial groups to become more cohesive? In what kinds of situations might people come to identify more strongly with their groups? In his book *The Ethnic Myth* (1981), Steinberg contended that ethnic diversity and strength of group identification may be a result of group conflict over valued goods and services, a way of defending privilege and position. Unlike Greeley or Glazer and Moynihan, Steinberg argued that white ethnic groups would soon be assimilated. He analyzed the "ethnic resurgence" of the 1960s: an apparent increase in interest in and commitment to white ethnicity. According to Steinberg, the resurgence was essentially a defensive reaction to the perceived advances of African Americans and other racial minorities. The white ethnic groups organized around their common heritage as a way of protecting their control of resources.

More recently, Gallagher (2001) reported a series of interviews that seem to confirm Steinberg's point regarding the demise of white ethnicity. He interviewed 92 white ethnic respondents from all walks of life and found very little evidence or trace of ethnic identity. Only 13% of his respondents, usually those who had a parent born in Europe or lived in ethnic neighborhoods, said that their ethnicity was an important part of their identity. This finding supports Steinberg's (1981) prediction that white ethnic identity would fade away.

Consistent with Steinberg's other conclusion, that ethnic identity can be a defensive reaction against other groups, Gallagher found that his respondents often used their understanding of the struggles of their own ethnic ancestors as a context for criticizing and disparaging blacks and other racial minorities today. The understanding of these respondents was that their ancestors succeeded in America against odds just as formidable as those faced by blacks (a very dubious equation, as we shall see).

Furthermore, they used their (sometimes exaggerated) family tales of immigrant success as a rhetorical device for denigrating other groups: "My family came with nothing and succeeded; why can't blacks?"

Although some of their conclusions differ, Glazer and Moynihan, Greeley, and Steinberg all found that white ethnic groups played important roles in intergroup conflicts and remained viable and important social entities late in the 20th century, even though they changed form and function as the surrounding society changed. New groupings appeared even as old ones declined in importance. Gallagher found that ethnic identity has faded in salience and importance to people but still retains a role as a rhetorical device for expressing disdain for other groups, especially African Americans.

In the current era of multiculturalism and high rates of immigration, ethnicity is frequently celebrated, and people are encouraged to know and express their heritage. Pluralism is seen as sophisticated and progressive because it seems to be associated with increased tolerance for diversity and respect for all peoples and ways of life. Steinberg and Gallagher remind us that ethnicity has a negative as well as a positive side: It may be the result of conflict and a disguise for expressing prejudice and denying opportunity to other groups.

OTHER GROUP GOALS

Although this book concentrates on assimilation and pluralism, there are, of course, other possible group relationships and goals. Two minority group goals that are commonly noted are separatism and revolution (Wirth, 1945). The goal of *separatism* is for the group to sever *all* ties (political, cultural, geographic) with the larger society. Thus, separatism goes well beyond pluralism. Native Americans have expressed both separatist and pluralist goals, and separatism also has been pursued by some African American organizations, such as the Black Muslims.

A minority group promoting *revolution* seeks to switch places with the dominant group and become the ruling elite or create a new social order, perhaps in alliance with members of the dominant group. Although revolutionary activity can be found among some American minority groups (e.g., the Black Panthers), this goal has been relatively rare for minority groups in the United States. Revolutionary minority groups are more commonly found in situations such as those in colonial Africa, in which one nation conquers and controls another racially or culturally different nation.

The dominant group may also pursue goals other than assimilation and pluralism, including forced migration or expulsion, extermination or genocide, and continued subjugation of the minority group. Chinese immigrants, for example, were the victims of a policy of expulsion beginning in the 1880s (see Chapter 8), and Native Americans also have been the victims of this policy (see Chapter 6). The most infamous example of genocide is the Holocaust in Nazi Germany, during which 6 million Jews were murdered. The dominant group pursues "continued subjugation" when, as in slavery in the antebellum South, it attempts to maintain the status quo. A dominant group may simultaneously pursue different policies with different minority groups and may, of course, change policies over time.

CONTEMPORARY IMMIGRANTS: SEGMENTED ASSIMILATION

Recall that the theories of assimilation and pluralism presented to this point focus on European immigrants who arrived between the 1820s and 1920s and their descendants. Although their experiences were varied, all these groups eventually acculturated and integrated. Today, white ethnic groups are equal to national norms in terms of average income, education, unemployment, and other measures of economic success (see Chapter 9).

What relevance do the experiences of these groups have for the immigrants who have arrived in recent decades? How are the complex forces of American assimilation and pluralism shaping the fate of these new arrivals (and their children)? Contemporary immigrants are unlikely simply to duplicate the experiences of earlier groups. Present-day immigrants are much more diverse racially and culturally than immigrants from Europe, and they come (literally) from all over the globe. In addition, the United States today is a very different place from the society European immigrants confronted in the 19th and 20th centuries. Industrialization has advanced, and relatively fewer of the blue-collar, manual labor jobs that sustained European immigrants are now available. Economic inequality is greater and social mobility more difficult than in previous generations.

Will religion and social class be important forces in the lives of these newest immigrants? Will these groups acculturate before they integrate? Will they take as many as three (or more) generations to assimilate? What will their patterns of intermarriage look like? Will they follow the pattern of the European groups and eventually achieve socioeconomic parity with the dominant group? When? How?

To deal with these and other questions, one group of researchers has proposed the concept of *segmented assimilation* (Portes & Rumbaut, 2001; Portes & Zhou, 1993). These scholars argue that assimilation in the United States today is fragmented and can have a number of different outcomes. Some contemporary immigrants will follow the pattern established by the earlier European immigrants and analyzed by Gordon: Eventually, they will integrate into the white, middle-class mainstream. Others will become part of the urban poor and will find themselves mired in permanent poverty. Still other immigrant groups will form close-knit enclaves based on their traditional cultures and become successful in the United States by *resisting* acculturation (Portes & Rumbaut, 2001, p. 45).

The key factors that shape the fate of current immigrants include the degree of racial discrimination and rejection directed at them, the degree of cohesion and solidarity they maintain, the physical and monetary resources and human capital they bring with them (e.g., wealth, education, business skills), and the nature of the job market. For example, immigrants who are nonwhite, less educated, and unskilled (e.g., many Latin American immigrants) will be forced by racial discrimination and by their relatively low levels of human capital into the lower social and economic classes of American society. On the other hand, immigrants who bring high levels of education (e.g., many Asians) will be able to penetrate the mainstream job market and achieve socioeconomic equality, regardless of their race.

Furthermore, U.S. society and American culture are more fragmented and diverse today. The traditional perspective on assimilation assumes a "two-group" model: immigrant groups on one hand and middle-class, white, mainstream society and culture on the other. Today, new groups can assimilate into one of the varieties of African American subcultures or into any number of other niches and spaces in American society (Alba & Nee, 1997). Thus, the notion of the triple melting pot (already expanded to four melting pots by Gordon in the 1960s) might have to be multiplied many times to accommodate the various types of ethnic and racial intermixing in contemporary society.

COMPARATIVE FOCUS

IMMIGRATION, EMIGRATION, AND IRELAND

Immigration and assimilation are among the most wrenching, exciting, disconcerting, exhilarating, and heartbreaking of human experiences. Immigrants have recorded these feelings—along with the adventures and experiences that sparked them—in every possible medium, including letters, memoirs, poems, photos, stories, movies, jokes, and music. These immigrant tales recount the traumas of leaving home, adjusting to a new society, coping with rejection and discrimination, and thousands of other experiences. Some of the most poignant of these stories express the sadness of parting with family and friends, perhaps forever. Peter Jones captured some of these feelings in his song "Killkelly," based on letters written nearly 150 years ago by an Irish father to his immigrant son—Jones's great-grandfather—in the United States. Each verse of the song paraphrases a letter and includes news of the family and community left behind. The song expresses, in simple but powerful language, the deep sadness of separation and the longing for reunion.

Kilkelly, Ireland, 18 and 90, my dear and loving son John
I guess that I must be close on to eighty,

it's thirty years since you're gone.
Because of all of the money you send me,
I'm still living out on my own.
Michael has built himself a fine house and Brigid's daughters have grown.
Thank you for sending your family picture,
they're lovely young women and men.
You say that you might even come for a visit,
what joy to see you again.[1]

It is particularly appropriate to use an Irish song to illustrate the sorrows of immigration. Just as the United States has been a major receiver of immigrants for the last 200 years, Ireland has been a major supplier. Mass immigration from Ireland began with the potato famines of the 1840s and continued through the end of the 20th century, motivated by continuing hard times, political unrest, and unemployment. The sadness of Peter Jones's ancestors has been repeated over and over as the youth of Ireland left for jobs in Great Britain, the United States, and hundreds of other places, never expecting to return. The famines of the 1840s and the continuing immigration in the decades that followed cut the Irish population of 7 million in half; today, the population is still less than 4 million.

History rarely runs in straight lines, however. Today, after nearly 200 years of supplying immigrants, Ireland (along with the other nations of Northern and Western Europe) has become a consumer. The number of immigrants *entering* Ireland has nearly tripled since the late 1980s, and, in 2001, more than 45,000 newcomers arrived. This is a tiny number compared to the hundreds of thousands of immigrants entering the United States, but as a proportion of the population, immigration to Ireland actually is larger. By one count, Ireland received 5.3 immigrants per 1,000 population in the year 2000, while the United States received only 3.5 per 1,000 population (Central Intelligence Agency, 2001).

What explains this switch from immigration to emigration? The answers are not hard to find. After decades of unemployment and depression, the Irish economy entered a boom phase in the early 1990s. Spurred by the investments of multinational corporations (many headquartered in the United States) and the benefits of joining the European Economic Union, the Irish economy and the job supply have grown rapidly. In fact, there is now a labor shortage in Ireland. One estimate from the year 2000 was that the nation would need 200,000 more workers—about 10% of the present workforce—by the year 2005 to fill the jobs that would become available ("A Sorry Tale," 2000, p. 51). To fill this gap, the Irish government has mounted a worldwide recruiting effort, and many of the recent immigrants are ethnic Irish returning home. Others come from the same pool of workers in the developing world who are flowing to the United States. In addition, Ireland is receiving refugees and people seeking asylum from the former Yugoslavia, the Middle East, Nigeria, and other trouble spots around the globe.

What awaits these newcomers when they arrive on the Emerald Isle? Will they be subjected to the Irish version of "Anglo-conformity"? Will Irish society become a melting pot? Will Gordon's ideas about assimilation be applicable to their experiences? Will their assimilation be segmented? Will the Irish—such immigrants themselves—be especially understanding of and sympathetic to the traumas faced by the newcomers?

Of course, it is too early to answer any of these questions. We can note, however, that the Irish are responding to this wave of immigration in a variety of ways. The national government is officially supportive of immigrants and stresses tolerance for diversity and a welcoming attitude. The attitudes of the Irish public are more mixed. Unlike the United States, Ireland has no experience in dealing with newcomers and strangers (at least in modern times). Compared to the United States, Ireland is extremely homogenous in race (virtually 100% Caucasian), religion (92% Roman Catholic), and language (Gaelic is an official language, along with English, but few Irish speak Gaelic exclusively). This homogeneity no doubt makes the newcomers feel even more isolated, and it also means that the Irish do not have a backlog of experiences to draw on when confronted with language, cultural, and racial differences in their own country.

Many Irish are very sympathetic to the immigrants and refugees. For others, predictably, the influx of newcomers has aroused racist sentiments and demands for exclusion—reactions that ironically echo the rejection experienced by Irish immigrants to the United States in the 19th century (for example, jobs advertisements that included the stipulation that "No Irish Need Apply"). Irish radio and TV talk shows commonly discuss issues of immigration and assimilation, and they frequently evoke prejudiced statements from the audience. Spokespersons for "Keeping Ireland for the Irish" have found a ready audience and have spread their views in political campaigns, in newspaper interviews, and on the Internet.

Like the United States, Ireland finds itself dealing with diversity and debating what kind of society it should become. It is far too early to tell if the Irish experience will parallel the American or if the sociological concepts presented in this chapter will prove useful in analyzing the Irish immigrant experience. We can be sure, however, that the experience of the immigrants in Ireland will be laced with plentiful doses of the loneliness and longing experienced by Peter Jones's ancestors. Times have changed, but today's immigrants will yearn for Abuja, Riga, or Baku with the same melancholy as previous waves of immigrants yearned for Kilkelly, Dublin, or Galway. Who knows what songs and poems will come from this?

IMPLICATIONS FOR EXAMINING DOMINANT-MINORITY RELATIONS

Chapters 1 and 2 have introduced many of the terms, concepts, and themes that form the core of this text. Although the connections between the concepts are not simple, some key points can be made to summarize these chapters and anticipate the material to come.

First, minority group status has much more to do with power and the distribution of resources than with simple numbers or the percentage of the population in any particular category. We saw this notion expressed in Chapter 1, in the definition of minority group and in our exploration of inequality. The themes of inequality and differentials in status were also covered in our discussion of prejudice, racism, and discrimination. To understand minority relations, we have to examine some very basic realities of human society: inequalities in wealth, prestige, and the distribution of power. To discuss changes in minority group status, we must be prepared to discuss changes in the way society does business, makes decisions, and distributes income, jobs, health care, and opportunity.

A second focus of our attention in the rest of the book is the question of how our society should develop. Assimilation and pluralism, with all their variations, define two broad directions. Each has been extensively examined and discussed by social scientists, by leaders and decision makers in American society, and by ordinary people from all groups and all walks of life. The analysis and evaluation of these two broad directions, assimilation and pluralism, is a thread running throughout this book.

MAIN POINTS

- Assimilation and pluralism are two broad pathways of development for intergroup relations. Assimilation and pluralism are in some ways contrary processes, but they may appear together in a variety of combinations.
- Two types of assimilation are the melting pot and Anglo-conformity. The latter historically has been the dominant value in the United States.
- Gordon theorized that assimilation occurs through a series of stages, with integration being the crucial stage. In his view, it is common for American minority groups, especially racial minority groups, to be acculturated but not integrated. Once a group has begun to integrate, in his view, all other stages will follow in order.
- The past few decades have shown increased interest in pluralism. The three types of pluralistic situations are cultural or full pluralism, structural pluralism, and enclave or middleman minority groups.
- According to many scholars, white ethnic groups survived decades of assimilation, albeit in altered forms. New ethnic (and racial) minority groups continue to appear, and old

ones change form and function as the society changes. At the dawn of the 21st century, however, white ethnicity may well be fading in <u>salience</u> for most people, except perhaps as a context for criticizing other groups.

- In the United States today, assimilation may be segmented and have outcomes other than equality with and acceptance into the middle class.

QUESTIONS FOR REVIEW AND STUDY

1. Summarize Gordon's model of assimilation. Identify and explain each stage and how the stages are linked together. Explain Exhibits 2.2 and 2.3 in terms of Gordon's model.
2. "Human capital theory is not so much wrong as it is incomplete." Explain this statement. What does the theory leave out? What questionable assumptions does it make?
3. What are the major dimensions along which the experience of assimilation varies? Explain how and why.
4. Define pluralism and explain the ways in which it differs from assimilation. Why has interest in pluralism increased? Explain the difference between and cite examples of structural and cultural pluralism. Describe enclave minority groups in terms of pluralism and in terms of Gordon's model of assimilation. How have contemporary theorists added to the concept of pluralism?
5. Define and explain "segmented assimilation" and explain how it differs from Gordon's model.
6. Do the American theories and understandings of assimilation apply to the case of Ireland?

INTERNET RESEARCH PROJECT

Investigate the debate on language and assimilation in American society. You might begin with Web sites for major American newspapers (e.g., *The New York Times*), newsmagazines (e.g., *U.S. News and World Report*), and other news sources (e.g., CNN) and search for relevant items from their home pages, or, perhaps, do a general search on the Internet itself using key terms such as "English first" or "language diversity." Search for a diversity of opinions and analyze the information you find in terms of Gordon's model of assimilation and the concepts of Americanization, the melting pot, acculturation, integration, pluralism, and human capital theory.

FOR FURTHER READING

Alba, Richard. (1990). *Ethnic Identity: The Transformation of White America*. New Haven, CT: Yale University Press.
 A useful analysis of the changing meanings of ethnic identity for the descendants of European immigrants.

Gordon, Milton. (1964). *Assimilation in American Life*. New York: Oxford University Press.
Herberg, Will. (1960). *Protestant-Catholic-Jew: An Essay in American Religious Sociology*. New York: Anchor.
 Two classic works of scholarship on assimilation, religion, and white ethnic groups.

Portes, Alejandro, & Rumbaut, Richard. (1996). *Immigrant America: A Portrait*. Berkeley: University of California Press.

Portes, Alejandro, & Rumbaut, Richard. (2001). *Legacies: The Story of the Immigrant Second Generation*. Berkeley: University of California Press.

Zhou, Min, & Bankston, Carl. (1998). *Growing Up American: How Vietnamese Children Adapt to Life in the United States*. New York: Russell Sage Foundation.

Three outstanding works analyzing the new immigrants and the concept of segmented assimilation.

NOTE

1. Copyright ©1983 by Green Linnet Music. Used with permission.

Part II

The Evolution of Dominant-Minority Relations in the United States

The chapters in Part II will explore several questions: Why do some groups become minorities? How and why do dominant-minority relations change over time? These questions are more than casual or merely academic. Understanding the dynamics that created and sustained prejudice, racism, and discrimination in the past will build understanding about group relations in the present and future, and such understanding is crucial if we are ever to deal effectively with these problems. Both chapters in Part II use African Americans as the primary case study. Chapter 3 focuses on the preindustrial United States and the creation of slavery but also considers the fate of Native Americans and Mexican Americans during the same time period. Chapter 4 analyzes the changes in group relations that were caused by the industrial revolution and focuses on the shift from slavery to segregation for African Americans and their migration out of the South. Throughout the 20th century, industrial technology continued to evolve and shape American society and group relationships. We begin to explore the consequences of these changes in Chapter 4, and we continue the investigation in the case studies of contemporary minority groups in Part III.

The concepts introduced in Part I are used throughout Chapters 3 and 4, and some very important new concepts and theories are introduced as well. By the end of Part II, you will be familiar with virtually all the conceptual framework that will guide us through the remainder of this text.

A NOTE ON MORALITY AND THE HISTORY OF MINORITY RELATIONS IN AMERICA: GUILT, BLAME, UNDERSTANDING, AND COMMUNICATION

Very often, when people confront the kind of material presented in the next few chapters, they react on a personal level. Some might feel a sense of guilt for America's less-than-wholesome history of group relations. Others might respond with anger and increased impatience to the injustice and unfairness that remains in American society. Still others might respond with denial or indifference, refusing to acknowledge certain events or feeling that these events are so distant in time that they have no importance or meaning for them.

These reactions—guilt, anger, denial, and indifference—are common, and I ask you to consider them. First, the awful things I will discuss did happen, and they were done largely by members of a particular racial/ethnic group: white Europeans and their descendants in America. No amount of denial, distancing, or disassociation can make these facts go away. African Americans, Native Americans, Mexican Americans, and other groups were victims, and they paid a terrible price for the early growth and success of American society.

Second, the successful domination and exploitation of these groups were made easier by the cooperation of members of each of the minority groups. The slave trade relied on agents and slavers, some of whom were black Africans; some Native Americans aided and abetted the cause of white society; and some Mexicans helped to cheat other Mexicans. There's plenty of guilt to go around, and Anglo-Americans do not have a monopoly on greed, bigotry, or viciousness. Indeed, some white Southerners opposed slavery and fought for the abolition of the "peculiar institution." Many of the ideas and values on which the United States was founded (justice, equality, liberty) had their origins in European intellectual traditions, and minority group protest has often involved little more than insisting that the nation live up to these ideals. Segments of the white community were appalled at the treatment of Native Americans and Mexicans. Some members of the dominant group devoted (and sometimes gave) their lives to end oppression, bigotry, and racial stratification.

My point is to urge you to avoid, insofar as is possible, a "good-guy/bad-guy" approach to this subject matter. Guilt, anger, denial, or indifference are common reactions to this material, but these emotions do little to advance understanding, and often they impede communication between members of different groups. I believe that an understanding of America's racial past is vitally important for understanding the present. Historical background provides a perspective for viewing the present and allows us to identify important concepts and principles that we can use to disentangle the intergroup complexities surrounding us.

The goal of the chapters to come is not to make you feel any particular emotion. I will try to present the often ugly facts neutrally and without extraneous editorializing. As scholars, your goal should be to absorb the material, understand the principles, and apply them to your own life and the society around you—not to feel guilt, indulge yourself in elaborate moral denunciations of American society, develop apologies for the past, or deny the realities of what happened. By dealing objectively with this material, we can begin to liberate our perspectives and build an understanding of the realities of American society and American minority groups.

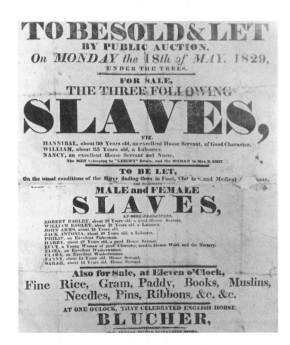

3

The Development of Dominant-Minority Group Relations in Preindustrial America

The Origins of Slavery

From the first settlements in the 1600s until the 19th century, most people living in what was to become the United States relied directly on farming for food, shelter, and other necessities of life. In an agricultural society, land and labor are central concerns, and the struggle to control these resources led directly to the creation of minority group status for three groups: African Americans, Native Americans, and Mexican Americans. Why did the colonists create slavery? Why were Africans enslaved, but not Native Americans or Europeans? Why did Native Americans lose their land and most of their population by the 1890s? How did the Mexican population in the Southwest become "Mexican Americans"? How did the experience of becoming a subordinated minority group vary by gender?

In this chapter, the concepts introduced in Chapters 1 and 2 will be used to answer these questions. Some new ideas and theories will also be introduced, and, by the end of this chapter, we will have developed a theoretical model of the process that leads to the creation of a minority group. The creation of black slavery in colonial America, arguably the single most significant event in the early years of this nation, will be used to illustrate the process of minority group creation. We will also consider the subordination of Native Americans and Mexican Americans—two more historical events of great significance—as additional case studies. We will follow the experiences of African Americans through the days of segregation in Chapter 4 and into the contemporary era in Chapter 5. The story of the development of minority group status for Native Americans and Mexican Americans will be picked up again in Chapters 6 and 7, respectively.

Two broad themes underlie this chapter and, indeed, the remainder of the text:

1. *The nature of dominant-minority group relations at any point in time is largely a function of the characteristics of the society as a whole.* The situation of a minority group will reflect the realities of everyday social life and, particularly, the subsistence technology (the means by which a society satisfies basic needs such as food and shelter). As explained by Gerhard Lenski (see Chapter 1), the subsistence technology of a society acts as a foundation, shaping and affecting every other aspect of the social structure, including minority group relations.

2. *The contact situation—the conditions under which groups first come together—is the single most significant factor in the creation of minority group status.* The nature of the contact situation has long-lasting consequences for the extent of racial or ethnic stratification experienced by the minority group, the levels of racism and prejudice it will face, the possibilities for assimilation and pluralism, and virtually every other aspect of the dominant-minority relationship.

THE ORIGINS OF SLAVERY IN AMERICA

By 1600, Spanish explorers had conquered much of Central and South America, and the influx of gold, silver, and other riches from the New World had made Spain a powerful nation. Following Spain's lead, England proceeded to establish its presence in the Western Hemisphere, but its efforts at colonization were more modest than those of Spain. By the early 1600s, only two small colonies had been established: Plymouth, settled by pious Protestant families, and Jamestown, populated primarily by males seeking their fortunes.

By 1619, the British colony at Jamestown, Virginia, had survived for more than a decade. The residents of the settlement had fought with the local Native Americans and struggled continuously to eke out a living from the land. Starvation, disease, and death were frequent visitors, and the future of the enterprise continued to be in doubt.

In August of that year, a Dutch ship arrived in colonial Virginia. The master of the ship needed provisions and offered to trade his only cargo: about 20 black Africans. Many of the details of this transaction have been lost, and we probably will never know the names of these people, their exact origins in Africa, or how they came to be chained in the hold of a ship. Regardless, this brief episode was a landmark event in the formation of what would become the United States. In combination with the strained relations between the English settlers and Native Americans, the presence of these first few Africans raised an issue that has never been fully resolved: How should different groups in this society relate to each other?

The colonists at Jamestown had no ready answer. In 1619, England and its colonies did not practice slavery, so these first Africans probably were incorporated into colonial society as *indentured servants,* contract laborers who were obligated to serve a master for a specific number of years. At the end of the indenture, or contract, the servant became a free citizen. The colonies depended heavily on indentured servants from the British Isles for labor, and this status apparently provided a convenient way of defining the newcomers from Africa, who were, after all, treated as commodities and exchanged for food and water.

The position of African indentured servants in the colonies remained ambiguous for several decades. American slavery evolved gradually and in small steps; in fact, there was little demand for African labor during the years following 1619. By 1625, there still were only 23 blacks in Virginia, and that number had increased to perhaps 300 by midcentury (Franklin & Moss, 1994, p. 57). In the decades before the dawn of slavery, we know that some African indentured servants did become free citizens. Some became successful farmers and landowners and, like their white neighbors, purchased African and white indentured servants themselves (Smedley, 1999, p. 97). By the 1650s, however, many African Americans (and their offspring) were being treated as the property of others, or, in other words, as slaves (Morgan, 1975, p. 154).

It was not until the 1660s that the first laws defining slavery were enacted in the American colonies. In the century that followed, hundreds of additional laws were passed to clarify and formalize the status of Africans in colonial America. By the 1750s, slavery had been clearly defined in law and in custom, and the idea that a person could own another person—not just the labor or the energy or the work of a person, but the actual person—had been thoroughly institutionalized.

What caused slavery? The gradual evolution and low demand for indentured servants from Africa suggest that slavery was not somehow inevitable or preordained. Why did the colonists deliberately create this repressive system? Why did they reach out all the way to Africa for their slaves? If they wanted to create a slave system, why didn't they enslave the Native Americans nearby or the white indentured servants already present in the colonies?

The Labor Supply Problem

American colonists of the 1600s saw slavery as a solution to several problems they faced. The business of the colonies was agriculture, and farm work at this time was *labor intensive,* or performed almost entirely by hand. The industrial revolution was two centuries in the future, and there were few machines or labor-saving devices available to ease the everyday burden of work. A successful harvest depended largely on human effort.

As colonial society grew and developed, a specific form of agricultural production began to emerge. The *plantation system* was based on cultivating and exporting crops such as sugar, tobacco, and rice raised on large tracts of land with a large, cheap labor force. Profit margins tended to be small, so planters sought to stabilize their income by farming in volume and keeping the costs of production as low as possible. Profits in the labor-intensive plantation system could be maximized if a large, disciplined, and cheap workforce could be maintained by the landowners (Curtin, 1990; Morgan, 1975).

At about the same time that the plantation system began to emerge, the supply of white indentured servants from the British Isles began to dwindle. Furthermore, the white indentured servants who did come to the colonies had to be released from their indenture every few years. Land was available, and these newly freed citizens tended to strike out on their own. Thus, landowners who relied on white indentured servants had to deal with high turnover rates in their workforce and faced a continually uncertain supply of labor.

Attempts to solve the labor supply problem by using Native Americans failed. The tribes closest to the colonies occasionally were exploited for manpower. However, by the time the plantation system evolved, the local tribes had dwindled in numbers as a result of warfare and disease. Other Indian nations across the continent retained enough power to resist enslavement, and it was relatively easy for Native Americans to escape back to their kinfolk.

This left black Africans as a potential source of labor. The slave trade from Africa to the Spanish and Portuguese colonies of South America was firmly established by the mid-1600s and could be expanded to fill the needs of the British colonies as well. The colonists came to see slaves imported from Africa as the most logical, cost-effective way to solve their vexing shortage of labor. The colonists created slavery to cultivate their lands and generate profits, status, and success. The paradox at the core of U.S. society had been established: The construction of a social system devoted to freedom and individual liberty "in the New World was made possible only by the revival of an institution of naked tyranny foresworn for centuries in the Old" (Lacy, 1972, p. 22).

The Contact Situation

The conditions under which groups first come into contact determine the immediate fate of the minority group and shape intergroup relations for years to come. Two theories serve as analytical guides in understanding this crucial phase of group relationships.

The Noel Hypothesis

Sociologist Donald Noel identified three features of the contact situation that, in combination, lead to some form of inequality between groups. The *Noel hypothesis* states: *If two or more groups come together in a contact situation characterized by ethnocentrism, competition, and a differential in power, then some form of racial or ethnic stratification will result* (Noel, 1968, p. 163). If the contact situation has all three characteristics, some dominant-minority group structure will be created.

Noel's first characteristic, *ethnocentrism,* is the tendency to judge other groups, societies, or lifestyles by the standards of one's own culture. Ethnocentrism probably is a universal component of human society, and some degree of ethnocentrism is essential to the maintenance of social solidarity and cohesion. Without some minimal level of pride in and loyalty to one's own society and cultural traditions, there would be no particular reason to observe the norms and laws, honor the sacred symbols, or cooperate with others in doing the daily work of society.

Regardless of its importance, ethnocentrism can have negative consequences. At its worst, it can lead to the view that other cultures and peoples are not only different but also inferior. At the very least, ethnocentrism creates a social boundary line that members of the groups will recognize and observe. When ethnocentrism exists in any degree, people will tend to sort themselves along

group lines and identify characteristics that differentiate "us" from "them."

Competition is a struggle over a scarce commodity. As we noted in Chapter 1, competition between groups often leads to harsh negative feelings (prejudice) and hostile actions (discrimination). In competitive contact situations, the victorious group becomes the dominant group, and the losers become the minority group. The competition may center on land, labor, jobs, housing, educational opportunities, political office, or anything else that is mutually desired by both groups or that one group has and the other group wants. Competition provides the eventual dominant group with the motivation to establish superiority. The dominant group serves its own interests by ending the competition and exploiting, controlling, eliminating, or otherwise dominating the minority group.

The third feature of the contact situation is a *differential in power* between the groups. Power, as you recall from Chapter 1, is the ability of a group to achieve its goals even in the face of opposition from other groups. The amount of power commanded by a group is a function of three factors. First, the size of the group can make a difference, and all other things being equal, larger groups are more powerful. Second, in addition to raw numbers, the degree of organization, discipline, and the quality of group leadership can make a difference in the ability of a group to pursue its goals. A third component of power is the group's supply of resources: anything that can be used to help the group achieve its goals. Depending on the context, resources might include anything from land to information to money. The greater the number and variety of resources at the disposal of a group, the greater its potential ability to dominate other groups. Thus, a larger, better-organized group with more resources at its disposal generally will be able to impose its will on smaller, less well-organized groups with fewer resources. The Noel hypothesis is diagrammed in Exhibit 3.1.

Note the respective functions of each of the three factors in shaping the contact situation and the emergence of inequality. If ethnocentrism is present, the groups will recognize their

Exhibit 3.1   A Model of the Establishment of Minority Group Status

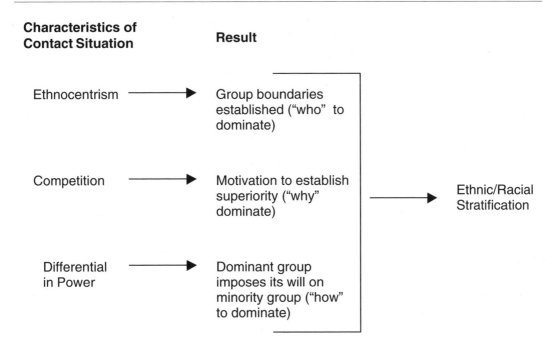

Characteristics of Contact Situation	Result
Ethnocentrism	Group boundaries established ("who" to dominate)
Competition	Motivation to establish superiority ("why" dominate)
Differential in Power	Dominant group imposes its will on minority group ("how" to dominate)

Ethnic/Racial Stratification

differences and maintain their boundaries. If competition also is present, the eventual dominant group will attempt to maximize its share of scarce commodities by controlling or subordinating the eventual minority group. The differential in power allows the dominant group to succeed in establishing a superior position. Ethnocentrism tells the dominant group *whom* to dominate, competition tells the dominant group *why* it should establish a structure of dominance, and power is *how* the dominant group's will is imposed on the minority group.

The Noel hypothesis can be applied to the creation of minority groups in a variety of situations. We will also use the model to analyze changes in dominant-minority structures over time.

The Blauner Hypothesis

The contact situation also has been analyzed by sociologist Robert Blauner in his book *Racial Oppression in America* (1972). Blauner identified two different initial relationships—colonization and immigration—and hypothesized that

minority groups created by colonization or conquest will experience more intense prejudice, racism, and discrimination than those created by immigration. Furthermore, the disadvantaged status of colonized groups will persist longer and be more difficult to overcome than the disadvantaged status faced by groups created by immigration.

Colonized or conquered minority groups, such as African Americans, are forced into minority status by the superior military and political power of the dominant group. At the time of contact with the dominant group, colonized groups are subjected to massive inequalities and attacks on their cultures. They are assigned to positions, such as slave status, from which any form of assimilation is extremely difficult and perhaps even forbidden by the dominant group. Frequently, members of the minority group are identified by highly visible racial or physical characteristics that maintain and reinforce the oppressive system. Thus, minority groups created by colonization or conquest experience harsher and more persistent rejection and oppression than groups created by immigration.

Immigrant minority groups are, at least in part, voluntary participants in the host society. That is, although the decision to immigrate may be motivated by extreme pressures, such as famine or political persecution, immigrant groups have at least some control over their destination and their position in the host society. As a result, they do not occupy such markedly inferior positions as do colonized groups. They retain enough internal organization and resources to pursue their own self-interests, and they commonly experience more rapid acceptance and easier movement to equality. The boundaries between groups are not so rigidly maintained, especially when the groups are racially similar. In discussing European immigrant groups, for example, Blauner (1972) stated that entering into American society "involved a degree of choice and self-direction that was for the most part denied to people of color. Voluntary immigration made it more likely that . . . European . . . ethnic groups would identify with America and see the host culture as a positive opportunity" (p. 56). Acculturation and, particularly, integration are significantly more possible for immigrant groups than for the groups formed under conquest or colonization.

Blauner stressed that these initial differences have consequences that persist long after the original contact. For example, based on measures of equality or integration into the secondary sector (see Chapter 2) such as average income, years of education, and unemployment rate, the descendants of the European immigrants are equal with national norms today (see Chapter 9 for specific data). In contrast, the descendants of colonized and conquered groups (e.g., African Americans) are, on average, below the national norms on virtually all measures of equality and integration (see Chapters 5–8 for specific data).

Blauner's two types of minority groups lie at opposite ends of a continuum; there are intermediate positions between the extremes. Enclave and middleman minorities (see Chapter 2) often originate as immigrant groups who bring some resources and thus have more opportunities than colonized minority groups to carve out a place for themselves in the host society. Many of these minorities, however, are racially distinguishable from the dominant group, and certain kinds of opportunities may be closed to them. For instance, citizenship was expressly forbidden to immigrants from China for much of the 20th century. Federal laws restricted the entrance of Chinese immigrants, and state and local laws restricted their opportunities for education, jobs, and housing. For these and other reasons, the Asian immigrant experience cannot be equated with European immigrant patterns (Blauner, 1972, p. 55). Because enclave and middleman minority groups combine characteristics of both the colonized and the immigrant minority group experience, we can predict that in terms of equality, these groups will occupy an intermediate status between the more assimilated white ethnic groups and the colonized racial minorities (see Chapter 8).

Blauner's typology has proven to be an extremely useful conceptual tool for the analysis of U.S. dominant-minority relations and is used extensively throughout this text. In fact, the case studies that constitute Part III of this text are arranged in approximate order from groups created by colonization to those created by immigration. Of course, it is difficult to measure such things as the extent of colonization objectively or precisely, and the exact order of the groups is somewhat arbitrary.

The Creation of American Slavery

The Noel hypothesis helps explain why colonists enslaved black Africans instead of white indentured servants or Native Americans. First, all three groups were the objects of ethnocentric feelings on the part of the elite groups that dominated colonial society. Black Africans and Native Americans were perceived as being different on religious as well as racial grounds. Many white indentured servants were Irish Catholics, criminals, or paupers and were perceived as different from the British Protestants who dominated colonial society.

Exhibit 3.2 The Noel Hypothesis Applied to the Origins of Slavery

Potential Sources of Labor	Ethnocentrism	Competition	Differential in Power
White indentured servants	Yes	Yes	No
Native Americans	Yes	Yes	No
Black indentured servants	Yes	Yes	Yes

Second, competition of some sort existed between the colonists and all three groups. The competition with Native Americans was direct and focused on control of land. Competition with indentured servants, both white and black, was more indirect: These groups were the labor force that the landowners needed to work their plantations and become successful in the New World.

Noel's third variable, differential in power, is the key variable that explains why Africans rather than the other groups were enslaved. During the first several decades of colonial history, the balance of power between the colonists and Native Americans was relatively even, and, in fact, often favored Native Americans (Lurie, 1982, pp. 131–133). The colonists were outnumbered, and their muskets and cannons were only marginally more effective than bows and spears. The Native American tribes were well-organized social units capable of sustaining resistance to and mounting reprisals against the colonists, and it took centuries for the nascent United States to finally defeat Native Americans militarily.

White indentured servants, on one hand, had the advantage of being preferred over black indentured servants (Noel, 1968, p. 168). Their greater desirability gave them bargaining power and the ability to negotiate better treatment and more lenient terms than black indentured servants. If the planters had attempted to enslave white indentured servants, this source of labor would have dwindled even more rapidly.

Africans, on the other hand, had become indentured servants by force and coercion. In Blauner's terms, they were a colonized group that did not freely choose to enter the British colonies. Thus, they had no bargaining power. As opposed to Native Americans, they

had no nearby relatives, no knowledge of the countryside, and no safe havens to which to escape. Exhibit 3.2 summarizes the impact of these three factors on the three potential sources of labor in colonial America.

Paternalistic Relations

Recall the first theme stated at the beginning of this chapter: The nature of intergroup relationships will reflect the characteristics of the larger society. The most important and profitable unit of economic production in the colonial South was the plantation, and the region was dominated by a small group of wealthy landowners. A society with a small elite class and a plantation-based economy often will develop a form of minority relations called paternalism (van den Berghe, 1967; Wilson, 1973). The key features of paternalism are vast power differentials and huge inequalities between dominant and minority groups, elaborate and repressive systems of control over the minority group, castelike barriers between groups, elaborate and highly stylized codes of behavior and communication between groups, and low rates of overt conflict. We consider these characteristics in this section.

As slavery evolved in the colonies, the dominant group shaped the system to fit its needs. To solidify control of the labor of their slaves, the plantation elite designed and enacted an elaborate system of laws and customs that gave masters nearly total legal power over slaves. In these laws, slaves were defined as *chattel*, or personal property, rather than as persons, and they were accorded no civil or political rights. Slaves could not own property, sign contracts, bring lawsuits, or even testify in court (except against another slave). The masters were given the legal authority to determine almost every aspect of a slave's life, including work schedules, living arrangements, diets, and even names (Elkins, 1959; Franklin & Moss, 1994; Genovese, 1974; Jordan, 1968; Stampp, 1956).

Laws permitted the master to determine the type and severity of punishment for misbehavior. Slaves were forbidden by law to read or write, and marriages between slaves were not legally recognized. Masters could separate husbands from wives and parents from children if it suited them. Slaves had little formal decision-making ability or control over their lives or the lives of their loved ones.

In colonial America, slavery became synonymous with race. Race, slavery, inferiority, and powerlessness became intertwined in ways that, according to many analysts, still affect the ways that black and white Americans think about one another (Hacker, 1992). Slavery was a *caste system,* or a closed stratification system. In a caste system, there is no mobility between social positions, and the social class you are born into (your ascribed status) is permanent. Slave status was for life and was passed on to any children a slave might have. Whites, no matter what they did, could not become slaves.

Interaction between members of the dominant and minority groups in a paternalistic system is governed by a rigid, strictly enforced code of etiquette. Slaves were expected to show deference and humility and to visibly display their lower status when interacting with whites. These rigid behavioral codes made it possible for blacks and whites to work together, sometimes intimately, sometimes for their entire lives, without threatening the power and status differentials inherent in the system. Plantation and farm work required close and frequent contact between blacks and whites, and status differentials were maintained socially rather than physically.

The frequent but unequal interactions allowed the elites to maintain a *pseudotolerance,* or an attitude of benevolent despotism, toward their slaves. Their prejudice and racism often were expressed as *positive* emotions of affection for their black slaves. The attitude of the planters toward their slaves often was paternalistic and even genteel (Wilson, 1973, pp. 52–55).

For their part, black slaves often could not hate their owners as much as they hated the system that constrained them. The system defined slaves as pieces of property owned by their masters, yet they were, undeniably, human beings as well. Thus, slavery was based on a contradiction. "The master learned to treat his slaves both as property and as men and women, the slaves learned to express and affirm their humanity even while they were constrained in much of their lives to accept their status as chattel" (Parish, 1989, p. 1).

The powerlessness of slaves made it difficult for them to openly reject or resist the system. Slaves had few ways in which they could directly challenge the institution of slavery or their position in it. Open defiance was ineffective and could result in punishment or even death. In general, masters would not be prosecuted for physically abusing their slaves.

One of the few slave revolts that occurred in the United States illustrates both the futility of overt challenge and the degree of repression built into the system. In 1831, in Southhampton County, Virginia, a slave named Nat Turner led an uprising during which 57 whites were killed. The revolt was starting to spread when the state militia met and routed the growing slave army. More than a hundred slaves died in the armed encounter, and Nat Turner and 13 others were later executed. Slave owners and white Southerners in general were greatly alarmed by the uprising and consequently tightened the system of control over slaves, making it even more repressive (Franklin & Moss, 1994, p. 147). Ironically, the result of Nat Turner's attempt to lead slaves to freedom was greater oppression and control by the dominant group.

Others were more successful in resisting the system. Runaway slaves were a constant problem for slave owners, especially in the states bordering the free states of the North. The difficulty of escape and the low likelihood of successfully reaching the North did not deter thousands from attempting the feat, some of them repeatedly. Many runaway slaves received help from the Underground Railroad, an informal network of safe houses supported by African Americans and whites involved in *abolitionism,* the movement to abolish slavery. These escapes created colorful legends and heroic figures, including Frederick Douglass, Sojourner Truth, and Harriet Tubman.

Besides running away and open rebellion, slaves used the forms of resistance most readily available to them: sabotage, intentional carelessness, dragging their feet, and work slowdowns. As historian Peter Parish (1989) points out, it is difficult to separate "a natural desire to avoid hard work [from a] conscious decision to protest or resist" (p. 73), and much of this behavior may be categorized better as noncooperation than as deliberate political rebellion. Nonetheless, these behaviors were widespread and document the rejection of the system by its victims.

On an everyday basis, the slaves managed their lives and families as best they could. Most slaves were neither docile victims nor unyielding rebels. As the institution of slavery developed, a distinct African American experience accumulated, and traditions of resistance and accommodation developed side by side. Most slaves worked to create a world for themselves within the confines and restraints of the plantation system, avoiding the more vicious repression as much as possible while attending to their own needs and those of their families. An African American culture was forged in response to the realities of slavery and was manifested in folklore, music, religion, family and kinship structures, and other aspects of everyday life (Blassingame, 1972; Genovese, 1974; Gutman, 1976).

THE DIMENSIONS OF MINORITY GROUP STATUS

The situation of African Americans under slavery can be more completely described by applying some of the concepts developed in Part I.

Power, Inequality, and Institutional Discrimination

The key concepts for understanding the creation of slavery are power, inequality, and institutional discrimination. The plantation elite used its greater power resources to consign black Africans to an inferior status. The system of racial inequality was implemented and reinforced by institutionalized discrimination and became a central aspect of everyday life in the antebellum South. The legal and political institutions of colonial society were shaped to benefit the landowners and give them almost total control over their slaves.

Prejudice and Racism

What about the attitudes and feelings of the people involved? What was the role of personal prejudice? How and why did the ideology of anti-black racism start? As I mentioned in Chapter 1, most scholars agree that individual prejudices and ideological racism are not so important as *causes* for the creation of minority group status but are more the *results* of systems of racial inequality (Jordan, 1968, p. 80; Smedley, 1999, pp. 94–111). The colonists did not enslave black indentured servants because they were prejudiced or because they disliked blacks or thought them inferior. As we have seen, the decision to enslave black Africans was an attempt to resolve a labor supply problem. The primary roles of prejudice and racism in the creation of minority group status are to rationalize and "explain" the emerging system of racial and ethnic advantage (Wilson, 1973, pp. 76–78).

Prejudice and racism help to mobilize support for the creation of minority group status and to stabilize the system as it emerges. Prejudice and racism can provide convenient and convincing justifications for exploitation. They can help insulate a system like slavery from questioning and criticism and make it appear reasonable and even desirable. Thus, the intensity, strength, and popularity of anti-black Southern racism actually reached its height almost 200 years *after* slavery began to emerge. During the early 1800s, the American abolitionist movement brought slavery under heavy attack, and in response, the ideology of anti-black racism was strengthened (Wilson, 1973, p. 79). The greater the opposition to a system of racial stratification or the greater the magnitude of the exploitation, the greater the need of the beneficiaries and their apologists to justify, rationalize, and explain.

Once created, dominant group prejudice and racism become widespread and common ways of thinking about the minority group. In the case of colonial slavery, anti-black beliefs and feelings became part of the standard package of knowledge, understanding, and truths shared by members of the dominant group. As the decades wore on and the institution of slavery solidified, prejudice and racism were passed on from generation to generation. For succeeding generations, anti-black prejudice became just another piece of information and perspective on the world learned during socialization. Anti-black prejudice and racism began as part of an attempt to control the labor of black indentured servants, became embedded in early American culture, and were established as integral parts of the socialization process for succeeding generations.

These conceptual relationships are presented in Exhibit 3.3. Racial inequality arises from the contact situation, as specified in the Noel hypothesis. As the dominant-minority relationship begins to take shape, prejudice and racism develop as rationalizations. Over time, a vicious cycle (see Exhibit 1.3) develops as prejudice and racism reinforce the pattern of inequality between groups, which was the cause of prejudice and racism in the first place. Thus, the Blauner hypothesis states, the subordination of colonized minority groups is perpetuated through time.

Assimilation

There is an enormous literature on American slavery, and research on the causes, nature, and meaning of the system continues to this day. Many issues remain unsettled, and one of the more controversial, consequential, and interesting of these concerns the effects of slavery on the slaves.

Apologists for the system of slavery and some historians of the South writing early in the 20th century accepted the rationalizations inherent in anti-black prejudice and argued that slavery actually was beneficial for black Africans. According to this view, British-American slavery operated as a "school for civilization" (Phillips, 1918) that rescued savages from the jungles of Africa and exposed them to Christianity and Western civilization. Some argued that slavery was benevolent because it protected slaves from the evils and exploitation of the factory system of the industrial North. These racist views were most popular a century ago, early in the development of the social sciences. Since that time, scholars have established a number of facts (e.g., Western Africa, the area from which most slaves came, had been the site of a number of powerful, advanced civilizations) that make this view untenable for anyone but the most dedicated racist thinkers.

At the opposite extreme, slavery has been compared with Nazi concentration camps and likened to a "perverted patriarchy" that brainwashed, emasculated, and dehumanized slaves, stripping them of their heritage and culture. Historian Stanley Elkins provocatively argued this interpretation, now widely regarded as overstated, in his book *Slavery: A Problem in American Institutional and Intellectual Life* (1959). Although his conclusions might be overdrawn, Elkins's argument and evidence are important for any exploration of the nature of American slavery. In fact, much of the scholarship on slavery since the publication of Elkins's book has been an attempt to refute or at least modify the points he made.

Still a third view of the impact of slavery maintains that through all the horror and abuse of enslavement, slaves retained a positive sense of self and a firm anchor in their African traditions. This point of view stresses the importance of kinship, religion, and culture in helping African Americans cope. It has been presented most poignantly in Alex Haley's semifictional family history *Roots* (1976) but is also represented in the scholarly literature on slavery since Elkins (e.g., see Blassingame, 1972; Genovese, 1974).

The debate over the impact of slavery continues, and we cannot hope to resolve the issues here. However, it is clear that African Americans were, in Blauner's terms, a

Exhibit 3.3   A Model for the Creation of Prejudice and Racism

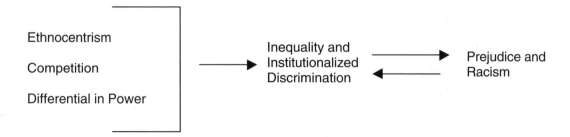

"colonized" minority group that was extensively—and coercively—acculturated. Language acculturation began on the slave ships, where different tribal and language groups were mixed together to inhibit communication and lower the potential for resistance and revolt (Mannix, 1962).

The plantation elite and their agents needed to communicate with their workforce and insisted on using English. Within a generation or two, African languages died out in America. Some scholars argue that some African words and language patterns persist to the present day, but even if this is true, the significance of this survival is trivial compared with the coerced adoption of English. To the extent that culture depends on language, Africans under slavery experienced massive acculturation.

Acculturation through slavery clearly was a process forced on African Americans. Because they were a colonized minority group and unwilling participants in the system, they had little choice but to adjust as best they could to the conditions established by the plantation elite. Their traditional culture was suppressed, and their choices for adjustment to the system were sharply constrained. Black slaves developed new cultural forms and social relationships, but they did so in a situation with few options or choices (Blauner, 1972, p. 66). The extent to which any African cultural elements survived the institution of slavery is a matter of some controversy, but given the power differentials inherent in the system, African Americans had few choices regarding their manner of adjustment.

Gender, Race, and Class

Southern agrarian society developed into a complex social system stratified by race and gender as well as by class. The plantation elite, small in number but wealthy and politically powerful, was at the top of the structure. Most whites in the South were small farmers, and relatively few of them owned slaves. In 1860, for example, only 25% of all Southern whites owned slaves (Franklin & Moss, 1994, p. 123).

The principal line of differentiation in the antebellum South was, of course, race, which was largely synonymous with slave versus nonslave status. Each of the racial groups was in turn stratified by gender. White women were subordinate to the males of the plantation elite, and the slave community echoed the patriarchal pattern of Southern society, except that the degree of gender inequality among blacks was sharply truncated by the fact that slaves had little autonomy and few resources. At the bottom of the system were African American female slaves. Minority women generally are in double jeopardy, oppressed through their gender as well as their race. For black female slaves, the constraints were triple: "Black in a white society, slave in a free society, women in a society ruled by men, female slaves had the least formal power and were perhaps the most vulnerable group of antebellum America" (White, 1985, p. 15).

The race/gender roles of the day idealized Southern white women and placed them on a pedestal. A romanticized conception of femininity was quite inconsistent with the roles women slaves were required to play. Besides domestic roles, female slaves also worked in the fields and did their share of the hardest, most physically demanding, least "feminine" farm work. Southern ideas about feminine fragility and daintiness were abandoned quickly when they interfered with work and the profit to be made from slave labor (Amott & Matthaei, 1991, p. 146).

Reflecting their vulnerability and powerlessness, women slaves sometimes were used to breed more slaves to sell. They were raped and otherwise abused by the males of the dominant group. John Blassingame (1972) expressed their vulnerability to sexual victimization:

> Many white men considered every slave cabin a house of ill-fame. Often through "gifts" but usually by force, white overseers and planters obtained the sexual favors of black women. Generally speaking, the women were literally forced to offer themselves "willingly" and receive a trinket for their compliance rather than a flogging for their refusal. (p. 83)

Note the power relationships implicit in this passage: Female slaves had little choice but to feign willing submission to their white owners.

The routines of work and everyday life differed for male and female slaves. Although they sometimes worked with the men, especially during harvest time, women more often worked in sex-segregated groups organized around domestic as well as farm chores. In addition to working in the fields, they attended the births and cared for the children of both races, cooked and cleaned, wove cloth and sewed clothes, and did the laundry. The women often worked longer hours than the men, doing housework and other chores long after the men retired (Robertson, 1996, p. 21; White, 1985, p. 122).

The group-oriented nature of their tasks gave female slaves an opportunity to develop same-sex bonds and relationships. Women cooperated in their chores, in caring for their children, in the maintenance of their quarters, and in myriad other domestic and family chores. These networks and interpersonal bonds could be used to resist the system. For

example, slave women sometimes induced abortions rather than bring more children into bondage. They often controlled the role of midwife and were able to effectively deceive slave owners and disguise the abortions as miscarriages (White, 1985, pp. 125–126). The networks of relationships among the female slaves provided mutual aid and support for everyday problems, solace and companionship during the travails of a vulnerable and exploited existence, and some ability to buffer and resist the influence and power of the slave owners (Andersen, 1993, pp. 164–165).

Slaves in the American system were brutally repressed and exploited, and females were even more subordinated than males. The oppression and exclusion of female slaves also sharply differentiated them from white females. The white "Southern belle," chaste, untouchable, and unremittingly virtuous, had little in common with African American women under slavery.

THE CREATION OF MINORITY STATUS FOR NATIVE AMERICANS AND MEXICAN AMERICANS

Two other groups became minorities during the preindustrial period. In this section, we will review the dynamics of these processes and make some comparisons with the experiences of African Americans. As you will see, both the Noel and Blauner hypotheses provide some extremely useful insights into these experiences.

Native Americans

As Europeans began to penetrate the New World, they encountered hundreds of societies that had lived on this land for thousands of years. Native American societies were highly variable in culture, language, size, and subsistence technology. Some were small, nomadic, hunter-gatherer bands, whereas others were more developed societies in which people lived in villages and tended large gardens. Regardless of their exact nature, the inexorable advance of white society eventually devastated them all. Contact began in the East and established a pattern of conflict and defeat for Native Americans that continued until the last of the tribes were defeated in the late 1800s. The continual expansion of white society into the West allowed many settlers to fulfill their dreams of economic self-sufficiency, but Native Americans, who lost not only their lives and their land but also much of their traditional way of life, paid an incalculable price.

An important and widely unrecognized point about Native Americans is that there is no such thing as *an* American Indian. Rather, there were—and are—hundreds of different tribes or nations, each with its own language, culture, home territory, and unique history. There are, of course, similarities from tribe to tribe, but there also are vast differences between, for example, the forest-dwelling tribes of Virginia, who lived in longhouses and cultivated gardens, and the nomadic Plains tribes, who relied on hunting to satisfy their needs. Each tribe was and remains a unique blend of language, values, and social structure. Because of space constraints, we will not always be able to take account of these differences. Nonetheless, it is important to be aware of the diversity and sensitive to the variety of peoples and histories subsumed within the general category of Native American.

A second important point is that many Native American tribes no longer exist or are vastly diminished in size. When Jamestown was established in 1607, it is estimated that there were anywhere from 1 million to more than 10 million Native Americans living in what became the United States. By 1890, when the Indian Wars finally ended, the number of Native Americans had fallen to fewer than 250,000. By the end of the nearly 300-year-long "contact situation," Native American populations had declined by 75% or more (Wax, 1971, p. 17; see also McNickle, 1973). Very little of this population loss was due directly to warfare and battle casualties. The greatest part was caused by European diseases brought over by the colonists and by the destruction of the food supplies on which Native American societies relied. Native Americans died by the thousands from measles, influenza, smallpox, cholera, tuberculosis, and a variety of other infectious diseases (Wax, 1971, p. 17; see also Oswalt & Neely, 1996; Snipp, 1989). Traditional hunting grounds and garden plots were taken over by the expanding American society, and game such as the buffalo was slaughtered to the point of extinction. The result of the contact situation for Native Americans very nearly approached genocide.

Native Americans and the Noel and Blauner Hypotheses

We already have used the Noel hypothesis to analyze why Native Americans were not enslaved during the colonial era. Their competition with whites centered on land, not labor, and the Indian nations often were successful in resisting domination (at least temporarily). As American society spread to the West, competition over land continued, and the growing power, superior technology, and greater resource base of the dominant group gradually pushed Native Americans to near extinction.

Various attempts were made to control the persistent warfare, the most important of which occurred before independence from Great Britain. In 1763, the British Crown ruled that the various tribes were to be considered "sovereign nations with inalienable rights to their land" (see Lurie, 1982; McNickle, 1973; Wax, 1971). In other words, each tribe was to be treated as a nation-state, like France or Russia, and the colonists could not simply expropriate tribal lands. Rather, negotiations had to take place, and treaties of agreement had to be signed by all affected parties. The tribes had to be compensated for any loss of land.

This policy was often ignored but was continued by the newborn federal government after the American Revolution. The principle of sovereignty is important because it established a unique relationship between the federal government and Native Americans. The fact that the policy was ignored in practice and that treaties were broken regularly or "renegotiated" unilaterally by white society gives Native Americans legal claims against the federal government that also are unique.

East of the Mississippi River, the period of open conflict was brought to a close by the Indian Removal Act of 1830, which required all eastern tribes to move to new lands west of the Mississippi. Some of the affected tribes went without resistance, others fought, and still others fled to Canada rather than move to the new territory. Regardless, the Indian Removal Act "solved" the Indian problem in the East. The relative scarcity of Native Americans in the eastern United States continues to the present, and the majority of Native Americans live in the western two thirds of the nation.

In the West, the grim story of competition for land accompanied by rising hostility and aggression repeated itself. Wars were fought, buffalo were killed, territory was expropriated, atrocities were committed on both sides, and the fate of the tribes became more and more certain. By 1890, the greater power and resources of white society had defeated the Indian nations. All the great warrior chiefs were dead or in prison, and almost all Native Americans were living on reservations controlled by agencies of the federal government. The reservations consisted of land set aside for the tribes by the government during treaty negotiations. Often, these lands were not the traditional homelands and were hundreds or even thousands of miles away from what the tribe considered to be "home." Not surprisingly, the reservations usually were on undesirable, often worthless land.

The 1890s mark a low point in American history, a time of great demoralization and sadness, especially for Native Americans, who had to find a way to adapt to reservation life and new forms of subordination to the federal government. Although elements of the tribal way of life have survived, the tribes were impoverished and without resources and had little ability to pursue their own interests.

Native Americans, in Blauner's terms, were a conquered minority group that faced high levels of prejudice, racism, and discrimination. Like African Americans, they were controlled by paternalistic systems (the reservations) and, in a variety of ways, were coercively acculturated. Furthermore, according to Blauner, the negative consequences of colonized minority

group status will persist long after the contact situation has been resolved. As we will see in Chapter 6, there is a great deal of evidence to support this prediction.

Gender Relations

In the centuries before contact with Europeans, Native American societies distributed resources and power in a wide variety of ways. At one extreme, some Native American societies were highly stratified, and many practiced various forms of slavery. Others stressed equality, sharing of resources, and respect for the autonomy and dignity of each individual, including women and children (Amott & Matthaei, 1991, p. 33). Native American societies generally were patriarchal and followed a strict gender-based division of labor, but this does not necessarily mean that women were oppressed or exploited. In many tribes, women held positions of great responsibility and controlled the wealth. For example, among the Iroquois (a large and powerful federation of tribes located in the Northeast), women controlled the land and the harvest, arranged marriages, supervised the children, and were responsible for the appointment of tribal leaders and decisions about peace and war (Oswalt & Neely, 1996, pp. 404–405). It was not unusual for women in many tribes to play key roles in religion, politics, warfare, and the economy. Some women even became highly respected warriors and chiefs (Amott & Matthaei, 1991, p. 36).

Gender relations were affected in a variety of ways during the prolonged contact period. In some cases, the relative status and power of women rose. For example, the women of the Navajo tribe (located mainly in what is now Arizona and New Mexico) traditionally were responsible for the care of herd animals and livestock. When the Spanish introduced sheep and goats into the region, the importance of this sector of the subsistence economy increased, and the power and status of women grew along with it.

In other cases, women were adversely affected. The women of the tribes of the Great Plains, for example, suffered a dramatic loss as a result of contact. The sexual division of labor in these tribes was such that women were responsible for gardening, whereas the men handled the hunting. When horses were introduced from Europe, the productivity of the male hunters was greatly increased. As their economic importance increased, males became more dominant, and women lost status and power. Women in the Cherokee nation—a large tribe whose original homelands were in the Southeast—similarly lost considerable status and power under the pressure to assimilate. Traditionally, Cherokee land was cultivated, controlled, and passed down from generation to generation by the women. This matrilineal pattern was abandoned in favor of the European pattern of male ownership when the Cherokee attempted (futilely, as it turned out) to acculturate and avoid relocation under the Indian Relocation Act of 1830 (Evans, 1989, pp. 12–18).

By the end of the contact period, the surviving Native American tribes were impoverished, powerless, and clearly subordinate to white society and the federal government. Like African Americans, they were sharply differentiated from the dominant group by race and, in many cases, internally stratified by gender. As was the case with African American slaves, the degree of gender inequality within the tribes was limited by the tribes' overall lack of autonomy and resources.

Mexican Americans

As the population of the United States increased and spread across the continent, contact with Mexicans inevitably occurred. Spanish explorers and settlers had lived in what is now the southwestern United States long before the wave of American settlers broke across this region. For example, Santa Fe, New Mexico, was founded in 1598, nearly a decade before Jamestown. As late as the 1820s, Mexicans and Native Americans were almost the sole residents of the region.

In the early 1800s, four areas of Mexican settlement had developed, roughly corresponding to what were to become Texas, California, New Mexico, and Arizona. These areas were sparsely settled, and most Mexicans lived in what was to become New Mexico (Cortes, 1980, p. 701). The economy of the regions was based on farming and herding. Most people lived in villages and small towns or on ranches and farms. Social and political life was organized around family and the Catholic church and tended to be dominated by an elite class of wealthy landowners.

Texas

Some of the first effects of U.S. expansion to the West were felt in Texas early in the 1800s. Mexico was no military match for its neighbor to the north, and the farmland of eastern Texas was a tempting resource for the cotton-growing interests in the American South. Anglo-Americans began to immigrate to Texas in sizable numbers in the 1820s, and by 1835, they outnumbered Mexicans six to one. The attempts by the Mexican government to control these immigrants were clumsy and ineffective, and they eventually precipitated a successful revolution by the Anglo-Americans, with some Mexicans also joining the rebels. At this point in time, competition between Anglos and Texans of Mexican descent (called *Tejanos*) was muted by the abundance of land and opportunity in the area. Population density was low, fertile land was readily available for all, and the "general tone of the time was that of inter-cultural cooperation" (Alvarez, 1973, p. 922).

Competition between Anglo Texans and *Tejanos* became increasingly intense. When the United States annexed Texas in the 1840s, full-scale war broke out, and Mexico was defeated. Under the Treaty of Guadalupe Hidalgo in 1848, Mexico ceded much of the Southwest to the United States. In the Gadsden Purchase of 1853, the United States acquired the remainder of the territory now composing the southwestern United States. As a result of these treaties, the Mexican population of this region had become, without moving an inch from their traditional villages and farms, both a conquered people and a minority group.

Following the war, intergroup relations continued to sour, and the political and legal rights of the *Tejano* community often were ignored in the hunger for land. Increasingly impoverished and powerless, the *Tejanos* had few resources with which to resist the growth of Anglo-American domination. They were badly outnumbered and stigmatized by the recent Mexican military defeat. Land that once had been Mexican increasingly came under Anglo control, and widespread violence and lynching reinforced the growth of Anglo dominance (Moquin & Van Doren, 1971, p. 253).

California

In California, the Gold Rush of 1849 spurred a massive population movement from the East. Early relations between Anglos and *Californios* (native Mexicans in the state) had been relatively cordial, forming the basis for a multiethnic, bilingual state. The rapid growth of an Anglo majority after statehood in 1850 doomed these efforts, however, and the *Californios,* like the *Tejanos,* lost their land and political power.

Laws were passed encouraging Anglos to settle on land traditionally held by *Californios.* In such situations, the burden was placed on the Mexican-American landowners to show that their deeds were valid. The *Californios* protested the seizure of their land but found it difficult to argue their cases in the English-speaking, Anglo-controlled court system. By the mid-1850s, a massive transfer of land to Anglo-American hands had taken place in California (Mirandé, 1985, pp. 20–21; see also Pitt, 1970).

Other laws passed in the 1850s made it increasingly difficult for *Californios* to retain their property and power as Anglo-Americans became the dominant group as well as the majority of the population. The Mexican heritage was suppressed and eliminated from public life and institutions such as schools and local government. For example, in 1855, California repealed a requirement in the state constitution that all laws be published in Spanish as well as English (Cortes, 1980, p. 706). Anglo-Americans used violence, biased laws, discrimination, and other means to exploit and repress *Californios,* and

the new wealth generated by gold mining flowed into Anglo hands.

Arizona and New Mexico

The Anglo immigration into Arizona and New Mexico was less voluminous than that into Texas and California, and both states retained Mexican numerical majorities for a number of decades. In Arizona, most of the Mexican population were immigrants themselves seeking work on farms, on ranches, in mines, and on railroads. The economic and political structures of the state quickly came under the control of the Anglo population.

Only in New Mexico did Mexican Americans retain some political power and economic clout, mostly because of the relatively large size of the group and their skill in mobilizing for political activity. New Mexico did not become a state until 1912, and Mexican Americans continued to play a prominent role in governmental affairs even after statehood (Cortes, 1980, p. 706).

Thus, the contact situation for Mexican Americans was highly variable by region. Although some areas were affected more rapidly and more completely than others, the ultimate result was the creation of minority group status for Mexican Americans (Acuna, 1999; Alvarez, 1973; McLemore, 1973; McWilliams, 1961; Moore, 1970; Stoddard, 1973).

Mexican Americans and the Noel and Blauner Hypotheses

The causal model we have applied to the origins of slavery and the domination of Native Americans also provides a way of explaining the development of minority group status for Mexican Americans. Ethnocentrism was clearly present from the very first contact between Anglo immigrants and Mexicans. Many American migrants to the Southwest brought with them the prejudices and racism they had acquired with regard to African Americans and Native Americans. In fact, many of the settlers who moved into Texas came directly from the South in search of new lands for the cultivation of cotton. They readily transferred their prejudiced views to at least the poorer Mexicans, who were stereotyped as lazy and shiftless (McLemore, 1973, p. 664). The visibility of group boundaries was heightened and reinforced by physical and religious differences. Mexicans were "racially" a mixture of Spanish and Native American, and the differences in skin color and other physical characteristics provided a convenient marker of group membership. In addition, the vast majority of Mexicans were Roman Catholic, whereas the vast majority of Anglo-Americans were Protestant.

Competition for land began with the first contact between the groups. However, for many years, population density was low in the Southwest, and the competition did not immediately or always erupt into violent domination and expropriation. Nonetheless, the loss of land and power for Mexican Americans was inexorable, although variable in speed.

The size of the power differential between the groups was variable and partly explains why domination was established faster in some places than others. In both Texas and California, the subordination of the Mexican American population followed quickly after a rapid influx of Anglos and the military defeat of Mexico in 1848. Anglo-Americans used their superior numbers and military power to acquire control of the political and economic structures and to expropriate the resources of the Mexican American community. In New Mexico, the groups were more evenly matched in size, and Mexican Americans were able to retain a measure of power for decades.

Unlike the case of Native Americans, however, the labor as well as the land of the Mexicans was coveted. On cotton plantations, ranches, and farms, and in mining and railroad construction, Mexican Americans became a vital source of inexpensive labor. During times of high demand, this labor force was supplemented by encouraging workers to emigrate from Mexico. When demand for workers decreased, these laborers were forced back to Mexico. Thus began a pattern of labor flow that continues to the present.

As in the case of African Americans and Native Americans, the contact period clearly established a colonized status for Mexican Americans in all areas of the Southwest. Their culture and language were suppressed even as their property rights were abrogated and their status lowered. In countless ways, they, too, were subjected to coercive acculturation. For example, California banned the use of Spanish in public schools, and bullfighting and other Mexican sports and recreational activities were severely restricted (Moore, 1970, p. 19; Pitt, 1970). In contrast to African Americans, however, Mexican Americans were in close proximity to their homeland and maintained close ties with villages and families. Constant movement across the border with Mexico kept the Spanish language and much of the Mexican heritage alive in the Southwest. Nonetheless, 19th-century Mexican Americans fit Blauner's category of a colonized minority group, and the suppression of their culture was part of the process by which the dominant culture was established.

Anglo-American economic interests benefited enormously from the conquest of the Southwest and the colonization of the Mexican people. Growers and other businessmen came to rely on the cheap labor pool formed by Mexican Americans and immigrant and day laborers from Mexico. The region grew in affluence and productivity, but Mexican Americans were now outsiders in their own land and did not share in the prosperity. In the land grab of the 1800s and the conquest of the indigenous Mexican population lay one of the roots of Mexican-American relations with the dominant U.S. society today.

Gender Relations

Prior to the arrival of Anglo-Americans, Mexican society in the Southwest was patriarchal and maintained a clear, gender-based division of labor. These characteristics tended to persist after the conquest and the creation of minority group status.

Most Mexican Americans lived in small villages or on large ranches and farms. The women devoted their energies to the family, child rearing, and household tasks. As Mexican Americans were reduced to a landless labor force, women along with men suffered the economic devastation that accompanied military conquest by a foreign power. The kinds of jobs available to the men (mining, seasonal farm work, railroad construction) often required them to be away from home for extended periods of time, and women, by default, began to take over the economic and other tasks traditionally performed by males.

Poverty and economic insecurity placed the family structures under considerable strain. Traditional cultural understandings about male dominance and patriarchy became moot when the men were absent for long periods of time and the decision-making power of Mexican-American women increased. Also, women were often forced to work outside the household for the family to survive economically. The economics of conquest led to increased matriarchy and more working mothers (Becerra, 1988, p. 149).

For Mexican American women, the consequences of contact were variable even though the ultimate result was a loss of status within the context of the conquest and colonization of the group as a whole. Like black female slaves, Mexican American women became the most vulnerable part of the social system.

COMPARATIVE FOCUS

MEXICO, CANADA, AND THE UNITED STATES

A major point of this chapter is that dominant-minority relations are profoundly shaped by the contact situation and by the characteristics of the groups involved (especially their subsistence technologies). We saw how these factors shaped relations with Native Americans and Mexican Americans and how they led British colonists to create a system of slavery to control the labor of African Americans. How do the experiences of the Spanish and the French in the Western Hemisphere compare with those of the British in what became the United States? What roles did the contact situation and subsistence technology play in the development of group relations in Mexico and Canada, the two closest neighbors of the United States?[1]

Spain was the first of three European nations to invade the Western Hemisphere, and the Spanish conquered much of what is now Central and South America in the century before Jamestown was founded. Their first encounter with a Native American society occurred in 1521, when they defeated the Aztec Empire, located in what is now central Mexico. Aztec society was large, highly organized, and complex. It was ruled by an emperor and included scores of different societies, each with its own language and identity, that had been conquered by the fiercely warlike Aztecs. The bulk of the population of the empire consisted of peasants or agricultural laborers who farmed small plots of land that were owned by members of the elite classes, to whom they paid rents. Peasants are a fundamental part of any labor-intensive, preindustrial agrarian societies and were just as common in Spain as they were in Mexico.

When the Spanish defeated the Aztecs, they destroyed their cities, their temples, and their leadership (the emperor, the nobility, priests, etc.). They did not destroy the Aztec social structure. Rather, they absorbed it and used it for their own benefit. For example, the Aztec Empire had financed its central government by collecting taxes and rents from citizens and tribute from conquered tribes. The Spanish simply grafted their own tax collection system onto this structure and diverted the flow from the Aztec elite classes (which they had, at any rate, destroyed) to themselves (Russell, 1994, pp. 29–30).

The Spanish tendency to absorb rather than destroy operated at many levels. Aztec peasants became Spanish (and then Mexican) peasants, occupying roughly the same role in the new societies that they had in the old, save for paying their rents to different landlords. There was also extensive interbreeding between the Spanish and the conquered tribes of Mexico but, unlike the English colonists, the Spanish recognized the resultant racial diversity and developed an elaborate system for classifying people by race. They recognized as many as 56 racial groups, including whites, mestizos (mixed European-Indian), and mulattos (mixed European-African) (Russell, 1994, p. 35). The society that emerged was very race conscious, and race was highly correlated with social class: The elite classes were white, and the lower classes were nonwhite. However, the large-scale intermarriage and the official recognition of mixed-race peoples did establish the foundation for a racially mixed society. Today, the huge majority of the Mexican population is mestizo, although there remains a very strong correlation between race and class, and the elite positions in the society tend to be monopolized by people of "purer" European ancestry.

The French began to colonize Canada at about the same time the English established their colonies further south. The dominant economic enterprise in the early days was not farming but trapping and the fur trade. The French developed a lucrative trade in this area by allying themselves with some Native American tribes. The Indians produced the furs and traded them to the French, who in turn sold them on the world market. Like the Spanish in Mexico, the French in Canada tended to link to and absorb Native American social structures. There was also a significant amount of intermarriage between the French and Native Americans, resulting in a mixed-race group, called Métis, who had their own identities and, indeed, their own settlements along the Canadian frontier (Russell, 1994, p. 39).

Note the profound differences in these three contact situations between Europeans and Native Americans. The Spanish confronted a large, well-organized social system and found it expeditious to adapt Aztec practices to their own benefit. The French developed an economy that required cooperation with at least some of the Native American tribes they encountered, and they too found benefits in adaptation. The tribes encountered by the English were much smaller and much less developed than the Aztecs, and there was no particular reason for the English to adapt to or absorb these social structures.

Furthermore, because the business of the English colonies was agriculture (not trapping), the competition at the heart of the contact situation was for land, and Native Americans were seen as rivals for control of that most valuable resource. Thus, the English tended to confront and exclude Native Americans, keeping them outside their emerging society and building strong boundaries between their own "civilized" world and the "savages" that surrounded them. Whereas the Spanish and French colonists had to adapt their society to fit with Native Americans, the English faced no such restraints. They could create their institutions and design their social structure to suit themselves (Russell, 1994, p. 30).

As we have seen, one of the institutions created in the English colonies was slavery based on African labor. Slavery also was practiced in New Spain (Mexico) and New France (Canada), but the institution evolved in very different ways in those colonies and never assumed the importance that it did in the United States. Why? As you might suspect, the answer has a lot to do with the nature of the contact situation. Like the English colonists, both the Spanish and French attempted large-scale agricultural enterprises that might have created a demand for imported slave labor. In the case of New Spain, however, there was a ready supply of Native American peasants available to fill the role played by blacks in the English colonies. Although Africans became a part of the admixture that shaped modern Mexico racially and socially, demand for black slaves never matched that of the English colonies. Similarly in Canada, slaves from Africa sometimes were used, but farmers there tended to rely on the flow of labor from France to fill their agricultural needs. While the British opted for slave labor from Africa over indentured labor from Europe, the French made the opposite decision.

Another difference between the three European nations that helps to explain the divergent development of group relations is their relative level of modernization. Compared to England, Spain and France were more traditional and feudalistic in their cultures and social structures. Among other things, this meant that they had to shape their agricultural enterprises in the New World around the ancient social relations between peasants and landlords that they brought from the Old World. Thus, the Spanish and French colonists were limited in their actions by these ancient customs, traditions, and understandings. Such old-fashioned institutions were much weaker in England, and the English colonists were much freer to design their social structures to suit their own needs. Whereas the Spanish and French had to shape their colonial societies to fit both Native American social patterns and European traditions, the English could improvise and attend only to their own needs and desires. The closed, complex, and repressive institution of American slavery—designed and crafted from scratch in the New World—was one result.

Finally, we should note that many of the modern racial characteristics of these three neighboring societies were foreshadowed in their colonial origins (for example, the greater concentration of African Americans in the United States and the more racially intermixed population of Mexico). The differences run much deeper than race alone, of course, and include differences in class structure and relative levels of industrialization and affluence. For our purposes, however, this brief comparison of the origins of dominant-minority relations underscores the importance of the contact situation in shaping group relations for centuries to come.

COMPARING U.S. MINORITY GROUPS

Native Americans and black slaves were the victims of the explosive growth of European power in the Western Hemisphere that began with Christopher Columbus's voyage in 1492. Europeans needed labor to fuel the plantations of the mid-17th-century American colonies and settled on slaves from Africa as the most logical, cost-effective means of resolving their labor supply problems. Black Africans had a commodity the colonists coveted (labor), and the colonists subsequently constructed a system to control and exploit this commodity.

To satisfy the demand for land created by the stream of European immigrants to North America, the threat represented by Native Americans had to be eliminated. Once their land was expropriated, Native Americans ceased to be of much concern. The only valuable resource they possessed—their land—was under the control of white society by 1890, and Native Americans were thought to be unsuitable as a source of labor.

Mexico, like the United States, had been colonized by a European power, in this case, Spain. In the early 1800s, the Mexican communities in the Southwest were a series of outpost settlements, remote and difficult to defend. Through warfare and a variety of other aggressive means, Mexican citizens living in this area were conquered and became an exploited minority group.

Each of these three groups—African Americans, Native Americans, and Mexicans—in their separate ways became involuntary players in the growth and development of European and, later, American economic and political power. None of these groups had much choice in their respective fates; all three were overpowered and relegated to an inferior, subordinate status. Many views of assimilation (such as the "melting pot"

metaphor discussed in Chapter 2) have little relevance to their situations. These minority groups had little control over their destiny, their degree of acculturation, or even their survival as a group. African Americans, Native Americans, and Mexican Americans were acculturated coercively in the context of paternalistic relations in an agrarian economy. Meaningful integration (structural assimilation) was not a real possibility, especially for African Americans and Native Americans. In Milton Gordon's terms (see Chapter 2), we might characterize these situations as "acculturation without integration" or structural pluralism. Given the grim realities described in this chapter, Gordon's terms seem a little antiseptic, and Blauner's concept of colonized and conquered minority groups seems far more descriptive.

MAIN POINTS

- Dominant-minority relations are shaped by the characteristics of society as a whole, particularly by subsistence technology. The contact situation is the single most important factor in the development of dominant-minority relations.

- The Noel and Blauner hypotheses provide powerful conceptual tools for analyzing the emergence of minority group status and its persistence over time. Together, they explain why Africans were enslaved in colonial America and why white indentured servants and Native Americans were not, and why racial inequality and anti-black racism and prejudice continue so many years after the initial contact situation.

- Prejudice and racism are more the results of systems of racial and ethnic inequality than they are causes. They serve to rationalize, "explain," and stabilize these systems.

- The competition between white Americans and Native Americans centered on control of the land. The Native American tribes were conquered and pressed into a paternalistic relationship with white society. Native Americans were a conquered minority group and were subjected to forced acculturation.

- Mexican Americans were the third minority group created during the preindustrial era. Mexican Americans competed with white settlers over both land and labor. Like African Americans and Native Americans, Mexican Americans were a colonized minority group subjected to forced acculturation.

- Conquest and colonization affected men and women differently. Women's roles changed, and sometimes the conquest of their nation released them from the constraints of patriarchal traditions. These changes always were in the context of increasing powerlessness and poverty for the group as a whole, however, and minority women have been doubly oppressed, by both their gender roles and their minority group status.

- In colonial Mexico and Canada, as well as in British America, the contact situation shaped initial relations between groups and continues to affect group relations in the present.

QUESTIONS FOR REVIEW AND STUDY

1. Two themes are stated at the beginning of this chapter. How exactly does the material presented in the chapter illustrate the usefulness of these themes?
2. Apply the Noel hypothesis to the origins of American slavery. Why did the colonists decide to create the institution of slavery? Why were Africans enslaved rather than Native Americans or white indentured servants? In your view, what was the single most important factor in the contact situation that led to the enslavement of Africans? Why?
3. Apply the Blauner hypothesis to the origins of American slavery. Explain the difference between immigrant and colonized or conquered minority groups. This hypothesis argues that the status of colonized groups will be more disadvantaged and persistent than the status of immigrant groups. How is this point illustrated by the history of African Americans?
4. Apply both the Noel and Blauner hypotheses to Native Americans and Mexican Americans. Compare and contrast the contact situations of these groups with that of African Americans. What important differences and similarities can you identify? How did the differences affect the respective fates of each of the three groups?
5. What are paternalistic relationships? In what specific ways were the early relations of African Americans, Native Americans, and Mexican Americans paternalistic?
6. What was the role of prejudice in the creation of minority status for African Americans, Native Americans, and Mexican Americans? Was it a cause or a result? How?
7. Compare and contrast the role of gender in the creation of minority status for African Americans, Native Americans, and Mexican Americans. How and why did the situation of male and female members of these minority groups vary?
8. Compare and contrast the contact situations for Mexico, the United States, and Canada. What important differences during the contact periods shaped the development of dominant-minority relations? How?

INTERNET RESEARCH PROJECT

"Slave Narratives" are one interesting source of information about the nature of everyday life under slavery. The narratives were compiled during the 1930s by interviewing former slaves, and although they are limited in many ways, the interviews do provide a close-up, personal view of the system of slavery from the perspective of its victims. To use this resource, go to www.newdeal. feri.org/asn/index.htm and read the home page carefully, especially the cautions. Select several of the narratives (the page provides a link to 13 more) and analyze them in terms of the concepts introduced in this chapter (e.g., paternalism, labor-intensive systems of work, or the Noel and Blauner hypotheses).

FOR FURTHER READING

Genovese, Eugene D. 1974. *Roll, Jordan, Roll.* New York: Pantheon.

Gutman, Herbert G. 1976. *The Black Family in Slavery and Freedom, 1750–1925.* New York: Vintage.

Levine, Lawrence. 1977. *Black Culture and Black Consciousness.* New York: Oxford University Press.

Rawick, George P. 1972. *From Sundown to Sunup: The Making of the Black Community.* Westport, CT: Greenwood Press.

Stuckey, Sterling. 1987. *Slave Culture: Nationalist Theory and the Foundations of Black America.* New York: Harper & Row.

A short list of vital sources on the origins and psychological and cultural impact of slavery in America.

Brown, Dee. 1970. *Bury My Heart at Wounded Knee*. New York: Holt, Rinehart & Winston.
An eloquent and moving account of the conquest of Native Americans.

Nabakov, Peter. (Ed.). 1991. *Native American Testimony*. New York: Penguin.
A collection of valuable and insightful Native American accounts of the last 500 years.

Wax, Murray. 1971. *Indian Americans: Unity and Diversity*. Englewood Cliffs, NJ: Prentice Hall.
A compact and informative analysis of the history and present situation of Native Americans.

Acuna, Rodolfo. 1999. *Occupied America* (4th ed.). New York: Harper & Row.
Acuna examines a broad sweep of Mexican American experiences and argues that the status of Mexican Americans is comparable to that of other colonized groups.

McWilliams, Carey. 1961. *North from Mexico: The Spanish Speaking People of the United States*. New York: Monthly Review Press.
A classic overview of the historical development of Mexican Americans.

Mirandé, Alfredo. 1985. *The Chicano Experience: An Alternative Perspective*. Notre Dame, IN: University of Notre Dame Press.
A passionate argument for a new sociological approach to the study of Mexican Americans. Many useful insights into Mexican American family structures, the problem of crime, and other areas.

NOTE

1. This analysis is based largely on the work of sociologist James W. Russell, especially on *After the Fifth Sun: Class and Race in North America* (1994).

4

Industrialization and Dominant-Minority Relations

From Slavery to Segregation and the Coming of Postindustrial Society

One theme stated at the beginning of Chapter 3 was that a society's subsistence technology profoundly affects the nature of dominant-minority group relations. A corollary of this theme, explored in this chapter, is that *dominant-minority group relations change as the subsistence technology changes.* As we saw in Chapter 3, agrarian technology and the concern for control of land and labor profoundly shaped dominant-minority relations in the formative years of the United States. The agrarian era ended in the 1800s, and since that time, the United States has experienced two major transformations in subsistence technology, each of which has, in turn, transformed the relationships between the dominant group and minority groups.

The first transformation began in the early 1800s as American society began to experience the effects of the *industrial revolution,* or the shift from agrarian technology to machine-based, manufacturing technology. In the agrarian era, as we saw in Chapter 3, work was *labor intensive:* done by hand or with the aid of draft animals. As industrialization proceeded, work became *capital intensive* as machines replaced people and animals.

The new industrial technology rapidly increased productivity and efficiency and quickly began to change every aspect of U.S.

society, including the nature of work, politics, communication, transportation, family life, birth rates and death rates, the system of education, and, of course, dominant-minority relations. The groups that had become minorities during the agrarian era (African Americans, Native Americans, and Mexican Americans) faced new possibilities and new dangers. Industrialization also created new minority groups, new forms of exploitation and oppression, and, for some, new opportunities to rise in the social structure and succeed in America. In this chapter, we will explore this transformation in general terms and illustrate its effects by analyzing the changing status of African Americans after the abolition of slavery. Industrialization's impact on other minority groups will be considered in the case studies presented in Part III.

The second transformation in subsistence technology brings us to more recent times. Industrialization is a continuous process, and beginning in the mid-20th century, the United States entered a stage of late industrialization (also called *deindustrialization* or the *postindustrial* era). This shift in subsistence technology is marked by a decline in the manufacturing sector of the economy and a decrease in the supply of blue-collar, manual labor jobs. At the same time, there was an expansion in the service and information-based sectors of the economy and an increase in the proportion of white-collar and "high-tech" jobs. Like the 19th-century industrial revolution, these 20th-century changes have profound implications not only for dominant-minority relations but for every aspect of modern society. Work, family, politics, popular culture, and thousands of other characteristics of American society are being transformed as the subsistence technology continues to develop and modernize. In the latter part of this chapter, we examine this most recent transformation in general terms and point out some of its implications for minority groups. We also present some new concepts and establish some important groundwork for the case studies in Part III, in which the effects of late industrialization on America's minority groups will be considered in detail.

INDUSTRIALIZATION AND THE SHIFT FROM PATERNALISTIC TO RIGID COMPETITIVE GROUP RELATIONS

The industrial revolution began in England in the mid-1700s and spread from there to the rest of Europe, to the United States, and eventually to the rest of the world. The key innovations associated with the industrial revolution were the application of machine power to production and the harnessing of inanimate sources of energy, such as steam and coal, to fuel the machines (Nolan & Lenski, 1999). As machines replaced humans and animals, work became many times more productive, the economy grew, and the volume and variety of goods produced increased dramatically.

As the industrial economy grew, the close, paternalistic control of minority groups found in agrarian societies gradually became irrelevant. Paternalistic relationships such as slavery are found in societies with labor-intensive technologies and are designed to organize and control a large, involuntary, geographically immobile labor force. An industrial economy, in contrast, requires a workforce that is geographically and socially mobile, skilled, and literate. Furthermore, with industrialization comes urbanization, and close, paternalistic controls are difficult to maintain in a city.

Thus, as industrialization progresses, agrarian paternalism tends to give way to *rigid competitive* group relations. Under this system, minority group members are free to compete for jobs and other valued commodities with dominant group members, especially the lower-class segments of the dominant group. As competition increases, the threatened members of the dominant group become more hostile, and attacks on the minority groups tend to increase. Whereas paternalistic systems seek to directly dominate and control the minority group (and its labor), rigid competitive systems are more defensive in nature. The threatened segments of the dominant group seek to minimize or eliminate minority group encroachment on jobs, housing, or other valuable goods or services (van den Berghe, 1967; Wilson, 1973).

Paternalistic systems such as slavery required members of the minority group to be active, if involuntary, participants. In rigid competitive systems, the dominant group seeks to preserve its advantage by handicapping the minority group's ability to compete effectively or, in some cases, by eliminating competition from the minority group altogether. For example, in a rigid competitive system, the dominant group might make the minority group politically powerless by depriving it of (or never granting it) the right to vote. The lower the power of the minority group, the lower the threat to the interests of the dominant group.

THE IMPACT OF INDUSTRIALIZATION ON AFRICAN AMERICANS: FROM SLAVERY TO SEGREGATION

Industrial technology began to transform American society in the early 1800s, but its effects were not felt equally in all regions. The northern states industrialized first, while the South remained primarily agrarian. This economic diversity was one of the underlying causes of the regional conflict that led to the Civil War. Because of its more productive technology, the North had more resources and, in a bloody war of attrition, was able to defeat the Confederacy. Slavery was abolished, and black-white relations in the South entered a new era when the Civil War ended in April of 1865.

The southern system of race relations that ultimately emerged after the Civil War was designed in part to continue the control of black labor institutionalized under slavery. It also was intended to eliminate any political or economic threat from the black community. This rigid competitive system grew to be highly elaborate and repressive, partly because of the high racial visibility and long history of inferior status and powerlessness of African Americans in the South and partly because of the particular needs of southern agriculture. In this section, we look at black-white relations from the end of the Civil War through the ascendancy of segregation in the South and the mass migration of African Americans to the cities of the industrializing North.

Reconstruction

The period of *Reconstruction,* from 1865 to the 1880s, was a brief respite in the long history of oppression and exploitation of African Americans. The Union army and other agencies of the federal government such as the Freedman's Bureau were used to enforce racial freedom in the defeated Confederacy. Black Southerners took advantage of the 15th Amendment to the Constitution, passed in 1870, which states that the right to vote cannot be denied on the grounds of "race, color, or previous condition of servitude." They registered to vote in large numbers and turned out on election days, and some were elected to high political office. Schools for the former slaves were opened, and African Americans purchased land and houses and founded businesses.

The era of freedom was short, however, and Reconstruction began to end when the federal government demobilized its armies of occupation and turned its attention to other matters. By the 1880s, the federal government had withdrawn from the South, Reconstruction was over, and black Southerners began to fall rapidly into a new system of exploitation and inequality.

Reconstruction was too brief to change two of the most important legacies of slavery. First, the centuries of bondage left black Southerners impoverished, largely illiterate and uneducated, and with few power resources. When new threats of racial oppression appeared, African Americans found it difficult to defend their group interests.

These developments are, of course, highly consistent with the Blauner hypothesis. Because colonized minority groups confront greater inequalities and have fewer resources at their disposal, they will face greater difficulties in improving their disadvantaged status.

Second, slavery left a strong tradition of racism in the white community. Anti-black prejudice and racism originated as rationalizations for slavery but had taken on lives of their own over the generations. After two centuries of slavery, the heritage of prejudice and racism was thoroughly ingrained in southern culture. White Southerners were predisposed by this cultural legacy to see racial inequality and exploitation of African Americans as normal and desirable, and after Reconstruction ended and the federal government withdrew, they were able to act on these assumptions.

De Jure Segregation

The system of race relations that replaced slavery in the South was *de jure segregation,* sometimes referred to as the *Jim Crow* system. Under segregation, the minority group is physically and socially separated from the dominant group and consigned to an inferior position in virtually every area of social life. The phrase *de jure* ("by law") means that the system is sanctioned and reinforced by the legal code. In other words, the inferior status of African Americans actually was mandated or required by state and local laws. For example, southern cities passed laws requiring blacks to ride in the back of vehicles used for public transportation (horse-drawn street cars at first, buses later). If an African American refused to comply with this seating arrangement, he or she could be arrested.

De jure segregation came to encompass all aspects of southern life. Neighborhoods, jobs, stores, restaurants, and parks were segregated. When new social forms, such as movie theaters, sports stadiums, and interstate buses appeared in the South, they were quickly segregated.

The logic of segregation created another vicious cycle (see Exhibits 1.3 and 3.3). The more African Americans were excluded from the mainstream of society, the greater became their abject poverty and powerlessness. The more inferior their status, the easier it was to mandate even more inequality. High levels of inequality reinforced racial prejudice and made it easy to use racism to justify further separation. The system kept turning on itself, finding new social niches to segregate and reinforcing the inequality that was its starting point. For example, at the height of the Jim Crow era in the mid-20th century, the system had evolved to the point that some courtrooms maintained separate bibles for black witnesses to swear on. Also, in Birmingham, Alabama, it was against the law for blacks and whites to play checkers and dominoes together (Woodward, 1974, p. 118).

What were the causes of this massive separation of the races? Once again, the concepts of the Noel hypothesis prove useful. Because strong anti-black prejudice already existed when segregation began, we don't need to account for ethnocentrism. The post-Reconstruction competition between the racial groups was reminiscent of the origins of slavery in that black Southerners had something that white Southerners wanted: labor. In addition, a free black electorate threatened the political and economic dominance of the elite segments of the white community. Finally, after the withdrawal of federal troops and the end of Reconstruction, white Southerners had sufficient power resources to end the competition on their own terms and construct repressive systems of control over black Southerners.

The Origins of Jim Crow

Although the South lost the Civil War, its basic class structure and agrarian economy remained intact. The plantation elite, with their huge tracts of land, remained the dominant class, and cotton remained the primary cash crop. As was the case before the Civil War, the landowners needed a workforce to farm the land. Because of the depredations and economic disruptions of the war, the old plantation elite were short on cash and liquid capital. Hiring workers on a wage system was not feasible for them. In fact, almost as soon as the war ended, southern legislatures attempted to force African Americans back into involuntary servitude by passing a series of laws known as the Black Codes. Only the beginning of Reconstruction and the active intervention of the federal government halted the implementation of this legislation (Geschwender, 1978, p. 158; Wilson, 1973, p. 99).

The plantation elite solved their manpower problem this time by developing a system of *sharecropping,* or tenant farming. The sharecroppers worked the land, which was owned by the planters, in return for payment in shares of the profit when the crop was taken to market. The landowner would supply a place to live, along with food and clothing, on credit. After the harvest, tenant and landowner would split the profits (sometimes very unequally), and the tenant's debts would be deducted from his share. The accounts were kept by the landowner. Black sharecroppers lacked political and civil rights and found it difficult to keep unscrupulous white landowners honest. The landowner could inflate the indebtedness of the sharecropper and claim that he was still owed money even after profits had been split. Under this system, sharecroppers had few opportunities to improve their situation and could be bound to the land until their "debt" was paid off (Geschwender, 1978, p. 163).

By 1910, more than half of all employed African Americans worked in agriculture, and more than half of the remainder (25% of the total) worked in domestic occupations such as maid and janitor (Geschwender, 1978, p. 169). The manpower shortage in southern agriculture was solved, and the African American community once again found itself in a subservient status. At the same time, the white southern working class was protected from direct job competition with African Americans. As the South began to industrialize, white workers were able to monopolize the better-paying jobs. With a combination of direct discrimination by whites-only labor unions and strong anti-black laws and customs, white workers erected barriers that excluded black workers and reserved the better industrial jobs in cities and mill towns for themselves. White workers took advantage of the new jobs brought by industrialization, while black Southerners remained a rural peasantry, excluded from participation in this process of modernization.

In some sectors of the changing southern economy, the status of African Americans actually fell lower than it had been during slavery. For example, in 1865, 83% of the artisans in the South were African Americans; by 1900, this percentage had fallen to 5% (Geschwender, 1978, p. 170). By the early years of the 20th century, the Jim Crow system of legally sanctioned segregation confined African Americans to the agrarian and domestic sectors of the labor force, denied them the opportunity for a decent education, and excluded them from politics. The system was reinforced by still more laws and customs that drastically limited the options and life courses available to black Southerners.

A final force behind the creation of de jure segregation was more political than economic. As the 19th century drew to a close, a wave of agrarian radicalism known as *populism* spread across the country. This anti-elitist movement was a reaction to changes in agriculture caused by industrialization. The movement attempted to unite poor whites and blacks in the rural South against the traditional elite classes. The economic elite was frightened by the possibility of a loss of power, and it split the incipient coalition between poor whites and blacks by fanning the flames of racial hatred. The strategy of "divide and conquer" proved to be effective (as it often has both before and since that time), and states throughout the South eliminated the possibility of future threats by depriving African Americans of the right to vote (Woodward, 1974).

The disenfranchisement of the black community was accomplished by measures such as literacy tests, poll taxes, and property requirements. The literacy tests were officially justified as promoting a better-informed electorate but were shamelessly rigged to favor white voters. The requirement that voters pay a tax or prove ownership of a certain amount of property could also disenfranchise poor whites, but again, the implementation of these policies was racially biased.

The policies were extremely effective, and by the early 20th century, the southern black community was virtually powerless politically. For example, as late as 1896 in Louisiana, there had been more than 100,000 registered black voters, and black voters were a majority in 26 parishes (counties). In 1898, the state adopted a new constitution containing stiff educational and property requirements for voting *unless* the voter's father or grandfather had been eligible to vote as of January 1, 1867. At that time, the 14th and 15th Amendments, which guaranteed suffrage for black males, had not yet been passed. Such "grandfather clauses" made it easy for white males to register while disenfranchising blacks. By 1900, only about 5,000 African Americans were registered to vote in Louisiana, and black voters were not a majority in any parish. A similar decline occurred in Alabama, where an electorate of more than 180,000 black males was reduced to 3,000 by a provision within the new state constitution. This story repeated itself throughout the South, and black political powerlessness had become a reality by 1905 (Franklin & Moss, 1994, p. 261).

This system of legally mandated racial privilege was approved by the U.S. Supreme Court, which ruled in the case of *Plessy v. Ferguson* (1896) that it was constitutional for states to require separate facilities (schools, parks, etc.) for African Americans as long as the separate facilities were fully equal. The southern states paid close attention to *separate* but ignored *equal*.

Reinforcing the System

Under de jure segregation, as under slavery, the subordination of the African American community was reinforced and supplemented by an elaborate system of racial etiquette. Everyday interactions between blacks and whites proceeded according to highly stylized and rigidly followed codes of conduct intended to underscore the inferior status of the African American community. Whites were addressed as "Mister" or "Ma'am," whereas blacks were called by their first names or perhaps by an honorific title such as Aunt, Uncle, or Professor. Blacks were expected to assume a humble and deferential manner, remove their hats, cast their eyes downward, and enact the role of the subordinate in all interactions with whites. If an African American had reason to call on anyone in the white community, he or she was expected to go to the back door.

These expectations and "good manners" for black Southerners were systematically enforced. Anyone who ignored them ran the risk of reprisal, physical attacks, and even death by lynching. During the decades in which the Jim Crow system was imposed, there were thousands of lynchings in the South. From 1884 until the end of the 19th century, lynchings averaged almost one every other day (Franklin & Moss, 1994, p. 312). The bulk of this violent terrorism was racial and intended to reinforce the system of racial advantage or punish real or imagined transgressors. In addition, various secret organizations, such as the Ku Klux Klan, engaged in terrorist attacks against the African American community and anyone else who failed to conform to the dictates of the system.

Increases in Prejudice and Racism

As the system of racial advantage formed and solidified, levels of prejudice and racism increased (Wilson, 1973, p. 101). The new system needed justification and rationalization, just as slavery did, and anti-black sentiment, stereotypes, and ideologies of racial inferiority grew stronger. At the start of the 20th century, American society in general—not just the South—was highly racist and intolerant. This spirit of rejection and scorn for all out-groups coalesced with the need for justification of the Jim Crow system and created an especially negative brand of racism in the South.

THE "GREAT MIGRATION"

Although African Americans lacked the power resources to withstand the resurrection of southern racism and oppression, they did have one option that had not been available under slavery: freedom of movement. African Americans were no longer legally tied to a specific master or to a certain plot of land, and in the early 20th century, a massive population movement out of the South began. Slowly at first, African Americans began to move to other regions of the nation and from the countryside to the city. The movement increased when hard times hit southern agriculture and

Exhibit 4.1   Population Characteristics of African Americans (percentages)

	Regional Distribution				Percentage Urban		
	South	North East	North Central	West	United States	South	Non-South
1890	90	4	6	<1	20	15	62
1920	85	7	8	<1	34	25	85
1940	77	11	11	1	50	25	89
1960	60	16	18	6	73	58	95
1990	53	19	19	9	84	NA	NA
2000	55	18	19	9	82	NA	NA

SOURCE: 1890–1960: Geschwender (1978, p. 173); 1990 (Regional Distribution): U.S. Bureau of the Census (1997, p. 31); 1990 (urbanization): O'Hare, Pollard, Mann, & Kent (1991, p. 9); 2000 (Regional Distribution): U.S. Bureau of the Census (2002, p. 24); 1990 (Urbanization): U.S. Bureau of the Census (2000q).

slowed down during better times. It has been said that African Americans voted against southern segregation with their feet.

As Exhibit 4.1 shows, an urban black population living outside the South is a 20th-century phenomenon. A slight majority of African Americans continue to live in the South, but the group is more evenly distributed across the nation and much more urbanized than a century ago. The significance of this population redistribution is manifold. Most important, perhaps, is the fact that by moving out of the South and from rural to urban areas, African Americans moved from areas of great resistance to racial change to areas of lower resistance. In the northern cities, for example, it was far easier to register and to vote. Black political power began to grow and eventually provided many of the crucial resources that fueled the Civil Rights movement of the 1950s and 1960s.

Life in the North

What did African American migrants find when they got to the industrializing cities of the North? There is no doubt that life in the North was better for the vast majority of black migrants. The growing northern black communities relished the absence of Jim Crow laws and oppressive racial etiquette, the relative freedom to pursue jobs, and the greater opportunities to educate their children. Inevitably, however, life in the North fell short of utopia. Many aspects of African American culture—literature, poetry, music—flourished in the heady new atmosphere of freedom, but on other fronts, Northern black communities faced discrimination in housing, schools, and the job market. Along with freedom and such cultural flowerings as the Harlem Renaissance came the first black ghettoes and new forms of oppression that, although different from and subtler than those of the South, were still devastating in their impact.

Competition With White Ethnic Groups

It is useful to see this population movement of African Americans in terms of their relationship with other groups. Southern blacks began to migrate to the North at about the same time that a huge, century-long wave of immigration from Europe came to an end. By the time substantial numbers of black Southerners began arriving in the North, European immigrants and their descendants had had decades and generations to establish themselves in the job markets, political systems, labor unions, and neighborhoods of the North. Many of the European ethnic groups also had been the victims of discrimination and rejection in America, and their hold on economic security and status was tenuous for much of the 20th century. They saw the newly arriving black migrants as a threat to their status, a perception that was reinforced by the fact that industrialists and factory owners often used blacks as strikebreakers and "scabs" during strikes. The white ethnic groups responded by developing defensive strategies to limit the dangers presented by these migrants from the South. They tried to exclude blacks from their labor unions and other associations and to limit their impact on the political system. They also attempted, often successfully, to maintain segregated neighborhoods and schools (although the legal system outside the South did not sanction de jure segregation).

This competition led to hostile relations between black southern migrants and white ethnic groups, especially the lower- and working-class segments of those groups. Ironically, however, the newly arriving African Americans helped white ethnic groups to become upwardly mobile. Sociologist Stanley Lieberson (1980) compared black migrants from the South with immigrants from southern and Eastern Europe in the early 20th century, focusing especially on the relatively faster rise of white ethnic groups. He concluded that the arrival of African Americans from the South actually *aided* the European immigrants and their descendants in their rise up the social class structure. Whites in the dominant group became less vocal about their contempt for the white ethnic groups as their alarm over the presence of blacks increased. The greater antipathy of the white community toward African Americans made the immigrants less undesirable and thus hastened their admittance to the institutions of the larger society. For many white ethnic groups, the increased tolerance of the larger society coincided happily with the coming of age of the more educated and skilled descendants of the original immigrants.

For more than a century, each newly arrived European immigrant group had helped to push previous groups up the ladder of socioeconomic success and out of the old, ghettoized neighborhoods. The Irish pushed the Germans up and were, in turn, pushed up

by Italians and Poles. However, black Southerners got to the cities last, after immigration from Europe had been curtailed. Large-scale immigration did not resume until the mid-1960s, and no newly arrived immigrants appeared to continue the pattern of succession. Instead, American cities developed a concentration of low-income blacks who were economically vulnerable and politically weak, and whose position was further solidified by anti-black prejudice and discrimination (Wilson, 1987, p. 34).

THE ORIGINS OF BLACK PROTEST

As we pointed out in Chapter 3, African Americans have always resisted their oppression and protested their situation. Under slavery, however, the inequalities they faced were so vast and their resources so meager that their protests were ineffective. With the increased freedom that followed slavery, a national black leadership developed and began to speak out against oppression. They helped to found the organizations that eventually led the fight for freedom and equality. Even at its birth, the black protest movement was diverse and incorporated a variety of viewpoints and leaders.

Booker T. Washington was the most prominent African American leader prior to World War I. Washington had been born in slavery and was the founder and president of Tuskegee Institute, a college in Alabama dedicated to educating African Americans. His public advice to African Americans in the South was to be patient, to accommodate to the Jim Crow system for now, to raise their levels of education and job skills, and to take full advantage of whatever opportunities became available. This nonconfrontational stance earned Washington praise and support from the white community and widespread popularity in the nation. Privately, he worked behind the scenes to end discrimination and implement full racial integration and equality (Franklin & Moss, 1994, pp. 272–274; Hawkins, 1962; Washington, 1965).

Washington's most vocal opponent was W. E. B. Du Bois, a black intellectual and activist who was born in the North and educated at some of the leading universities of the day. Among his many other accomplishments, Du Bois was part of a coalition of blacks and white liberals that founded the National Association for the Advancement of Colored People (NAACP) in 1909. Du Bois rejected Washington's accommodationist stance and advocated immediate pursuit of racial equality and a direct assault on de jure segregation. Almost from the beginning of its existence, the NAACP filed lawsuits that challenged the legal foundations of Jim Crow segregation (Du Bois, 1961). As we shall see in Chapter 5, this legal strategy eventually succeeded and was instrumental in the demise of the Jim Crow system.

Washington and Du Bois may have differed on matters of strategy and tactics, but they agreed that the only acceptable ultimate goal for African Americans was an integrated, racially equal United States. A third leader who emerged early in the 20th century called for a very different approach to the problems of U.S. race relations. Marcus Garvey was born in Jamaica and immigrated to the United States during World War I. He argued that the white-dominated U.S. society was hopelessly racist and would never truly support integration and racial equality. He advocated separatist goals, including a return to Africa. Garvey founded the Universal Negro Improvement Association (UNIA) in 1914 in his native Jamaica and founded the first U.S. branch in 1916. Garvey's organization was very popular for a time in African American communities outside the South, and he helped to establish some of the themes and ideas of black nationalism and pride in African heritage that would become prominent again in the pluralistic 1960s (Essien-Udom, 1962; Garvey, 1969, 1977; Vincent, 1976).

These early leaders and organizations established some of the foundations for later protest movements, but prior to midcentury, they made few actual improvements in the situation of black Americans in the North or the South. Jim Crow was a formidable opponent, and the black community lacked the resources to successfully challenge the status quo until the

century was well along and some basic structural features of American society had changed.

APPLYING CONCEPTS

Acculturation and Integration

During this era of southern segregation and migration to the North, assimilation was not a major factor in the African American experience. Rather, black-white relations are better described as a system of structural pluralism combined with great inequality. Excluded from the mainstream but freed from the limitations of slavery, African Americans constructed a separate subsociety and subculture. In all regions of the nation, black Americans built an institutional life around family, the neighborhood, church, schools, businesses, and other organizations of all types. Like immigrants from Europe in the same era, they organized their communities to cater to their own needs and problems and to pursue their agenda as a group.

During the era of segregation, a small, black middle class emerged based on leadership roles in the church, education, and business. A network of black colleges and universities was constructed to educate the children of the growing middle class as well as other classes. Through this infrastructure, African Americans began to develop the resources and leadership that, in the decades ahead, would attack, head-on, the structures of racial inequality.

Gender and Race

For African American men and women, the changes wrought by industrialization and the population movement to the North created new possibilities and new roles. However, as African Americans continued to be the victims of exploitation and exclusion in both the North and the South, black women continued to be among the most vulnerable groups in society.

Following Emancipation, there was a flurry of marriages and weddings among African Americans as they were finally able to legitimate their family relationships (Staples, 1988, p. 306). African American women continued to have primary responsibility for home and children. Historian Herbert Gutman (1976) reported that it was common for married women to drop out of the labor force and attend solely to household and family duties because being a working wife was too reminiscent of a slave role. This pattern became so widespread that it created serious labor shortages in many areas (Gutman, 1976; see also Staples, 1988, p. 307).

The former slaves were hardly affluent, however, and as sharecropping and segregation began to shape race relations in the South, women often had to return to the fields or to domestic work in order for their families to survive. One former slave woman noted that women "do double duty, a man's share in the field and a woman's part at home" (Evans, 1989, p. 121). During the bleak decades following the end of Reconstruction, southern black families and black women in particular lived "close to the bone" (Evans, 1989, p. 121).

In the cities and in the growing black neighborhoods in the North, African American women played a role that in some ways paralleled the role of immigrant women from Europe. The men often moved north first and sent for the women after they had attained some level of financial stability or after the pain of separation became too great (Almquist, 1979, p. 434). In other cases, black women by the thousands left the South to work as domestic servants; they often replaced European immigrant women who had moved up in the job structure (Amott & Matthaei, 1991, p. 168).

In the North, discrimination and racism created constant problems of unemployment for black men, and families often relied on the income supplied by the women to make ends meet. It was comparatively easy for women to find work, but only in the low-paying, less desirable areas, such as domestic work. In both the South and the North, African American women worked outside the home in larger proportions than did white women. For example, in 1900, 41% of black women

were employed, compared with only 16% of white women (Staples, 1988, p. 307).

In 1890, more than a generation after the end of slavery, 85% of all black men and 96% of black women were employed in just two occupational categories: agriculture and domestic or personal service. By 1930, 90% of employed black women were still in these same two categories, whereas the corresponding proportion for employed black males had dropped to 54% (although nearly all the remaining 46% were unskilled workers) (Steinberg, 1981, pp. 206–207). Since the inception of segregation, African American women have had consistently higher unemployment rates and lower incomes than black men and white women (Almquist, 1979, p. 437). These gaps, as we shall see in Chapter 5, persist to the present day.

During the years following Emancipation, some issues did split men and women, within both the black community and the larger society. Prominent among these was suffrage, or the right to vote, which was still limited to men only. The abolitionist movement, which had been so instrumental in ending slavery, also supported universal suffrage. Efforts to enfranchise women, though, were abandoned by the Republican Party and large parts of the abolitionist movement, which turned their attention to efforts to secure the vote for black males in the South. Ratification of the 15th Amendment in 1870 extended the vote, in principle, to African American men, but the 19th Amendment, enfranchising women, would not be passed for another 50 years (Almquist, 1979, pp. 433–434; Evans, 1989, pp. 121–124).

INDUSTRIALIZATION, THE SHIFT TO POSTINDUSTRIAL SOCIETY, AND DOMINANT-MINORITY GROUP RELATIONS: GENERAL TRENDS

The process of industrialization that began in the 19th century continued to shape the larger society and dominant-minority relations throughout the 20th century. At the start of the 21st century, the United States bears little resemblance to the society it was a century ago. The population has more than tripled in size and has urbanized even more rapidly than it has grown. New organizational forms (bureaucracies, corporations, multinational businesses) and new technologies (nuclear power, computers) dominate everyday life. Levels of education have risen, and public schools have produced one of the most literate populations and best-trained workforces in the history of the world.

Minority groups also grew in size, and most became even more urbanized than the general population. Minority group members have come to participate in an increasing array of occupations, and their average levels of education have also risen. Despite these real improvements, however, virtually all U.S. minority groups continue to face racism, poverty, discrimination, and exclusion. In this section, we outline the ways in which industrialization has changed American society and examine some of the implications for minority groups in general. We also note some of the ways in which industrialization has aided minority groups and address some of the barriers to full participation in the larger society that continue to operate in the present era. The impact of industrialization and the coming of postindustrial society will be considered in detail in the case studies that constitute Part III of this text.

Urbanization

We already have noted that urbanization made close, paternalistic controls of minority groups irrelevant. For example, the racial etiquette required by southern de jure segregation, such as African Americans deferring to whites on crowded sidewalks, tends to disappear in the chaos of an urban rush hour. Besides weakening dominant group controls, urbanization also created the potential for minority groups to mobilize and organize large numbers of people. As stated in Chapter 1, the sheer size of a group is a source of power. Without the freedom to organize, however, size means little, and urbanization increased *both* the concentration of populations and the freedom to organize.

Occupational Specialization

One of the first and most important results of industrialization, even in its earliest days, were increases in occupational specialization and in the variety of jobs available in the workforce. The growing needs of an urbanizing population increased the number of jobs available in the production, transport, and sale of goods and services. Occupational specialization also was stimulated by the very nature of industrial production. Complex manufacturing processes could be performed more efficiently if they were broken down into narrower component tasks. It was easier and more efficient to train the workforce in the simpler, specialized jobs. Assembly lines were invented, the work was subdivided, the division of labor became increasingly complex, and the number of different occupations continued to grow.

The sheer complexity of the industrial job structure made it difficult to maintain rigid, caste-like divisions of labor between dominant and minority groups. Rigid competitive forms of group relations, such as Jim Crow segregation, became less viable as the job market became more diversified and changeable. Simple, clear rules about which groups could do which jobs disappeared. As the more repressive systems of control weakened, job opportunities for minority group members sometimes increased.

As the relationships between group memberships and positions in the job market became more blurred, conflict between groups also increased. For example, as we have noted, African Americans moving from the South often found themselves in competition for jobs with white ethnic groups, labor unions, and elements of the dominant group.

Bureaucracy and Rationality

As industrialization continued, privately owned corporations and businesses came to have workforces numbering in the hundreds of thousands. Gigantic factories employing thousands of workers became common. To coordinate the efforts of these huge workforces, bureaucracy became the dominant form of organization in the economy and, indeed, throughout the society. Bureaucracies are large-scale, impersonal, formal organizations that run "by the book." They are governed by rules and regulations (i.e., "red tape") and are "rational" in that they attempt to find the most efficient ways to accomplish their tasks. Although they typically fail to attain the ideal of fully rational efficiency, bureaucracies tend to recruit, reward, and promote employees on the basis of competence and performance (Gerth & Mills, 1946).

An emphasis on rationality and objectivity can counteract the more blatant forms of racism and increase the array of opportunities available to members of minority groups. Although they are often nullified by other forces (see Blumer, 1965), these antiprejudicial tendencies do not exist at all or are much weaker in preindustrial economies.

The history of the concept of race illustrates the effect of rationality and scientific ways of thinking. Today, virtually the entire scientific community regards race as a biological triviality, a conclusion based on decades of research. This scientific finding undermined and contributed to the destruction of the formal systems of privilege based solely on race (e.g., segregated school systems) and individual perceptual systems (e.g., traditional prejudice), which themselves were based on the assumption that race was a crucial personal characteristic.

Growth of White-Collar Jobs and the Service Sector

Industrialization changed the composition of the labor force. As work became more complex and specialized, the need to coordinate and regulate the production process increased, and as a result, bureaucracies and other organizations grew larger still. Within these organizations, white-collar occupations—those that coordinate, manage, and deal with the flow of paperwork—continued to expand. As industrialization progressed, mechanization and automation reduced the number of manual or blue-collar workers, and white-collar occupations became the dominant sector of the job market in the United States.

The changing nature of the workforce can be illustrated by looking at the proportional representation of three different types of jobs:

1. Extractive (or primary) occupations are those that produce raw materials, such as food and agricultural products, minerals, and lumber. The jobs in this sector often involve unskilled manual labor, require little formal education, and generally offer low compensation.

2. Manufacturing (or secondary) occupations transform raw materials into finished products ready for sale in the marketplace. Like jobs in the extractive sector, these blue-collar jobs involve manual labor, but they tend to require higher levels of skill and are more highly rewarded. Examples of occupations in this sector include the assembly line jobs that transform steel, rubber, plastic, and other materials into finished automobiles.

3. Service (or tertiary) occupations don't produce "things," but, rather, provide services. As urbanization increased and self-sufficiency decreased, opportunities for work in this sector grew. Examples of tertiary occupations include police officer, clerk, waiter, teacher, nurse, doctor, and cab driver.

The course of industrialization is traced in the changing structure of the labor market depicted in Exhibit 4.2. In 1840, when industrialization was just beginning in the United States, most of the workforce was in the extractive sector, with agriculture being the dominant occupation. As industrialization progressed, the manufacturing, or secondary, sector grew, reaching a peak after World War II. Today, the large majority of jobs are in the service, or tertiary, sector.

This shift away from blue-collar jobs and manufacturing is sometimes referred to as deindustrialization or discussed in terms of the emergence of postindustrial society. The

Exhibit 4.2   The Changing Job Market in the United States, 1840–2000

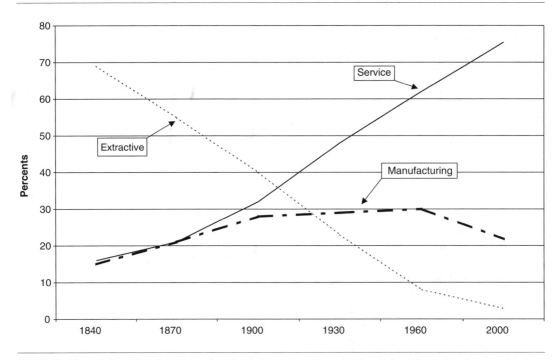

SOURCE: 1840–1990: Adapted from Lenski, Nolan, & Lenski (1995); 2000 calculated from U.S. Bureau of the Census (2002, p. 384). Adaptation is with permission.

U.S. economy has lost millions of unionized, high-paying factory jobs over the past several decades, and the downward trend will continue. The industrial jobs that sustained so many generations of American workers have moved to other nations where wages are considerably lower than in the United States or have been eliminated by robots or other automated manufacturing processes (see Rifkin, 1996).

The changing structure of the job market helps to clarify the nature of intergroup competition and the sources of wealth and power in society. Job growth in the United States today is largely in the service sector, in which occupations are highly variable. At one end are low-paying jobs with few, if any, benefits or chances for advancement (e.g., washing dishes in a restaurant). At the upper end are high-prestige, lucrative positions, such as Supreme Court justice, scientist, and

financial analyst. The new service sector jobs are either highly desirable technical, professional, or administrative jobs with demanding entry requirements (e.g., physician or nurse) or low-paid, low-skilled jobs with few benefits and little security (e.g., receptionist, nurse's aide). For the last half century, job growth in the United States has been either in areas in which educationally deprived minority group members find it difficult to compete or in areas that offer little compensation, upward mobility, or security. As we will see in Part III, the economic situation of contemporary minority groups reflects these fundamental trends.

The Growing Importance of Education

Education has become an increasingly important prerequisite for employability as

American society moves into the postindustrial era. A high school or, increasingly, a college degree has become the minimum entry-level requirement for employment. However, opportunities for high-quality education are not distributed equally across the population. Some minority groups, especially those created by conquest or colonization, have been systematically excluded from the schools of the dominant society. Today, they are less likely to have the educational backgrounds needed to compete for better jobs. Access to education is a key issue for almost all U.S. minority groups, and the average educational levels of these groups have been rising since World War II. Still, minority children continue to be much more likely to attend segregated, underfunded, deteriorated schools and to receive an inferior education (see Orfield, 2001).

A Dual Labor Market

The changing composition of the labor force and increasing importance of educational credentials has split the U.S. labor market into two segments or types of jobs. The *primary labor market* includes jobs usually located in large, bureaucratic organizations. These positions offer higher pay, more security, better opportunities for advancement, health and retirement benefits, and other amenities. Entry requirements often include college degrees, even when people with fewer years of schooling could competently perform the work.

The *secondary labor market,* sometimes called the competitive market, includes low-paid, low-skilled, insecure jobs. Many of these jobs are in the service sector. They do not represent a career and offer little opportunity for promotion or upward mobility. Very often, they do not offer health or retirement benefits, have high rates of turnover, and are part-time, seasonal, or temporary.

Many American minority groups are concentrated in the secondary job market. Their exclusion from better jobs is perpetuated not so much by direct or obvious discrimination as by educational and other credentials

required to enter the primary sector. The differential distribution of educational opportunities, in the past as well as in the present, effectively protects workers in the primary sector from competition from minority groups.

Globalization

Over the past century, the United States became an economic, political, and military world power with interests around the globe. These worldwide ties have created new minority groups through population movement and have changed the status of existing minority groups. Immigration to this country has been considerable for the past three decades. The American economy is one of the most productive in the world, and jobs, even those in the low-paid secondary sector, are the primary goals for millions of newcomers. For other immigrants, this country continues to play its historic role as a refuge from political and religious persecution.

Many of the wars, conflicts, and other disputes in which the United States has been involved have had consequences for American minority groups. For example, both Puerto Ricans and Cuban Americans became U.S. minority groups as the result of processes set in motion during the Spanish-American War of 1898. Both World War I and World War II created new job opportunities for many minority groups, including African Americans and Mexican Americans. After the Korean War, international ties were forged between the United States and South Korea, and this led to an increase in immigration from that nation. In the 1960s and 1970s, the military involvement of the United States in Southeast Asia led to the arrival of Vietnamese, Cambodian, and other immigrants from Southeast Asia.

Dominant-minority relations in the United States increasingly have been played out on an international stage as the world has effectively "shrunk" in size and become more interconnected by international organizations such as the United Nations, by ties of trade and commerce, and by modern means of transportation and communication. In a world in which two thirds of the population is nonwhite and many important nations (such as China, India, and Nigeria) represent peoples of color, the treatment of racial minorities by the U.S. dominant group has come under increased scrutiny. It is difficult to preach principles of fairness, equality, and justice—which the United States claims as its own—when domestic realities suggest an embarrassing failure to fully implement these standards. Part of the pressure for the United States to end blatant systems of discrimination such as de jure segregation came from the desire to maintain a leading position in the world.

THE SHIFT FROM RIGID TO FLUID COMPETITIVE RELATIONSHIPS

The recent changes in the structure of American society are so fundamental and profound that they are often described in terms of a revolution in subsistence technology: from an industrial society, based on manufacturing, to a postindustrial society, based on information processing and computer-related or other new technologies.

As the subsistence technology has evolved and changed, so have American dominant-minority relations. The rigid competitive systems (such as Jim Crow) associated with earlier phases of industrialization have given way to *fluid competitive systems* of group relations. In fluid competitive relations, there are no formal or legal barriers to competition such as Jim Crow laws. Both geographic and social mobility are greater, and the limitations imposed by minority group status are less restrictive and burdensome. Rigid caste systems of stratification, in which group membership determines opportunities, adult statuses, and jobs, are replaced by more open class systems, in which there are weaker relationships between group membership and wealth, prestige, and power. Because fluid competitive systems are more open and the position of the minority group is less fixed, the fear of competition from minority groups becomes more widespread for the dominant

group, and intergroup conflict increases. Exhibit 4.3 compares the characteristics of the three systems of group relations.

Compared with previous systems, the fluid competitive system is closer to the American ideal of an open, fair system of stratification in which effort and competence are rewarded and race, ethnicity, gender, religion, and other "birthmarks" are irrelevant. However, as we will see in chapters to come, race and ethnicity continue to affect life chances and limit opportunities for minority group members even in fluid competitive systems. As suggested by the Noel hypothesis, people continue to identify themselves with particular groups (ethnocentrism), and competition for resources continues to play out along group lines. Consistent with the Blauner hypothesis, the minority groups that were formed by colonization remain at a disadvantage in the pursuit of opportunities, education, prestige, and other resources.

Modern Institutional Discrimination

Virtually all American minority groups continue to lag behind national averages in income, employment, and other measures of equality despite the greater fluidity of group relations, the greater openness in the U.S. stratification system, dramatic declines in overt, traditional prejudice, and the introduction of numerous laws designed to ensure that all people are treated without regard to race, gender, or ethnicity. After all this change, shouldn't there be less minority group inequality? In fact, many Americans attribute the persisting patterns of inequality to the minority groups' lack of willpower or motivation to get ahead. In the remaining chapters of this text, however, I argue that the major barrier facing minority groups in late industrial, post–Jim Crow America is a more subtle but still powerful form of discrimination: *modern institutional discrimination.*

As you recall from Chapter 1, institutional discrimination is built into the everyday operation of the social structure of society. The routine procedures and policies of institutions

Exhibit 4.3   Characteristics of Three Systems of Group Relations

	Paternalistic	Competitive	
		Rigid	Fluid
Subsistence technology	Agrarian	Early industrial	Advanced industrial
Stratification	Caste. Group determines status.	Mixed. Elements of caste and class. Group determines status.	Variable. Class more important. Group strongly affects status but inequality varies within groups.
Division of labor	By group. Simple division of labor.	Mostly by group. Some sharing of jobs by different groups.	Group moderately related to job. Complex specialization. Great variation within groups.
Contact between groups	High rates but contact is unequal.	Lower rates of contact, mostly unequal and often conflictual.	Higher rates of contact, more often between status equals. Conflict common.
Power differential	Maximum. Minority group has little or no ability to pursue self-interest.	Less. Minority group has some ability to pursue self interest.	Least. Minority group has more ability to pursue self-interest.

SOURCE: Based on Farley (1995, p. 81).

and organizations are arranged so that minority group members are automatically put at a disadvantage. In the Jim Crow era in the South, for example, African Americans were deprived of the right to vote by overt institutional discrimination and could acquire little in the way of political power.

The forms of institutional discrimination that persist in the present are more subtle and less overt than those that defined the Jim Crow system. In fact, they are often unintentional or unconscious and exist more in the results for minority groups than in the intentions or prejudices of dominant group members. Modern institutional discrimination is not necessarily linked to prejudice, and the decision makers who implement it may sincerely think of themselves as behaving rationally and in the best interests of their organizations.

When employers make hiring decisions based solely on educational criteria, they may be putting minority group members at a disadvantage. When banks use strictly economic criteria to deny money for home mortgages or home improvement loans in certain "rundown" neighborhoods, they may be handicapping the efforts of minority groups to cope with the results of the blatant, legal housing segregation of the past. When businesspeople decide to reduce their overhead by moving their operations away from center cities, they may be reducing the ability of America's highly urbanized minority groups to earn a living and educate their children. When educators rely solely on standardized tests of ability that have been developed from white, middle-class experiences to decide who will be placed in college preparatory courses, they may be limiting the ability of minority group children to compete for jobs in the primary sector.

Any and all of these decisions can and do have devastating consequences for minority individuals, even though decision makers may be entirely unaware of the discriminatory effects. Employers, bankers, and educators do not have to be personally prejudiced for their actions to have negative consequences for minority groups. Modern institutional discrimination helps to perpetuate systems of inequality that can be just as pervasive and stifling as those of the past.

To illustrate, consider the effects of *past-in-present institutional discrimination*, which involves practices in the present that have discriminatory consequences because of some pattern of discrimination or exclusion in the past (Feagin & Feagin, 1986, p. 32). One form of this discrimination is found in workforces organized around the principle of seniority. In these systems, which are quite common, workers who have been on the job longer have higher incomes, more privileges, and other benefits, such as longer vacations. The "old-timers" often have more job security and are designated in official, written policy as the last to be fired or laid off in the event of hard times. Workers and employers alike may think of the privileges of seniority as just rewards for long years of service, familiarity with the job, and so forth.

Personnel policies based on seniority may seem perfectly reasonable, neutral, and fair. However, they can have discriminatory results in the present, because in the past, members of minority groups and women were excluded from specific occupations by racist or sexist labor unions, discriminatory employers, or both. As a result, minority group workers and women may have fewer years of experience than dominant group workers and may be the first to go when layoffs are necessary. The adage "last hired, first fired" describes the situation of minority group and female employees who are more vulnerable not because of some overtly racist or sexist policy but because of the routine operation of the seemingly neutral principle of seniority.

It is much more difficult to identify, measure, and eliminate this more subtle form of institutional discrimination, and some of the most heated disputes in recent group relations have concerned public policy and law in this area. Among the most controversial issues are affirmative action programs that attempt to ameliorate the legacy of past discrimination or increase diversity in the workplace or in schools. In many cases, the Supreme Court has found that programs designed to favor minority employees as a strategy for overcoming overt discrimination in the past are constitutional (e.g., *Firefighters Local Union No. 1784 v. Stotts*, 1984; *Sheet Metal Workers v. EEOC*, 1986; *United Steelworkers of America, AFL-CIO-CLC v. Weber*, 1979). Virtually all these decisions, however, were based on narrow margins (votes of 5 to 4) and featured acrimonious and bitter debates. More recently, the Court narrowed the grounds on which such past grievances could be redressed and, in the eyes of many observers, dealt serious blows to affirmative action programs (e.g., *Adarand Constructors Inc. v. Pena*, 1995).

One of the more prominent battlegrounds for affirmative action programs has been in higher education. Since the 1960s, it has been common for colleges and universities to implement programs to increase the number of minority students on campus at both the undergraduate and graduate levels, sometimes admitting minority students who had lower GPAs or test scores than dominant group students who were turned away. In general, these programs have been justified in terms of redressing the discriminatory practices of the past or increasing diversity on campus and making the student body a more faithful representation of the surrounding society. To say the least, these programs have been highly controversial and the targets of frequent lawsuits, some of which have found their way to the highest courts in the land.

The future of these programs remains unclear. At present, a number of states have banned affirmative action programs in their universities and colleges, but the legality of these outright bans remains in some doubt. For example, in 1996, voters in California passed an amendment to the state constitution that banned all use of racial, ethnic, or gender preferences in education, in hiring, and in the conduct of state business. In the spring of 2001, after years of protest and pressure by a variety of groups, the governing body of the California system of higher education ended the ban on affirmative action. This decision was mainly symbolic, however, because the university system cannot exempt itself from the state constitution.

The future of affirmative action will be determined by a number of lawsuits currently working their way through the system. No one can say for sure what the future will bring, but affirmative action appears to be very much in danger, and there is very little social support for these programs. According to a public opinion survey conducted in 2000, affirmative action was supported by only 13% of white respondents. More surprising, perhaps, it was supported by less than a majority of black respondents (44%) and only 20% of female respondents (National Opinion Research Council, 2000). At the highest levels of society, support is likewise scarce. The administration of President George W. Bush has registered its opposition to affirmative action in documents related to a Supreme Court case involving the University of Michigan (Lewis, 2003), and many assume that his administration will appoint judges to the bench who will be unsympathetic to affirmative action. It would not be surprising to see all affirmative action programs end in the next 5 to 10 years, and if they do, one of the few tools available to combat modern institutional discrimination will be eliminated.

FOCUS ON GENDER

GENDER INEQUALITY IN A GLOBALIZING, POSTINDUSTRIAL WORLD

Deindustrialization and globalization are transforming gender relations along with dominant-minority relations. Everywhere, even in the most traditional and sexist societies, women are moving away from their traditional "wife/mother" roles, taking on new responsibilities, and facing new challenges. Some women are also encountering new dangers and new forms of exploitation that perpetuate their lower status and extend it into new areas.

In the United States, the transition to a postindustrial society has changed gender relations and the status of women on a number of levels. Women and men are now nearly equal in terms of levels of education (U.S. Bureau of the Census, 2002, pp. 139–140), and the shift to fluid competitive group relations has weakened the barriers to gender equality along with the barriers to racial equality. The changing role of women is also shaped by other characteristics of a modern society: smaller families, high divorce rates, and rising numbers of single mothers who must work to support their children as well as themselves.

Many of the trends have coalesced to motivate women to enter the paid labor force in unprecedented numbers over the past half century. Women are now employed at almost the same levels as men. In the year 2000, for example, 69% of single women (vs. about 74% of single men) and about 61% of married women (vs. about 77% of married men) had jobs outside the home (U.S. Bureau of the Census, 2002, p. 372). Furthermore, between 1970 and 2000, the participation of married women with children in the workforce increased from a little less than 40% to a little more than 70% (U.S. Bureau of the Census, 2002, p. 373).

Many of these "new" women workers entered the paid labor force to compensate for the lower earning power of men. Before deindustrialization began to transform U.S. society, men monopolized the more

Exhibit 4.4 Median Earnings for Full-Time, Year-Round Workers Over Age 15 by Gender, 1966–2000

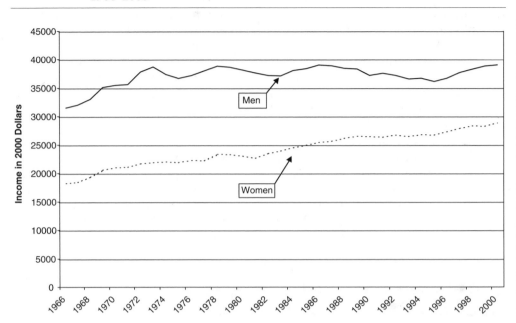

desirable, higher-paid, unionized jobs in the manufacturing sector. For much of the 20th century, these blue-collar jobs paid well enough to subsidize a comfortable lifestyle, a house in the suburbs, and vacations, with enough money left over to save for a rainy day or for college for the kids. However, when deindustrialization began, many of these desirable jobs were lost to automation and to cheaper labor forces outside the United States and were replaced, if at all, by low-paying jobs in the service sector. Thus, deindustrialization tended to drive men's wages down, and many women were forced to take jobs to supplement the family income. This trend is reflected in Exhibit 4.4, which shows that average wages for men have been stagnant or actually declining since the early 1970s.

A large number of the "new" women workers have taken jobs in a limited number of female-dominated occupations, most of which are in the less well-paid service sector, and this pattern of occupational segregation is one important reason for the continuing gender gap in income. For example, Exhibit 4.5 lists some of the occupations that were dominated by females in 1983 and 2000. For comparison, the percentages of females in comparable but higher-status occupations are also included in the table where possible.

In part, this occupational segregation is a result of the choices women make to balance the demands of their jobs with their family obligations. Whereas men are expected to make a total commitment to their jobs and careers, women are expected to find ways to continue to fulfill their domestic roles even while working full-time, and many "female jobs" offer some flexibility in this area (Shelton & John, 1996). For example, many women become elementary educators despite the lower salaries because the job offers predictable hours and long summer breaks, both of which can help women meet their child care and other family responsibilities.

Exhibit 4.5   Selected Occupations With High Concentrations of Females, 1983 and 2000

	Percentage Female	
Occupation	*1983*	*2000*
Registered nurse	96%	93%
(*Physician*)	(*16%*)	(*28%*)
Pre-kindergarten and kindergarten teacher	98%	99%
Elementary school teacher	83%	83%
(*College and university teacher*)	(*36%*)	(*44%*)
Dental hygienist	99%	99%
(*Dentist*)	(*7%*)	(*19%*)
Legal assistant	74%	84%
(*Lawyer*)	(*15%*)	(*30%*)
Secretary	99%	99%

SOURCE: U.S. Bureau of the Census (2002, pp. 380–382).

NOTE: Occupations in italics and parentheses are comparable but higher-status occupations.

This pattern of gender occupational segregation testifies to the lingering effects of minority status for women and the choices they make to reconcile the demands of career and family.

Exhibit 4.5 also shows that gender segregation in the world of work is declining, at least in some areas. Women are rapidly moving into traditionally male (and higher-paid) occupations, as reflected by the rising percentages of female physicians, dentists, college professors, and lawyers. In addition, some of the occupational areas that have traditionally had high concentrations of women—for example, the so-called FIRE sector, or finance, insurance, and real estate—actually benefited from deindustrialization and the shift to a service economy. Job opportunities in the FIRE sector have expanded rapidly since the 1960s and have provided opportunities for women to rise in the social structure; the good fortune of these women has in turn tended to elevate the average salaries for women in general (Farley, 1996, pp. 95–101). The movement of females into these more lucrative occupations is

one reason why the gender gap in income is decreasing, as reflected in Exhibit 4.4.

How have deindustrialization and globalization affected women internationally? In part, the trends worldwide parallel those in the United States. According to a recent United Nations report (United Nations, 2000), indicators such as rising education levels for women and lower rates of early marriage and childbirth show that women around the world are moving out of their traditional (and often highly controlled and repressed) status. They are entering the labor force in unprecedented numbers virtually everywhere, and women now constitute at least a third of the global workforce.

Although the status of women is generally rising, the movement away from traditional gender roles also brings an exposure to new forms of exploitation. Around the globe, women have become a source of cheap labor, often in jobs that have recently been exported from the U.S. economy. For example, many manufacturing jobs formerly held by men in the United States have migrated just south of the border to Mexico, where they are held by women. *Maquiladoras* are assembly plants built by corporations, often headquartered in the United States, to take advantage of the plentiful supply of working-class females who will work for low wages and in conditions that would not be tolerated in the United States (see Parrado and Zenteno, 2001, for a recent analysis of the Mexican female labor force and the maquiladora phenomenon).

The weakening of traditional gender roles has increased women's vulnerability in other areas as well. According to one report, many Filipino women (and children) have become ensnared in an increasingly international sex trade. The trade focuses on impoverished women who have been pushed out of the subsistence rural economy by industrialization and globalization and who move to urban areas in the Philippines. They are forced into prostitution or other jobs in the growing sex industry, where their lack of resources and power makes them easy targets for exploitation (Women's International Network, 1998).

Across all these changes and around the globe, women commonly face the challenge of reconciling their new work demands with their traditional family responsibilities. Women also face challenges and issues, such as sexual harassment and domestic violence, that clearly differentiate their status from that of men. In this context, minority group women face a double disadvantage: The issues they face as women are overlaid on the barriers of racial and ethnic prejudice and discrimination. Minority group women are often the poorest, most vulnerable, and most exploited groups both in U.S. society and around the globe.

CONCLUSION

This chapter has focused on the continuing industrial revolution and its impact on minority groups in general and black-white relations in particular. For the most part, changes in group relations have been presented as the results of the fundamental transformation of the U.S. economic institution from agrarian to industrial to late industrial (or postindustrial). However, the changes in the situation of black Americans and other minority groups didn't "just happen" as society modernized. Although the *opportunity* to pursue favorable change was the result of broad structural changes in American society, the *realization* of these opportunities came from the efforts of the many who gave their time, their voices, their resources, and sometimes their lives in pursuit of racial justice in America. Since World War II, African Americans often have been in the vanguard of protest activity, and we focus on the contemporary situation of this group in the next chapter.

MAIN POINTS

- Group relations change as the subsistence technology and the level of development of the larger society change. As nations industrialize and urbanize, dominant-minority relations change from paternalistic to rigid competitive forms.
- In the South, slavery was replaced by de jure segregation, a system that combined racial separation with great inequality. The Jim Crow system was motivated by a need to control labor and was reinforced by coercion and intense racism and prejudice.
- Black Southerners responded to segregation in part by moving to northern urban areas. The northern black population enjoyed greater freedom and developed some political and economic resources, but a large concentration of low-income, relatively powerless African Americans developed in the ghetto neighborhoods.

- In response to segregation, the African American community developed a separate institutional life centered on family, church, and community. A black middle class emerged, as well as a protest movement.
- African American women remain one of the most exploited groups. Combining work with family roles, black females were employed mostly in agriculture and domestic service during the era of segregation.
- Industrialization continued throughout the 20th century and has profoundly affected dominant-minority relations. Urbanization, specialization, bureaucratization, and other trends have changed the shape of race relations, as have the changing structure of the occupational sector and the growing importance of education. Group relations have shifted from rigid competitive to fluid competitive. Modern institutional discrimination is one of the major challenges facing minority groups.

QUESTIONS FOR REVIEW AND STUDY

1. A corollary to two themes from Chapter 3 is presented at the beginning of Chapter 4. How exactly does the material in the chapter illustrate the usefulness of this corollary?
2. Explain paternalistic and rigid competitive relations and link them to industrialization. How does the shift from slavery to de jure segregation illustrate the dynamics of these two systems?
3. What was the "Great Migration" to the North? How did it change American race relations?
4. Explain the transition from rigid competitive to fluid competitive relations and explain how this transition is related to the coming of postindustrial society. Explain the roles of urbanization, bureaucracy, the service sector of the job market, and education in this transition.
5. What is modern institutional discrimination? How does it differ from "traditional" institutional discrimination? Explain the role of affirmative action in combating each.
6. Explain the impact of industrialization and globalization on gender relations. Compare and contrast these changes with the changes that occurred for racial and ethnic minority groups.

INTERNET RESEARCH PROJECT

A. *Everyday Life Under Jim Crow*

The daily workings of the Jim Crow system of segregation are analyzed and described in a collection of interviews and memories archived at www.americanradioworks.org/features/remembering/. Listen to the clips and analyze them in terms of the concepts introduced in this chapter.

B. *The Debate Over Affirmative Action*

Update and supplement the debate over affirmative action. Start with the newspaper Web sites including the *New York Times* (www.nytimes.com), the *Washington Post* (www.washingtonpost.com), and the *Los Angeles Times* (www.latimes.com) and search for recent news items or opinion pieces on the issue. Search the Internet for other viewpoints and perspectives from other groups and positions on the political spectrum. One place you might start is www.aad.english.ucsb.edu/, a Web site that presents diverse opinions on the topic and brings many different voices to the debates. Analyze events and opinions in terms of the concepts introduced in this chapter, especially *modern institutional discrimination*.

FOR FURTHER READING

Bluestone, Barry, & Harrison, Bennett. 1982. *The Deindustrialization of America.* New York: Basic Books.

An important analysis of the shift from a manufacturing to a service-based, information society.

Feagin, Joe R., & Feagin, Clairece Booher. 1986. *Discrimination American Style: Institutional Racism and Sexism.* Malabar, FL: Robert E. Krieger.

A comprehensive and provocative look at modern institutional discrimination.

Geschwender, James A. 1978. *Racial Stratification in America.* Dubuque, IA: William C. Brown.

Wilson, William J. 1973. *Power, Racism, and Privilege: Race Relations in Theoretical and Sociohistorical Perspectives.* New York: Free Press.

Woodward, C. Vann. 1974. *The Strange Career of Jim Crow* (3rd rev. ed.). New York: Oxford University Press.

Three outstanding analyses of black-white relations in the United States, with a major focus on the historical periods covered in this chapter.

Part III

Understanding Dominant-Minority Relations in the United States Today

In Part III, we turn to contemporary intergroup relations and the major minority groups in the United States. The emphasis is on the present situation of these groups, but the recent past also is investigated to see how present situations developed. We explore how minority and dominant groups respond to a changing American society and to each other and how minority groups define and pursue their own self-interest in interaction with other groups, American culture and values, and the institutions of the larger society.

The themes and ideas developed in the first two parts of this text will continue to be central to the analysis. For example, the five case study chapters are presented in an order that roughly follows the Blauner hypothesis: Colonized groups are presented first, and we end with groups created by immigration. We also will continue to rely on the concepts of the Noel hypothesis to analyze and explain contemporary dominant-minority patterns.

The history and present conditions of each minority group are unique, and no two groups have had the same experiences. To help identify and understand these differences, a common comparative frame of reference—stressing assimilation and pluralism;

inequality and power; and prejudice, racism, and discrimination—is used throughout these case studies.

Much of the conceptual frame of reference employed in these case studies can be summarized in six themes. The first five themes are based on material from previous chapters; the last is covered in forthcoming chapters.

1. Consistent with the Noel hypothesis, the present condition of America's minority groups reflects their contact situations, especially the nature of their competition with the dominant group (e.g., competition over land vs. competition over labor) and the size of the power differential between groups at the time of contact.

2. Consistent with the Blauner hypothesis, minority groups created by conquest and colonization experience economic and political inequalities that have lasted longer and been more severe than those experienced by minority groups created by immigration.

3. Power and economic differentials and barriers to upward mobility are especially pronounced for groups identified by racial or physical characteristics, as opposed to cultural or linguistic traits.

4. Consistent with the themes stated in Chapters 3 and 4, dominant-minority relations reflect the economic and political characteristics of the larger society and change as those characteristics change. Changes in the subsistence technology of the larger society are particularly consequential for dominant-minority relations. The shift from a manufacturing to a service economy ("deindustrialization") is one of the key factors shaping dominant-minority relations in the United States today.

5. The development of group relations, both in the past and for the future, can be analyzed in terms of assimilation (more unity) and pluralism (more diversity). Group relations in the past (e.g., the degree of assimilation permitted or required of the minority group) primarily reflected the needs and wishes of the dominant group. Although the pressure for Americanization remains considerable, there is more flexibility and variety in group relations today.

6. Since World War II, minority groups have gained significantly more control over the direction of group relationships. This trend reflects the decline of traditional prejudice in the larger society and the successful efforts of minority groups to protest, resist, and change patterns of exclusion and domination. These successes have been possible, in large part, because American minority groups have increased their share of political and economic resources.

5

African Americans

From Segregation to Modern Institutional Discrimination and Modern Racism

At the dawn of the 20th century, African Americans were a southern rural peasantry, victimized by de jure segregation, enmeshed in the sharecropping system of agriculture, and blocked from the better-paying industrial and manufacturing jobs in urban areas. Segregation had disenfranchised them and stripped them of the legal and civil rights they had enjoyed briefly during Reconstruction. As we saw in Chapter 4, the huge majority of African Americans had very limited access to quality education; few political rights; few occupational choices; and few vehicles for expressing their views, grievances, and concerns. Today, at the dawn of the 21st century, African Americans are highly urbanized, dispersed throughout the United States, and represented in virtually every occupational grouping. Members of the group are visible at the highest levels of American society, from the U.S. Supreme Court to corporate boardrooms and the most prestigious universities. Some of the best-known, most successful, and most respected (and wealthiest) people in the world have been African Americans: Martin Luther King Jr., Malcolm X, Michael Jordan, Shirley Chisholm, Jesse Jackson, Bill Cosby, Toni Morrison, Maya Angelou, Muhammad Ali, Oprah Winfrey, Barbara Jordan, and Secretary of State Colin Powell, to name only a few. Furthermore, some of the most important and prestigious American corporations (including Merrill

Lynch, American Express, and AOL Time Warner) are currently led by African Americans (Roberts, 2002, p. 44).

How did these changes come about, and what do they signify? What problems are obscured by these glittering success stories? Do racism, prejudice, and discrimination continue to be significant problems? Is there any support for the view that the barriers to racial equality have been eliminated? How do the Noel and Blauner hypotheses and the other concepts developed earlier in this text help us understand contemporary black-white relations?

To understand the trajectories of change that have led to the present, we must deal with the watershed events in black-white relations: the end of de jure segregation, the triumph (and the limitations) of the Civil Rights movement of the 1950s and 1960s, the urban riots and Black Power movement of the 1960s, and the continuing racial divisions within U.S. society since the 1970s. Behind these events lie the powerful pressures of industrialization and modernization, the shift from rigid to fluid competitive group relations, changing distributions of power and forms of intergroup competition, declining levels of traditional prejudice, and new ideas about assimilation and pluralism. In less academic terms, black-white relations changed as a direct result of protest, resistance, and the concerted actions of thousands of individuals, both blacks and whites.

THE END OF DE JURE SEGREGATION

As a colonized minority group, African Americans entered the 20th century facing extreme inequality, relative powerlessness, and sharp limitations on their freedom. Their most visible enemy was the system of de jure segregation in the South, the rigid competitive system of group relations that controlled the lives of most black Americans. Why and how did de jure segregation come to an end? Recall from Chapter 4 that dominant-minority relationships change as the larger society and its subsistence technology change. As the United States industrialized and urbanized during the

20th century, a series of social, political, economic, and legal processes were set in motion that ultimately destroyed Jim Crow segregation.

The mechanization and modernization of agriculture in the South had a powerful effect on race relations. As farm work became less labor intensive and machines replaced people, the need to maintain a large, powerless workforce declined (Geschwender, 1978, pp. 175–177). Thus, one of the primary motivations for maintaining Jim Crow segregation and the sharecropping system of farming lost force.

In addition, the modernization of southern agriculture helped to spur migration northward and to urban areas as discussed in Chapter 4. Outside the rural South, African Americans found it easier to register to vote and pursue other avenues for improving their situation. The weight of the growing black vote was first felt in the 1930s and was large enough by the 1940s to make a difference in local, state, and even national elections. In 1948, for example, President Harry Truman recognized that his reelection could hinge on the support of African American voters. As a result, the Democratic Party adopted a civil rights plank in the party platform, the first time since Reconstruction that a national political party had taken a stand on race relations (Wilson, 1973, p. 123).

The weight of these changes accumulated slowly, and no single date or specific event marks the end of de jure segregation. The system ended as it had begun: gradually and in a series of discrete episodes and incidents. By the mid-20th century, resistance to racial change was weakening, and the power resources of African Americans were increasing. This enhanced freedom and strength fueled a variety of efforts that sped the demise of Jim Crow segregation. Although a complete historical autopsy is not necessary here, a general understanding of the reasons for the death of Jim Crow segregation is essential for an understanding of modern black-white relations.

The Civil Rights Movement

The Civil Rights movement was a multifaceted campaign to end legalized segregation and ameliorate the massive inequalities faced by African Americans. Although it is usually said to have begun in the 1950s, the movement was foreshadowed by a number of separate protests in the 1930s and 1940s. One such precursor, for example, was the March on Washington movement in 1941 that protested the racial discrimination that was common in the defense industry even as the nation mobilized for World War II.

The Civil Rights movement lasted for decades and included lawsuits and court-room battles as well as protest marches and demonstrations. We begin our examination with a look at a successful challenge to the laws of racial segregation.

Brown v. Board of Education of Topeka

Undoubtedly, the single most powerful blow to de jure segregation was delivered by the U.S. Supreme Court in *Brown v. Board of Education of Topeka* in 1954. The Court reversed the *Plessy v. Ferguson* decision of 1896 and ruled that racially separate facilities are inherently unequal and therefore unconstitutional. Segregated school systems—and all other forms of legalized racial segregation—would have to end. The landmark *Brown* decision was the culmination of decades of planning and effort by the National Association for the Advancement of Colored People (NAACP) and individuals such as Thurgood Marshall, the NAACP's chief counsel (who was appointed to the Supreme Court in 1967).

The strategy of the NAACP was to attack Jim Crow by finding instances in which the civil rights of an African American had been violated and then bringing suit against the relevant governmental agency. These lawsuits were intended to extend far beyond the specific case being argued. The goal was to persuade the courts to declare segregation unconstitutional not only in the specific instance being tried but in all similar cases. The *Brown* decision was the ultimate triumph of this strategy. The significance of the Court's decision lies in the rejection of the *principle* of de jure segregation in the South and, by implication, throughout the nation. The *Brown* decision changed the law and dealt a crippling blow to Jim Crow segregation.

Nonviolent Direct Action Protest

The principle established by *Brown* was assimilationist: It ordered the educational institutions of the dominant group to be opened up, freely and equally, to all. Southern states and communities overwhelmingly rejected the principle of equal access and shared facilities, and they responded to the Court's decision by stalling and mounting a campaign of "massive resistance." Centuries of racist tradition and privilege were at stake, and white Southerners used a variety of means, including violence and intimidation, to defend their system of racial privilege. The Ku Klux Klan (KKK), largely dormant since the 1920s, reappeared along with other racist and terrorist groups, such as the White Citizens' Councils. White politicians and other leaders competed with each other to express the most adamant statements of racist resistance (Wilson, 1973, p. 128).

It quickly became clear that considerable effort would be required to overcome Southern defiance and resistance. The central force in this struggle was a protest movement, the beginning of which is often traced to Montgomery, Alabama, where on December 1, 1955, Rosa Parks, a seamstress and NAACP member, rode the city bus home from work, as she usually did. As the bus filled, she was ordered to surrender her seat to a white male passenger. When she refused, the police were called, and Rosa Parks was jailed for violating a local segregation ordinance. Although Parks was hardly the first African American to be subjected to such indignities, her case galvanized the black community, and a boycott of the city buses was organized. Participants in the boycott set up car pools, shared taxis, and walked (in some cases, for miles) to and from work. They stayed off the buses for more than a year, until victory was achieved and the city was ordered to desegregate its buses. The Montgomery boycott was led by the Reverend Martin Luther King Jr., the new minister of a local Baptist church.

From these beginnings sprang the protest movement that eventually defeated de jure segregation. The central strategy of the movement involved *nonviolent direct action,* a method by which the system of de jure segregation was confronted head-on—not in the courtroom or in the state legislature, but in the streets. The movement's principles of nonviolence were adopted from the tenets of Christianity and from the teachings of Mohandas Gandhi, Henry David Thoreau, and others. Dr. King expressed the philosophy in a number of books and speeches (King, 1958, 1963, 1968). Nonviolent protest was intended to confront the forces of evil rather than the people who happened to be doing evil, and it attempted to win the friendship and support of its enemies rather than to defeat or humiliate them. Above all, nonviolent protest required courage and discipline; it was not a method for cowards (King, 1958, pp. 83–84).

The movement used different tactics for different situations, including sit-ins at segregated restaurants, protest marches and demonstrations, prayer meetings, and voter registration drives. The police and terrorist groups such as the KKK often responded to these protests with brutal repression and violence, and protesters were routinely beaten, attacked by police dogs, and imprisoned. The violent resistance sometimes escalated to acts of murder, including the 1963 bombing of a black church in Birmingham, Alabama, that took the lives of four little girls, and the 1967 assassination of Dr. King. Resistance to racial change in the South was intense. It would take more than protests and marches to finally extirpate de jure segregation, and the U.S. Congress finally provided the necessary tools (see D'Angelo, 2001; Killian, 1975; King, 1958, 1963, 1968; Morris, 1984).

Landmark Legislation

The successes of the protest movement, changing public opinion, and the legal principles established by the Supreme Court coalesced in the mid-1960s to stimulate the passage of two laws that, together, ended Jim Crow segregation. In 1964, at the urging of President Lyndon B. Johnson, Congress passed the Civil Rights Act [Civil Rights Act of 1964, PL 88–352, 42 U.S.C. 2000, 1964] banning discrimination on the grounds of race, color, religion, national origin, or gender. The law applied to publicly owned facilities such as parks and municipal swimming pools, businesses and other facilities open to the public, and any programs that received federal aid. Congress followed up with the Voting Rights Act in 1965 [42 U.S.C. 1971, 1965]. This law required that the same standards be used to register all citizens for federal, state, and local elections. The act banned literacy tests, whites-only primaries, and other means that had been used to prevent African Americans from registering to vote. The Voting Rights Act gave the franchise back to black Southerners and laid the groundwork for increasing black political power. Added to the court decisions and the protest movement, this landmark federal legislation finally succeeded in crushing Jim Crow.

The Successes and the Limitations of the Civil Rights Movement

Why did the Civil Rights movement succeed? A comprehensive list of reasons would be legion, but we can cite some of the most important, especially those consistent with the general points about dominant-minority relations that were made in previous chapters.

1. The continuing industrialization and urbanization of the society as a whole—and the South in particular—weakened the Jim Crow, rigid competitive system of minority group control and segregation.

2. Following World War II, the United States enjoyed a period of prosperity that lasted into the 1960s. Consistent with the Noel hypothesis, these good economic times reduced the intensity of intergroup competition and resistance to change (at least outside the South). When the economic "pie" is expanding, the "slices" claimed by minority groups can increase without threatening the size of anyone else's portions, and

the prejudice generated during intergroup competition (à la Robber's Cave—see Chapter 1) is held in check. Thus, prosperity and growth muted the sense of threat experienced in the dominant group as a result of the demands for equality made by the Civil Rights movement.

Also, some of the economic prosperity found its way into African American communities and increased their pool of economic and political resources. Networks of independent, African American–controlled organizations and institutions, such as churches and colleges, were created or grew in size and power. The increasingly elaborate infrastructure of the black community included protest organizations and provided material resources, leadership, and the "people power" to lead the fight against segregation and discrimination.

3. The goals of the Civil Rights movement were assimilationist, and they embraced the traditional American values of liberty, equality, freedom, and fair treatment. The movement demanded civil, legal, and political rights for African Americans, rights available to whites automatically. Thus, many whites did not feel threatened by the movement because they saw it as consistent with mainstream American values, especially in contrast with the intense, often violent resistance of southern racism. The perceived legitimacy of the goals of the movement also opened up the possibility of alliances with other groups (white liberals, Jews, college students). The support of others was crucial because black Southerners had few resources of their own other than their numbers and their courage. By mobilizing the resources of other, more powerful groups, black Southerners increased the strength of their movement and brought more pressure to bear on their opponents.

4. Finally, widespread and sympathetic coverage from the mass media, particularly television, was crucial to the success of the movement. The oft-repeated scenario of African Americans being brutally attacked while demonstrating for their rights outraged many Americans and reinforced a moral consensus that helped to reject traditional racial prejudice along with Jim Crow segregation.

The southern Civil Rights movement ended de jure segregation, but the movement found it difficult to survive the demise of its primary enemy. The confrontational tactics that had been so effective against the abstract principles that legalized de jure segregation proved less useful when attention turned to the actual distribution of jobs, wealth, political power, and other valued goods and services. Outside the South, the allocation of opportunity and resources had always been the central concern of the African American community. We now turn to those concerns.

DEVELOPMENTS OUTSIDE THE SOUTH

De Facto Segregation

Chapter 4 discussed some of the difficulties encountered by African Americans as they left the rural South. Discrimination by labor unions, employers, industrialists, and white ethnic groups was common. Racial discrimination outside the South was less blatant but was still pervasive, especially in housing, education, and employment.

The pattern of racial separation and inequality outside the South is often called *de facto segregation*: segregation resulting from the apparently voluntary choices of dominant and minority groups alike. Theoretically, no person, law, or specific group is responsible for de facto segregation; it "just happens" as people and groups make decisions about where to live and work.

The distinction between de facto and de jure segregation can be misleading, however, and the de facto variety often is the de jure variety in thin disguise. Although cities and states outside the South may not have had actual Jim Crow laws, de facto segregation often was the direct result of intentionally racist decisions made by governmental and quasi-governmental agencies such as real estate boards, school boards, and zoning boards (see Massey & Denton, 1993, pp. 74–114). For example, shortly after World War I, the Real Estate Board in the city of Chicago adopted a policy that required its members, on penalty of "immediate expulsion," to follow a policy of racial residential segregation (Cohen & Taylor, 2000, p. 33).

Regardless of who or what was responsible for these patterns, African Americans living outside the South faced more poverty, higher unemployment, and lower-quality housing and schools than did whites, but there was no clear equivalent of Jim Crow to attack or to blame for these patterns of inequality. In the 1960s, the African American community outside the South expressed its frustration over the slow pace of change in two ways: urban unrest and a movement for change that rose to prominence as the Civil Rights movement faded.

Urban Unrest

In the mid-1960s, the frustration and anger of urban black communities erupted into a series of violent uprisings. The riots began in the summer of 1965 in Watts, a neighborhood in Los Angeles, and over the next 4 years, virtually every large black urban community experienced similar outbursts.

Racial violence was hardly a new phenomenon in America. Race riots had occurred as early as the Civil War, and various time periods had seen racial violence of considerable magnitude. The riots of the 1960s were different, however. Most race riots in the past had involved attacks by whites against blacks, often including the invasion and destruction of African American neighborhoods (e.g., see D'Orso, 1996; Ellsworth, 1982). The urban unrest of the 1960s, in contrast, consisted largely of attacks by blacks against the symbols of their oppression and frustration. The most obvious targets were white-owned businesses operating in black neighborhoods and the police, who were seen as an army of occupation and whose excessive use of force often was the immediate precipitator of riots (Conot, 1967; National Advisory Commission, 1968).

The Black Power Movement

The urban riots of the 1960s were an unmistakable sign that the problems of race relations had not been resolved with the end of Jim Crow segregation. Outside the South, the problems were different and called for different solutions. Even as the Civil Rights movement was celebrating its victory in the South, a new protest movement rose to prominence to express some of these grievances. The Black Power movement was a loose coalition of organizations and spokespersons that encompassed a variety of ideas and views, many of which differed sharply from those of the Civil Rights movement. Some of the central ideas included racial pride ("Black is beautiful" was a key slogan of the day), interest in African heritage, and black nationalism. In contrast to the assimilationist goals of the Civil Rights movement, black power groups worked to increase African American control over schools, police, welfare programs, and other public services operating in black neighborhoods.

Most adherents of the Black Power movement felt that white racism and institutional discrimination, forces buried deep in the core of American culture and society, were the causes of racial inequality in America. Thus, if African Americans were ever to be truly empowered, they would have to liberate themselves and do it on their own terms. Some black power advocates specifically rejected the goal of assimilation into white society, arguing that integration would require blacks to become part of the very system that had for centuries oppressed, denigrated, and devalued them and other peoples of color.

The Nation of Islam

The themes of black power voiced so loudly in the 1960s were decades, even centuries, old. Marcus Garvey had popularized many of these ideas in the 1920s (see Chapter 4), and they were espoused and further developed by the Nation of Islam, popularly known as the Black Muslims, in the 1960s.

The Black Muslims, one of the best-known organizations within the Black Power movement, were angry, impatient, and outspoken. They denounced the hypocrisy, greed, and racism of American society and advocated staunch resistance and racial separation. The Black Muslims did more than talk, however. Pursuing the goals of autonomy and self-determination, they worked hard to create a separate, independent black economy within the United States. They opened businesses and stores in African American neighborhoods and tried to deal only with other Black Muslim–owned firms. Their goal was to develop the black community economically and supply jobs and capital for expansion solely by using their own resources (Essien-Udom, 1962; Lincoln, 1961; Malcolm X, 1964; Wolfenstein, 1993).

The Nation of Islam and other black power groups distinguished between racial separation and racial segregation. The former is a process of empowerment whereby a group becomes stronger as it becomes more autonomous and self-controlled. The latter is a system of inequality in which the African American community is held powerless and is controlled by the dominant group. Thus, the black power groups were working to find ways in which African Americans could develop their own resources and deal with the dominant group from a more powerful position, a strategy similar to that followed by minority groups that formed ethnic enclaves (see Chapter 2).

The best-known spokesman for the Nation of Islam was Malcolm X, one of the most charismatic figures of the 1960s and a powerful exponent of the themes of black power. He became the chief spokesperson for the Black Muslims and a well-known but threatening figure to the white community. After a dispute with Elijah Muhammad, the leader of the Nation of Islam, Malcolm X founded his own organization, in which he continued to express and develop the ideas of black nationalism. Like so many other protest leaders of the era, Malcolm X was assassinated in 1965.

Black power leaders like Malcolm X advocated autonomy, independence, and a pluralistic direction for the African American protest movement. They saw the black community as a colonized, exploited population in need of liberation from the unyielding racial oppression of white America, rather than integration into the system that was the source of its oppression.

PROTEST, POWER, AND PLURALISM

The Black Power Movement in Perspective

By the end of the 1960s, the riots had ended, and the most militant and dramatic manifestations of the Black Power movement had faded. The nation's commitment to racial change wavered and weakened as other concerns, such as the Vietnam War, competed for attention. Richard M. Nixon was elected president in 1968 and made no pretense of being an ally of the black protest movement. Pressure from the federal government for racial equality was reduced. The boiling turmoil of the mid-1960s faded, but the idea of black power had become thoroughly entrenched in the African American community.

In some part, the pluralistic themes of black power were a reaction to the failure of assimilation and integration in the 1950s and 1960s. Laws had been passed; court decisions had been widely publicized; and presidents, members of Congress, governors, mayors, and other leaders had made promises and pledges. For many African Americans, though, little had changed. The problems of their parents and grandparents continued to constrain and limit their lives and, as far into the future as they could see, the lives of their children. The pluralistic black power ideology was a response to the failure to go beyond the repeal of Jim Crow laws and fully implement the promises of integration and equality.

But black nationalism was, and remains, more than simply a reaction to a failed dream. It also was a different way of defining what it means to be black in America. In the context of black-white relations in the 1960s, the Black Power movement served a variety of purposes. First, along with the Civil Rights movement, it helped carve out a new identity for African Americans. The cultural stereotypes of black Americans stressed laziness, irresponsibility, and inferiority. This image needed to be refuted, rejected, and buried. The black protest movements supplied a view of African Americans that emphasized power, assertiveness, seriousness of purpose, intelligence, and courage. Second, black power served as a new rallying cry for solidarity and unified action. Following the success of the Civil Rights movement, these new themes and ideas helped to focus attention on "unfinished business": the black-white inequalities that remained in U.S. society. Finally, the ideology provided a new analysis of the problems of American race relations in the 1960s. The Civil Rights movement had, of course, analyzed race relations in terms of integration, equality of opportunity, and an end to exclusion. After the demise of Jim Crow, that analysis became less relevant. A new language was needed to describe and analyze the continuation of racial inequality. Black power argued that the continuing problems of U.S. race relations were structural and institutional, not individual or legal. To take the next steps toward actualizing racial equality and justice would require a fundamental and far-reaching restructuring of society.

One profound implication of the analysis developed by the Black Power movement was that, ultimately, white Americans would not support such restructuring because they were the beneficiaries of the system. The necessary energy and commitment for change had to come from black Americans pursuing their own self-interest and acting by and for themselves.

The nationalistic and pluralistic demands of the Black Power movement evoked defensiveness and a sense of threat in white society. By questioning the value of assimilation and celebrating a separate African heritage, equal in legitimacy with white European heritage, the Black Power movement questioned the legitimacy and worth of Anglo-American values. In fact, many black power spokespersons condemned Anglo-American values, fiercely and openly, and implicated them in the creation and maintenance of a centuries-long system of racial repression. Today, nearly 40 years after the success of the Civil Rights movement, assertive and critical demands by the black community continue to be perceived as threatening.

Gender and Black Protest

Both the Civil Rights movement and the Black Power movement tended to be male dominated. African American women often were viewed as supporters of men rather than as equal partners in liberation. Although African American women were heavily involved in the struggle, they often were denied leadership roles and decision-making positions in favor of men. In fact, the women in one organization, the Student Nonviolent Coordinating Committee (SNCC), openly protested their relegation to lowly clerical positions and the frequent references to them as "girls" (Andersen, 1993, p. 284). The Nation of Islam emphasized female subservience, imposed a strict code of behavior and dress for women, and separated the genders in many temple and community activities. This pattern of male dominance illustrates a larger point: The battle against racism and the battle against sexism can be separate struggles with separate and often contradictory agendas (Amott & Matthaei, 1991, p. 177).

When the protest movements began, however, African American women already were heavily involved in community and church work, and they often used their organizational skills and energy to further the cause of black liberation. In the view of many, African American women were the backbone of the movement, even if they were often relegated to less glamorous but vital organizational work (Evans, 1979).

Fannie Lou Hamer of Mississippi, an African American who became a prominent leader in the black liberation movement, illustrates the importance of the role played by women. Hamer was born in 1917 to sharecropper parents. Her life was so circumscribed that until she attended her first rally at the beginning of the Civil Rights movement, she was unaware that blacks could—even theoretically—register to vote. The day after the rally, she quickly volunteered to register:

> I guess I'd had any sense I'd a-been a little scared, but what was the point of being scared? The only thing they could do to me was kill me and it seemed like they'd been trying to do that a little bit at a time ever since I could remember. (quoted in Evans, 1989, p. 271)

As a result of her activism, Hamer lost her job, was evicted from her house, and was jailed and beaten on a number of occasions. She devoted herself entirely to the Civil Rights movement and founded the Freedom Party, which successfully challenged the racially segregated Democratic Party and the all-white political structure of the state of Mississippi (Evans, 1979; Hamer, 1967).

CONTEMPORARY BLACK-WHITE RELATIONS

Since the heady days of the 1960s, significant progress has been made in integrating U.S. society and reducing racial inequality. Still, the problems that continue to confront African Americans are enormous, deep-rooted, and inextricably mixed with the structure and functioning of modern American society. As was the case in earlier eras, racism and racial inequality today cannot be addressed apart from the trends of change in the larger society, especially changes in subsistence technology. This section examines the racial separation that continues to characterize so many areas of U.S. society and applies many of the concepts from previous chapters to present-day black-white relations.

Continuing Separation, Continuing Violence

Although progress has been made in many areas, African Americans and white Americans continue to live in worlds that are separate, unequal, and often hostile. Each group has committed violence and hate crimes against the other, but the power differentials and the

patterns of inequality that are the legacy of our racist past guarantee that African Americans are more often seen as "invaders" pushing into areas where they do not belong and are not wanted. Sometimes the reactions to these perceived intrusions are immediate and bloody, but other, subtler attempts to maintain the exclusion of African Americans continue to be part of everyday life, even at the highest levels of society. For example, in a lawsuit reminiscent of Jim Crow days, Denny's, a national restaurant chain, was accused of discriminating against African American customers by systematically providing poor service. In 1994, the company agreed to pay $54 million to settle the lawsuit (Labaton, 1994). In another example, Texaco was sued for discrimination in 1996 by several of its minority employees. The case was settled out of court after a tape recording was made public; on the tape, company executives could be heard plotting to destroy incriminating documents and heard making racist remarks (Eichenwald, 1996).

Many African Americans mirror the hostility of whites, and as the goals of full racial equality and justice continue to seem remote, frustration and anger continue to run high. The unrest and discontent have been manifested in violence and riots, the most widely publicized example of which had origins in the 1991 beating and arrest of Rodney King by police officers in Los Angeles. The attack on King was videotaped by a civilian onlooker and shown repeatedly on national and international news. Contrary to the expectations of most people who saw the videotape, the police officers accused of beating King were acquitted of almost all criminal charges in April 1992. On hearing word of the acquittals, African Americans and others in several cities erupted in violence. The worst disturbance occurred in the Watts section of Los Angeles, where 58 people lost their lives and millions of dollars of property damage was done (Wilkens, 1992).

In some ways, the riot following the 1992 King verdict was different from the riots of the 1960s. The more recent event was multiracial and involved Hispanics as well as African Americans. In fact, most of the 58 fatalities were from these two groups. In addition, many of the businesses looted and burned were owned by Korean Americans, and many of the attacks were against whites directly, as in the beating of truck driver Reginald Denny (also, ironically, captured on videotape).

In other ways, the events were similar. Both were spontaneous and expressed diffuse but bitter discontent with the racial status quo. Both signaled continuing racial inequality, urban poverty and despair, and the reality of separate nations, unequal and hostile (see Gooding-Williams, 1993, for more on these urban uprisings).

The Criminal Justice System and African Americans

No area of race relations is more volatile and controversial than the relationship between the black community and the criminal justice system. There is considerable mistrust and resentment of the police among African Americans, and the perception that the entire criminal justice system is stacked against them is widespread. These perceptions are not without justification: Black people continue to be victimized by the police in a variety of ways—some petty, some involving deadly violence. The police attack on Rodney King is echoed in more recent murders in New York City in 1999 and in Cincinnati in 2001.

In the New York case, Amadou Diallo, an unarmed immigrant from West Africa, was gunned down in a hail of 41 bullets fired by four undercover police officers on a drug stakeout. The officers testified that they believed that Diallo was reaching for a gun when they opened fire, a defense that led to their acquittal. In the Cincinnati case, the shooting of Timothy Thomas, an unarmed 19-year-old black man, by a white police officer set off a storm of protest and days of rioting in the city.

On another level, more pervasive if less dramatic, is the issue of racial profiling: the police use of race as an indicator of suspiciousness and danger (Kennedy, 2001, p. 3). The tendency to focus more on blacks and to disproportionately stop, question, and follow them is a form of discrimination that generates resentment and increases the distrust (and fear) many black Americans feel toward their local police forces. According to some, humiliating encounters with police (for example, being stopped and questioned for "driving while black") are virtually a rite of passage for black men (Kennedy, 2001, p. 7). A recent national survey found that more than half of all black men and 25% of black women feel that they have been unfairly stopped by police (Morin & Cottman, 2001).

Black males are much more likely to be involved in the criminal justice system than white males, and in many communities, as many as one third of all young black men are under the supervision of the system: in jail or prison or on probation or parole (Mauer & Huling, 2000, p. 417). This phenomenal level of imprisonment is largely the result of a national "get tough" policy on drugs, especially crack cocaine, that began in the 1980s. Crack cocaine is a cheap form of the drug that has devastated certain, largely minority, neighborhoods. The street level dealers who have felt the brunt of the national antidrug campaign have been disproportionately young black males. Some see this crackdown as a not-so-subtle form of racial discrimination. For example, a 1986 federal law required a minimal prison sentence of 10 years for anyone convicted of possession with intent to distribute 50 grams or more of crack, a drug much more likely to be dealt by blacks. At the same time, comparable levels of sentencing for dealing powder cocaine—the more expensive form of the drug—was not reached until the accused possessed a minimum of 5,000 grams (Kennedy, 2001, p. 15). The result was a double victimization of the black community: first from the drug itself and then from the attempt to police the drug.

These charges of racial profiling and discrimination in the war against drugs are controversial. Many argue that racial profiling is, at some level, based on the fact that blacks statistically are more likely to be involved in street crime and in the illegal drug trade (for example, see Taylor & Whitney, 1999). At another level, these patterns sustain the ancient perceptions of black Americans as dangerous outsiders, and they feed the tradition of resentment and anger against the police in the black community.

Urbanization and Increasing Class Differentiation

As black Americans moved out of the rural South and as the repressive force of de jure segregation receded, social class inequality within the African American population increased. Since the 1960s, the black middle class has grown, but black poverty continues to be a serious problem.

The Black Middle Class

A small black middle class, based largely on occupations and businesses serving only the black community, had been in existence since before the Civil War (Frazier, 1957). Has this more affluent segment benefited from increasing tolerance in the larger society, civil rights legislation, and affirmative action programs? Is the black middle class growing in size and affluence?

The answers to these questions are not entirely clear. Although the percentage of African Americans who might be considered middle class has increased, research suggests that the size and affluence of this group are less than often assumed. For example, one nationwide research project found that middle-class blacks lag far behind middle-class whites in economic resources. Using white-collar occupations as their indicator of middle-class membership, Oliver and Shapiro (1995) found that the median income of middle-class blacks was only about 70% of the median income of middle-class whites. Even more dramatically, they found a huge racial gap in total net worth (home equity, stocks, savings, etc.): For every dollar owned by the white middle class, middle-class blacks owned only 15¢ (Oliver & Shapiro, 1995, p. 96). Other research (Oliver & Shapiro, 2001, pp. 230–231; Pollard & O'Hare, 1999, pp. 37–38) has shown similar large gaps in wealth between black and white households.

These economic differences are due partly to discrimination in the present and partly to the racial gaps in income, wealth, and economic opportunity in past generations. Economically more advantaged white families can pass along a larger store of resources, wealth, and property to the present generation. Thus, the greater economic marginality of the black middle class today is a form of "past-in-present" institutional discrimination (see Chapter 4) that reflects the greater ability of white parents (and grandparents) to finance higher education and to subsidize business ventures and home mortgages (Oliver & Shapiro, 2001).

Not only is their economic position more marginal, but middle-class blacks also commonly report that they are unable to escape the narrow straitjacket of race. No matter what their level of success, occupation, or professional accomplishments, race continues to be seen as their primary defining characteristic in the eyes of the larger society (Cose, 1993). Without denying the advances of some, many analysts argue that the stigma of race continues to set sharp limits on the life chances of African Americans.

There is also a concern that greater class differentiation may decrease solidarity and cohesion within the black community. There is greater income variation among African Americans than ever before, with the urban poor at one extreme and some of the wealthiest, most recognized figures in the world—millionaires, celebrities, business moguls, politicians, and sports and movie stars—at the other. Will the more affluent members of the black community disassociate themselves from the plight of the less fortunate and move away from the urban neighborhoods, taking with them their affluence, eloquence, and leadership skills? If this happens, it would reinforce the class division and further seal the fate of impoverished African Americans, who are largely concentrated in urban areas.

Urban Poverty

African Americans have become an urban minority group, and the fate of the group is bound inextricably to the fate of America's cities. The issues of black-white relations cannot be addressed successfully without dealing with urban issues, and vice versa.

As we saw in Chapter 4, automation and mechanization in the workplace have eliminated many of the manual labor jobs that sustained city dwellers in earlier decades (Kasarda, 1989). The manufacturing, or secondary, segment of the labor force has declined in size, while the service sector has continued to expand (see Exhibit 4.2). The more desirable jobs in the service sector have increasingly demanding educational prerequisites. The service sector jobs available to people with lower educational credentials often pay low wages and offer no benefits, no security, and no links to more rewarding occupations. This form of past-in-present institutional discrimination constitutes a powerful handicap for colonized groups such as African Americans, who have been excluded from educational opportunities for centuries.

Furthermore, many of the blue-collar jobs that have escaped automation have migrated away from the cities. Industrialists have been moving their businesses to areas where labor is cheaper, unions have less power, and taxes are lower. This movement to the suburbs, to the Sunbelt, and "offshore" has been devastating for inner cities. Poor transportation systems, lack of car ownership, the absence of affordable housing outside the center city, and outright housing discrimination have combined to keep urban poor people of color confined to center-city neighborhoods, distant from opportunities for jobs and economic improvement (Feagin, 2001, pp. 159–160; Kasarda, 1989; Massey & Denton, 1993).

These industrial and economic forces affect all poor urbanites, not just minority groups or African Americans in particular. The issues facing many African Americans are not limited to racism or discrimination; the impersonal forces of evolving industrialization and social class structures contribute as well. However, when immutable racial stigmas and centuries of prejudice are added to these economic and urban developments, the forces limiting and constraining many African Americans become extremely formidable.

For the past 60 years, the African American poor have been increasingly concentrated in narrowly delimited urban areas ("the ghetto") in which the scourge of poverty has been compounded and reinforced by a host of other problems, including joblessness, high rates of school dropout, crime, drug use, teenage pregnancy, and welfare dependency. These increasingly isolated neighborhoods are fertile grounds for the development of *oppositional cultures*, which reject or invert the values of the larger society. The black urban counterculture may be most visible in music, fashion, speech, and other forms of popular culture but is also manifest in widespread lack of trust in the larger society and in whites in particular. An urban underclass, barred from the mainstream economy and the primary labor force and consisting largely of poor African Americans and people from other minority groups of color, is quickly becoming a permanent feature of the American landscape (Kasarda, 1989; Massey & Denton, 1993; Wilson, 1987, 1992, 1996).

Under the Jim Crow system of race relations, black Southerners were excluded from opportunities for success and growth by a rigid code of laws, harsh customs, and intense prejudice. Today, the exclusion of many African Americans is perpetuated by economic and educational deficits that are the legacy of our racist past, deindustrialization, and continuing racism and discrimination. While many members of the black middle and working classes enjoy unprecedented opportunities, a large segment of the group remains colonized, isolated, marginalized, and burdened with a legacy of powerlessness and poverty.

Race vs. Class

One of the livelier debates in contemporary race relations concerns the relative importance of race and class in shaping the lives of African Americans and other minority groups. One position argues that race is no longer the primary controlling influence in the lives of African Americans and that blacks and whites at the same social class level or with the same educational credentials have the same opportunities. The playing field is level, it is argued, and what matters are competence and willingness to work hard, not skin color. The increase in the size of the black middle class has been used frequently as proof that modern American society is open and fair.

This position is often associated with *The Declining Significance of Race,* a book written in the late 1970s by William J. Wilson, an African American and a prominent sociologist. Wilson concluded that there is a segmented job market for blacks. The black urban underclass is restricted to the low-wage sector and faces high rates of unemployment and crushing poverty. Talented and educated African Americans, in contrast, have job prospects that are "at least comparable to those of whites with equivalent qualifications" (Wilson, 1980, p. 151). Wilson attributed the improved situation of the black middle class partly to the expansion of white-collar occupations and partly to affirmative action programs and pressure from the federal government to include African Americans and other minorities in colleges, universities and professional schools, and the job market.

Wilson's assessment may have been accurate for the 1970s. It follows, however, that these improvements would be sustained only to the extent that white-collar jobs continued to grow in number and affirmative action programs continued to be enforced. In the decade following the publication of Wilson's book, neither of these conditions was fulfilled. Economic growth slowed in the 1980s, the racial gap in wages actually widened (especially among younger workers), and, under the administrations of Presidents Ronald Reagan and George H. W. Bush, federal affirmative action programs were de-emphasized (Cancio, Evans, & Maume, 1996, pp. 551–554). There is some evidence of a closing of the race and gender gaps during the economic boom of the 1990s (see Exhibits 5.2 and 5.10 later in this chapter), but these gains may not persist. At any rate, Wilson's conclusion that race is declining in significance seems, at best, premature (Hughes & Thomas, 1998; Thomas, 1993; Wilson, 1996).

Other critics of Wilson's thesis argue that the forces of institutional discrimination and racism remain strong in modern America, even though they may be less blatant than in the past. Race remains the single most important feature of a person's identity and the most important determinant of life chances. Contrary to the beliefs of many white Americans, reports of the death of racism and the coming of a color-blind society have been greatly exaggerated (Feagin, 2001; Margolis, 1989, p. 99; Willie, 1989).

Closed Networks and Racial Exclusion

The continuing importance of race in American society is dramatically illustrated in a recent research project. Royster (in press) interviewed black and white graduates of a trade school in Baltimore. Her respondents had completed the same curricula and earned similar grades. In other words, they were nearly identical in terms of the credentials they brought to the world of work. Nonetheless, the black graduates were employed less often in the trades for which they had been educated, had lower wages, got fewer promotions, and experienced longer periods of unemployment. Virtually every white graduate found secure and reasonably lucrative employment; the black graduates, in stark contrast, usually were unable to stay in the trades and became, instead, low-skilled, low-paid workers in the service sector.

What accounts for these differences? Based on extensive interviews with the subjects, Royster concluded that the differences could not be explained by training or by personality characteristics. Instead, she found that what really mattered was not "what you know" but rather "who you know." The white graduates had access to networks of referrals and recruitment that linked them to the job market in ways that simply were not available to black graduates. In their search for jobs, whites were assisted more fully by their instructors and were able to use intraracial networks of family and friends, connections so powerful that they "assured even the worst [white] troublemaker a solid place in the blue collar fold" (Royster, in press).

Needless to say, these results run contrary to some deeply held American values, most notably the widespread, strong support for the idea that success in life is due to individual effort, self-discipline, and the other attributes enshrined in the Protestant ethic. The strength of this faith is documented in a recent survey that was administered to a representative sample of adult Americans. The respondents were asked if they thought that people got ahead by hard work, luck, or a combination of the two. Fully 65% of the sample choose "hard work," and another 25% choose "hard work and luck equally" (National Opinion Research Council, 2000). This overwhelming support for the importance of individual effort is echoed in human capital theory and many "traditional" sociological perspectives on assimilation (see Chapter 2).

Royster's results demonstrate that this view is simply wrong. To the contrary, access to the world of work is controlled by nepotism, cronyism, personal relationships, and networks of social relations that are decidedly not open to everyone. These subtle patterns of exclusion and closed intraracial networks are more difficult to document than the blatant discrimination that was at the core of Jim Crow segregation, but they can be just as devastating in their effects and just as powerful as mechanisms for perpetuating racial gaps in income and employment.

The Family Institution and the Culture of Poverty

The nature of the African American family institution has been a continuing source of concern and controversy. On one hand, some analysts see the black family as structurally weak, a cause of continuing poverty and a variety of other problems. No doubt the most famous study in this tradition was the Moynihan report (1965), which focused on the higher rates of divorce, separation, desertion, and illegitimacy among African American families and the fact that black families were far more likely to be female-headed than were white families. Moynihan concluded that the fundamental barrier facing black Americans was a family structure that he saw as crumbling, a condition that would

perpetuate the cycle of poverty entrapping black Americans (Moynihan, 1965, p. iii). Today, most of the differences between black and white family institutions identified by Moynihan are even more pronounced. Exhibit 5.1, for example, compares the percentages of households headed by females (black and white) with the percentages of households headed by married couples. (Note, however, that the percentage of female-headed-households in the black community began a slight decline in the mid-1990s.)

The line of analysis implicit in the Moynihan report locates the problem of urban poverty in the characteristics of the black community, particularly in the black family. These structures of community and family are "broken" in important ways and need to be "fixed." This argument is consistent with the *culture of poverty theory*, which argues that poverty is perpetuated by the particular characteristics of the poor. Specifically, poverty is said to encourage fatalism (the sense that one's destiny is beyond one's control) and an orientation to the present rather than to the future. The desire for instant gratification is a central trait of the culture of poverty, as opposed to the ability to defer gratification, which is thought to be essential for middle-class success. Other characteristics include violence, authoritarianism, and high rates of alcoholism and family desertion by males (Lewis, 1959, 1965, 1966). The culture of poverty theory leads to the conclusion that the problem of urban poverty would be resolved if female-headed family structures and other cultural characteristics correlated with poverty could be changed. Note that this approach is consistent with the traditional assimilationist perspective and human capital theory: The poor have "bad" or inappropriate values. If they could be equipped with "good" (i.e., white, middle-class) values, the problems would be resolved.

An opposed perspective, more consistent with the concepts and theories that underlie this text, sees the matriarchal structure of the African American family as the *result* of urban poverty—rather than a cause—and a reflection of racial discrimination and the

Exhibit 5.1   Percentage of Family Households With Married Couples and Headed by Females, by Race, 1970–2002

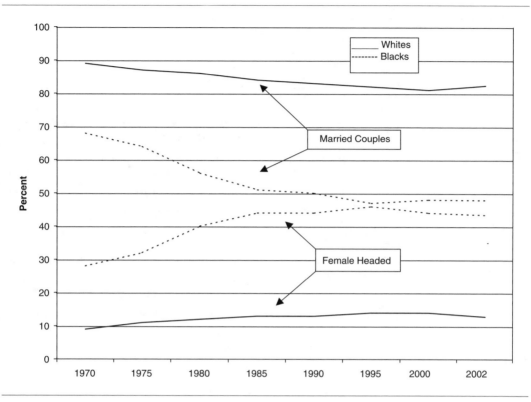

SOURCE: U.S. Bureau of the Census (2003c, p. 51).

scarcity of jobs for urban black males. In impoverished black urban neighborhoods, the supply of men able to support a family is reduced by high rates of unemployment, incarceration, and violence, and these conditions are in turn created by the concentration of urban poverty and the growth of the "underclass" (Massey & Denton, 1993; Wilson, 1996). Thus the burden of child rearing tends to fall on females, and female-headed households are more common than in more advantaged neighborhoods.

Female-headed African American families tend to be poor not because of any structural weakness but because of the lower wages paid to women in general and to African American women in particular (see Exhibit 5.2). Rather than reflecting a weak or pathological family structure, the poverty associated with black female-headed households is the result of complex interactions of past and present institutional discrimination, American racism and prejudice, the precarious position of African American women in the labor force, and continuing urbanization and industrialization. The African American family is not in need of "fixing," and the attitudes and values of the urban underclass are more the results of impoverishment and hopelessness than they are the causes (Farley, 2000, p. 94).

Prejudice and Discrimination

Traditional Prejudice and Modern Racism

Public opinion polls and other sources of evidence document a dramatic decline in

Exhibit 5.2   Median Income by Race and Sex, 1967–1999

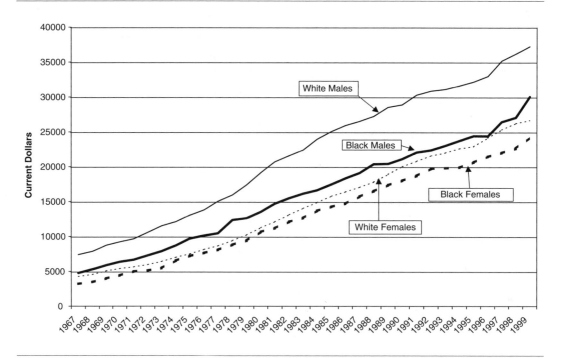

SOURCE: U.S.Bureau of the Census (2003b).

traditional, overt, anti-black prejudice since the mid-20th century. Exhibit 5.3 displays this trend using a number of survey items administered to representative samples of U.S. citizens over the past 60 years. In 1942, a little more than 70% of white Americans thought that black and white children should attend different schools; 40 years later, support for separate schools had dropped to less than 10%. Similarly, support for the right of white people to maintain separate neighborhoods declined from 65% in 1942 to 18% in the early 1990s. In more recent decades, the percentage of white respondents who support laws against interracial marriage decreased from almost 40% in the early 1970s to only 12% in 2000, and the percentage who believe that blacks are inferior fell from 26% to 12% in the same time period.

These trends document a genuine decline in levels of prejudice in the United States. However, we should not accept these changes at face value and leap to the conclusion that

racial prejudice is no longer a problem in society. First of all, these survey items also show that prejudice has not vanished. A percentage of the white population continues to endorse highly prejudicial sentiments and opinions. Second, the polls show only what people *say* they feel and think, which might be different from what they truly believe. Exhibit 5.3 may document a decline in people's willingness to admit their prejudice rather than a genuine improvement in intergroup attitudes and feelings.

A third possibility is that prejudice remains strong but has taken on new forms and expressions. This possibility is being investigated by a number of researchers who are studying *symbolic* or *modern racism,* a more subtle, complex, and indirect way to express negative feelings toward minority groups and opposition to change in dominant-minority relations (see Bobo, 1988, 2001; Kinder & Sears, 1981; Kluegel & Smith, 1982; McConahy, 1986; Sears, 1988). People

Exhibit 5.3   Declining Prejudice in the United States

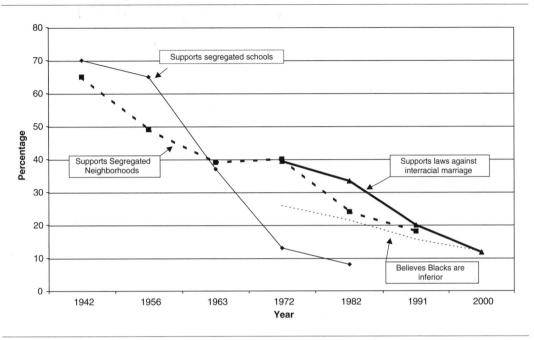

SOURCE: 1942, 1956, 1963: Hyman and Sheatsley (1964); 1972–2000: National Opinion Research Council, *General Social Survey*. Data are used with permission.

NOTE: Results are accurate to within 3 or 4 percentage points.

affected by modern racism have negative feelings (the affective aspect of prejudice) toward minority groups but reject the idea of genetic or biological inferiority and do not think in terms of the traditional stereotypes. Instead, their prejudicial feelings are expressed indirectly and subtly. The attitudes that define modern racism tend to be consistent with some tenets of the traditional assimilation perspective discussed in Chapter 2, especially human capital theory, and the "Protestant ethic": the traditional American value system that stresses individual responsibility and the importance of hard work. Specifically, modern racism assumes that (a) there is no longer any serious or important racial, ethnic, or religious discrimination in American society; (b) any remaining racial or ethnic inequality is the fault of members of the minority group; and (c) demands for preferential treatment or affirmative action for minorities are therefore unjustified. Modern racism tends to "blame

the victim" and place the responsibility for change and improvements on minority groups, not on society.

To illustrate the difference between traditional prejudice and modern racism, consider the results of a recent public opinion survey administered to a representative sample of Americans (National Opinion Research Council, 2000). Respondents were asked to choose from among four explanations of why black people, on the average, have "worse jobs, income, and housing than white people." Respondents could choose as many explanations as they wanted. One explanation, consistent with traditional anti-black prejudice, attributed racial inequality to the genetic or biological inferiority of African Americans ("The differences are mainly because blacks have less in-born ability to learn"). About 12% of the white respondents chose this explanation. A second explanation attributed continuing racial inequality to discrimination and a third to the lack of opportunity for an education. Of white respondents, 33% chose the former and 45% chose the latter.

A fourth explanation, consistent with modern racism, attributes racial inequality to a lack of effort by African Americans ("The differences are because most blacks just don't have the motivation or willpower to pull themselves up out of poverty"). Of the white respondents, 51% chose this explanation, the most popular of the four. Thus, support for modern racism—the view that the root of the problem of continuing racial inequality lies in the black community, not the society as a whole—has a great deal of support among white Americans.

What makes this view an expression of prejudice? Besides blaming the victim, it deflects attention away from centuries of oppression and continuing inequality and discrimination in modern society. It stereotypes African Americans and encourages the expression of negative feelings against them (but without invoking the traditional image of innate inferiority). Furthermore, researchers consistently have found that modern racism is correlated with opposition to policies and programs intended to reduce racial inequality (Bobo, 2001, p. 292). In the survey summarized earlier, for example, respondents who blamed continuing racial inequality on the lack of motivation or willpower of blacks—the "modern racists"—were the least likely to support government help for African Americans and affirmative action programs. In fact, as Exhibit 5.4 shows, the modern racists were less supportive of these programs than the traditional racists (those who chose the "in-born ability" explanation)!

Modern Institutional Discrimination

Paralleling the softening of traditional prejudice are changes in discrimination from blunt and overt to subtle and covert. The clarity of Jim Crow has yielded to the ambiguity of modern institutional discrimination (see Chapter 4) and the continuing legacy of past discrimination in the present. The dilemmas of the black urban underclass provide a clear, if massive, example of modern institutional discrimination. As long as American businesses and financial and political institutions continue to operate as they do, jobs will continue to migrate, cities will continue to lack the resources to meet the needs of their poorer citizens, and urban poverty will continue to sustain itself, decade after decade. The individual politicians, bankers, industrialists, and others who perpetuate and benefit from this system are not necessarily prejudiced and may not even be aware of these minority group issues, yet their decisions can and do have profound effects on the perpetuation of racial inequality in America.

The effects of past discrimination on the present can be illustrated by the relatively low level of black business ownership. From the beginning of slavery through the end of Jim Crow segregation less than 40 years ago, the opportunities for black Americans to start their own businesses were severely restricted (even forbidden) by law. The black-owned businesses that did exist were confined to the relatively less affluent market provided by the black community, a market they had to share with firms owned by dominant group members. At the same time, customs and laws prevented the black-owned businesses from competing for more affluent white customers. The lack of opportunity to develop and maintain a strong business base in the past—and the consequent inability to accumulate wealth, experience, and other resources—limits the ability of African Americans to compete successfully for economic opportunities in the present (Oliver & Shapiro, 2001, p. 239).

Assimilation and Pluralism

Acculturation

The Blauner hypothesis states that the culture of groups created by colonization will be attacked, denigrated, and, if possible, eliminated—an assertion that seems well validated by the experiences of African Americans. African cultures and languages were largely eradicated under slavery. As a powerless, colonized minority group, slaves had few opportunities to preserve their heritages even

Exhibit 5.4   Support for Government Help for Blacks and Affirmative Action by Explanation for Racial Inequality

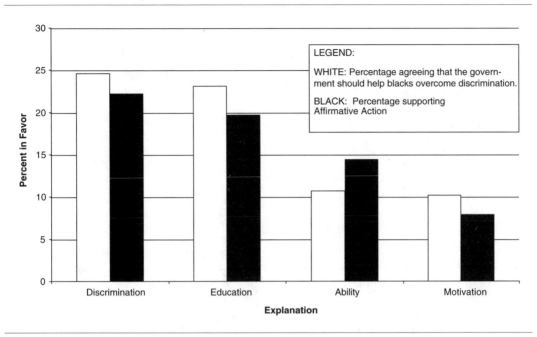

SOURCE: National Opinion Research Council, *General Social Survey* (2000). Data are used with permission.

though some traces of African homelands have been found in black language patterns, kinship systems, music, folk tales, and family legends (see Levine, 1977; Stuckey, 1987).

Cultural domination continued under the Jim Crow system, albeit through a different structural arrangement. Under slavery, slaves and their owners worked together, and interracial contact was common. Under de jure segregation, intergroup contact diminished, and the structural separation between blacks and whites generally widened. After slavery ended, the African American community had somewhat more autonomy (although still few resources) to define itself and develop a distinct culture.

The centuries of cultural domination and separate development have created a unique black experience in America. African Americans share language, religion, values, beliefs, and norms with the dominant society but have developed distinct variations on the general themes.

The acculturation process may have been slowed (or even reversed) by the Black Power movement. Beginning in the 1960s, there has been an increased interest in African culture, language, clothing, and history and a more visible celebration of unique African American experiences (e.g., Kwanzaa) and the innumerable contributions of African Americans to the larger society.

Secondary Structural Assimilation

Structural assimilation, or integration, involves several different phases. According to Gordon (see Chapter 2), the first occurs in more public areas such as the job market, schools, and political institutions and is called secondary structural assimilation. We can assess integration in this area by comparing residential patterns, income distributions, job profiles, political power, and levels of education of the different groups. Each of these areas is addressed in the text that follows. We then discuss assimilation at the primary level (integration in intimate associations such as friends) and in marriage patterns.

Exhibit 5.5   Number of People, 2000: One or More Races Including Black or African American

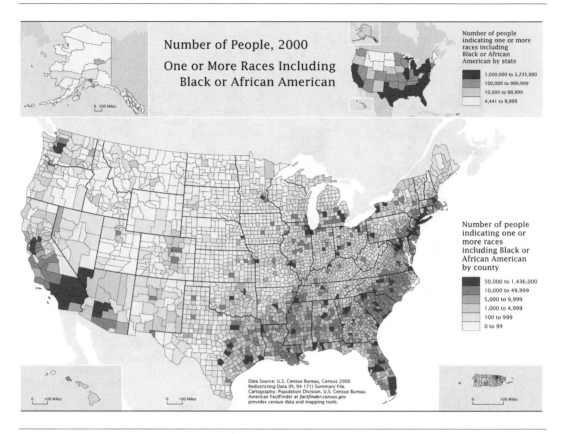

SOURCE: U.S. Bureau of the Census (2000i).

Residential Patterns. Even after a century of migration to other parts of the nation, a slim majority of African Americans continues to reside in the South (about 55% today vs. almost 90% in 1910). About 36% of African Americans now live in the Northeast and Midwest (overwhelmingly in urban areas), and about 9% live in the West (Pollard & O'Hare, 1999, p. 23). Exhibit 5.5 clearly shows the concentration of African Americans in the states of the old Confederacy; the urbanized East Coast corridor from Washington, D.C., to Boston; the industrial centers of the Midwest; and to a lesser extent, California.

In the decades since Jim Crow segregation ended in the 1960s, residential integration has advanced slowly, if at all. Black and white Americans have continued to live in separate areas, and residential segregation has been the norm even for blacks and whites of similar income levels (O'Hare, Pollard, et al., 1991, p. 9; O'Hare & Usdansky, 1992). This pattern of racial separation at the level of neighborhoods has been reinforced by the pattern illustrated in Exhibit 5.6: African Americans are heavily concentrated in urban areas and especially in the center city, whereas whites are more dispersed and more suburban.

Residential segregation has declined over the past several decades and, today, its extent varies around the nation. African Americans continue to be the most isolated of minority groups, especially in the older industrial cities of the Northeast and Midwest (Iceland, Weinberg, & Steinmetz. 2002; Pollard & O'Hare, 1999, p. 29).

Exhibit 5.6   Residential Patterns by Race, 2002

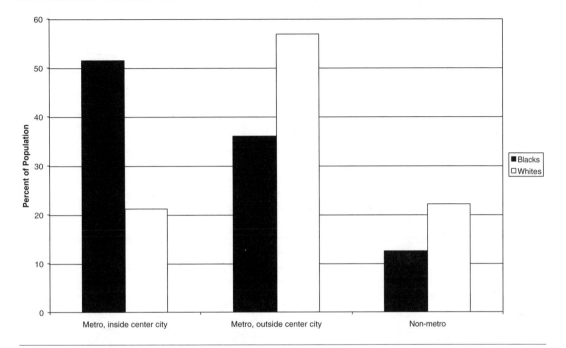

SOURCE: Compiled from data presented in U.S. Bureau of the Census (2003b, p. 2).

These continuing patterns of residential segregation reflect the social class differences between the races and are reinforced by a variety of discriminatory practices. Realtors practice racial steering—guiding clients to same-race housing areas—a practice that is illegal today but widely documented in research. For example, in an investigation of housing discrimination in the rental apartment market conducted over the telephone, Massey demonstrated that compared with speakers of "white English," speakers of "black English" were less likely to be told that an advertised unit was available, more likely to be required to pay an application fee, and more likely to have credit mentioned as an issue (Massey, 2000, p. 4). In addition, banks and other financial institutions are more likely to refuse home mortgages to black applicants than to white applicants and are more likely to "redline," or deny home improvement loans, for houses in minority group neighborhoods (Feagin, 2001, pp. 155–159). "White flight" away from

integrated areas also contributes to the pattern of racial separation as whites flee from even minimal neighborhood integration. Harassment and violence against African Americans who move into white-majority neighborhoods frequently supplement these practices.

School Integration. In 1954, the year of the landmark *Brown* desegregation decision, the great majority of African Americans lived in states operating segregated school systems. Compared with white schools, Jim Crow schools were severely underfunded and had less qualified teachers, shorter school years, and inadequate physical facilities. Today, 70% of African American children still attend schools with a black majority, and one third attend schools that are 90% to 100% minority. The pressure from the federal government to integrate the schools has eased over the past several decades, and one recent report found that schools are being resegregated today at the fastest rate since the 1950s. For example,

Exhibit 5.7   Percentage of Persons 25 Years of Age and Older Completing High School, 1960–2002, by Race and Gender

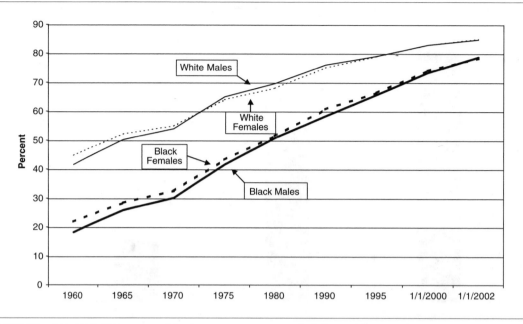

SOURCE: 1960–2000: U.S. Bureau of the Census (2002). *Statistical Abstract of the United States* (2001, p. 139); 2002: U.S. Bureau of the Census (2003a).

schools in the southern states actually reached their highest levels of racial integration in the mid-1980s—almost 20 years ago—when 44% of black students attended white-majority schools. Since that time, this percentage has drifted downward and reached a low of about 33% in 1998 (Orfield, 2001).

Underlying and complicating the difficulty of school integration is the widespread residential segregation mentioned previously. The challenges for school integration are especially evident in those metropolitan areas, such as Washington, D.C., that consist of a largely black inner city surrounded by largely white rings of suburbs. Even with busing, political boundaries would have to be crossed before the school systems could be substantially integrated. Without a renewed commitment to integration, American schools will continue to re-segregate. This is a particularly ominous trend because it directly affects the quality of education. For example, years of research

demonstrate that the integration of schools—by social class as well as by race—is related to improved test scores (Orfield, 2001).

In terms of the quantity of education, the gap between whites and blacks generally decreased over the 20th century. Exhibit 5.7 displays the percentage of the population over age 25, by race and sex, who have high school diplomas and clearly shows a shrinking (though still noticeable) racial gap in education. Part of the remaining difference in educational attainment is due to social class factors. For example, African American students are more likely to drop out of high school. Research has shown that "students are more likely to drop out . . . when they get poor grades, are older than their classmates, come from a single-parent family, have parents who dropped out . . . or live in a central city" (O'Hare, Pollard, et al., 1991, p. 21). On the average, black students are more exposed to these risk factors than are

Exhibit 5.8   Percentage of Persons Age 25 and Older Completing 4 Years of College or More, 1960–2002

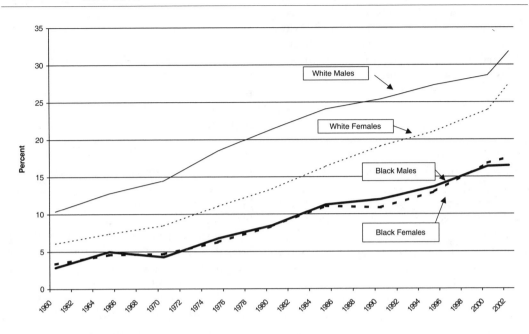

SOURCE: 1960–2000: U.S. Bureau of the Census (2002, p. 139); 2002: U.S. Bureau of the Census (2003a, p. 2).

white students. When the effects of social class background are taken into account, differences in dropout rates nearly disappear (O'Hare, Pollard, et al., 1991, p. 21).

At the college level, the trends somewhat parallel the narrowing gap in levels of high school education, as shown in Exhibit 5.8. For example, in 1960, white males were about 3½ times as likely to have a college degree than were black males. By 2000, the advantage of white males had shrunk to a factor of less than 2. These racial differences become even larger for more advanced degrees, and differences such as these will be increasingly serious in an economy in which jobs increasingly require an education beyond high school (Pollard & O'Hare, 1999, p. 30).

Political Power. Two trends have increased the political power of African Americans since World War II. One is the movement out of the rural South, a process that concentrated

African Americans in areas where it was easier for people to register to vote and that resulted in greater representation of African Americans at all levels of government. Today, black communities are virtually guaranteed some political representation by their high degree of geographical concentration at local levels. Today, most large American cities, including Los Angeles, Chicago, Atlanta, New York, and Washington, D.C., have elected African American mayors at least once.

The number of black elected officials at all levels of government increased from virtually zero at the beginning of the 20th century to 9,001 in 2000 (U.S. Bureau of the Census, 2003c, p. 252). The first African American representative to the U.S. Congress (other than those elected during Reconstruction) was elected in 1928 (Franklin, 1967, p. 614). In 2001, there were 39 African Americans serving in the House of Representatives (about 9% of the total) but none in the Senate. (U.S.

Bureau of the Census, 2003c, p. 247). In Virginia in 1989, Douglas Wilder became the first African American to be elected to a state governorship, and in 2001, retired Army General Colin Powell was appointed Secretary of State, the highest governmental office—along with Supreme Court Justice—ever held by an African American.

The other trend is the dismantling of the institutions and practices that disenfranchised Southern blacks during Jim Crow segregation (see Chapter 4). In particular, the Voting Rights Act of 1965 specifically prohibited many of the practices (poll taxes, literacy tests, and whites-only primaries) traditionally used to keep blacks politically powerless. The effect of these repressive policies can be seen in the fact that as late as 1962, only 5% of the African American population of Mississippi and 13% of the African American population of Alabama were registered to vote (O'Hare, Pollard, et al., 1991, p. 33).

Since the 1960s, the number of African Americans in the nation's voting age population has increased from slightly less than 10% to almost 13%. This increasing potential for political power was not fully mobilized, however, and actual turnout on election days generally has been low. In presidential elections from 1972 to 2000, for example, between 56% and 65% of eligible whites voted. The comparable percentages for black voters ranged from 48% to 56% (U.S. Bureau of the Census, 1992, p. 269; U.S. Bureau of the Census, 2002, p. 251). It should be noted, though, that the black vote figured prominently in the elections of John F. Kennedy in 1960, Jimmy Carter in 1976, and Bill Clinton in 1992 and 1996.

In the closely contested 2000 presidential race, the turnout for African Americans was almost 54%, just 3 percentage points below the white turnout. Led by the NAACP and Jesse Jackson, a concerted effort was made to get the black vote out, and the democratic candidate (Al Gore) probably received more African American votes than any political candidate in history. Black turnout rose in virtually every state and, in the view of many,

might have been the margin of victory for Gore in the bitterly contested state of Florida had the votes been counted differently (White, 2000).

Jobs and Income. Integration in the job market and racial equality in income follow the trends established in other areas of social life: The situation of African Americans has improved since the end of de jure segregation but has stopped well short of equality. Exhibits 5.9a and 5.9b show the differences in occupation by race and sex. White males are much more likely to be employed in the highest-rated occupational area, whereas black males are overrepresented in the service sector and in unskilled labor. Although huge gaps remain, we should also note that the present occupational distribution represents a rapid and significant upgrading. As recently as the 1930s, the majority of black males were unskilled agricultural laborers (Steinberg, 1981, pp. 206–207).

A similar improvement has occurred for black females. In the 1930s, about 90% of employed black women worked in agriculture or in domestic service (Steinberg, 1981, pp. 206–207). The percentage of African American women in these categories has dropped dramatically, and the majority of black females are employed in the two highest occupational categories, although typically at the lower levels of these categories. For example, in the "managerial and professional" category, women are more likely to be concentrated in less-well-paid occupations such as nurse or elementary school teacher, whereas men are more likely to be physicians and lawyers.

Unemployment has been at least twice as high for blacks as for whites since the 1940s. Unemployment rates vary by sex and by age, and black males frequently have higher unemployment rates than black females. Among white Americans, females have always had a higher unemployment rate. The reasons for greater unemployment among African Americans are various and complex. As we have seen, lower levels of education

Exhibit 5.9a Occupation by Race, 2000, Males

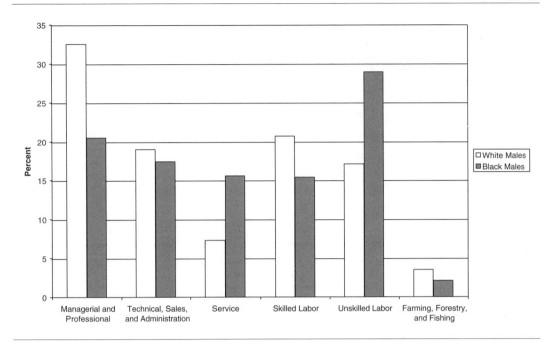

Exhibit 5.9b Occupation by Race, 2000, Females

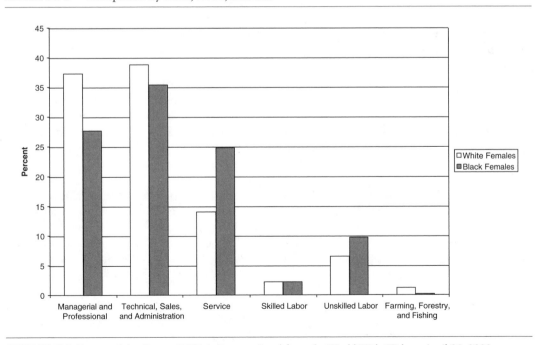

Exhibit 5.10   Median Family Income by Race, 1947–2001 (current dollars)

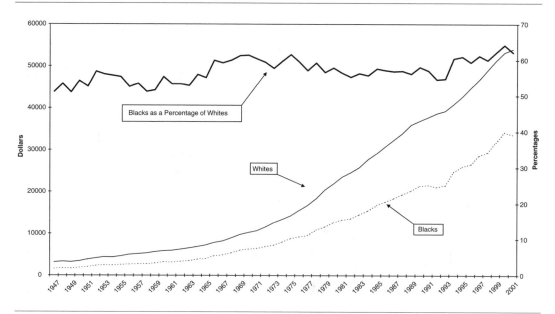

SOURCE: U.S. Bureau of the Census (2000d).

and concentration in the job-poor center cities play a part. So, too, does lower seniority (because integration is so recent, black workers have less seniority and are more often the victims of the "last hired, first fired" pattern), along with the fact that African Americans are more concentrated in positions more likely to become obsolete in a developing economy. At the core of these patterns of unemployment and disadvantage, however, are discrimination, both individual and institutional, and the continuing presence of prejudice and racism (Feagin, 2001, pp. 159–166).

The differences in education and jobs are reflected in a persistent racial income gap, as shown in Exhibit 5.10. In 1947, black median family income was about 51% of white median family income. By the mid-1970s, black median family income rose to about 60% of white median family income; it stabilized at that figure for nearly 30 years, then rose sharply during the economic "boom" of the 1990s. However, after reaching an all-time high of 64% in 2000, the percentage fell

to 62% in 2001, the most recent year for which data is available.

As we saw in Exhibit 5.2, sex as well as race affects the distribution of income, and black females continue to be one of the lowest-paid groups in society. Also as noted earlier, when total net worth (including savings, stocks, real estate, etc.) is taken into account, the racial gap widens dramatically (Oliver & Shapiro, 2001).

Finally, poverty affects black Americans at much higher rates than it does white Americans. Exhibit 5.11 shows the percentages of white and black Americans living below the federally established, "official" poverty level from 1970 through 2001. The poverty rate for blacks runs at about three times the rate for whites, even though the rate for both groups trends down. For example, in 1970, the rate of black poverty was more than 3.3 times the rate of white poverty (about 33% vs. 10%). By 2001, fewer families of both races were living in poverty (about 22% for blacks and 8% for whites), but the racial differential was still on the order of 3 times more poverty for black families. Tragically,

Exhibit 5.11 Percentages of Families and of Children Below the Poverty Level, by Race, 1970–2001

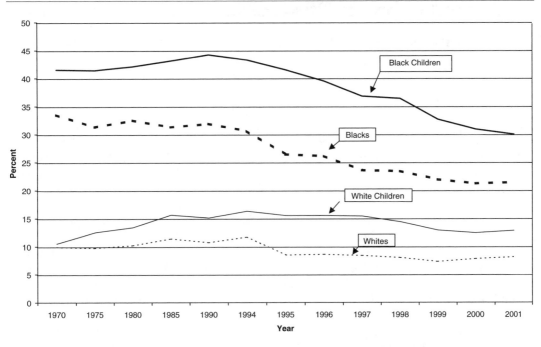

SOURCE: 1970–1997: U.S. Bureau of the Census (1999, p. 483, 487); 1998-1999: www.census.gov/hhes/poverty

although they are also declining, the highest rates of poverty continue to be found among children, especially black children.

Primary Structural Assimilation

Interracial contact in the more public areas of society, such as schools and the workplace, is certainly more common today, and as Gordon's model of assimilation predicts, this has led to increases in more intimate contacts across racial lines. For example, the percentage of blacks who say that they have "good friends" who are white increased from 21% in 1975 to 78% in 1994. Comparable increases have occurred for whites: In 1975, only 9% said they had "good friends" who were black, and that percentage rose to 73% in 1995 (Thernstrom & Thernstrom, 1997, p. 521). These figures are from public opinion polls, and they may very well exaggerate the actual number of interracial friendships (see Lach, 2000). Nonetheless, they document an increase in integration at the primary level. On the other hand, continuing structural pluralism and separate black and white institutional and organizational structures limit further increases in this area.

Interracial marriages are increasing in number but still make up a tiny percentage of all marriages. According to the U.S. Bureau of the Census (2002), there were 65,000 black-white married couples in 1970 (including persons of Hispanic origin), about one tenth of 1% of all married couples. By 2000, the number of black-white married couples had increased more than fivefold, to 363,000, but this was still only about 0.7% of all married couples (U.S. Bureau of the Census, 2002, p. 47).

FOCUS ON RACE AND GENDER

MODERN RACISM AND SEXISM IN THE MASS MEDIA

The changing nature of American racism and sexism is mirrored in the mass media and popular culture, which are presenting more diversified and more positive images of people of color and of women. For example, in 2002, African Americans Halle Berry and Denzel Washington won the Academy Awards for best actress and best actor. An African American had won either top award only once before (Sidney Poitier in 1963) in the 73-year history of the Oscars.

Just as in the larger society, such events signal not the disappearance but the evolution of traditional anti-minority and anti-female sentiment and patterns of discrimination. The mass media (movies, television, music, and so forth) are more open and egalitarian than in the past, but the old attitudes, stereotypes, and behavior atterns continue to haunt these societal institutions, as they do many others. To illustrate, consider how images of race and gender are presented in television commercials. Historically, when presented at all, both nonwhites and women have been depicted in derogatory or stereotypical roles. To see how these patterns have changed, researchers Coltrane and Messineo (2000) examined a representative sample of TV ads from the mid-1990s. They found some evidence of progress in the portrayal of minority group members and women, but they also found patterns consistent with modern racism and a parallel set of attitudes toward women that can be called modern sexism.

For example, they found that blacks were included in commercials in rough proportion to their actual representation in the population: About 11% of the TV characters were black, and African Americans make up about 12% of the population (see Exhibit 1.1). However, the researchers also found that the characters in the commercials they studied varied sharply by race and gender and did so in ways that are consistent with traditional stereotypes. Men were more likely to be depicted in active/instrumental roles (e.g., as leaders or people of high status and accomplishment or as people who gave orders), and black men were more likely to be presented as aggressive and menacing (e.g., bold, forceful, competitive). Black males often were depicted as "hypermasculine" (particularly in connection with sports) and were less likely than white males to be seen as gentle, romantic, or domestic (Coltrane & Messineo, 2000, p. 383).

White females were much more likely than black females to be depicted as sex objects and to have their beauty and sexuality bent to commercial ends. This pattern reflects the larger culture's lower regard for African American standards of beauty, a bias that has its origins in the days of slavery (see Chapter 3). In the stilted world of TV commercials, the role of white women is still strongly linked to love, sex, and marriage. The relative absence of black females from these associations reflects continuing bias in the perceptions of the larger society and the stereotype that disassociates blacks from "images of happy parents, well-scrubbed children, and sparkling homes" (Coltrane & Messineo, 2000, p. 383).

The researchers found that in TV commercials, as in the real world, race and gender continue to shape opportunity, image, and access to sexual and domestic fulfillment. Furthermore, they found that race and gender images did not vary by the intended audience: Commercials broadcast in shows aimed at African American audiences were very similar in images and themes to those included in shows intended for white audiences.

How significant are these findings? Does it really matter what television commercials show? Coltrane and Messineo (2000) argued that the power of TV comes from its pervasive presence in the American home. According to the Bureau of the Census (U.S. Bureau of the Census, 2002, p. 705), more than 98% of homes have at least one television set—more than have telephones (about 94%). The world represented on TV helps to shape our view of the "real world" in countless, sometimes subtle ways. It reinforces and helps maintain both modern racism and modern sexism, and "by inundating people with images of race and gender that presuppose differential access to authority, romance, sex, and domestic fulfillment, commercial television promotes and protects existing social hierarchies" (Coltrane & Messineo, 2000, p. 387).

IS THE GLASS HALF EMPTY OR HALF FULL?

The contemporary situation of African Americans is perhaps what might be expected for a group so recently "released" from exclusion and subordination. The average situation of African Americans improved vastly during the latter half of the 20th century in virtually every area of social life. As demonstrated by the data presented in this chapter, however, racial progress stopped well short of equality. In assessing the present situation, one might stress the improved situation of the group ("the glass is half full") or the challenges that remain before full racial equality and justice are achieved ("the glass is half empty"). Perhaps the most reasonable approach is to recognize that in many ways, the overall picture of racial progress is "different" rather than "better" and that a large percentage of the African American population has traded rural peasantry for urban poverty and faces an array of formidable and deep-rooted problems.

The situation of black Americans is intimately intermixed with the plight of our cities and the changing nature of the labor force. It is the consequence of nearly 400 years of prejudice, racism, and discrimination, but it also reflects broader social forces, such as urbanization and industrialization. Consistent with their origin as a colonized minority group, black Americans have seen their relative poverty and powerlessness persist long after other groups (e.g., the descendants of the European immigrants who arrived between the 1820s and 1920s) achieved equality and acceptance. African Americans were enslaved to meet the labor demands of an agrarian economy, became a rural peasantry under Jim Crow segregation, were excluded from the opportunities created by early industrialization, and remain largely excluded from the better jobs in the emerging postindustrial economy.

Progress toward racial equality has slowed considerably since the heady days of the 1960s, and in many areas, earlier advances seem hopelessly stagnated. Public opinion polls indicate that there is little support or sympathy for the cause of black Americans. Traditional prejudice has declined, only to be replaced by modern racism. In the court of public opinion, African Americans often are held responsible for their own plight. Biological racism has been replaced by indifference to racial issues or by blaming the victims.

Of course, in acknowledging the challenges that remain, we should not downplay the real improvements that have been made in the lives of African Americans. Compared with the days of Jim Crow, African Americans are on the average more prosperous and more politically powerful, and some are among the most revered of current popular heroes ("the glass is half full"). However, the increases in average income and education and the glittering success of the few obscure a tangle of problems for the many, problems that may well grow worse as America moves further into the postindustrial era. Poverty, unemployment, a failing educational system, residential segregation, racism, discrimination, and prejudice continue to be inescapable realities for millions of black Americans. In many black neighborhoods, crime, drugs, violence, poor health care, malnutrition, and a host of other factors compound these problems ("the glass is half empty").

Given this gloomy situation, it should not be surprising to find significant strength in pluralistic, nationalistic thinking, as well as resentment and anger in the black community. Black nationalism and black power remain powerful ideas, but their goals of development and autonomy for the black community remain largely rhetorical sloganeering without the resources to bring them to actualization.

The situation of the African American community in the early days of the 21st century might be characterized as structural pluralism combined with inequality. The former characterization testifies to the failure of assimilation and the latter to the continuing effects, in the present, of a colonized origin. The problems that remain are less visible (or perhaps just better hidden from the average white middle-class American) than those of previous eras. Responsibility is more diffused, the moral certainties of opposition to slavery or to Jim Crow laws are long gone, and contemporary racial issues must be articulated and debated in an environment of subtle prejudice and low levels of sympathy for the grievances of African Americans. Urban poverty, modern institutional discrimination, and modern racism are less dramatic and more difficult to measure than an overseer's whip, a lynch mob, or a sign that says "Whites Only," but they are just as real and can be just as deadly in their consequences.

MAIN POINTS

- At the beginning of the 20th century, the racial oppression of African Americans took the form of a rigid competitive system of group relations, de jure segregation. This system ended because of changing economic and political conditions, changing legal precedents, and a mass movement of protest initiated by African Americans.

- The U.S. Supreme Court decision in *Brown v. Board of Education of Topeka* (1954) was the single most powerful blow struck against legalized segregation. A nonviolent direct action campaign was launched in the South to challenge and defeat segregation. The U.S. Congress delivered the final blows to de jure segregation in the 1964 Civil Rights Act and the 1965 Voting Rights Act.

- Outside the South, the concerns of the African American community had centered on access to schooling, jobs, housing, health care, and other opportunities. Their frustration and anger was expressed in the urban riots in the 1960s. The Black Power movement addressed the massive problems of racial inequality remaining after the victories of the Civil Rights movement.

- Black-white relations since the 1960s have been characterized by continuing inequality, separation, and hostility, along with substantial improvements in the status for some African Americans. Class differentiation within the black community is greater than ever before.

- The African American family has been perceived as weak, unstable, and a cause of continuing poverty. The culture of poverty theory attributes poverty to certain characteristics of the poor. An alternative view sees problems such as high rates of family desertion by men as the result of poverty rather than the cause.

- Anti-black prejudice and discrimination are manifested in more subtle, covert forms (modern racism and institutional discrimination) in contemporary society.

- African Americans are largely acculturated, but centuries of separate development have created a unique black experience in American society.

- Despite real improvements in their status, the overall secondary structural assimilation of African Americans remains low. Evidence of racial inequalities in residence, schooling, politics, jobs, income, unemployment, and poverty is massive and underlines the realities of the urban underclass.
- In the area of primary structural assimilation, interracial interaction and friendships appear to be rising. Interracial marriages are increasing, although they remain a tiny percentage of all marriages.
- Compared with their situation at the start of the 20th century, African Americans have made considerable improvements in quality of life. The distance to true racial equality remains enormous.

QUESTIONS FOR REVIEW AND STUDY

1. What forces led to the end of de jure segregation? To what extent was this change a result of broad social forces (e.g., industrialization), and to what extent was it the result of the actions of African Americans acting against the system (e.g., the Southern Civil Rights movement). By the 1960s and 1970s, how had the movement for racial change succeeded, and what issues were left unresolved? What issues remain unresolved today?

2. What are the differences between de jure segregation and de facto segregation? What are the implications of these differences for movements to change these systems? That is, how must movements against de facto segregation differ from movements against de jure segregation in terms of tactics and strategies?

3. Describe the differences between the Southern Civil Rights movement and the Black Power movement. Why did these differences exist? Do these movements remain relevant today? How?

4. How does gender affect contemporary black-white relations and the African American protest movement? Is it true that African American women are a "minority group within a minority group?" How?

5. What are the implications of increasing class differentials among African Americans? Does the greater affluence of middle-class blacks mean that they are no longer a part of a minority group? Must future protests by African Americans be confined only to working-class and lower-class blacks?

6. Define and explain modern racism. How does this differ from "traditional" prejudice? How is it related to modern institutional discrimination?

7. How are African Americans presented in the mass media? In what ways do these portrayals sustain traditional prejudice and modern racism?

8. Regarding contemporary black-white relations, is the glass half empty or half full? Considering the totality of evidence presented in this chapter, would you agree more with statement A or statement B? Why?
   A. American race relations are the best they've ever been; racial equality has been essentially achieved (even though some problems remain).
   B. American race relations have a long way to go before society achieves true racial equality.

INTERNET RESEARCH PROJECT

In the year 2000, a team of reporters from the *New York Times* conducted a year-long investigation of how black-white relations are being lived out by ordinary people in churches, schools, neighborhoods, and other venues. A series of 15 articles detailing and analyzing these experiences were published, and all are available online at www.nytimes.com/library/national/race/. Read at least three or four of these stories and analyze them in terms of the concepts and conclusions presented in this chapter. What do these stories imply about black-white inequality, prejudice, discrimination, assimilation, pluralism, and racial separation? Is the glass half empty or half full?

FOR FURTHER READING

Feagin, Joe. 2001. *Racist America: Roots, Current Realities, and Future Reparations.* New York: Routledge.

Hacker, Andrew. 1992. *Two Nations: Black and White, Separate, Hostile, Unequal.* New York: Scribner's.
Two very readable overviews of contemporary race relations.

Massey, Douglas, & Denton, Nancy. 1993. *American Apartheid: Segregation and the Making of the Underclass.* Cambridge, MA: Harvard University Press.
The authors argue powerfully that residential segregation is the key to understanding urban black poverty.

Morris, Aldon D. 1984. *The Origins of the Civil Rights Movement.* New York: Free Press.
An indispensable source.

Smelser, Neil J., Wilson, William Julius, & Mitchell, Faith. (Eds.). 2001. *America Becoming: Racial Trends and Their Consequences.* Washington, DC: National Academy Press.
A two-volume collection of articles by leading scholars that, together, present a comprehensive analysis of black-white relations in America.

Thernstrom, Stephan, & Thernstrom, Abigail. 1997. *America in Black and White.* New York: Simon & Schuster.
A comprehensive review of American race relations.

Williams, Juan. 1987. *Eyes on the Prize: America's Civil Rights Years, 1954–1965.* New York: Penguin.
See also the acclaimed television documentary of the same name.

6

Native Americans

From Conquest to Tribal
Survival in a Postindustrial Society

The contact period for Native Americans began in the earliest colonial days and lasted nearly 300 years, ending only with the final battles of the Indian Wars in the late 1800s. The Indian nations fought for their land and to preserve their cultures and ways of life. The tribes had enough power to win many battles, but they eventually lost all the wars. The superior resources and power of the burgeoning white society made the eventual defeat of Native Americans inevitable, and by 1890, the last of the tribes had been conquered, their leaders killed or in custody, and their people living on government-controlled reservations.

In Blauner's (1972) terms, American Indians were a conquered and colonized minority group. Like the slave plantations, the reservations were paternalistic systems on which Native Americans were controlled; the tools used against them were federally mandated regulations and government-appointed Indian agents. For the bulk of the 20th century, while industrialization and urbanization transformed the situations of other American minority groups, Native Americans subsisted on the fringes of development and change, marginalized, relatively powerless, and isolated. As the century wore on and especially in the most recent decades, their situation changed and, in some ways, improved. Compared with other minority groups, however, they tended to be less connected to the larger society and less affected by its economic and social evolution.

At the dawn of the 21st century, Native Americans remain among the most disadvantaged and isolated of minority groups. Their present status reflects the long, bitter competition with the dominant group, their colonized origins, and their lengthy exclusion from mainstream society. As we shall see, however, the group is not without resources and strategies for improving its situation.

NATIVE AMERICAN CULTURES

The dynamics of Native American and Anglo-American relationships have been shaped by the vast differences in culture, values, and norms between the two groups. These differences have hampered communication in the past and continue to do so in the present, even though contemporary differences have been diminished by centuries of contact with and domination by white civilization. A comprehensive analysis of Native American cultures is well beyond the scope of this text, but the past experiences and present goals of the group can be appreciated only with some understanding of their views of the world. We must note here, as we did in Chapter 3, that there are hundreds of different tribes in what is now the United States—each with its own language and heritage—and that a complete analysis of Native American culture would have to take this diversity into account. However, some patterns and cultural characteristics are widely shared across the tribes, and we will concentrate on these similarities.

Perhaps the most obvious difference between Native American and Western cultures lies in their respective conceptions of the relationship between human beings and the natural world. In the traditional view of many Native American cultures, the universe is a unity. Humans are simply a part of a larger reality, no different from or more important than other animals, plants, trees, and the earth itself. The goal of many Native

American tribes was to live in harmony with the natural world, not "improve" it or use it for their own selfish purposes. That goal differs sharply from Western concepts of development, commercial farming, and bending the natural world to the service of humans. The gap between the two worldviews is evident in the reaction of one Native American to the idea that his people should become farmers: "You ask me to plow the ground. . . . Shall I take a knife and tear my mother's bosom? You ask me to cut grass and make hay . . . but how dare I cut my mother's hair?" (Brown, 1970, p. 273).

The concept of private property, or the ownership of things, was not prominent in Native American cultures and was, from the Anglo-American perspective, most notably absent in conceptions of land ownership. The land simply existed, and the notion of owning, selling, or buying it was foreign to Native Americans. In the words of Tecumseh, a chief of the Shawnee, a man could no more sell the land than the "sea or the air he breathed" (Josephy, 1968, p. 283).

Native American cultures and societies also tended to be more oriented toward groups (e.g., the extended family, clan, or tribe) than toward individuals. The interests of the self are subordinated to those of the group, and child-rearing practices strongly encouraged group loyalty (Parke & Buriel, 2002, p. 22). Cooperative, group activities were stressed over those of a competitive, individualistic nature. The bond to the group remains so strong that "students go hungry rather than ask their parents for lunch money, for in asking they would be putting their needs in front of the group's needs" (Locust, 1990, p. 231).

Many Native American tribes were organized around egalitarian values that stressed the dignity and worth of every man, woman, and child. Virtually all tribes had a division of labor based on gender, but women's work was valued, and they often occupied far more important positions in tribal society than was typical for women in Anglo-American society at the time of first contact. In many of the Native American societies that practiced gardening, women controlled the land. In other tribes, women wielded considerable power and held the most important political and religious offices. Among the Iroquois, for example, a council of older women appointed the chief of the tribe and made decisions about when to wage war (Amott & Matthaei, 1991, pp. 34–35).

These differences in values, compounded by the power differentials that emerged, often placed Native Americans at a disadvantage when dealing with the dominant group. The Native Americans' conception of land ownership and their lack of experience with deeds, titles, contracts, and other Western legal concepts often made it difficult for them to defend their resources from Anglo-Americans. At other times, cultural differences led to disruptions of traditional practices, further weakening or disrupting Native American societies. For example, Christian missionaries and government representatives tried to reverse the traditional Native American division of labor in which women were responsible for gardening. In the Western view, only males did farm work. In addition, the military and political representatives of the dominant society usually ignored female tribal leaders and imposed Western notions of patriarchy and male leadership on the tribes (Amott & Matthaei, 1991, p. 39).

RELATIONS WITH THE FEDERAL GOVERNMENT AFTER THE 1890S

By the end of the Indian Wars in 1890, American Indians had few resources with which to defend their self-interest. In addition to being confined to the reservations, the group was scattered throughout the western two thirds of the United States and split by cultural and linguistic differences. Politically, the power of Native Americans was further limited by the facts that the huge majority of the group were not U.S. citizens and that most tribes lacked a cultural basis for understanding representative democracy as practiced in the larger society.

Economically, Native Americans were among the most impoverished groups in the society. Reservation lands generally were of poor quality; traditional food sources, such

as buffalo and other game, had been destroyed; and traditional hunting grounds and gardening plots had been lost to white farmers and ranchers. The tribes had few means of satisfying even their most basic needs. Many became totally dependent on the federal government for food, shelter, clothing, and other necessities.

Prospects for improvement seemed slim. Most reservations were in remote areas, far from the sites of industrialization and modernization, and Native Americans had few of the skills (knowledge of English, familiarity with Western work habits and routines) that would have enabled them to compete for places in the increasingly urban and industrial American society of the early 20th century. Off the reservations, racial prejudice and strong intolerance limited them. On the reservations, they were subjected to policies designed either to maintain their powerlessness and poverty or to force them to Americanize. Either way, the future of Native Americans was in serious jeopardy, and their destructive relations with white society continued in peace as they had in war.

Reservation Life

The reservations were intended to closely supervise the recently conquered and still hostile Native Americans and maintain their powerlessness. Relationships with the federal government were paternalistic and featured a variety of policies designed to coercively acculturate the tribes.

Paternalism and the Bureau of Indian Affairs

The reservations were run not by the tribes, but by an agency of the federal government: the Bureau of Indian Affairs (BIA) of the U.S. Department of the Interior. The BIA and its local superintendent controlled virtually all aspects of everyday life, including the reservation budget, the criminal justice system, and the schools. The BIA (again, not the tribes) even determined tribal membership.

The traditional leadership structures and political institutions of the tribes were ignored as the BIA executed its duties with little regard for, and virtually no input from, the people it supervised. The BIA superintendent of the reservations "ordinarily became the most powerful influence on local Indian affairs, even though he was a government employee, not responsible to the Indians but to his superiors in Washington" (Spicer, 1980, p. 117). The superintendent controlled the food supply and communications to the world outside the reservation. This control was used to reward tribal members who cooperated and to punish those who did not.

Coercive Acculturation: The Dawes Act and Boarding Schools

Consistent with the Blauner hypothesis, Native Americans on the reservations were subjected to coercive acculturation or forced Americanization. Their culture was attacked, their languages and religions were forbidden, and their institutions were circumvented and undermined. The centerpiece of U.S. Indian policy was the Dawes Allotment Act of 1887, a deeply flawed attempt to impose white definitions of land ownership and to transform Native Americans into independent farmers by dividing their land among the families of each tribe. The intention of the act was to give each Indian family the means to survive like its white neighbors.

Although the law might seem benevolent in intent (certainly, thousands of immigrant families would have been thrilled to own land), it was flawed by a gross lack of understanding of Native American cultures and needs, and in many ways, it was a direct attack on those cultures. Most Native American tribes did not have a strong agrarian tradition, and little or nothing was done to prepare the tribes for their transition to peasant yeomanry. More important, Native Americans had little or no concept of land as private property, and it was relatively easy for settlers, land speculators, and others to separate Indian families from the land allocated to them by this legislation. By allotting land to families and individuals, the legislation sought to

destroy broader kinship, clan, and tribal social structures and replace them with Western systems that featured individualism and the profit motive (Cornell, 1988, p. 80).

About 140 million acres were allocated to the tribes in 1887. By the 1930s, nearly 90 million of those acres—almost 65%—had been lost to the land hunger of whites, often in deals marred by fraud or the threat of violence. Most of the remaining land was desert or otherwise nonproductive (Wax, 1971, p. 55). From the standpoint of the Indian Nations, the Dawes Allotment Act was a disaster and a further erosion of their already paltry store of resources (for more details, see Josephy, 1968; Lurie, 1982; McNickle, 1973; Wax, 1971).

Coercive acculturation operated through a variety of other avenues as well. Whenever possible, the BIA sent Native American children to boarding schools, sometimes hundreds of miles away from parents and kin, where they were required to speak English, convert to Christianity, and become educated in the ways of Western civilization. Consistent with the Blauner hypothesis, tribal languages, dress, and religion were forbidden, and to the extent that native cultures were mentioned at all, they were attacked and ridiculed. Children of different tribes were mixed together as roommates to speed the acquisition of English. When school was not in session, children often were boarded with local white families, usually as unpaid domestic helpers or farmhands, and were prevented from visiting their families and revitalizing their tribal ties (Hoxie, 1984; Spicer, 1980; Wax, 1971).

Native Americans were virtually powerless to change the reservation system or avoid the campaign of acculturation. Nonetheless, they resented and resisted coerced Americanization, and many languages and cultural elements survived the early reservation period, although often in altered form. For example, the traditional tribal religions remained vital through the period despite the fact that by the 1930s, the great majority of Indians had affiliated with one Christian faith or another. Furthermore, many new religions were founded, some combining Christian and traditional elements (Spicer, 1980, p. 118).

The Indian Reorganization Act

By the 1930s, the failure of the reservation system and the policy of forced assimilation had become obvious to all who cared to observe. The quality of life for Native Americans had not improved, and there was little economic development and few job opportunities on the reservations. Health care was woefully inadequate, and education levels lagged far behind national standards.

The plight of Native Americans eventually found a sympathetic ear in the administration of Franklin D. Roosevelt, who was elected president in 1932, and John Collier, the man he appointed to run the Bureau of Indian Affairs. Collier was knowledgeable about Native American issues and concerns and was instrumental in securing the passage of the Indian Reorganization Act (IRA) in 1934.

This landmark legislation contained a number of significant provisions for Native Americans and broke sharply with the federal policies of the past. In particular, the IRA rescinded the Dawes Act and the policy of individualizing tribal lands. It also provided means by which the tribes could expand their land holdings. Many of the mechanisms of coercive Americanization in the school system and elsewhere were dismantled. Financial aid in various forms and expertise were made available for the economic development of the reservations. In perhaps the most significant departure from earlier policy, the IRA proposed an increase in Native American self-governance and a reduction of the paternalistic role of the BIA and other federal agencies.

Although sympathetic to Native Americans, the IRA had its limits and shortcomings. Many of its intentions were never realized, and the empowerment of the tribes was not unqualified. The move to self-governance generally took place on the dominant group's terms and in conformity with the values and practices of white society. For example, the proposed increase in the decision-making power of the tribes was contingent on their adoption of Anglo-American political forms, including secret ballots, majority rule, and written constitutions. These concepts were alien to the tribes that selected leaders by procedures other than popular election (e.g., leaders might be selected by councils of elders) or that made decisions by open discussion and consensus building (i.e., decisions required the agreement of *everyone* with a voice in the process, not a simple majority). The incorporation of these Western forms of governance illustrates the basically assimilationist intent of the IRA.

The IRA had variable effects on Native American women. In tribes that were male dominated, the IRA gave women new rights to participate in elections, run for office, and hold leadership roles. In other cases, new political structures replaced traditional forms, some of which, as in the Iroquois culture, had accorded women considerable power. Although the political effects were variable, the programs funded by the IRA provided opportunities for women on many reservations to receive education and training for the first time. Many of these opportunities were oriented toward domestic tasks and other traditionally Western female roles, but some prepared Native American women for jobs outside the family and off the reservation, such as clerical work and nursing (Evans, 1989, pp. 208–209).

In summary, the Indian Reorganization Act of 1934 was a significant improvement over prior federal Indian policy but was bolder and more sympathetic to Native Americans in intent than in execution. On one hand, not all tribes were capable of taking advantage of the opportunities provided by the legislation, and some ended up being further victimized. For example, in the Hopi tribe—located in the Southwest—the act allowed a westernized group of Indians to be elected to leadership roles, with the result that business firms run by the dominant group were allowed to have access to the mineral resources, farmland, and water rights controlled by the tribe. The resultant development generated wealth for the white firms and their Hopi allies while most of the tribe continued to languish in poverty (Churchill, 1985, pp. 112–113). On the other hand, some tribes prospered (at least comparatively speaking) under the IRA. One impoverished, landless group of Cherokee in Oklahoma acquired land, equipment, and expert advice through the IRA and between 1937 and 1949, developed a prosperous, largely debt-free farming community (Debo, 1970, pp. 294–300). Many tribes remained suspicious of the IRA, and by 1948, fewer than 100 tribes had voted to accept its provisions.

Termination and Relocation

The IRA's stress on the legitimacy of tribal identity seemed "un-American" to many. There was constant pressure on the federal government to return to an individualistic policy that encouraged (or required) Americanization. Some viewed the tribal structures and communal property-holding patterns as relics of an earlier era and as impediments to modernization and development. Not so incidentally, some elements of dominant society still coveted the remaining Indian lands and resources, which could be more easily exploited if property ownership were individualized.

In 1953, the assimilationist forces won a victory when Congress passed a resolution calling for an end to the reservation system and to the special relationships between the tribes and the federal government. The proposed policy, called *termination,* was intended to get the federal government "out of the Indian business." It rejected the IRA and proposed a return to the system of private land ownership imposed on the tribes by the Dawes Act. Horrified at the notion of termination, the tribes opposed the policy strongly and vociferously. Under this policy, all special relationships—including treaty obligations—between the federal government and the tribes would end. Tribes would no longer exist as legally recognized entities, and tribal lands and other resources would be placed in private hands (Josephy, 1968, pp. 353–355).

About 100 tribes, most of them small, were terminated. In virtually all cases, the termination process was administered hastily, and fraud, misuse of funds, and other injustices were common. The Menominee of Wisconsin and the Klamath on the West Coast were the two largest tribes to be terminated. Both suffered devastating economic losses and precipitous declines in quality of life. Neither tribe had the business base or tax base needed to finance the services (e.g., health care and schooling) formerly provided by the federal government, and both were forced to sell land, timber, and other scarce resources to maintain minimal standards of living. Many poor Native American families were forced to turn to local and state agencies, placing severe strains on welfare budgets. The experience of the Menominee was so disastrous that, following concerted requests of the tribe, reservation status was restored in 1973 (Deloria, 1969, pp. 60–82; McNickle, 1973, pp. 103–110; Raymer, 1974). The Klamath reservation was restored in 1986 (Snipp, 1996, p. 394).

At about the same time that the termination policy came into being, various programs were established to encourage Native Americans to move to urban areas. The movement to the city had already begun in the 1940s, spurred by the availability of factory jobs during World War II. In the 1950s, the movement was further encouraged with programs of assistance and by the declining government support for economic development on the reservation, the most dramatic example of which was the policy of termination (Green, 1999, p. 265). Centers for Native Americans were established in many cities, and various services (e.g., job training, housing assistance, English instruction) were offered to assist in the adjustment to urban life. The urbanization of the Native American population is displayed in Exhibit 6.1. Note the rapid increase in the movement to the city that began in the 1950s. More than half of all Native Americans are now urbanized, and since 1950, Indians have urbanized faster than the general population. Nevertheless, Native Americans are still the least urbanized minority group. The population as a whole is about 80% urbanized; in contrast, African Americans (see Exhibit 5.6) are about 86% urbanized.

As with African Americans, Native Americans arrived in the cities after the mainstream economy had begun to de-emphasize blue-collar or manufacturing jobs.

Exhibit 6.1   Urbanization of Native Americans, 1900–2000

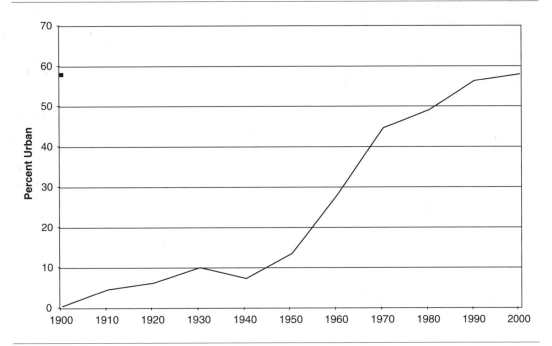

SOURCE: 1900–1990: Thornton (2001, p. 142); 2000: Calculated from the U.S. Bureau of the Census (2000q, Table DP-1).

Because of their relatively low average levels of educational attainment and their racial and cultural differences, Native Americans in the city tended to encounter the same problems experienced by African Americans and other minority groups of color: high rates of unemployment, inadequate housing, and all the other travails of the urban underclass.

Native American women also migrated to the city in considerable numbers. The discrimination, unemployment, and poverty of the urban environment often made it difficult for the men of the group to fulfill the role of breadwinner; thus, the burden of supporting the family and caring for the children has tended to fall more on the women. The difficulties inherent in combining child rearing and a job outside the home are compounded by isolation from the support networks provided by extended family and clan back on the reservations. Nevertheless, one study found that Native American women in the city continue to practice their traditional cultures and maintain the tribal identity of their children (Joe & Miller, 1994, p. 186).

Native Americans living in the city are, on the average, better off than those living on reservations, where unemployment can reach 80% or even 90%. But the improvement is relative. Although many individual Indians prosper in the urban environment, income figures for urban Indians as a whole are comparable to those for African Americans and well below those for whites. Native American unemployment rates run about twice the national average (Cornell, 1988, p. 132). Thus, moving to the city often involves trading rural poverty for the urban variety, with little net improvement in life chances.

Native Americans probably will remain more rural than other minority groups for years to come. Despite the poverty and lack of opportunities for schooling and jobs, the reservation offers some advantages in services and lifestyle. On the reservation, there may be opportunities for political participation and leadership roles that are not available in the cities, where Native Americans are a tiny minority. Reservations also offer kinfolk, friends, religious services, and tribal celebrations (Snipp, 1989, p. 84). Lower levels of education, work experience, and financial resources combine with the prejudice, discrimination, and racism of the larger society to lower the chances of success in the city and probably will sustain the pattern of return to the reservations.

Although the economic benefits of urbanization have been slim for the group as a whole, other advantages have accrued from life in the city. It was much easier to establish networks of friendship and affiliation across tribal lines in the cities, and urban Indians have been one of the sources of strength and personnel for a movement of protest that began early in the 20th century. Virtually all the organizational vehicles of Indian protest have had urban roots.

Self-Determination

Termination aroused so much opposition from Native Americans and was such an obvious disaster that the pressure to enforce it faded in the late 1950s, although the policy itself was not repealed until 1975. Since the 1960s, federal Indian policy generally has returned to the tradition set by the IRA. Termination and forced assimilation continue to be officially rejected, and within limits, the tribes have been granted more freedom to find their own way, at their own pace, of relating to the larger society.

Several federal programs and laws have benefited the tribes during the past few decades, including the antipoverty and "Great Society" campaigns launched in the 1960s. In 1970, President Richard Nixon affirmed the government's commitment to fulfilling treaty obligations and the right of the tribes to govern themselves. This policy was further advanced in the Indian Self-Determination and Education Assistance Act, which was passed in 1975. This legislation increased aid to reservation schools and Native American students and increased the

tribes' control over the administration of the reservations, from police forces to schools and road maintenance.

The Self-Determination Act primarily benefited the larger tribes and those that had well-established administrative and governing structures. Smaller and less well-organized tribes continue to rely heavily on the federal government (Snipp, 1996, p. 394). Nonetheless, at least in some cases, this new phase of federal policy has allowed Native American tribes to plot their own courses free of paternalistic regulation, and just as important, it gave them the tools and resources to address their problems and improve their situations. We will look at some of these developments after examining the Native American protest movement.

PROTEST AND RESISTANCE

Early Efforts

As BIA-administered reservations and coercive Americanization came to dominate tribal life in the 20th century, new forms of Indian activism appeared. The modern protest movement was tiny at first and, with few exceptions, achieved a measure of success only in recent decades. In fact, the Native American protest movement in the past was not so much unsuccessful as simply ignored. The movement has focused on several complementary goals: protecting Native American resources and treaty rights, striking a balance between assimilation and pluralism, and finding a relationship with the dominant group that would permit a broader array of life chances without sacrificing tribal identity and heritage.

Formally organized Native American protest organizations have existed since the 1910s, but the modern phase of the protest movement began during World War II. Many Native Americans served in the military or moved to the city to take jobs in aid of the war effort and were thereby exposed to the world beyond the reservation. In addition, political activism on the reservation was stimulated by the passage of the IRA and continued through the war years along with the recognition that many problems were shared across tribal lines.

These trends helped to stimulate the founding of the National Congress of American Indians (NCAI) in 1944. This organization was pan-tribal (i.e., included members from many different tribes); its first convention was attended by representatives of 50 different tribes and reservations (Cornell, 1988, p. 119). The leadership consisted largely of Native Americans educated and experienced in the white world. However, the NCAI's program stressed the importance of preserving the old ways and tribal institutions as well as protecting Indian welfare. An early victory for the NCAI and its allies came in 1946 when an Indian Claims Commission was created by the federal government. This body was authorized to hear claims brought by the tribes with regard to treaty violations. The commission has settled hundreds of claims resulting in awards of millions of dollars to the tribes, and it continues its work today (Weeks, 1988, pp. 261–262).

In the 1950s and 1960s, the protest movement was further stimulated by the threat of termination and by the increasing number of Native Americans living in the cities who developed friendships across tribal lines. Awareness of common problems, rising levels of education, and the examples set by the successful protests of other minority groups also increased readiness for collective action.

Red Power

By the 1960s and 1970s, Native American protest groups were finding new ways to express their grievances and problems to the nation. The Red Power movement, like the Black Power movement (see Chapter 5), encompassed a coalition of groups, many considerably more assertive than the NCAI, and a varied collection of ideas, most of which stressed self-determination and pride in race and cultural heritage.

Red power protests included a "fish-in" in the state of Washington in 1965, an episode that also illustrates the nature of Native American demands. The state of Washington

had tried to limit the fishing rights of several different tribes on the grounds that the supply of fish was diminishing and needed to be protected. The tribes depended on fishing for subsistence and survival, and they argued that their right to fish had been guaranteed by treaties signed in the 1850s and that it was the pollution and commercial fishing of the dominant society that had depleted the supply of fish. They organized a fish-in in violation of the state's policy and were met by a contingent of police officers and other law officials. Violent confrontations and mass arrests ensued. Three years later, after a lengthy and expensive court battle, the tribes were vindicated, and the U.S. Supreme Court confirmed their treaty rights to fish the rivers of Washington State (Nabakov, 1999, pp. 362–363).

Another widely publicized episode took place in 1969, when Native Americans from various tribes occupied Alcatraz Island in San Francisco Bay, the site of a now-closed federal prison. The protesters were acting on an old law that granted Native Americans the right to reclaim abandoned federal land. The occupation of Alcatraz was organized, in part, by the American Indian Movement (AIM), founded in 1968. More militant and radical than the previously established protest groups, AIM aggressively confronted the BIA, the police, and other forces that were seen as repressive. With the backing of AIM and other groups, Alcatraz was occupied for nearly 4 years. The incident generated a great deal of publicity for the Red Power movement and the plight of Native Americans.

In 1972, AIM helped to organize a march on Washington, D.C., called the "Trail of Broken Treaties." Marchers came from many tribes and represented both urban and reservation Indians. The intent of the marchers was to dramatize the problems of the tribes. The leaders demanded the abolition of the BIA, the return of illegally taken land, and increased self-governance for the tribes, among other things. When they reached Washington, some of the marchers forcibly occupied the BIA offices. Property was damaged (by which side is disputed), and records and papers were destroyed. The march generated a great deal of publicity but, ultimately, none of the demands of the leadership were met.

The following year, AIM occupied the village of Wounded Knee in South Dakota to protest the violation of treaty rights. Wounded Knee was the site of the last armed confrontation between Indians and whites, in 1890, and was selected by AIM for its deep symbolic significance. The occupation lasted more than 2 months and involved several armed confrontations with federal authorities. Again, the protest ended without achieving any of the demands made by the Indian leadership (Olson & Wilson, 1984, pp. 172–175). Since the early 1970s, the level of protest activity has declined, just as it has for the black protest movement, and lawsuits and court cases have predominated over dramatic, direct confrontations.

Ironically, the struggle for red power encouraged assimilation as well as pluralism. The movement linked members of different tribes and forced Indians of diverse heritages to find common ground, often in the form of a "generic" Native American culture. Inevitably, the protests were conducted in English and the grievances were expressed in ways that were understandable to white society, in an acknowledgment of the pressure to acculturate even while arguing for the survival of the tribes. Furthermore, mounting successful protests required that Native Americans be fluent in English, trained in the law and other professions, skilled in dealing with bureaucracies, and knowledgeable about the formulation and execution of public policy. Native Americans who became proficient in these areas thereby took on the characteristics of their adversaries (Hraba, 1994, p. 235).

As the pan-tribal protest movement forged ties between members of diverse tribes, the successes of the movement and changing federal policy and public opinion encouraged a rebirth of commitment to tribalism and "Indian-ness." Native Americans were simultaneously stimulated to assimilate (by stressing their common characteristics and creating organizational forms that united the tribes) and to retain a pluralistic relationship with the larger society (by working for self-determination and

enhanced tribal power and authority). Thus, part of the significance of the Red Power movement was that it encouraged both pan-tribal unity and a continuation of tribal diversity (Olson & Wilson, 1984, p. 206). Today, Native Americans continue to seek a way of existing in the larger society that merges assimilation with pluralism.

Exhibit 6.2 summarizes this discussion of federal policy and Indian protest. The four major policy phases since the end of overt hostilities in 1890 are listed on the left. The thrust of the government's economic and political policies are listed in the next two columns, followed by a brief characterization of tribal response. The last column shows the changing bases for federal policy, sometimes aimed at weakening tribal tribes and individualizing Native Americans and sometimes (and most recently) aimed at working with and preserving tribal structures.

THE CONTINUING STRUGGLE FOR DEVELOPMENT IN CONTEMPORARY INDIAN-WHITE RELATIONS

Conflicts between Native Americans and the larger society are far from over. Although the days of deadly battle are (with occasional exceptions) long gone, the issues that remain are serious, difficult to resolve, and, in their way, just as much matters of life and death. American Indians face enormous challenges in their struggle to improve their status, but largely as a result of their greater freedom from stifling federal control since the 1970s, they also have some resources, some opportunities, and a leadership that is both talented and resourceful (Bordewich, 1996, p. 11).

Natural Resources

Ironically, land allotted to Native American tribes in the 19th century sometimes turned out to be rich in resources that became valuable in the 20th century. These resources include 3% of U.S. oil and natural gas reserves, 15% of U.S. coal reserves, and 55% of U.S. uranium reserves (Amott & Matthaei,

Exhibit 6.2   Federal Policy and Native American Response

Period	Economic Impact	Political Impact	Native American Response	Government Approach
Reservation (late 1800s to 1930s)	Land loss (Dawes Act, 1887) and welfare dependency	Government control of reservations and coercive acculturation	Some limited resistance and protest	Individualistic; creation of self-sufficient farmers
Reorganization (IRA: 1930s to 1940s)	Stabilized land base and supported some development of reservation	Established tribal governments sponsored by the federal government	Increased political participation in many tribes, some pan-tribal activity	Incorporate tribes as groups, creation of self-sufficient "Americanized" communities
Termination and relocation (late 1940s to early 1960s)	Withdrawal of government support for reservations, promotion of urbanization	New assaults on tribes, new forms of coercive acculturation	Increased pan-tribalism, widespread and intense opposition to termination	Individualistic; dissolve tribal ties and promote incorporation into modern, urban labor market
Self-determination (1960s to present)	Develop reservation economies, increase integration of Native American labor force	Support for tribal governments	Greatly increased political activity	Incorporate tribes as self-sufficient communities with access to federal programs of support and welfare

SOURCE: Based on Cornell, Kalt, Krepps, and Taylor (1998, p. 5). Adapted with permission.

1991, p. 54). In addition (and despite the devastation wreaked by the Dawes Act), some tribes hold title to water rights, fishing rights, woodlands that could sustain a lumbering industry, and wilderness areas that could be developed for camping, hunting, and other forms of recreation. These resources are likely to become more valuable as the earth's natural resources and undeveloped areas are further depleted in the future.

The challenge faced by Native Americans is to retain control of these resources and to develop them for the benefit of the tribes. Threats to the remaining tribal lands and assets are common. Mining and energy companies continue to cast envious eyes, while other tribal assets are coveted by real estate developers, fishermen (recreational as well as commercial), backpackers and campers, and cities facing water shortages (Harjo, 1996).

Some tribes have succeeded in developing their resources for their own benefit. For example, the White Mountain Apaches of Arizona operate nine tribally owned enterprises, including a major ski resort, a logging operation and sawmill, and a small casino. These businesses are the primary economic engines of the local area, and unemployment on the White Mountain reservation is only one fourth of the national reservation average (Cornell & Kalt, 2000, pp. 445–446). On many other reservations, however, even rich stores of resources lie dormant, awaiting the right combination of tribal leadership, expertise, and development capital. The Crow tribe of Montana, for example, controls a huge supply of coal and has extensive timber, water, mineral, and other resources. Yet unemployment on the reservation runs nearly 80%, and more than half of the tribe gets public assistance of some kind. "The last two tribal chief executives have been convicted of federal felonies, and the current chief executive has had to have armed guards surrounding her when addressing the tribal council" (Cornell & Kalt, 2000, p. 444).

On a broader level, tribes are banding together to share expertise and negotiate more effectively with the larger society. For example, 25 tribes founded the Council of Energy Resource Tribes (CERT) in 1975 to coordinate and control the development of mineral resources on reservation lands. Since its founding, CERT has successfully negotiated a number of agreements with dominant group firms, increasing the flow of income to the tribes and raising their quality of life (Cornell, 1988; Snipp, 1989).

Attracting Industry to the Reservation

Many efforts to develop the reservations have focused on creating jobs by attracting industry through such incentives as low taxes, low rents, and a low-wage pool of labor—not unlike the package of benefits offered to employers by less-developed nations in Asia, South America, and Africa. With some notable exceptions, these efforts have not been particularly successful (for a review, see Vinje, 1996). Reservations often are so geographically isolated that transportation costs become prohibitive. The jobs that have materialized typically offer low wages and have few benefits; usually, non-Indians fill the more lucrative managerial positions. Thus, the opportunities for building economic power or improving the standard of living from these jobs are sharply limited. These new jobs may transform "the welfare poor into the working poor" (Snipp, 1996, p. 398), but their potential for raising economic vitality is low.

As an illustration of the problems of developing reservations by attracting industry, consider the Navajo, the second largest Native American tribe. The Navajo reservation spreads across Arizona, New Mexico, and Utah and encompasses about 20 million acres, an area a little smaller than either Indiana or Maine. Although the reservation seems huge on a map, much of the land is desert not suitable for farming or other uses. As they have for the past several centuries, the Navajo today rely heavily on the cultivation of corn and sheepherding for sustenance.

Most wage-earning jobs on the reservation are with agencies of the federal government (e.g., the BIA) or with the tribal government. Tourism is large and growing, but the jobs available in that sector typically are low wage and seasonal. There are reserves of coal, uranium, and oil on the reservation, but these resources have not generated many jobs. In some cases, the Navajo have resisted the damage to the environment that would be caused by mines and oil wells, acting on their traditional values and respect for the land. When exploitation of these resources has been permitted, the companies involved often have used highly automated technologies that generate few jobs (Oswalt & Neely, 1996, pp. 317–351). As of 1990 (the last year for which data is available), the median family income for the Navajo was $13,940—about one-third the median family income for white Americans in that year—and nearly half the tribe lived below the poverty line. The tribe runs an extensive school system, and almost all Navajo children attend day school (as opposed to the boarding schools of the past). The schools mix a standard curriculum with Navajo culture and language. Only about half of all Navajo have high school degrees, and fewer than 5% have college degrees (U.S. Bureau of the Census, 1997, p. 50).

On the other hand, some tribes have managed to achieve relative prosperity by bringing jobs to their people. The Choctaw Nation of Mississippi, for example, has become one of the largest employers in the state. Tribal leaders have been able to attract companies such as Xerox and Harley-Davidson to the reservation by promising (and delivering) high-quality labor for relatively low wages. Incomes have risen; unemployment is relatively low; and the tribe has built schools, hospitals, and a television station; the tribe also administers numerous other services for its members (Bordewich, 1996, pp. 300–305). As of 1990, median family income for the Choctaw was $24,467 ($10,500 more than the Navajo but less than 60% of the national norm for that year), and fewer than 20% of Choctaw families lived below the poverty line. As for education, 70% of the Choctaw had high school diplomas, and 13% were college graduates (U.S. Bureau of the Census, 1997, p. 50).

The Choctaw are not the most affluent tribe, and the Navajo are far from being the most destitute. These two tribes illustrate the mixture of partial successes and failures that typify efforts to bring prosperity to the reservations; together, these two cases suggest that attracting industry and jobs to the reservations is a possible, but difficult and uncertain, strategy for economic development.

Broken Treaties

For many tribes, the treaties signed with the federal government in the 19th century offer another potential resource. These treaties often were violated by white settlers, the military, state and local governments, the BIA, and other elements and agencies of the dominant group, and many tribes are pursuing this trail of broken treaties and seeking compensation for the wrongs of the past. For example, in 1972, the Passamaquoddy and Penobscot tribes filed a lawsuit demanding the return of 12.5 million acres of land—more than half the state of Maine—and $25 billion in damages. The tribes argued that this land had been illegally taken from them more than 150 years earlier. After 8 years of litigation, the tribes settled for a $25 million trust fund and 300,000 acres of land. Although far less than their original demand, the award gave the tribes control over resources that could be used for economic development, job creation, upgrading educational programs, or developing other

programs that would enhance human and financial capital (Worsnop, 1992, p. 391).

Virtually every tribe has similar grievances, and if pursued successfully, the long-dead treaty relationship between the Indian nations and the government could be a significant fount of economic and political resources. Of course, lawsuits require considerable (and expensive) legal expertise and years of effort to bring to fruition. Because there are no guarantees of success, this avenue has some sharp limitations and risks.

Gambling and Other Development Possibilities

Another potential resource for Native Americans is the gambling industry, the development of which was made possible by federal legislation passed in 1988. Currently, more than 144 tribes have gaming establishments (Cornell, Kalt, et al., 1998, p. 12), and the industry has grown nearly 50-fold, from $212 million in revenues in 1988 to nearly $10 billion in 2000 (Spilde, 2001).

The single most profitable Indian gambling operation is the Foxwoods Casino in Connecticut, operated by the Pequot tribe. The casino attracts as many as 35,000 gamblers per day and generates more revenue than the casinos of Atlantic City. The profits from the casino are used to benefit tribal members in a variety of ways, including the repurchase of tribal lands, housing assistance, medical benefits, educational scholarships, and public services, including a tribal police force (Bordewich, 1996, p 110). Other tribes have used gambling profits to purchase restaurants and marinas and to finance the development of outlet malls, aquacultural programs, manufacturing plants, and a wide variety of other businesses and enterprises (Spilde, 2001).

Various tribes have sought other ways to capitalize on their freedom from state regulation and taxes. Some have established small but profitable businesses selling cigarettes tax-free. Because they are not subject to state and federal environmental regulations, some reservations are exploring the possibility of housing nuclear waste and other refuse of industrialization—a somewhat ironic and not altogether attractive use of the remaining Indian lands.

Many individual Native Americans may benefit from a lawsuit brought by Elouise Cobell, a banker and member of the Blackfeet tribe of Montana, against the Department of the Interior. The suit concerns perhaps as much as $10 billion collected by the federal government in leases for the land allocated to individual Native Americans in the 1880s but never dispersed to the legal owners. Cobell's suit represents more than 300,000 descendants of the original owners and, if successful, could result in a significant flow of resources to Native Americans ("A Long Overdue Scalping," 2002).

Clearly, the combination of increased autonomy, treaty rights, natural resources, and gambling means that Native Americans today have an opportunity to dramatically raise their standards of living and creatively take control of their own destinies. For many tribes, however, these assets remain a potential waiting to be actualized (Vinje, 1996). Without denying the success stories such as the Choctaw and the Pequot, we must recognize that the lives of most Native Americans continue to be limited by poverty and powerlessness, prejudice, and discrimination.

COMPARATIVE FOCUS

AUSTRALIAN ABORIGINES AND NATIVE AMERICANS

The history of Native Americans—their conquest and domination by a larger, more powerful society—has a number of parallels from around the globe, a reflection of the rise of European societies to power and their frequent conquests of indigenous societies in Africa, North and South America, and Asia. A comparative analysis of these episodes suggests that similar dynamics have come into play in these situations, even though each has its own unique history. To illustrate, we will use some of the concepts developed in this text to compare the impact of European domination on Australian Aborigines and the indigenous peoples of North America.

Australia came under European domination in the late 1700s, nearly two centuries after the establishment of Jamestown and the beginning of Anglo–Native American relations. In other ways, however, the two contact situations shared many features. In both cases, the colonial power was Great Britain, and first contacts occurred in the preindustrial era (although Britain had begun to industrialize by the late 1700s). In addition, the indigenous peoples of both North America and Australia were thinly spread across vast areas and were greatly inferior to the British in their technological development.

The Aboriginal peoples had lived in Australia for 50,000 years by the time the British arrived. Estimates of their population size vary, but there may have been as many as a million Aborigines at the time of contact with the British ("A Sorry Tale," 2000, p. 12). They were organized into small, nomadic hunting and gathering bands and generally were much less developed than the tribes of North America. They lacked the population base, social organization, and resources that would have permitted sustained resistance to the invasion of their land. There was plenty of violence in the contact situation, but unlike the situation in North America, no sustained military campaigns pitting large armies against each other.

The initial thrust of colonization was motivated by Great Britain's need for a place to send its convicts after losing the Revolutionary

War to the fledgling United States. The European population in Australia grew slowly at first and consisted mostly of prisoners. The early economic enterprises centered on subsistence farming and sheepherding, not large-scale enterprises that required forced labor (at least not on the same scale as the plantations of colonial America).

Relations between the English and the Aborigines were hostile and centered on competition for land. In their ethnocentrism, the invaders denied that the Aborigines had any claims to the land and simply pushed them aside or killed them if they resisted. As in the Americas, European diseases took their toll, and the indigenous population declined rapidly. Because they were not desired as laborers (although many became semi-unfree servants), they were pushed away from the areas of white settlement into the fringes of development, where they and their grievances could be ignored. As in North America, they were seen as "savages," a culture that would (and in the view of the emerging dominant group, should) wither away and disappear.

To the extent that there was contact with the larger society, it was often in the form of coercive acculturation. For example, throughout much of the 20th century, the Australian government, aided by various church organizations, actually removed children of mixed parentage from their Aboriginal mothers and placed them in orphanages. The idea behind this program was to give these children a chance to leave their Aboriginal culture behind, marry whites, and enter the larger society. This policy, not abandoned until the 1960s, resulted in the state-sponsored orphaning of thousands of Aboriginal children. Some of the angriest and most militant members of the current generation of Aborigines belong to this "stolen generation." (For a report on this program, see Australian Human Rights and Equal Opportunity Commission, 1997.)

The contemporary situation of Australian Aborigines has many parallels with that of Native Americans, as does their past. The group is largely rural and continues to live on land that is less desirable. After the initial—and dramatic—declines following first contact with Europeans, their numbers have been increasing of late, partly because of higher birth rates and partly because of changing perceptions, growing sympathy for their plight, and increased willingness of people to claim their Aboriginal heritage. The population fell to a low of less than 100,000 at the start of the 20th century but is now estimated at 427,000, or about 2% of the total population (Australian Bureau of Statistics, 2002).

Just as in North America, there is a huge gap between the indigenous population and the rest of society on every statistic that measures quality of life, equality, and access to resources. Life expectancy for Aborigines is as much as 20 years lower than for the general population, and their infant mortality rate is 2 to 3 times as high. They have much less access to health care, and Aboriginal communities are much more afflicted with alcoholism, suicide, and malnutrition than the general population. Unemployment rates are double the rate in the general population, average income is about 65% of the national average, and only about one third as many Aboriginal people (13.6%) as the national population (34.4%) are in school at age 19 (Brace, 2001; see also the Web site of the Australian Bureau of Statistics at www.abs.gov.au). The issues animating Aboriginal affairs have a familiar ring for anyone familiar with Native Americans. They include concerns for the preservation of Aboriginal culture, language, and identity; self-determination and autonomy; the return of lands illegally taken by the Anglo invaders; and an end to discrimination and unequal treatment.

As in North America, Aboriginal relations are in flux, and the overall picture is mixed. For example, in 1998, the federal government of Australia was condemned by the United Nations Committee on the

Elimination of Racial Discrimination for its handling of Aboriginal land claims. Australia is the only developed nation ever to have received this censure (Pilger, 2000). On the other hand, the opening ceremonies of the 2000 Olympic Games in Sydney featured a celebration of Aboriginal culture, dance, music, and art, and Aboriginal athlete Cathy Freeman lit the Olympic flame.

The Aboriginal peoples of Australia, like Native Americans, face many—often overwhelming—challenges to secure a better future for themselves and for their children. Their history and their present situation clearly validate both the Blauner and Noel hypotheses: They are a colonized minority group, victims of European domination, with all that that status implies.

CONTEMPORARY NATIVE AMERICAN–WHITE RELATIONS

This section uses many of the concepts developed in the first five chapters to analyze the contemporary situation of Native Americans. Compared with other groups, information about Native Americans is scant. Nevertheless, a relatively clear picture of the Indian nations emerges. The portrait that follows stresses many of the themes of this chapter: continued colonization, marginalization, and impoverishment for a large segment of the group; continuing discrimination and exclusion; and the search for a meaningful course between integration and separation.

Prejudice and Discrimination

Anti-Indian prejudice has been a part of American society from the beginning. Historically, negative feelings such as hatred and contempt have been widespread and strong, particularly during the heat of war, and various stereotypes of Indians have been common. One stereotype, especially strong during periods of conflict, depicts Indians as bloodthirsty, ferocious, and inhumanly cruel savages capable of any atrocity. The other image of Native Americans is the image of "the noble redman" who lives in complete harmony with nature and symbolizes goodwill and pristine simplicity (Bordewich, 1996, p. 34). Although the first stereotype tended to fade away as hostilities drew to a close, the latter image retains a good deal of strength in the modern views of Indians found in popular culture and among environmentalist and New Age spiritual organizations.

A variety of studies have documented continued stereotyping of Native Indians in the popular press, textbooks, the media, cartoons, and various other places (for example, see Bird, 1999; Rouse & Hanson, 1991). In the tradition of "the noble redman," Native Americans often are portrayed as bucks and squaws, complete with headdresses, bows, tepees, and other such "generic" Indian artifacts. These portrayals obliterate the diversity of Native American culture and lifestyles. Native Americans often are referred to in the past tense, as if their present situation were of no importance or, worse, as if they no longer existed. Many history books continue to begin the study of American history in Europe or with the "discovery" of America, omitting the millennia of civilization prior to the arrival of European explorers and colonizers. Contemporary portrayals of Native Americans, such as in the movie *Dances With Wolves* (1990), are more sympathetic but still treat the tribes as part of a bucolic past forever lost, not as peoples with real problems in the present.

The persistence of stereotypes and the extent to which they have become enmeshed in modern culture is illustrated by continuing controversies surrounding nicknames for athletic teams (e.g., the Washington Redskins, the Cleveland Indians, and the Atlanta Braves) and the use of Native American mascots, "tomahawk chops," and other practices offensive to many Native Americans. Protests have been staged at some athletic events to increase awareness of these derogatory depictions, but, as was the case so often in the past, the protests have been attacked, ridiculed, or simply ignored. Public opinion polls indicate that the public sees the issue as trivial and regards the protesters as attention-seeking troublemakers (Giago, 1992).

There are relatively few studies of anti-Indian prejudices in the social science literature, and it is therefore difficult to characterize changes over the past several decades. We don't know whether there has been a shift to more symbolic or "modern" forms of anti-Indian racism, as there has been for anti-black prejudice, or if the stereotypes of Native Americans have declined in strength or changed in content.

One of the few records of national anti-Indian prejudice over time are social distance scale scores (see Exhibit 1.4). When the scales were first administered in 1926, Native Americans were ranked in the middle third of all groups (18th out of 28), at about the same level as Southern and Eastern Europeans and slightly above Mexicans, another colonized group. The ranking of Native Americans remained stable until 1977, when there was a noticeable rise in their position relative to other groups. In the 1993 poll, Native Americans dropped in rank relative to other groups but actually had a lower average score compared with 1977. These shifts may reflect a decline in levels of prejudice, a change from more overt forms to more subtle modern racism, or both. Remember, however, that the samples for the social distance research were college students for the most part and do not necessarily reflect trends in the general population (see also Hanson & Rouse, 1987; Smith & Dempsey, 1983).

Research also is unclear about the severity or extent of discrimination against Native Americans. Certainly, the group's lower average levels of education limits their opportunities for upward mobility, choice of occupations, and range of income. This is a form of institutional discrimination in the sense that the opportunities to develop human capital are much less available to Native Americans than to much of the rest of the population. In terms of individual discrimination or more overt forms of exclusion, there is simply too little evidence to sustain clear conclusions (Snipp, 1992, p. 363). The situation of Native American women also is underresearched, but Snipp (1992) reported that like their counterparts in other minority groups and the dominant group, they "are systematically paid less than their male counterparts in similar circumstances" (p. 363).

The very limited evidence available from social distance scales suggests that overt anti-Indian prejudice has declined, perhaps in parallel with anti-black prejudice. A great deal of stereotyping remains, however, and demeaning, condescending, or negative portrayals of Native Americans are common throughout the dominant culture. Institutional discrimination is a major barrier for Native Americans, who have not had equal access to opportunities for education and employment.

Assimilation and Pluralism

Acculturation

Despite more than a century of coercive Americanization, many tribes have been able to preserve large portions of their traditional cultures. For example, many tribal languages continue to be spoken on a daily basis. According to Census Bureau data, 23% of Native Americans speak a language other than English, and of those, about 38% do not speak English "very well" (U.S. Bureau of the Census, 1995). These figures suggest that the tribal language remains the primary tongue for as many as 10% of the group.

Snipp (1989) reported that the strength of native languages varies by region. He found that less than 10% of the Native Americans living along the eastern seaboard are familiar with their native language. In contrast, nearly two thirds of the Native Americans in the mountain states, which include many large reservations, speak their tribal languages at home (Snipp, 1989, p. 176). The greater the extent to which the traditional languages are spoken, the more likely the traditional culture is to survive.

Traditional culture is retained in forms other than language. Religions and value systems, political and economic structures, cuisine, and recreational patterns all have survived the military conquest and the depredations of reservation life; each pattern has been altered, however, by contact with the dominant group. Cornell (1987), for example, argued that although Native Americans have been affected by the "American dream" of material success through hard, honest work, their individual values continue to reflect their greater orientation to the group rather than to the individual.

The tendency to filter the impact of the larger society through the continuing, vital Native American cultures is also illustrated by the Native American Church (NAC). The NAC is an important Native American religion with congregations across the nation (Wax, 1971, pp. 141–144). This religion combines elements from both cultures, and church services freely mix Christian imagery and the Bible with attempts to seek personal visions by using peyote, a hallucinogenic drug. The latter practice is consistent with the spiritual and religious traditions of many tribes.

Native Americans have been considerably more successful than African Americans in preserving their traditional cultures. The differences in the relationship between each minority group and the dominant group help explain this pattern. African Americans were exploited for labor, whereas the competition with Native Americans involved land. African cultures could not easily survive because the social structures that transmitted the cultures and gave them meaning were destroyed by slavery and sacrificed to the exigencies of the plantation economy.

In contrast, Native Americans confronted the dominant group as tribal units, intact and whole. The tribes maintained integrity throughout the wars and throughout the reservation period. Tribal culture was indeed attacked and denigrated during the reservation era, but the basic social unit that sustained the culture survived, albeit in altered form. The fact that Native Americans were placed on separate reservations, isolated from one another and the "contaminating" effects of everyday contact with the larger society, also abetted the preservation of traditional languages and culture (Cornell, 1990).

Indian cultures seem healthy and robust in the current atmosphere of greater tolerance and support for pluralism in the larger society combined with increased autonomy and lower government regulation on the reservations. However, a number of social forces are working against pluralism and the survival of tribal cultures. Pan-tribalism may threaten the integrity of individual tribal cultures even as it successfully represents Native American grievances and concerns to the larger society. Opportunities for jobs, education, and higher incomes draw Native Americans to more developed urban areas and will continue to do so as long as the reservations are underdeveloped. Many aspects of the tribal cultures can be fully expressed and practiced only with other tribal members on the reservations. Thus, many Native Americans must make a choice between "Indian-ness" on the reservation and "success" in the city. The younger, more educated Native Americans will be most likely to confront this choice, and the future vitality of traditional Native American cultures and languages will hinge on which option is chosen.

Secondary Structural Assimilation

This section assesses the degree of integration of Native Americans into the various institutions of public life, following the general outlines of the parallel section in Chapter 5.

Population Size. The changing fortunes of Native Americans are reflected in their population size. In 1492, the group numbered at least 1 million in what is now the continental United States. Some estimates put the Indian population at 2 to 4 million; one estimate is as high as 18 million (Snipp, 1992, p. 354).

Exhibit 6.3   Native American Population, 1900–2000

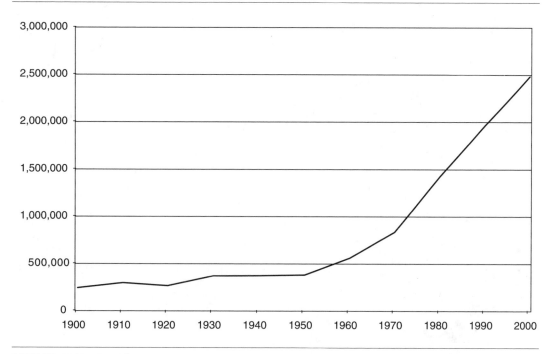

SOURCE: 1900–1990: Thornton (2001, p. 137); 2000: U.S. Bureau of the Census (2000q, Table DP-1).

Losses suffered during the contact period reduced the population to less than 250,000 by 1900, a loss of at least 75%. Since that time, the population generally has increased, dramatically so in recent decades.

Exhibit 6.3 charts the changes in Native American population during the 20th century. The recent population growth is partly due to higher birth rates but mainly reflects changing definitions of race in the larger society and a much greater willingness of people to claim Indian ancestry (Thornton, 2001, p. 137). The 2000 U.S. Census, as you recall, allowed people to classify themselves in more than one racial group. If we included people who choose American Indian as their "second race," the number of identified Indians would increase by over 60%, from 2.5 million to more than 4 million. (U.S. Bureau of the Census, 2000q). These patterns again underscore the basically social nature of race (see Chapter 1).

Residence. Since the Indian Removal Act of 1830 (see Chapter 3), Native Americans have been concentrated in the western two thirds of the nation, as illustrated in Exhibit 6.4, although some pockets of population still can be found in the East. The states with the largest concentrations of Native Americans—California, New Mexico, and Arizona—together include about one third of all Native Americans, and another 10% live in Oklahoma. Native Americans belong to hundreds of different tribes, the 10 largest of which are listed in Exhibit 6.5.

Education. As a result of the combined efforts of missionaries and federal agencies, Native Americans have had a long but not necessarily productive acquaintance with Western education. Until the last few decades, schools for Native Americans focused primarily on Americanizing children, not on educating them. Although the

Exhibit 6.4   Number of People, 2000: One or More Races Including American Indian and Alaska Native

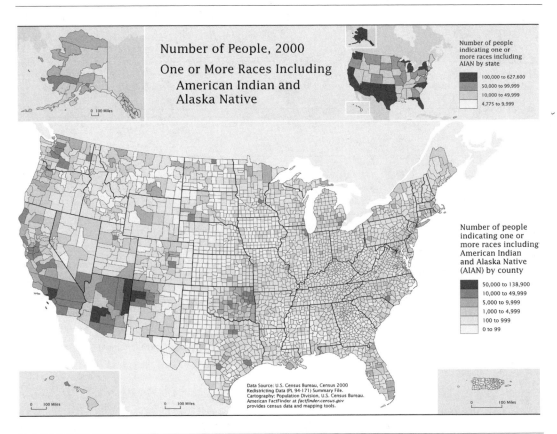

SOURCE: U.S. Bureau of the Census (2000g).

Exhibit 6.5   10 Largest Native American Tribes, 1995

Tribe	Number	Percentage of All Native Americans
Cherokee	369,035	19.0
Navajo	225,298	11.6
Sioux	107,321	5.5
Chippewa	105,988	5.5
Choctaw	86,231	4.5
Pueblo	55,330	2.9
Apache	53,330	2.8
Iroquois	52,557	2.7
Lumbee	50,888	2.6
Creek	45,872	2.4

SOURCE: U.S. Bureau of the Census (1995).

Exhibit 6.6   Educational Attainment of Adults Aged 25–44 for Non-Hispanic Whites and Native Americans

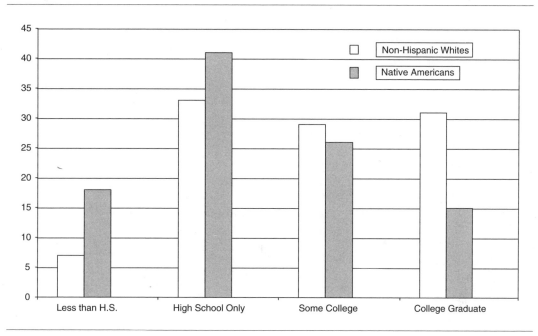

SOURCE: Pollard and O'Hare (1999, p. 32).

percentage of high school graduates has increased dramatically over the past 30 years, levels of education are still lower than for the nation as a whole. In 1997, about 82% of younger American Indians (age 25–44) had graduated from high school, compared with 93% of non-Hispanic whites in the same age group. The number of Native Americans enrolled in college also has increased, and in 1998, 15% of Indians age 25 to 44 had a college degree, still only half the graduation rate for non-Hispanic whites (Pollard & O'Hare, 1999, p. 31). The educational levels of Native Americans are displayed in Exhibit 6.6. The differences in schooling are especially important because the lower levels of educational attainment limit mobility and job opportunities in the postindustrial job market.

One positive development for the education of American Indians is the rapid increase in tribally controlled colleges, more than 30 of which have been built since the 1960s. These institutions are mostly 2-year community colleges located on or near a reservation, and some have been constructed with funds generated in the gaming industry. They are designed to be more sensitive to the educational and cultural needs of the group, and tribal college graduates who transfer to 4-year colleges are more likely to graduate than other American Indian students (Pego, 1998).

Political Power. The ability of Native Americans to exert power as a voting bloc or to otherwise directly influence the political structure is very limited by group size; they are a tiny percentage of the electorate. Furthermore, their lower average levels of education, language differences, and lack of economic resources, along with the factional differences within and between tribes and reservations limit their political power. The number of Native Americans holding elected office is minuscule, far less than 1% (Pollard & O'Hare, 1999, p. 41). In 1992, however, Ben Nighthorse Campbell of Colorado became the first Native American to

Exhibit 6.7   Occupational Distributions of Native Americans and Alaska Natives and White Americans

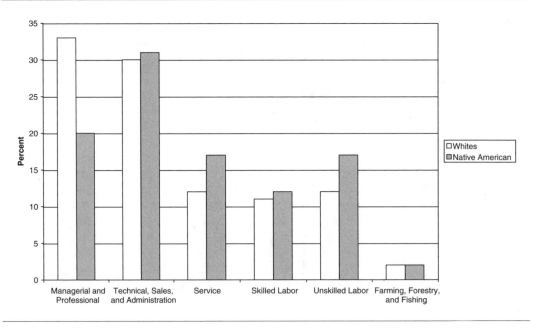

SOURCE: Pollard and O'Hare (1999, p. 33).

be elected to the U.S. Senate, and he continues to hold his seat in 2002. There is currently only one Native American in the House of Representatives (see www.lexis-nexis.com/congcomp).

Jobs and Income. Some of the most severe challenges facing Native Americans relate to work and income. The problems are especially evident on the reservations, where jobs traditionally have been scarce and affluence rare. Like African Americans, the overall unemployment rate for all Native Americans is about double the rate for whites. For Indians living on or near reservations, however, the rate is much higher. It averaged 50% in 1997 (U.S. Bureau of Indian Affairs, 1997) but ranged up to 70% or 80% on the smaller, more isolated reservations.

Nationally, Exhibit 6.7 shows an employment picture with Native Americans underrepresented in the higher-status, more lucrative professions and overrepresented in

unskilled labor and service jobs. As is the case for African Americans, American Indians who hold white-collar jobs are more likely than whites to work in relatively low-level occupations such as typist or retail salesperson (Pollard & O'Hare, 1999, p. 33).

Income data reflect these higher levels of unemployment and lower levels of education. In 1979, median household income for Native Americans was $20,500, 68% of median household income for non-Hispanic whites (O'Hare, 1992, p. 34). By 1997, this figure had risen to $29,200, still only 72% of median household income for non-Hispanic whites (Pollard & O'Hare, 1999, p. 36). In 1969, about one third of all Native American families had incomes below the federal poverty line, and the percentage living in poverty was higher on the reservations (Snipp, 1992, pp. 362–363). By 1997, the percentage had fallen to 25% but was still almost three times the poverty rate for whites (Pollard & O'Hare, 1999, p. 41).

The interlocking forces of past discrimination, lack of development on the reservation, and lower levels of educational attainment have severely limited the range of job opportunities and career possibilities for Native Americans. Over the past 20 years, the situation of the group has improved on many indicators, and as we have seen, there is some promise for the future (e.g., natural resources, treaty rights, gambling). However, the rural isolation of the reservations and their distance from the centers of growth and development limit these possibilities for improvement and raise the likelihood that many reservations will remain the rural counterpart to the urban underclass ghettoes.

Primary Structural Assimilation

Rates of intermarriage for Native Americans are quite high compared with those of other groups. In 1980, only about half of all married Indians were married to other Indians. In contrast, the rate of within-group marriage for whites and blacks was about 99%. The higher rate of marriage outside the group for Native Americans is partly the result of the small size of the group. In New England, which has the lowest relative percentage of Native Americans in any region, less than 10% of Indian marriages are within the group. By contrast, in the mountain states, which have a greater number of Native Americans who are also highly concentrated on reservations, more than 60% of Indian marriages are within the group (Snipp, 1989, pp. 156–159). The higher rate of marriage outside the group is also an indication of the extent of acculturation and integration for Native Americans. Marriages with non-Indians are much more common in metropolitan areas, away from the reservations. They are also associated with higher levels of education, greater participation in the labor force, higher income levels, and lower rates of poverty (Snipp, 1989, pp. 160–164). Thus, marriage with non-Indians is more characteristic for Native Americans who have left the reservation to pursue opportunities for education and career in the cities.

COMPARING MINORITY GROUPS

This chapter focused on Native Americans, but comparing their experiences with other groups will further our understanding of the complexities of dominant-minority relationships and permit us to test the explanatory power of the concepts and theories that are central to this text. No two minority groups have had the same experiences, and our concepts and theories should help us understand the differences and the similarities. At this point, we can compare only Native Americans with African Americans, but we will expand our comparisons as we examine other groups.

First, note the differences in the stereotypes attached to the two groups during the early years of European colonization. While Indians were seen as "cruel savages," African Americans under slavery were seen as lazy, irresponsible, and in constant need of supervision and direction. The two stereotypes are consistent with the outcomes of the contact period. The supposed irresponsibility of blacks under slavery helped justify their subordinate, highly controlled status, while the alleged savagery of Native Americans helped to justify their near extermination by white society.

Second, both Native and African Americans were colonized minority groups, but their contact situations were governed by very different dynamics (competition for labor vs. land) and a very different dominant group agenda (the capture and control of a large, powerless work force vs. the elimination of a military threat). These differing contact situations shaped subsequent relationships with the dominant group and the place of the groups in the larger society.

For example, consider the situations of the two groups a century ago. For African Americans, the most visible enemy was de jure segregation, the elaborate system of repression in the South that controlled them politically, economically, and socially. In particular, the southern system of agriculture needed the black population—but only as a powerless, cheap work force. The goals of African Americans centered on dismantling this oppressive system, assimilation, and equality.

Native Americans, in contrast, were not viewed as a source of labor and were far too few in number and too dispersed geographically to constitute a political threat. Thus, there was little need to control them in the same way African Americans were controlled. The primary enemies of the tribes were the reservation system, various agencies of the federal government (especially the Bureau of Indian Affairs), rural isolation, and the continuing attacks on their traditional cultures and lifestyles, which are typical for a colonized minority group. Native Americans had a different set of problems, different resources at their disposal, and different goals in mind. They have always been more oriented toward a pluralistic relationship with the larger society and preserving what they could of their autonomy, their institutions, and their heritage. While African Americans spent much of the 20th century struggling for inclusion and equality, Native Americans were fighting to maintain or recover their traditional cultures and social structures. This difference in goals reflects the different histories of the two groups and the different circumstances surrounding their colonization.

PROGRESS AND CHALLENGES

What does the future hold for Native Americans? Their situation certainly has changed over the past 100 years, but is it "better" or just "different," as is the case for large segments of the African American community? The answer seems to be a little of both as the group grows in size and becomes even more diversified. To reach some conclusions, we'll look at several aspects of the situation of Native Americans and assess the usefulness of our theoretical models and concepts.

Since the 1960s, the decline of intolerance in the society at large, the growth of pride in ancestry in many groups (e.g., black power), and the shift in federal government policy to encourage self-determination all helped to spark a reaffirmation of commitment to tribal cultures and traditions. As was the case with black Americans and the Black Power movement, the Red Power movement

asserted a distinct and positive Indian identity, a claim for the equal validity of Native American cultures within the broad framework of the larger society. During the same time period, the favorable settlements of treaty claims, the growth in job opportunities, and the gambling industry enhanced the flow of resources and benefits to the reservations. In popular culture, Native Americans have enjoyed a strong upsurge of popularity and sympathetic depictions. This enhanced popularity accounts for much of the growth in population size, as people of mixed ancestry resurrect and reconstruct their Indian ancestors and their own ethnic identity.

Linear or simplistic views of assimilation do not fit very well with the current situation or the past experiences of Native Americans. Some Native Americans are intermarrying with whites and integrating into the larger society; others strive to retain a tribal culture in the midst of an urbanized, industrialized society; while still others labor to use the profits from gaming and other enterprises for the benefit of their tribe as a whole. Members of the group can be found at every degree of acculturation and integration, and the group seems to be moving toward assimilation in some ways and away from it in others.

From the standpoint of the Noel and Blauner hypotheses, we can see that Native Americans have struggled from conquest and colonization, an experience made more difficult by the loss of so much of their land and other resources and by the concerted, unrelenting attacks on their culture and language. The legacy of conquest and colonization was poor health and housing, inadequate education, and slow (or nonexistent) economic development. For most of the 20th century, Native Americans were left to survive as best they could on the margins of the larger society, too powerless to establish meaningful pluralism and too colonized to pursue equality.

Today, the key to further progress for many, if not all, members of this group is economic development on reservation lands and the further strengthening of the tribes as functioning social units. Some tribes do have assets—natural resources, treaty rights, and the gambling industry—that could fuel development. However, they often do not have the expertise or the capital to finance the exploitation of these resources. They must rely, in whole or in part, on non-Indian expertise and white-owned companies and businesses. Thus, non-Indians, rather than the tribes, may be the primary beneficiaries of some forms of development. (This would, of course, be quite consistent with American history.) For those reservations for which gambling is not an option and for those without natural resources, investments in human capital (education) may offer the most compelling direction for future development.

Even though research is scant, it is clear that urban Indians confront the same patterns of discrimination and racism that confront other minority groups of color. Members of the group with lower levels of education and job skills face the prospect of becoming a part of a permanent urban underclass. More educated and skilled Native Americans share with African Americans the prospect of a middle-class lifestyle that is more partial and tenuous than that of comparable segments of the dominant group.

The situation of Native Americans today is superior to the status of the group a century ago. Given the depressed and desperate conditions of the reservations in the early 20th century, however, it wouldn't take much to show an improvement. Native Americans are growing rapidly in numbers and are increasingly diversified by residence, education, and degree of assimilation. Some tribes have made dramatic progress over the past several decades, but enormous problems remain, both on and off the reservations. The challenge for the future, as it was in the past, is to find a course between pluralism and assimilation, pan-tribalism and traditional lifestyles, that will balance the issues of quality of life against the importance of retaining an Indian identity.

MAIN POINTS

- Native American and Anglo-American cultures are vastly different, and these differences have hampered communication and understanding, usually in ways that harmed Native Americans or weakened the integrity of their tribal structures.
- At the beginning of the 20th century, Native Americans faced the paternalistic reservation system, poverty and powerlessness, rural isolation and marginalization, and the BIA. Native Americans continued to lose land and other resources.
- The Indian Reorganization Act (IRA) of 1934 attempted to increase tribal autonomy and to provide mechanisms for improving the quality of life on the reservations. The policy of termination was proposed in the 1950s. The policy was a disaster, and the tribes that were terminated suffered devastating economic losses and drastic declines in quality of life.
- Native Americans began to urbanize rapidly in the 1950s but are still less urbanized than the population as a whole. They are the least urbanized American minority group.
- The Red Power movement rose to prominence in the 1960s and had some successes but often was simply ignored. The Red Power movement was partly assimilationist even while it pursued pluralistic goals and greater autonomy for the tribes.
- Current conflicts between Native Americans and the dominant group center on control of natural resources, preservation of treaty rights, and treaties that were broken in the past. Another possible source of development and conflict lies in the potentially lucrative gambling industry.
- There is some indication that anti-Indian prejudice has shifted to more "modern" forms. Institutional discrimination and access to education and employment remain major problems confronting Native Americans.

- Native Americans have preserved much of their traditional culture, although in altered form. The secondary structural assimilation of Native Americans is low; on many measures of quality of life, they are the most impoverished American minority group. Primary structural assimilation is comparatively high.
- Over the course of the 20th century, Native Americans have struggled from a position of powerlessness and isolation. Today, Native Americans face an array of problems similar to those faced by all American colonized minority groups of color as they try to find ways to raise their quality of life while continuing their commitment to their tribes and an Indian identity.

QUESTIONS FOR REVIEW AND STUDY

1. What were the most important cultural differences between Native American tribes and the dominant society? How did these affect relations between the two groups?
2. Compare and contrast the effects of paternalism and coercive acculturation on Native Americans after the end of the contact period with those of African Americans under slavery. What similarities and differences existed in the two situations? Which system was more oppressive and controlling? How? How did these different situations shape the futures of the groups?
3. How did federal Indian policy change over the course of the 20th century? What effects did these changes have on the tribes? Which were more beneficial? Why? What was the role of the Indian protest movement in shaping these policies?
4. What options do Native Americans have for improving their position in the larger society and developing their reservations? Which strategies seem to have the most promise? Which seem less effective? Why?
5. Compare and contrast the contact situations of Native Americans, African Americans, and Australian Aborigines. What are the most crucial differences in the situations? What implications did these differences have for the development of each group's situation after the initial contact situation?
6. Characterize the present situation of Native Americans in terms of acculturation and integration. How do they compare to African Americans? What factors in the experiences of the two groups might help explain contemporary differences?
7. What gender differences can you identify in the experiences of Native Americans? How do these compare to the gender differences in the experiences of African Americans?
8. Given the information and ideas presented in this chapter, speculate about the future of Native Americans. How likely is it that Native American cultures and languages will survive? What are the prospects for achieving equality? What strategies for development seem most promising?

INTERNET RESEARCH PROJECT

Use the Internet to develop a profile of Native Americans by answering the questions below. Some addresses are provided as starting points, but you will have to use your own initiative to cruise the Internet and answer all questions fully.

A. Numbers

Refer to these Web sites: U.S. Bureau of the Census, www.census.gov; Bureau of Indian Affairs, www.doi.gov/bureau-indian-affairs.html.

1. Counting people who select only one racial category, how many Native Americans are there?
2. How does the number change when people who selected more than one category are counted as members of the group?
3. Which of these two totals (if either) should be regarded as the "true" number of Native Americans? Why?
4. How many separate tribes are recognized by the federal government?
5. How many federal reservations are there? In what regions of the nation are they concentrated? Which is the largest? Which is the smallest?

B. Gambling

Refer to this Web site: National Indian Gaming Association, www.indiangaming.org/.

1. How many reservations are involved in gaming or gambling?
2. What is the approximate annual revenue from these enterprises?
3. How is that revenue used?

C. Health

Refer to this Web site: Indian Health Services, www.ihs.gov.

1. What are the birth rates and death rates for Native Americans?
2. Are these higher or lower than national norms or the rates for white Americans?
3. What are the mortality rates for various age groups compared with national norms?

D. Issues

Refer to this Web site: National Congress of American Indians, www.ncai.org. Also, search for Native American newspapers or periodicals that are on-line. For example, *Indian Country Today*, "America's Leading Indian News Source," is available at www.indiancountry.com.

1. Cite and briefly explain three current issues in *Indian Country Today*.
2. Analyze each issue in terms of the concepts used in the text (especially assimilation, pluralism, self-determination or development of the reservation, institutional discrimination, protest and resistance, and inequality).
3. How would members of other groups (e.g., white or black Americans) view each issue?

FOR FURTHER READING

Amott, Teresa, & Matthaei, Julie. 1991. "I Am the Fire of Time: American Indian Women." In Teresa Amott & Julie Matthaei (Eds.), *Race, Gender, and Work: A Multicultural History of Women in the United States.* Boston: South End.
   A good overview of the history and present situation of Native American women.

Bordewich, Fergus. 1996. *Killing the White Man's Indian.* New York: Doubleday.
   A comprehensive, dispassionate analysis of current problems and future possibilities.

Brown, Dee. 1970. *Bury My Heart at Wounded Knee.* New York: Holt, Rinehart, & Winston.
   A passionately written, highly readable account of the military defeat and the establishment of dominance over Native Americans.

Deloria, Vine. 1995. *Red Earth, White Lies.* New York: Scribner's.

Deloria, Vine. 1970. *We Talk, You Listen.* New York: Macmillan.

Deloria, Vine. 1969. *Custer Died for Your Sins.* New York: Macmillan.
   The major works of the well-known Native American activist, writer, and professor of Indian studies.

Nabakov, Peter (Ed.). 1999. *Native American Testimony.* (Rev. ed.) New York: Penguin.
   A collection of personal accounts by Native Americans from pre-Columbian times to the present day.

Snipp, C. Matthew. 1989. *American Indians: The First of This Land.* New York: Russell Sage.
   A valuable scholarly study covering a variety of aspects of the Native American condition.

Wax, Murray. 1971. *Indian Americans: Unity and Diversity.* Englewood Cliffs, NJ: Prentice Hall.
   A leading authority's view of the history and contemporary situation of Native Americans.

7

Hispanic Americans
Colonization, Immigration, and Ethnic Enclaves

The United States is home to many different Spanish-origin groups. Before the Declaration of Independence was signed, before slavery began, even before Jamestown was founded, the ancestors of some of these groups were already in North America. Other Hispanic groups are recent immigrants and new members of U.S. society. The label *Hispanic American* includes a number of groups that are diverse and distinct from each other. The members of these groups connect themselves to a diversity of traditions; like the larger society, they are dynamic and changeable, unfinished and evolving. Hispanic Americans share a language and some cultural traits but do not generally think of themselves as a single social entity. Many identify with their national-origin groups (e.g., Mexican American) rather than broader, more encompassing labels, and politically, the group has not acted as a united voting bloc (Camarillo & Bonilla, 2001, p. 119).

In this chapter, we look at the development of Hispanic American groups over the past century, examine their contemporary relations with the larger society, and assess their current status. We focus on the three largest Hispanic groups—Mexican Americans, Puerto Ricans, and Cuban Americans—but immigrants from Latin America and the Caribbean also are discussed.

Exhibit 7.1 shows the sizes of the Latino groups and some information on growth since 1980. Although Mexican Americans are more than 7% of the total U.S. population (and 58%

Exhibit 7.1   Size and Recent Growth of Hispanic American Groups

Group	1980	1990	2000	Increase in Population, 1980–2000	Percentage of Total U.S. Population, 2000
Mexican Americans	8,740,000	13,496,000	20,640,000	236%	7.3%
Puerto Ricans[a]	2,014,000	2,728,000	3,406,000	169%	1.2%
Cuban Americans	803,000	1,044,000	1,242,000	155%	0.4%
Other Hispanics[b]	3,051,000	5,086,000	10,017,000	328%	3.6%
Total population	226,546,000	248,710,000	281,422,000	124%	

SOURCE: 1980 and 1990: del Pinal and Singer (1997, p. 13); 2000: U.S. Bureau of the Census (2002, p. 24).

a. Living on U.S. mainland only.

b. Includes people from the Dominican Republic, El Salvador, Colombia, Peru, and many other nations.

of all Hispanic Americans), the other groups are small in size. Considered as a single group, however, Hispanic Americans are 12.5% of the total population, and they became the largest U.S. minority group, surpassing African Americans, in the spring of 2001.

The Latino population is growing rapidly, partly because of Latinos' relatively high birth rates but mainly because of immigration. The Mexican American population increased in size by 236% between 1980 and 2000, and all Hispanic groups are growing at rates above the national average. The growth is projected to continue well into the century. Clearly, Hispanic Americans will become an increasingly important part of American life and culture. Today, about 1 out of every 8 Americans is Hispanic, but by 2050, this ratio will increase to 1 out of every 4 (see Exhibit 1.1).

It is appropriate to discuss Hispanic Americans at this point because they include both colonized and immigrant groups, and in that sense, they combine elements of the polar extremes of Blauner's typology of minority groups. We would expect that the Hispanic groups that have been more colonized in the past would have much in common with African and Native Americans today. Hispanic groups whose experiences more closely model those of immigrants would have different characteristics and follow different pathways of adaptation. We test these ideas by reviewing the histories of the groups and by analyzing

their current status and degree of acculturation and integration.

Two additional introductory comments can be made about Hispanic Americans.

• Hispanic Americans are partly an ethnic minority group (i.e., identified by cultural characteristics such as language) and partly a racial minority group (identified by their physical appearance). Latinos bring a variety of racial backgrounds to U.S. society. For example, most Mexican Americans combine European and Native American ancestry and are identifiable by their physical traits as well as by their cultural and linguistic characteristics. Puerto Ricans, in contrast, are a mixture of white and black ancestry. The original inhabitants of the island, the Arawak and Caribe tribes, were decimated by the Spanish conquest, and the proportion of Native American ancestry is much smaller for Puerto Ricans than for Mexicans. Africans were first brought to the island as slaves, and there has been considerable intermarriage between whites and blacks. The Puerto Rican population today varies greatly in its racial characteristics, combining every conceivable combination of Caucasian and African ancestry. Hispanic Americans are often the victims of racial discrimination in the United States. Racial differences often (but not always) overlap with the cultural distinctions and reinforce the separation of Hispanic Americans from

Anglo-American society. Even members of the group who are completely acculturated may still experience discrimination based on their physical appearance.

- As is the case with most American minority groups, labels and group names are important. The term *Hispanic American* is widely applied to this group and might seem neutral and inoffensive to non-Hispanics. In fact, a recent survey shows that a sizable majority (67%) of the group prefer this label to *Latino* (Jones, 2001). However, depending on context, the term can have negative meanings and controversial connotations. For one thing, this label is similar to *American Indian* in that it was invented and applied by the dominant group and may reinforce the mistaken perception that all Spanish-speaking peoples are the same. Also, the term *Hispanic* highlights Spanish heritage and language but does not acknowledge the roots of these groups in African and Native American civilizations. On the other hand, the "Latino"[1] label stresses the common origins of these groups in Latin America and the fact that each culture is a unique blend of diverse traditions. In this chapter, "Latino" and "Hispanic" are used interchangeably.

MEXICAN AMERICANS

We applied the Noel and Blauner hypotheses to this group in Chapter 3. Mexicans were conquered and colonized in the 19th century and used as a cheap labor force in agriculture, ranching, mining, railroad construction, and other areas of the dominant group economy in the Southwest. In the competition for control of land and labor, they became a minority group, and the contact situation left them with few power resources with which to pursue their self-interest.

By the dawn of the 20th century, the situation of Mexican Americans resembled that of Native Americans in some ways. Both groups were small, numbering about one half of 1% of the total population (Cortes, 1980, p. 702). Both differed from the dominant group in culture and language, and both were impoverished, relatively powerless, and isolated in rural areas distant from the centers of industrialization and modernization. In other ways, Mexican Americans resembled African Americans in the South. Both groups supplied much of the labor power for the agricultural economy in their respective regions, and both were limited to low-paying occupations and a subordinate status in the social structure. All three groups were colonized and, at least in the early decades of the 20th century, lacked the resources to end their exploitation and protect their cultural heritages from continual attack by the dominant society (Mirandé, 1985, p. 32).

There were also some important differences between the situations of Mexican Americans and the other two colonized minority groups. Perhaps the most crucial difference was the proximity of the sovereign nation of Mexico. Population movement across the border was constant, and Mexican culture and the Spanish language were continually rejuvenated, even as they were attacked and disparaged by Anglo-American society.

Cultural Patterns

Mexican American and Anglo-American cultures differ in many ways besides language differences. Whereas the dominant society is largely Protestant, the overwhelming majority of Mexican Americans are Catholic, and the Church remains one of the most important institutions in any Mexican American community. Religious practices also vary: Mexican Americans (especially the men) are relatively inactive in church attendance, preferring to express their spiritual concerns in more spontaneous, less routinized ways.

In the past, everyday life among Mexican Americans often was described in terms of the "culture of poverty" (see Chapter 5), an idea originally based on research in several different Hispanic communities (see Lewis, 1959, 1965, 1966). This perspective asserts that Mexican Americans suffer from an unhealthy value system that includes a weak work ethic, fatalism, and other negative attitudes. Today, this characterization is widely regarded as exaggerated or simply mistaken. More recent research shows that the traits associated with the culture of poverty tend to characterize people who are poor and uneducated, rather than any particular racial or ethnic group. In fact, a number of studies show that there is little difference between the value systems of Mexican Americans and other Americans of similar length of residence in the United States, social class, and educational backgrounds (e.g., see Buriel, 1993; Moore & Pinderhughes, 1993; Valentine & Mosley, 2000).

Another area of cultural difference involves *machismo*, a value system that stresses male dominance, honor, virility, and violence. The stereotypes of the dominant group exaggerate the negative aspects of machismo and often fail to recognize that machismo also can be expressed through being a good provider or a respected father, and in other nondestructive ways. In fact, the concern for male dignity is not unique to Hispanics and can be found in varying strengths and expressions in many cultures, including Anglo-American. Thus, this difference is one of degree rather than kind (Moore & Pachon, 1985).

Compared with Anglo-Americans, Mexican Americans tend to place more value on family relations and obligations. Strong family ties can be the basis for support networks and cooperative efforts but also can conflict with the emphasis on individualism and individual success in the dominant culture. For example, strong family ties may inhibit geographical mobility and people's willingness to pursue educational and occupational opportunities distant from their home communities (Moore, 1970, p. 127).

These cultural and language differences have inhibited communication with the dominant group and have served as the basis for excluding Mexican Americans from the larger society. However, they also have provided a basis for group cohesion and unity that has sustained common action and protest activity.

Immigration

Although Mexican Americans originated as a colonized minority group, their situation since the early 1900s (and especially since the 1960s) has been largely shaped by immigration. The numbers of legal border crossings from Mexico to the United States are shown in Exhibit 7.2.[2] The fluctuations in the rate of immigration can be explained by conditions in Mexico; the varying demand for labor in the low-paying, unskilled sector of the U.S. economy; and changes in federal immigration policy. As you will see, competition, one of the key variables in Noel's hypothesis, has shaped the relationships between Mexican immigrants and the larger American society.

Leaving Mexico

Since the early 1900s, a variety of events in Mexico have motivated people to immigrate. The Mexican Revolution began in 1910, and the resulting political turmoil and instability created a strong "push" to the North. Mexico also began to industrialize at about this time, and its rural population was displaced by the mechanization of agriculture. Over the course of the 20th century, the population of Mexico has grown, and unemployment frequently has been widespread (Cortes, 1980, p. 702; Moore, 1970, pp. 39–41). In recent years, the rising levels of immigration have been sustained by the strong demand for cheap labor in the United States and the continuing wage gap between the two nations that makes even menial work in the North attractive.

Fluctuating Demand for Labor and Federal Immigration Policy

For the last century, Mexico has served as a reserve pool of cheap labor for the benefit of U.S. businesses, agricultural interests, and other groups, and the volume of immigration reflects changing economic conditions in the United States. By and large, the policies of the federal government have responded to these conditions and have encouraged immigration

Exhibit 7.2   Legal Immigration From Mexico

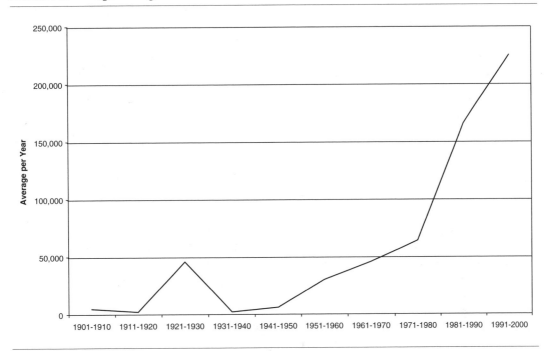

SOURCE: U.S. Immigration and Naturalization Service (2002, pp. 16-21).

NOTE: Numbers are average per year for each decade.

during good times and clamped down during hard times.

In the earliest decades of the 20th century, movement across the southern border was informal and largely unrestricted (Grebler, Moore, & Guzman, 1970, p. 63). In the 1910s and 1920s, the demand for cheap labor from Mexico increased because World War I and restrictive immigration legislation reduced or eliminated the flow of labor from Europe and Asia. Whereas employers in the East recruited African American workers from the South to solve the labor shortages, those in the West, the Southwest, and even the Midwest turned to Mexico. During this time, Mexicans were not only encouraged to immigrate, they were actively recruited by U.S. employers.

When hard times came to the United States (and the world) during the Great Depression of the 1930s, demand for labor decreased, the flow of immigration slowed, recruiting stopped, and Mexicans in the United States returned home, sometimes voluntarily but often by force. As unemployment rates soared and competition for jobs increased, efforts began to expel Mexican laborers, just as the Noel hypothesis would predict. The federal government instituted a *repatriation* campaign aimed specifically at deporting illegal Mexican immigrants. In many localities, repatriation was pursued with great zeal, and the campaign intimidated many legal immigrants and native-born Mexican Americans into moving to Mexico. The result was that the Mexican American population of the United States declined by an estimated 40% during the 1930s (Cortes, 1980, p. 711).

When the depression ended and U.S. society began to mobilize for World War II, federal policy toward immigrants from Mexico changed once more as employers again turned to Mexico for workers. In 1942, a formal program was initiated to bring in contract laborers. Called the *bracero* ("laborer") *program*, the policy permitted contract laborers—usually employed in agriculture or as unskilled laborers in other areas—to work in the United States for a limited amount of time. When their contracts expired, the workers were required to return to Mexico.

The bracero program continued for several decades after the end of the war and was a crucial source of labor for the American economy. In 1960 alone, braceros supplied 26% of the nation's seasonal farm labor (Cortes, 1980, p. 703). The program generated millions of dollars of profit for growers and other employers by paying braceros much less than American workers would have received (Amott & Matthaei, 1991, pp. 79–80).

At the same time that the bracero program permitted immigration from Mexico, other programs and agencies worked to deport undocumented (or illegal) immigrants, large numbers of whom entered the United States with the braceros. Government efforts reached a peak in the early 1950s with the insultingly named "Operation Wetback," a program under which federal authorities deported almost 4 million Mexicans (Grebler et al., 1970, p. 521).

During Operation Wetback, raids on the homes and places of business of Mexican Americans were common, and authorities often ignored their civil and legal rights. In an untold number of cases, U.S. citizens of Mexican descent were deported along with illegal immigrants. These violations of civil and legal rights have been a continuing grievance of Mexican Americans (and other Latinos) for decades (Mirandé, 1985, pp. 70–90).

In 1965, a new U.S. immigration policy came into effect that gave a high priority to immigrants who were family and kin of U.S. citizens (Bouvier & Gardner, 1986, pp. 13–15; Rumbaut, 1991, p. 215). Immigrants have always tended to move along chains of kinship and other social relationships, and the new policy reinforced those tendencies. The social networks connecting Latin America with the United States expanded, and the rate of immigration from Mexico increased sharply after 1965 (see Exhibit 7.2).

Most of these more recent Mexican immigrants, legal as well as undocumented, continue the pattern of seeking work in the low-wage, unskilled sectors of the labor market in the cities and fields of the Southwest. For many, work is seasonal or temporary. When the work ends, they often return to Mexico, commuting across the border as has been done for decades (for estimates of the circular nature of Mexican immigration, see Massey & Singer, 1995).

In 1986, Congress attempted to deal with illegal immigrants, most of whom were thought to be Mexican, by passing the Immigration Reform and Control Act (IRCA). This legislation allowed illegal immigrants who had been in the country continuously since 1982 to legalize their status. According to the U.S. Immigration and Naturalization Service (1993, p. 17), about 3 million people, 75% of them Mexican, have taken advantage of this provision, but this program has not slowed the volume of illegal immigration. In 1988, at the end of the amnesty application period, there were still almost 3 million undocumented immigrants in the United States, and this number grew to an estimated 5 million in 1996 (del Pinal & Singer, 1997, pp. 20, 22). In 2001, the number may have been as high as 8 million (Cohn, 2001), and perhaps as many as half of these illegal immigrants are from Mexico.

Immigration, Colonization, and Intergroup Competition

Three points can be made about Mexican immigration to the United States. First, the flow of population from Mexico was and is stimulated and sustained by powerful political and economic interests in the United States. Systems of recruitment and networks of communication and transportation have been established to routinize the flow of people and make it a predictable source of labor for the benefit of U.S. agribusiness and other employers. The flow of people back and forth across the border was well established long before current efforts to regulate and control that movement. Depending on U.S. policy, this immigration is sometimes legal and encouraged and sometimes illegal and discouraged. Regardless of the label, the river of people has been flowing steadily for decades in response to opportunities for work in the North (Portes, 1990, pp. 160–163).

Second, Mexican immigrants entered a social system in which a colonized status for the group already had been established. The paternalistic traditions and racist systems that were established in the 19th century shaped the positions that were open to Mexican immigrants in the 20th century. Mexican Americans continued to be treated as a colonized group despite the streams of new arrivals, and the history of the group in the 20th century has many parallels with African Americans and Native Americans. Thus, Mexican Americans might be thought of as a colonized minority group that happens to have a large number of immigrants or, alternately, as an immigrant group that incorporates a strong tradition of colonization.

Third, this brief review of the twisting history of U.S. policy on Mexican immigration should serve as a reminder that levels of prejudice, racism, and discrimination tend to fluctuate with the dominant group's sense of threat. The very qualities that make Mexican labor attractive to employers have caused bitter resentment among those segments of the Anglo population who feel that their own jobs and financial security are threatened. Often caught in the middle, Mexican immigrants and Mexican Americans have not had the resources to avoid exploitation by employers or rejection and discrimination by others. The ebb and flow of the efforts to regulate the flow of immigration can be understood in terms of competition, differentials in power, and prejudice.

Developments in the United States

While the flow of immigration from Mexico fluctuated with the need for labor, Mexican Americans struggled to improve their status. In the early decades of the 20th century, like other colonized minority groups, they faced a system of repression and control in which they were accorded few rights and had little political power.

Continuing Colonization

Throughout much of the 20th century, Mexican Americans have been limited to the less desirable, low-wage jobs. Split labor markets, in which Mexican Americans are paid less for the same jobs than are Anglos, have been common. The workforce often has been further split by gender, with Mexican American women assigned to the worst jobs and receiving the lowest wages in both urban and rural areas (Takaki, 1993, pp. 318–319).

Men's jobs often took them away from their families to work in the mines and fields. In 1930, 45% of all Mexican American men worked in agriculture, and another 28% in unskilled nonagricultural jobs (Cortes, 1980, p. 708). The women often were forced by economic necessity to enter the job market; in 1930, they were concentrated in farm work (21%), unskilled manufacturing jobs (25%), and domestic and other service work (37%) (Amott & Matthaei, 1991, pp. 76–77). They typically were paid less than both Mexican American men and Anglo women. In addition to their job responsibilities, Mexican American women had to maintain their households and raise their children, often facing these tasks without a spouse (Zinn & Eitzen, 1990, p. 84).

As the United States industrialized and urbanized during the 20th century, employment patterns became more diversified. Mexican Americans found work in manufacturing, construction, transportation, and other sectors of the economy. Some Mexican Americans, especially those of the third generation or later, moved into middle- and upper-level occupations, and some began to move out of the Southwest. Still, Mexican Americans in all regions (especially recent immigrants) tended to be concentrated at the bottom of the occupational ladder. Women increasingly worked outside the home, but their employment was limited largely to agriculture, domestic service, and the garment industry (Amott & Matthaei, 1991, pp. 76–79; Cortes, 1980, p. 708).

Like African Americans in the segregated South, Mexican Americans were excluded from the institutions of the larger society by law and by custom for much of the 20th century. There were separate (and unequal) school systems for Mexican American children, and in many communities, Mexican Americans were disenfranchised and accorded few legal or civil rights. There were "whites-only" primary elections modeled after the Jim Crow system, and residential segregation was widespread. The police and the court system generally abetted or ignored the rampant discrimination against the Mexican American community. Discrimination in the criminal justice system and civil rights violations were continual grievances of Mexican Americans throughout the century.

Protest and Resistance

Like all minority groups, Mexican Americans have attempted to improve their collective position whenever possible. The beginnings of organized resistance and protest stretch back to the original contact period in the 19th century, when protest usually was organized on a local level. Regional and national organizations made their appearance in the 20th century (Cortes, 1980, p. 709).

As with African Americans, the early protest organizations were integrationist and reflected the assimilationist values of the larger society. For example, one of the earlier and more significant groups was the League of United Latin American Citizens (LULAC), founded in Texas in 1929. LULAC promoted Americanization and greater educational opportunities for Mexican Americans. The group also worked to expand civil and political rights and to fight for equality for Mexican Americans. LULAC fought numerous court battles against discrimination and racial segregation (Moore, 1970, pp. 143–145).

As the 20th century progressed, the number and variety of groups pursuing the Mexican American cause increased. During World War II, Mexican Americans served in the armed forces, and, as with other minority groups, this experience increased their impatience with the constraints on their freedoms and opportunities. After the war ended, a number of new Mexican American organizations were founded, including the Community Service Organization in Los Angeles and the American GI Forum in Texas. Compared with older organizations such as LULAC, the new groups were less concerned with assimilation per se, addressed a broad range of community problems, and attempted to increase Mexican American political power (Grebler et al., 1970, pp. 543–545).

Chicanismo

The 1960s were a time of intense activism and militancy for Mexican Americans. A protest movement guided by an ideology called *Chicanismo* began at about the same time as the Black Power and Red Power movements. Chicanismo encompassed a variety of organizations and ideas, united by a heightened militancy and impatience with the racism of the larger society and by strongly stated demands for justice, fairness, and equal rights. The movement questioned the value of assimilation and sought to increase awareness of the continuing exploitation of Mexican Americans; it adapted many of the tactics and strategies (marches, rallies, voter registration drives, etc.) of the Civil Rights movement of the 1960s.

Chicanismo is similar in some ways to the black power ideology (see Chapter 5). It is partly a reaction to the failure of U.S. society to implement the promises of integration and equality. It rejected traditional stereotypes of Mexican Americans, proclaimed a powerful and positive group image and heritage, and analyzed the group's past and present situation in American society in terms of victimization, continuing exploitation, and institutional discrimination. The inequalities that separated Mexican Americans and the larger society were seen as the result of deep-rooted, continuing racism and the cumulative effects of decades of exclusion. According to Chicanismo, the solution to these problems lay in group empowerment, increased militancy, and group pride, not in assimilation to a culture that had rationalized and abetted the exploitation of Mexican Americans (Acuna, 1988, pp. 307–358;

Grebler et al., 1970, p. 544; Moore, 1970, pp. 149–154).

Some of the central thrusts of the 1960s protest movement are captured in the widespread adoption of *Chicano*, which had been a derogatory term, as the group name for Mexican Americans. Other minority groups underwent similar name changes at about the same time. For example, African Americans shifted from *Negro* to *black* as a group designation. These name changes were not merely cosmetic; they marked fundamental shifts in group goals and desired relationships with the larger society. The new names came from the minority groups themselves, not from the dominant group, and they expressed the pluralistic themes of group pride, self-determination, militancy, and increased resistance to exploitation and discrimination.

The Chicano movement saw the rise of new groups and leaders that reflected this new sense of militancy and adopted more confrontational tactics. Some examples include the *Alianza de Mercedes* (Alliance of Land Grants), founded by Reies Lopez Tijerina, which attempted to correct the illegal seizure of land from Mexicans during the 19th century; the Crusade for Justice, led by Rodolfo Gonzalez, which focused on abuses of Mexican American civil and legal rights; and *La Raza Unida* (the People United) party, led by Jose Angel Gutierrez, which tried to mobilize Mexican American political power, particularly at the local level.

Without a doubt, however, the best-known Chicano leader of the 1960s and 1970s was the late Cesar Chávez, who organized the United Farm Workers (UFW), the first union to successfully represent migrant workers. Chávez was primarily a labor leader, and he organized African Americans, Filipinos, and Anglo-Americans as well as Mexican Americans. Migrant farm workers have few economic or political resources, and many are undocumented immigrants. As a group, farm workers were nearly invisible in the social landscape of the United States in the 1960s, and organizing this group was a demanding task.

Like Dr. Martin Luther King Jr., Chávez was a disciple of Gandhi and a student of nonviolent direct protest (see Chapter 5). His best-known campaign was a grape pickers' strike and a national grape boycott that began in 1965. The boycott lasted 5 years and ended when the growers recognized the UFW as the legitimate representative for farm workers. Chávez and his organization achieved a major victory, and the agreement provided for significant improvements in the situation of the workers. (For a biography of Chávez, see Levy, 1975.)

Gender and the Chicano Protest Movement

Mexican American women were heavily involved in the Chicano protest movement. For example, Jessie Lopez and Dolores Huerta were central figures in the movement to organize farm workers and worked closely with Cesar Chávez. However, as was the case for African American women, Chicanas encountered sexism and gender discrimination within the movement, particularly when they tried to assume leadership roles (Amott & Mattaei, 1991, p. 83).

Despite these difficulties, Chicanas contributed to the movement in a variety of areas. They helped to organize poor communities and worked for welfare reform. Continuing issues include domestic violence, child care, the criminal victimization of women, and the racial and gender oppression that limits women of all minority groups (Amott & Matthaei, 1991, pp. 82–86; see also Mirandé & Enríquez, 1979, pp. 202–243).

Mexican Americans and Other Minority Groups

Like the Black Power and Red Power movements, Chicanismo began to fade from public view in the 1970s and 1980s. The movement could claim some successes, but perhaps the clearest victory was in raising awareness in the larger society about the grievances and problems of Mexican Americans. Today, many Chicanos continue to face poverty, powerlessness, and continuing exploitation as a cheap agricultural labor force. The less educated, urbanized segments of the group share the prospect of becoming a permanent urban underclass with other minority groups of color.

Like African Americans, the group has been systematically excluded from the institutions of the larger society. Continuing immigration from Mexico has increased the size of the group, but these immigrants bring few resources with them that could be directly or immediately translated into economic or political power in the United States.

Unlike immigrants from Europe, who settled in the urban centers of the industrializing East Coast, Mexican Americans tended to work and live in rural areas distant from and marginal to the urban centers of industrialization and opportunities for education, skill development, and upward mobility. They were a vitally important source of labor in agriculture and other segments of the economy but only to the extent that they were exploitable and powerless. As Chicanos moved to the cities, they continued to serve as a colonized, exploited labor force concentrated at the lower end of the stratification system. Thus, the handicaps created by discrimination in the past were reinforced by continuing discrimination and exploitation in the present, perpetuating the cycles of poverty and powerlessness.

At the same time, however, the flow of immigration and the constant movement of people back and forth across the border kept Mexican culture and the Spanish language alive. Unlike African Americans under slavery, Chicanos were not cut off from their homeland and native culture. Mexican American culture was attacked and disparaged, but it was not destroyed to the same extent as African culture.

Clearly, the traditional model of assimilation does not describe the experiences of Mexican Americans very well. They have experienced less social mobility than European immigrant groups and have maintained their traditional culture and language more completely. Although many Mexican Americans have acculturated and integrated, a large segment of the group continues to fill the same economic role as their ancestors: an unskilled labor force for the development of the Southwest, augmented with "immigrants" from Mexico at the convenience of U.S. employers. For the less educated and for recent immigrants, cultural and racial differences combine to increase their social visibility, mark them for exploitation, and rationalize their continuing exclusion from the larger society.

PUERTO RICANS

Puerto Rico became a territory of the United States after the defeat of Spain in the Spanish-American War of 1898. The island was small and impoverished, and it was difficult for Puerto Ricans to avoid domination by the United States. Thus, the initial contact between Puerto Ricans and U.S. society was made in an atmosphere of war and conquest. By the time Puerto Ricans began to migrate to the mainland in large numbers, their relationship to U.S. society was largely that of a colonized minority group, and they generally retained that status on the mainland.

Migration (Push and Pull) and Employment

At the time of initial contact, the population of Puerto Rico was overwhelmingly rural and supported itself by subsistence farming and by exporting coffee and sugar. Early in the 20th century, U.S. firms began to invest in and develop the island economy, especially the sugarcane industry. These agricultural endeavors took more and more of the land. Opportunities for economic survival in the rural areas declined, and many peasants were forced to move into the cities (Portes, 1990, p. 163).

Movement to the mainland began gradually and increased slowly until the 1940s. In 1900, there were about 2,000 Puerto Ricans living on the mainland. By the eve of World War II, this number had grown to only 70,000, a tiny fraction of the total population. Then, during the 1940s, the number of Puerto Ricans on the mainland increased more than fourfold to 300,000, and during the 1950s, it nearly tripled, to 887,000 (U.S. Commission on Civil Rights, 1976, p. 19).

This massive and sudden population growth was the result of a combination of circumstances. First, Puerto Ricans became citizens of the United States in 1917, so their movements were not impeded by international boundaries or immigration restrictions. Second, unemployment was a major problem on the island. The sugarcane industry continued to displace the rural population, urban unemployment was high, and the population continued to grow. By the 1940s, a considerable number of Puerto Ricans were available to seek work off the island and, like Chicanos, could serve as a cheap labor supply for U.S. employers.

Third, Puerto Ricans were "pulled" to the mainland by the same labor shortages that attracted Mexican immigrants during and after World War II. Whereas the latter responded to job opportunities in the West and Southwest, Puerto Ricans moved to the Northeast. The job profiles of these two groups were similar; both were concentrated in the low-wage, unskilled sector of the job market. However, the Puerto Rican migration began many decades after the Mexican migration, at a time when the United States was much more industrialized and urbanized. As a result, Puerto Ricans have been more concentrated in urban labor markets than Mexican immigrants (Portes, 1990, p. 164).

Economics and jobs were at the heart of the move to the mainland. The rate of Puerto Rican migration has followed the cycle of boom and bust, just as it has for Mexican immigrants. The 1950s, the peak decade for Puerto Rican migration, was a period of rapid U.S. economic growth. Migration was encouraged, and job recruiters traveled to the island to attract workers. By the 1960s, however, the supply of jobs on the island had expanded appreciably, and the average number of migrants declined from the peak of 41,000 per year in the 1950s to about 20,000 per year. In the 1970s, the U.S. economy faltered, unemployment grew, and the flow of Puerto Rican migration actually reversed itself, with the number of returnees exceeding the number of migrants in various years (U.S. Commission on Civil Rights, 1976, p. 25). The migrations

continue, and about 3.4 million Puerto Ricans, or about 44% of all Puerto Ricans, lived on the mainland in 2000.

As the U.S. economy expanded and migration accelerated after World War II, Puerto Ricans moved into a broad range of jobs and locations in society, and the group grew more economically diversified and more regionally dispersed. Still, the bulk of the group remains concentrated in lower-status jobs. Puerto Rican men often have found work as unskilled factory laborers or in the service sector, particularly in areas where English language facility was not necessary (e.g., janitorial work). The women often have been employed as domestics or seamstresses for the garment industry (Portes, 1990, p. 164).

Transitions

Although Puerto Ricans are not "immigrants," the move to the mainland does involve a change in culture and language (Fitzpatrick, 1980, p. 858). Despite nearly a century of political affiliation, Puerto Rican and Anglo cultures differ along many dimensions, including religious practices, cuisine, and family values (Fitzpatrick, 1987, pp. 117–138).

A particularly unsettling cultural difference between the island and the mainland involves skin color and perceptions of race. Puerto Rico has a long history of racial intermarriage. Slavery was less monolithic and total, and the island had no periods of systematic, race-based segregation like the Jim Crow system. Thus, although skin color prejudice still exists in Puerto Rico, it was never as categorical as on the mainland. On the island, race is perceived as a continuum of possibilities and combinations, not as a simple dichotomous split between white and black. Furthermore, in Puerto Rico, factors such as social class are considered to be more important than race as criteria for judging and classifying others. In fact, social class can affect perceptions of skin color, and regardless of actual color, people of higher status might be seen as "whiter" than those of lower status. Coming from this background, Puerto Ricans find the rigid racial thinking of U.S. culture disconcerting and even threatening (Rodriguez, 1989, pp. 60–61; see also Landale & Oropesa, 2002; Rodriguez & Cordero-Guzman, 1992).

In the racially dichotomized U.S. culture, many Puerto Ricans feel they have no clear place. They are genuinely puzzled when they first encounter prejudice and discrimination based on skin color and are uncertain about their own identity and self-image. The racial perceptions of the dominant culture can be threatening to Puerto Ricans to the extent that they are victimized by the same web of discrimination and disadvantage that affects African Americans. Combined with cultural and linguistic differences, traditional American racial prejudice can sharply limit opportunities and mobility for the group.

Puerto Ricans and Other Minority Groups

Puerto Ricans migrated primarily to the urban Northeast, but they arrived long after the great wave of European immigrants and several decades after African Americans began migrating from the South. They have often competed with these and other minority groups for housing, jobs, and other resources. A pattern of *ethnic succession* can be seen in some neighborhoods and occupational areas in which Puerto Ricans have replaced other groups that have moved out (and sometimes up).

Because of their more recent arrival, Puerto Ricans on the mainland were not subjected to repressive paternalistic or rigid competitive systems of race relations like slavery or Jim Crow. Instead, the subordinate status of the group is manifested in their occupational, residential, and educational profiles and by the institutionalized barriers to upward mobility that they face. Puerto Ricans share many problems with other urban minority groups of color, among them poverty, failing educational systems, and crime. Like African Americans, their fate depends on the future of the American city, and a large segment of the group is in danger of becoming part of a permanent urban underclass.

Like Mexican Americans, Puerto Ricans on the mainland combine elements of both an immigrant and a colonized minority experience. The movement to the mainland is voluntary in some ways, but in others, it is strongly motivated by the transformations in the island economy that resulted from modernization and U.S. domination. Like Chicanos, Puerto Ricans tend to enter the labor force at the bottom of the occupational structure and face similar problems of inequality and marginalization. Also similar to Chicano experience, Puerto Rican culture retains a strong vitality and is continually reinvigorated by the considerable movement back and forth between the island and the mainland.

CUBAN AMERICANS

The contact period for Cuban Americans, like Puerto Ricans, dates back to the Spanish-American War, and Cuba became an independent nation as a result of that war. Despite Cuba's nominal independence, the United States remained heavily involved in Cuban politics and economics for decades, and U.S. troops actually occupied the island on two different occasions.

The development of a Cuban American minority group bears little resemblance to the experience of either Chicanos or Puerto Ricans. Until the 1960s, there was little immigration from Cuba to the United States, even during times of labor shortages, and Cuban Americans were a very small group, numbering no more than 50,000 (Perez, 1980, p. 256).

Immigration (Push and Pull)

The conditions for a mass immigration were created in the late 1950s when a Marxist revolution brought Fidel Castro to power in Cuba. Castro's government was decidedly anti-American and began to restructure Cuban society along socialist lines. The middle and upper classes lost political and economic power, and the revolution made it difficult, even impossible, for Cuban capitalists to remain in business. Thus, the first Cuban immigrants to the United States tended to come from the more elite classes and included affluent and powerful people who controlled many resources.

The United States was a logical destination for those displaced by the revolution. Cuba is only 90 miles from southern Florida, the climates are similar, and the U.S. government, which was as anti-Castro as Castro was anti-American, welcomed the new arrivals as political refugees fleeing from communist tyranny. Prior social, cultural, and business ties also pulled the immigrants in the direction of the United States. Since gaining its independence in 1898, Cuba has been heavily influenced by its neighbor to the north, and U.S. companies helped to develop the Cuban economy. At the time of Castro's revolution, the Cuban political leadership and the more affluent classes were profoundly Americanized in their attitudes and lifestyles (Portes, 1990, p. 165). Furthermore, many Cuban exiles viewed southern Florida as an ideal spot from which to launch a counterrevolution to oust Castro.

Immigration was considerable for several years. More than 215,000 Cubans had arrived by 1962, when an escalation of hostile relations resulted in the cutoff of all direct contact between Cuba and the United States. In 1965, an air link was reestablished, and an additional 340,000 Cubans made the journey. When the air connection was terminated in 1973, immigration slowed to a trickle once more. In 1980, however, the Cuban government permitted another period of open immigration. Using boats of every shape, size, and degree of seaworthiness, about 124,000 Cubans crossed to Florida. These immigrants are often referred to as the *Marielitos,* after the port of Mariel from which many of them debarked. This wave of immigrants generated a great deal of controversy in the United States because the Cuban government used the opportunity to rid itself of a variety of convicted criminals and outcasts. The Marielitos included people from every segment of Cuban society, a fact that was lost in the clamor of concern about the "undesirables" (Portes & Manning, 1986, p. 58).

Regional Concentrations

The overwhelming majority of Cuban immigrants settled in southern Florida, especially in Miami and surrounding Dade County. Today, Cuban Americans remain one of the most spatially concentrated minority groups in the United States, with 67% of all Cuban Americans residing in Florida, and 52% in the Miami area alone (computed from data presented in U.S. Bureau of the Census, 2000q).

This dense concentration has led to a number of disputes and conflicts between the Hispanic, Anglo-, and African American communities in the area. Issues have centered on language, jobs, and discrimination by the police and other governmental agencies. The conflicts often have been intense, and on more than one occasion, they have erupted into violence and civil disorder.

Socioeconomic Characteristics

Cubans are, on the average, unusually affluent and well-educated compared with other streams of immigrants from Latin America. The immigrants of the 1960s included large numbers of professionals, landowners, and businesspeople. In later years, as Cuban society was transformed by the Castro regime, the stream included fewer elites (largely because there were fewer left in Cuba) and more political dissidents and working-class people. Today, Cuban Americans rank higher than other Latino groups on a number of socioeconomic dimensions, a reflection of the educational and economic resources they brought with them from Cuba and the favorable reception they enjoyed from the United States (Portes, 1990, p. 169).

These assets gave Cubans an advantage over Chicanos and Puerto Ricans, but the differences between the three Latino groups run deeper and are more complex than a simple accounting of initial resources would suggest. Cubans adapted to U.S. society in a way that is fundamentally different from the other two Latino groups.

The Ethnic Enclave

The minority groups we have discussed to this point have been concentrated in the unskilled, low-wage segments of the economy in which jobs are insecure and not linked to opportunities for upward mobility. Many Cuban Americans have bypassed this sector of the economy and much of the discrimination and many of the limitations associated with it. Like several other groups, Cuban Americans are an enclave minority (see Chapter 2). An ethnic enclave is a social, economic, and cultural subsociety controlled by the group itself. Located in a specific geographical area or neighborhood inhabited solely or largely by members of the group, the enclave encompasses sufficient economic enterprises and social institutions to permit the group to function as a self-contained entity largely independent of the surrounding community.

The first wave of Cuban immigrants generated enough economic activity to sustain restaurants, shops, and other small businesses that catered to the exile community. Over the years, the enclave economy has grown. Between 1967 and 1976, the number of Cuban-owned firms in Dade County increased ninefold, from 919 to about 8,000. Six years later, the number had reached 12,000. Most of these enterprises are small, but there are some factories employing hundreds of workers (Portes & Rumbaut, 1996, pp. 20–21). Over the decades, Cuban-owned firms have become increasingly integrated into the local economy and increasingly competitive with firms in the larger society. The growth in business firms has been paralleled by a growth in the number of other types of groups and organizations and in the number and quality of services available (schools, law firms, medical care, funeral parlors, etc.). The enclave has become a largely autonomous community capable of providing for its members from cradle to grave (Logan, Alba, & McNulty, 1994; Peterson, 1995; Portes & Bach, 1985, p. 59).

The fact that the enclave economy is controlled by the group itself is crucial because it distinguished the enclave from the "ghettoes,"

or neighborhoods that are impoverished and segregated. In ghettoes, members of other groups typically control the local economy, and the profits, rents, and other resources flow *out* of the neighborhood. In the enclave, profits are reinvested and kept *in* the neighborhood. Group members can avoid the discrimination and limitations imposed by the larger society and can apply their skills, education, and talents in an atmosphere free from language barriers and prejudice. Those who might wish to venture into business for themselves can use the networks of cooperation and mutual aid for advice, credit, and other forms of assistance. Thus, the ethnic enclave provides a platform from which Cuban Americans can pursue economic success independent of their degree of acculturation or English language ability.

The effectiveness of the ethnic enclave as a pathway for adaptation is illustrated by a study of Cuban and Mexican immigrants, all of whom entered the United States in 1973. At the time of entry, the groups were comparable in levels of skills, education, and English language ability. The groups were interviewed on several different occasions, and although they remained comparable on many variables, there were dramatic differences between the groups that reflected their different positions in the labor market. The majority of the Mexican immigrants were employed in the low-wage job sector. Less than 20% were self-employed or employed by another person of Mexican descent. Conversely, 57% of the Cuban immigrants were self-employed or employed by another Cuban (i.e., they were involved in the enclave economy). Among the subjects in the study, self-employed Cubans reported the highest monthly incomes ($1,495), and Cubans otherwise employed in the enclave earned the second-highest incomes ($1,111). The lowest incomes ($880) were earned by Mexican immigrants employed in small non-enclave firms; many of these people worked as unskilled laborers in seasonal, temporary, or otherwise insecure jobs (Portes, 1990, p. 173; see also Portes & Bach, 1985).

The ability of the Mexican immigrants to rise in the class system and compete for place and position was severely constrained by the weight of past discrimination, the preferences of employers in the present, and their own lack of economic and political power. Cuban immigrants who found jobs in the enclave did not need to expose themselves to American prejudices or rely on the job market of the larger society. They entered an ethnic community that had networks of mutual assistance and support and that linked them to opportunities more consistent with their ambitions and their qualifications.

The fact that success came faster to the group that was *less* acculturated reverses the prediction of many theories of assimilation. The pattern has long been recognized by some leaders of other groups, however, and is voiced in many of the themes of black power, red power, and Chicanismo that emphasize self-help, self-determination, nationalism, and separation. However, ethnic enclaves cannot be a panacea for all minority groups. They develop only under certain limited conditions; namely, when business and financial expertise and reliable sources of capital are combined with a disciplined labor force willing to work for low wages in exchange for on-the-job training, future assistance and loans, or other delayed benefits. Enclave enterprises usually start on a small scale and cater only to other ethnics. Thus, the early economic returns are small and prosperity follows only after years of hard work, if at all. Most important, eventual success and expansion beyond the boundaries of the enclave depend on the persistence of strong ties of loyalty, kinship, and solidarity. The pressure to assimilate might easily weaken these networks and the strength of group cohesion (Portes & Manning, 1986, pp. 61–66).

A final qualification on the Cuban "success story" is that for many members of the group, poverty and unemployment continue to be major problems. For example, although the poverty rate for Cuban Americans is much lower than that of Mexican Americans and Puerto Ricans, it is nearly triple the rate for non-Hispanic whites. Success has been selective, and inequality continues to be a problem for Cuban Americans.

Cuban Americans and Other Minority Groups

The adaptation of Cuban Americans contrasts sharply with the experiences of colonized minority groups and with the common understanding of how immigrants are "supposed" to acculturate and integrate. Cuban Americans are neither the first nor the only group to develop an ethnic enclave, and their success has generated prejudice and resentment from the dominant group and from other minority groups. Whereas Puerto Ricans and Chicanos have been the victims of stereotypes labeling them "inferior," higher-status Cuban Americans have been stereotyped as *too* successful, *too* clannish, and *too* ambitious. The former stereotype commonly emerges to rationalize exploitative relationships; the latter expresses disparagement and rejection of groups that are more successful in the struggle to acquire resources. Nonetheless, the stereotype of affluent Cubans is an exaggeration and a misperception that obscures the fact that poverty and unemployment are major problems for many members of this group.

RECENT IMMIGRANTS FROM LATIN AMERICA AND THE CARIBBEAN

Immigration from Central and South America and the Caribbean has been considerable since the 1960s, as demonstrated in Exhibit 7.3. These rising rates are in part a result of a new immigration policy instituted in 1965 that emphasizes family reunification and kinship ties. This stream of immigrants is diverse as well as large and includes French, British, and Portuguese traditions as well as Spanish. The immigrants come from more than a score of nations, and they reflect the cultural and racial diversity of their homelands. Some are highly educated professionals, whereas others are farmhands, political refugees, skilled technicians, or the wives and children of U.S. citizens. Mexico alone accounts for about half of these immigrants. Other large contingents have come from the Dominican Republic,

Exhibit 7.3   Immigration From Central and South America and the Caribbean (not including Mexico)

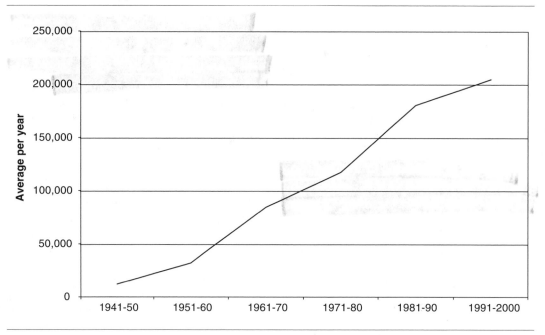

SOURCE: U.S. Immigration and Naturalization Service (2002, pp. 20-21).

Cuba, Jamaica, Haiti, and Colombia (U.S. Immigration and Naturalization Service, 2002, pp. 21–22). In this section, we examine the characteristics of these immigrants and their impact on U.S. society.

Socioeconomic Characteristics

Most of the Latin American and Caribbean sending nations are economically less developed, and most have long-standing relations with the United States. We have already discussed the role that Mexico and Puerto Rico have played historically as sources of cheap labor and the ties that led Cubans to immigrate to the United States. Each of the other sending nations has been similarly linked to the United States, the dominant economic and political power in the region (Portes, 1990, p. 162).

A large number of Latino immigrants are women and children, and the percentage of professionals, managers, and executives is relatively low, ranging between 10% and 20%. Although the majority of these immigrants bring educational and occupational qualifications that are modest by U.S. standards, they tend to be more educated, more urbanized, and more skilled than the average citizens of the nations from which they come. Most of these immigrants are not so much fleeing poverty or joblessness as they are attempting to pursue their ambitions and seek opportunities for advancement that simply are not available in their country of origin (Portes & Rumbaut, 1996, pp. 10–11).

This characterization applies to legal and unauthorized immigrants alike. The latter may illustrate the point more dramatically because the cost of illegally entering the United States can be considerable, much higher than the cost of a legal entry. The venture may require years of saving money or the combined resources of a large kinship group. Payment for forged papers and other costs of being smuggled into the country can easily run into thousands of dollars, a considerable sum in nations where the usual wage is a tiny fraction of the U.S. average (Orreniou, 2001, p. 7).

Location, Impact, and Illegal Immigrants

The current wave of Latino and Caribbean immigrants tends to follow the well-worn paths and networks of previous generations. New York City and Los Angeles remain major points of entry, and Houston and Miami also receive large numbers of Latino immigrants. The impact of these newcomers on local communities can be considerable, and immigration has generated a great deal of controversy in recent years.

Some of the common and most vociferous concerns are that immigrants take jobs away from U.S. citizens and that they slow economic growth, reduce economic vitality, and stress already overburdened welfare, health, and educational systems. These issues are complex, and they continue to be hotly debated. Some scholars find that the fears are exaggerated and that overall, the economic impact of immigration has been positive. For example, many studies have found that Latino immigrants tend to find low-wage jobs in areas of the economy in which few U.S. citizens work or in the enclave economies of their own groups, taking jobs that would not have existed without the economic activity of their co-ethnics. Further, some studies conclude that the presence of Latino immigrants in the low-wage sector actually pushes other native-born workers up into better jobs (Bouvier & Gardner, 1986, pp. 28–30; Heer, 1996, pp. 190–194; Smith & Edmonston, 1997). Other studies have found that rather than moving "up," native-born workers who must compete with immigrants for low-wage jobs move away to areas with fewer immigrants—a new form of "white flight" (Martin & Midgley, 1999, p. 27).

Another concern is the strain that immigrants place on taxes and services such as schools and welfare programs. Again, these issues are complex and far from settled. Some research projects suggest that immigrants cost less than they contribute. Taxes are deducted automatically from their paychecks, and their use of such services as unemployment compensation, Medicare, food stamps, Aid to Families with Dependent Children, and Social Security is actually lower than their proportional contributions. This is particularly true for undocumented immigrants, whose use of services is sharply limited by their vulnerable legal status (Marcelli & Heer, 1998; Simon, 1989). On the other hand, one recent study estimated that non-immigrant households paid an additional $200 in taxes in 1996 to finance the services used by immigrants, legal as well as unauthorized. Although $200 per household may not sound like much, the "immigrant deficit" totals up to $15 to $20 billion across the population (Martin & Midgley, 1999, p. 31).

Final conclusions about the impact and costs of immigration must await further research. For now, we can say that the fears and concerns, although not unfounded, may be confounded with and exaggerated by prejudice and racism directed at newcomers and strangers. The current opposition to immigration may be a reaction to *who* as much as to *how many* or *how much* the cost. To give some perspective to these concerns, we should remember that the percentage of the U.S. population that is foreign born is less today than it was at the turn of the 20th century. In 1920, toward the end of the last great wave of immigrants, 13.2% of the population was foreign-born (Daniels, 1990, p. 404). In 1999, the comparable figure was 9.5% (U.S. Bureau of the Census, 2000t).

The 1990s saw a number of efforts, at both the state and national levels, to curb immigration in general and illegal immigration in particular. For example, in 1994, the voters of California approved Proposition 187, which would have denied educational, health, and other services to illegal immigrants. The policy was declared unconstitutional and was never implemented. Federal efforts to decrease the flow of illegal immigration included new legislation limiting welfare benefits for immigrants, increases in the size of the Border Patrol, and building taller and wider walls along the border with Mexico.

As we have seen, immigration from Central and South America and from the Caribbean, illegal as well as legal, continued steadily throughout the 1990s despite these efforts to reduce the flow. In fact, the social networks are so well established and the demand for cheap labor in the United States is so strong that it seems unlikely that any attempts to stem the tide could have much success. In fact, denying services may make illegal immigrants *more* attractive as a source of labor by reducing their ability to resist exploitation. For example, if the children of illegal immigrants were not permitted to attend school, they might become more vulnerable to exploitation and more likely to join the army of cheap labor on which some employers depend. Who would benefit from closing public schools to the children of illegal immigrants?

Concern over the impact of immigration has been intense at various times in the history of our nation, and present-day arguments both for and against immigration have a familiar, even nostalgic flair. Two points seem clear in the midst of the frequently intense and continuing debate over immigration. First, prejudice and racism are part of what motivates people to oppose immigration, and second, immigrants, legal and illegal, continue to find work with Anglo employers and niches in American society in which they can survive. The networks that have delivered cheap immigrant labor for the low-wage sector continue to operate as they have for more than a century. Frequently, the primary beneficiaries of this long-established system are not the immigrants, but employers who benefit from a cheaper, more easily exploited workforce and American consumers who benefit from lower prices in the marketplace.

Recent Immigration in Historical Context

The current wave of immigration to the United States is part of a centuries-old process that spans the globe. Underlying this immense and complex population movement is the powerful force of the continuing industrial revolution. The United States and other industrialized nations are the centers of growth in the global economy, and immigrants flow to the areas of greater opportunity. In the 19th century, population moved largely from Europe to the Western Hemisphere. Over the past 50 years, the movement has been from South to North. This pattern reflects the simple geography of industrialization and opportunity and the fact that the more developed nations are in the Northern Hemisphere.

The United States has been the world's dominant economic, political, and cultural power for much of the past century and has been the preferred destination of most immigrants. Newcomers from Latin America and the Caribbean continue the collective, social nature of past population movements (see Chapter 2). The direction of their travels reflects contemporary global inequalities: Labor continues to flow from the less developed nations to the more developed nations. The direction of this flow is not accidental or coincidental. It is determined by the differential rates of industrialization and modernization across the globe. Immigration contributes to the wealth and affluence of the more developed societies and particularly to the dominant groups and elite classes of those societies.

COMPARING MINORITY GROUPS: WILL CONTEMPORARY IMMIGRANTS FROM CENTRAL AND SOUTH AMERICA AND THE CARIBBEAN ASSIMILATE AS EUROPEAN IMMIGRANTS DID?

In Chapter 2, we reviewed some of the patterns of acculturation and integration that typified the adjustment of Europeans who immigrated to the United States before the 1920s. Although the process of adjustment was anything but smooth or simple, these groups eventually Americanized and achieved levels of education and affluence comparable to national norms. Will contemporary immigrants from Latin America and the Caribbean experience similar success? Will their sons and daughters and grandsons and granddaughters rise in the occupational structure to a position of parity with the dominant group? Will the cultures and languages of these groups gradually fade and disappear?

The final answers to these questions must await future developments. In the meantime, some strong evidence suggests that the success stories of the white ethnic groups will *not* be repeated. Sociologist Douglas Massey (1995) argued that there are three crucial differences between the European assimilation experience of the past and the contemporary period. First, the flow of immigrants from Europe to the United States slowed to a mere trickle after the 1920s because of restrictive legislation, the worldwide depression of the 1930s, and World War II. For example, more than 14 million immigrants arrived from Europe between 1900 and 1930, an average of almost 500,000 each year. In the 1930s, immigration from Europe dropped to an average of about 35,000 per year, less than 10% of the earlier rate (U.S. Immigration and Naturalization Service, 2000, p. 21). Thus, as the children and grandchildren of the immigrants from Europe Americanized and grew to adulthood in the 1930s and 1940s, few new immigrants fresh from the old country replaced them in the ethnic neighborhoods. European cultural traditions and languages weakened rapidly with the passing of the first generation and the Americanization of their descendants.

As for contemporary immigration, the networks and the demand for cheap labor are so strong that it is unlikely that there will be a similar hiatus in the flow of people. Immigration has become continuous, and as some contemporary immigrants (or their descendants) Americanize and rise to affluence and success, new arrivals will replace them and continuously revitalize the ethnic cultures and languages. Thus, America's contemporary immigrant groups will strain toward both assimilation and pluralism simultaneously.

Second, the speed and ease of modern transportation and communication will help to maintain cultural and linguistic diversity. A century ago, immigrants from Europe could maintain contact with the old country only by mail, and most had no realistic expectation of ever returning. Most modern immigrants, in contrast, can return to their homes in a day or less and can use telephones, television, radio, e-mail, and the Internet to stay in intimate contact with the family and friends they left behind. Thus, the cultures of modern immigrants can be kept vital and whole in ways that were not available (and not even imagined) 100 years ago.

Third, and perhaps most important, contemporary immigrants face an economy and a labor market that are vastly different from those faced by European immigrants. The latter generally benefited from U.S. industrialization. As the economy matured and shifted from manufacturing to service (see Exhibit 4.2), the descendants of European immigrants rose in the occupational structure. Today, in contrast, we are in a period of growing income inequality and declining occupational mobility. Furthermore, "just at the point when public schools used by immigrants have fallen into neglect, the importance of education in the U.S. stratification system has increased" (Massey, 1995, pp. 645–646).

For the immigrants from Europe a century ago, assimilation meant a gradual rise to middle-class respectability and suburban comfort, even if it took four or five generations to accomplish. Assimilation today is segmented (see Chapter 2), and a large percentage of the descendants of contemporary immigrants—especially those from Latin America and from the Caribbean—face permanent membership in a growing underclass population and continuing marginalization and powerlessness.

This gloomy forecast does not, of course, apply to all contemporary immigrants. The current stream is diverse, and immigrants vary enormously in their cultural and racial backgrounds and in the resources they bring with them. Thus, different groups can expect to follow different pathways of incorporation into the larger society (Portes & Rumbaut, 2001; Portes & Zhou, 1993). The immigrant groups more likely to avoid underclass status are those that bring higher levels of human capital (e.g., education and occupational skills); are racially similar to the dominant group; and have stronger familial, social, and institutional networks. These principles would tend to favor groups closer to Blauner's immigrant type (e.g., Cuban Americans) over groups whose histories include strong elements of colonization (e.g., Mexican Americans or Puerto Ricans). We explore these patterns in the next section, and in the next chapter, we apply these ideas to immigrants from Asia.

FOCUS ON GENDER

IMAGES OF LATINAS

One part of the minority group experience is learning to deal with the stereotypes, images, and expectations of the larger society. Of course, everyone (even white males) has to respond to the assumptions of others, but given the realities of power and status, minority group members have fewer choices and a narrower range in which to maneuver: The images imposed by the society are harder to escape and more difficult to deny. In the analysis excerpted below, Judith Ortiz Cofer (1995), a writer, a poet, a professor of English, and a Puerto Rican, describes some of the images and stereotypes of Latinas with which she has had to struggle and some of the dynamics that have created and sustained those images. She writes from her own experiences, but the points she makes illustrate many of the sociological theories and concepts that guide this text.

On a bus trip from London to Oxford University . . . a young man, obviously fresh from a pub, spotted me and as if struck by inspiration went down on his knees in the aisle. With both hands over his heart he broke into an Irish tenor's rendition of "Maria" from *West Side Story*. My politely amused fellow passengers gave his lovely voice the round of gentle applause that it deserved. Though I was not quite as amused, I managed my version of an English smile: no show of teeth, no extreme contortions of the facial muscles—I was at this time in my life practicing reserve and cool. . . . But Maria had followed me to London, reminding me of a prime fact of my life: You can leave the Island, master the English language, and travel as far as you can, but if you are a Latina, . . . the Island travels with you.

This is sometimes a very good thing—it may win you the extra minute of somebody's attention. But with some people, the same things can make *you* an island—not so much a tropical paradise as an Alcatraz, a place nobody wants to visit. As a Puerto Rican girl growing up in the United States and wanting like most children to "belong," I resented the stereotypes that my Hispanic appearance called forth from many people I met.

Our family lived in a large urban center in New Jersey during the sixties, where life was designed as a microcosm of my parents' casas on the Island. We spoke Spanish, we ate Puerto Rican food bought at the bodega, and we practiced strict Catholicism. . . . As a girl, I was kept under strict surveillance, since virtue and modesty were, by cultural equation, the same as family honor.

At a Puerto Rican festival, neither the music nor the colors we wore could be too loud. I still experience a vague sense of letdown when I'm invited to a "party" and it turns out to be a marathon conversation in hushed tones rather than a fiesta with salsa, laughter, and dancing—the kind of celebration I remember from my childhood. . . .

Mixed cultural signals have perpetuated certain stereotypes—for example, that of the "Hot Tamale" or sexual firebrand. It is a . . . view that the media have found easy to promote. In their special vocabulary, advertisers have designated "sizzling" and "smoldering" as the adjectives of choice for describing not only the foods but the women of Latin America. . . .

It is custom, however, not chromosomes, that leads us to choose scarlet over pale pink. As young girls, we were influenced in our decisions about clothes and colors by the women . . . who had grown up on a tropical island where the natural environment was a riot of primary colors, where showing your skin was one way to keep cool as well as to look sexy. Most important of all, on the Island, women perhaps felt freer to dress and move more provocatively, since . . . they were protected by the traditions, mores, and laws of a Spanish/Catholic system of morality and machismo whose main rule was: *You may look at my sister, but if you touch her I will kill you.* The extended family and church structure could provide a young woman with a circle of safety in her small pueblo on the Island; if a man "wronged" a girl, everyone would close in to save her family honor. . . .

Because of my education and proficiency with the English language, I have acquired many mechanisms for dealing with the anger I experience. This was not true for my parents, nor is it true for the many Latin women working at menial jobs who must put up with stereotypes about our ethnic group such as: "They make good domestics." This is another facet of the myth of the Latin women in the United States. . . . The myth of the Hispanic menial has been maintained by the same media phenomenon that made "Mammy" from *Gone With the Wind* America's idea of a black woman for generations: Maria, the housemaid or counter girl, is now indelibly etched into the national psyche. The big and little screens have presented us with the picture of the funny Hispanic maid, mispronouncing words and cooking up a spicy storm in the kitchen. . . .

I am one of the lucky ones. My parents made it possible for me to acquire a stronger footing in the mainstream culture by giving me the chance at an education. . . . There are thousands of Latinas without the privilege of an education or the entrée into society that I have. For them, life is a struggle against the misconceptions perpetuated by the myth of the Latina as whore, domestic, or criminal. My personal goal in my public life is to try to replace the old pervasive stereotypes and myths about Latinas with a much more interesting set of realities. Every time I give a reading [of my poetry], I hope the stories I tell, the dreams and fears I examine in my work, can achieve some universal truth which will get my audience past the particulars of my skin color, my accent, or my clothes.

SOURCE: From Judith Ortiz Cofer (1995), "The Myth of the Latin Woman: I Just Met a Girl Named Maria," in *The Latin Deli: Prose and Poetry* (pp. 148–154). © Copyright 1995 by the University of Georgia Press. Reprinted with permission.

CONTEMPORARY HISPANIC-WHITE RELATIONS

As in previous chapters, we will use the central concepts of this text to review the status of Latinos in the United States. Where relevant, comparisons are made between the major Latino groups and with the minority groups discussed in previous chapters.

Prejudice and Discrimination

The American tradition of prejudice against Latinos was born in the 19th-century conflicts that created minority group status for Mexican Americans. The themes of the original anti-Mexican stereotypes and attitudes were consistent with the nature of the contact situation: As Mexicans were conquered and subordinated, they were characterized as inferior, lazy, irresponsible, low in intelligence, and dangerously criminal (McWilliams, 1961, pp. 212–214). The prejudice and racism, supplemented with the echoes of the racist ideas and beliefs brought to the Southwest by many Anglos, helped to justify and rationalize the colonized, exploited status of the Chicanos.

These prejudices were incorporated into the dominant culture and were transferred to Puerto Ricans when they began to arrive on the mainland. As we have already mentioned, this stereotype does not fit Cuban Americans. Instead, their affluence has been exaggerated and perceived as undeserved or achieved by unfair or "un-American" means, a characterization similar to the traditional stereotype of Jews, and just as prejudiced as the perception of Latino inferiority.

There is some evidence that the level of Latino prejudice has been affected by the decline of explicit American racism discussed in Chapter 5. For example, the social distance scale results reported in Exhibit 1.4 show a decrease in scores of Mexican Americans and an increase in rank position. On the other hand, prejudice and racism against Latinos tend to increase when the dominant group feels threatened by high rates of immigration.

Although discrimination of all kinds, institutional as well as individual, has been common against Latino groups, it has been neither as rigid nor as total as the systems that controlled African American labor under slavery and segregation. However, discrimination against Latinos has not dissipated to the same extent as it has against European immigrant groups and their descendants. Because of their longer tenure in the United States and their original status as a rural labor force, Mexican Americans probably have been more victimized by the institutionalized forms of discrimination than have other Latino groups.

Assimilation and Pluralism

Acculturation

Latino groups are highly variable in their extent of acculturation but often are seen as "slow" to change, learn English, and adopt Anglo customs. This perception is based partly on the assumption that Hispanics would follow the assimilation patterns of European immigrants and their descendants. Whereas white ethnic groups were largely acculturated after three or four generations, some Latino groups have been part of American society for many decades, and their language and culture remain prominently "unmelted."

Contrary to this perception, research shows that Hispanic groups are following many of the same patterns of assimilation as European groups. Their rates of acculturation increase with length of residence and are higher for the native born (Espinosa & Massey, 1997; Goldstein & Suro, 2000; Valentine & Mosley, 2000). One national study, for example, showed that Mexican Americans who are citizens of the United States are very similar to Anglos in terms of their support for economic individualism and patriotism (de la Garza, Falcon, & García, 1996). English language fluency increases as the generations pass, and most Hispanic Americans speak English or a combination of English and Spanish. Even those who speak Spanish at home report that they also speak English well or very well (de la Garza, DeSipio, García, García, & Falcon, 1992, p. 41; Portes & Rumbaut, 1996, pp. 199–231), and the percentage of Hispanics who are fluent in English increases with length of residence (for example, see Saenz, 1999, p. 223). The pattern of language acculturation and changing values by generation was also documented in Exhibit 2.3.

Even while acculturation continues, however, Hispanic culture and the Spanish language are revitalized by immigration. By its nature, assimilation is a slow process that can require decades or generations to complete. In contrast, immigration can be fast, often accomplished in less than a day. Thus, even as Hispanic Americans acculturate and integrate, Hispanic culture and language are sustained and strengthened. What is perceived to be slow acculturation for these groups is mostly the result of fast and continuous immigration.

Furthermore, colonized minority groups such as Chicanos and Puerto Ricans were not encouraged to assimilate in the past. Valued primarily for the cheap labor they supplied, they were seen as otherwise inferior or undesirable and as unfit for integration. Two sociologists put the point forcefully: "Non-white people were brought to this society precisely *because* of race: not to assimilate but to work in unfree, unskilled labor systems that were tightly controlled" (Zinn & Eitzen, 1990, p. 73). For much of the 20th century, Latinos were excluded from the institutions and experiences (e.g., school) that could have led to greater equality and higher rates of acculturation in the present. Prejudice, racism, and discrimination combined to keep most Latino groups away from the centers of modernization and change and away from opportunities to improve their situation.

Racial factors have complicated and slowed the process of assimilation for many Latinos, especially perhaps for darker-complexioned Puerto Ricans. Latinos who are less "Anglo" in appearance may retain or even emphasize their Spanish heritage to avoid classification as African American or Native American, along with all the disabilities associated with American racism. The same is true for Caribbean immigrants, such as Haitians and West Indians, who are seen as black (Fernandez-Kelly & Schauffler, 1994). Thus, the weight of our racist past (and present) may put some Latinos in a position in which they increase the salience of their ethnic identity and thus slow the process of Anglo-conformity as a way of avoiding the disadvantages associated with their racial identity.

Finally, for many Cubans and other groups, cultural differences reflect the fact that their immigration is very recent. Their first generations are alive and well, and as is typical for immigrant groups, they keep the language and traditions alive. Cuban Americans have been a sizable group in the

United States for only about 40 years, barely enough time for a third generation to develop.

Secondary Structural Assimilation

In this section, we survey the situation of Latinos in the public areas and institutions of American society, beginning with where people live.

Residence. Exhibit 7.4 shows the regional concentrations of Latinos in 2000. The legacies of their varied patterns of entry and settlement are evident. The higher concentrations in the Southwest reflect the presence of Mexican Americans, those in Florida are the results of the Cuban immigration, and those in the Northeast display the settlement patterns of Puerto Ricans.

Within each of these regions, Latino groups are highly urbanized, as shown in Exhibit 7.5. Virtually all Cuban Americans are city dwellers, and Puerto Ricans are more concentrated in central city areas than are the other two groups. Hispanics generally are less residentially segregated than African Americans but are more segregated than Asian Americans. However, the degree of segregation is variable across the nation, with the highest levels in the cities of the Northeast (Iceland et al., 2002; Pollard & O'Hare, 1999, p. 29).

Education. Levels of education for Hispanic Americans have risen in recent years but still lag behind national standards (see Exhibits 7.6a and 7.6b). The males and females of all three Hispanic groups have similar patterns. At the high school level, the groups—especially Cuban Americans—are comparable to non-Hispanic whites. The deficits appear at the lower levels of education (especially for Mexican Americans, who are more than 6 times as likely as non-Hispanic whites to have less than a 9th-grade education) and at the college level. The percentage of college-educated Cuban Americans is comparable to that of non-Hispanic whites, but the percentages for the other groups are dramatically lower. The level of college education for Puerto Ricans is similar to that of African

Exhibit 7.4   Number of People, 2000: Hispanic or Latino Origin, All Races

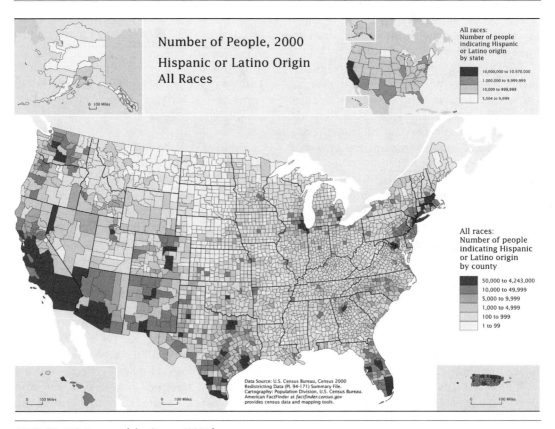

SOURCE: U.S. Bureau of the Census (2000f).

Exhibit 7.5   Residential Patterns of Hispanic Americans

	Mexican Americans	*Puerto Ricans*	*Cuban Americans*
Metropolitan area	89.4%	96.2%	98.4%
Inside central city	44.9%	61.2%	22.4%
Outside central city	44.5%	35.0%	76.0%
Nonmetropolitan area	10.6%	3.8%	1.2%

SOURCE: U.S. Bureau of the Census (2000k).

Americans (see Exhibit 5.8), but Mexican Americans lag far behind.

The lower levels of education are the cumulative results of decades of systematic discrimination and exclusion. They are further reduced, in the case of Mexican Americans, by the high percentage of recent immigrants who bring very modest educational backgrounds. Given the role that educational credentials have come to play in the job market, these figures support the idea that assimilation will be segmented for these groups and suggest that without substantial increases in the accessibility of schooling, opportunities for upward mobility will continue to be limited.

Exhibit 7.6a Educational Attainment for Three Hispanic Groups and Non-Hispanic Whites Aged 25 and Older (Males)

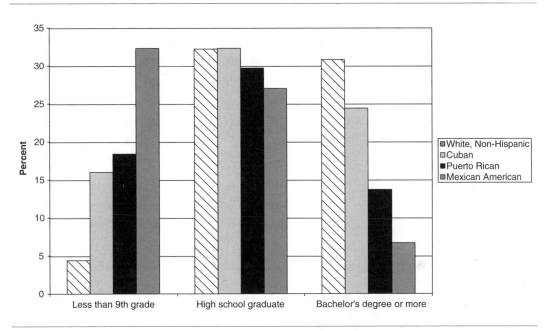

SOURCE: U.S. Bureau of the Census (2000b).

Exhibit 7.6b Educational Attainment for Three Hispanic Groups and Non-Hispanic Whites Aged 25 and Older (Females)

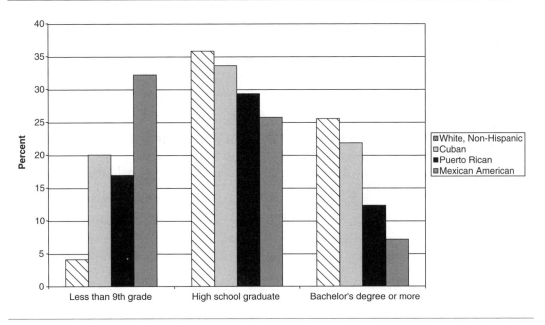

SOURCE: U.S. Bureau of the Census (2000b).

Political Power. The political resources available to Hispanic Americans have increased over the years, but the group is still proportionally underrepresented. There are currently 19 Hispanic Americans in the U.S. House of Representatives (up from 8 in 1983), but none in the Senate (U.S. Bureau of the Census, 2003c, p. 247). Hispanics still hold only 4% of the total House seats even though they make up about more than 12% of the population. On the local and state levels, the number of public officials identified as Hispanic increased by about 66% between 1985 and 2001, from 3,147 to 5,205 (U.S. Bureau of the Census, 2003c, p. 252).

The number of Hispanics of voting age has more than doubled in recent decades, and Hispanics today constitute more than 10% of the voting age population. Registration rates and turnout have been low, however, and the Hispanic community has not had an impact on the political structure proportionate to its size. For example, in the presidential elections between 1980 and 2000, actual voter turnout for Hispanic Americans generally was lower than 30% of those registered to vote, about half of the comparable rate for non-Hispanic whites (U.S. Bureau of the Census, 2002, p. 251). These lower participation rates are due to many factors, including the younger average age of the Hispanic population (younger people are the least likely to register and vote) and the large percentage of recent immigrants in the group (del Pinal & Singer, 1997, p. 42).

On a more positive note, Hispanic Americans are beginning to exert their political power as the 21st century dawns. The Hispanic vote figured prominently in the 2000 presidential election, and President George W. Bush has relied on support from the Hispanic community throughout his career. For example, Bush attracted the support of 38% of Hispanic voters in the 2000 presidential election, as opposed to only 9% of the African American vote (Wickham, 2000). With their rapid growth rate, it is clear that Hispanic voters will have a much greater impact on politics in the future, especially as second- and third-generation children reach voting age (del Pinal & Singer, 1997, p. 42)

Jobs and Income. The economic situation of Hispanic Americans is mixed. Many members of these groups, especially those who have been in the United States for several generations, are doing "just fine. They have, in ever increasing numbers, accessed opportunities in education and employment and have carved out a niche of American prosperity for themselves and their children" (Camarillo & Bonilla, 2001, pp. 130–131). For many others, however, the picture is not so promising. They face segmented assimilation (see Chapter 2) and, like African Americans and other minority groups of color, the possibility of becoming members of an impoverished, powerless, and economically marginalized urban underclass.

Exhibits 7.7a and 7.7b display the occupational profiles for Hispanic males and females. Looking first at males (see Exhibit 7.7a), we see that both Mexican Americans and Puerto Ricans are notably underrepresented in the highest status jobs and overrepresented in unskilled jobs.

Mexican Americans are overrepresented in the agricultural sectors, whereas Puerto Ricans are more overrepresented in the service sector, a difference that reflects the greater urbanization of Puerto Ricans. The profile for Cuban American males is similar to that of the other two groups except that they are less underrepresented in the highest occupational category (managerial and professional) and, along with Puerto Ricans, actually overrepresented in the next-highest occupational category (technical, sales, and administration). The females of all three groups (see Exhibit 7.7b), as well as dominant group females, are heavily concentrated in the "technical, sales, and administration" sector (mostly in clerical jobs) and in the service sector.

Unemployment, low income, and poverty continue to be issues for all three Hispanic groups. The unemployment rates for Hispanic Americans run about twice the rate for non-Hispanic whites, and the poverty rates for the group as a whole are comparable

Exhibit 7.7a Occupation by Ethnicity and Sex, 2000 (Males)

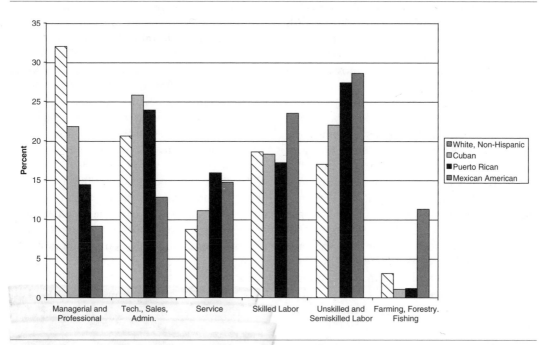

SOURCE: U.S. Bureau of the Census (2000j).

Exhibit 7.7b Occupation by Ethnicity and Sex, 2000 (Females)

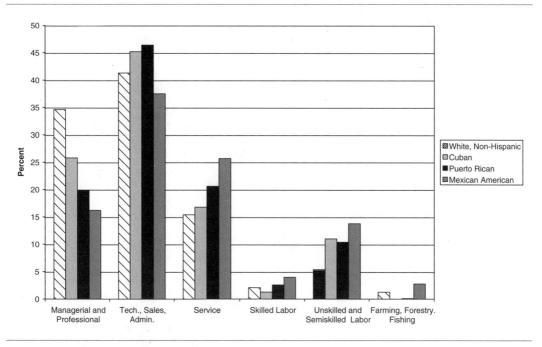

SOURCE: U.S. Bureau of the Census (2000j).

to those of African Americans (Camarillo & Bonilla, 2001, pp. 110–111). As shown in Exhibit 7.8, Cuban American households have the lowest poverty rates, and Puerto Ricans have the highest, especially for female-headed households. Exhibit 7.9 shows that all three groups, especially Mexican American and Puerto Rican females, are overrepresented in the lowest income groups and underrepresented in the highest income category. Cuban American males are the most concentrated in the highest income category, a pattern that is consistent with the relative degree of colonization experienced by each group and with the healthy Cuban enclave economy. The income figures suggest that Cuban American males are the primary beneficiaries of the enclave economy (as white males benefit from the national economy). Indeed, more than twice as many Cuban American males as Cuban American females reported earnings in excess of $50,000.

As was the case with African Americans and Native Americans, these economic differences are even wider when we consider wealth (savings, property, stocks and bonds, etc.) as opposed to income. As a group, the net worth of Hispanic Americans is about 10% that of whites, a gap that persists even for households that are similar in income. Among the households in the highest 20% of income, non-Hispanic whites are 2 to 3 times as wealthy as Hispanics (Pollard & O'Hare, 1999, pp. 37–38).

The socioeconomic profiles of Mexican Americans and Puerto Ricans reflect their concentration in the low-wage sector of the economy, the long tradition of discrimination and exclusion, and the lower amounts of human capital (education, job training) controlled by these groups. The higher rates of unemployment for these two groups reflect not only discrimination but also the insecurity and seasonal nature of many of the jobs they hold. Cuban Americans, buoyed by a more privileged social class background and their enclave economy, rank higher on virtually all measures of wealth and prosperity.

These figures point to a split labor market, differentiated by gender, within the dual market differentiated by race and ethnicity. Hispanic women—like minority group women in general—are among the lowest-paid, most exploitable, and least-protected segments of the U.S. labor force. The impact of poverty is especially severe for Latino women, who often find themselves with the responsibility of caring for their children alone. The percentage of female-headed households ranges from 36% for Puerto Rican families to about 20% for Mexican American and Cuban American families (U.S. Bureau of the Census, 2000p). This pattern is the result of many factors, among them the status of Latino men in the labor force. The jobs available to Latino men often do not pay enough to support a family, and many jobs are seasonal, temporary, or otherwise insecure.

Female-headed Latino families are affected by a triple economic handicap: They have only one wage earner, whose potential income is limited by discrimination against both women and Latinos. The result of these multiple disadvantages is an especially high rate of poverty. Whereas less than 20% of non-Hispanic, white female-headed households fall below the poverty line, the percentage is nearly 40% for Mexican female-headed households and more than 45% for Puerto Rican female-headed households.

The socioeconomic situation of Latinos is complex and diversified. Although members of all groups have successfully entered the mainstream economy, poverty and exclusion continue to be major issues. Highly concentrated in deteriorated urban areas (*barrios*), segments of these groups, like other minority groups of color, face the possibility of permanent poverty and economic marginality.

Primary Structural Assimilation

Overall, the extent of intimate contact between Hispanic Americans and the dominant group is probably higher than for either African Americans or Native Americans. This pattern may reflect the fact that Latinos are partly ethnic minority groups and partly

Exhibit 7.8 Households Below Poverty Level, 1999 (All Households and Female-Headed Households)

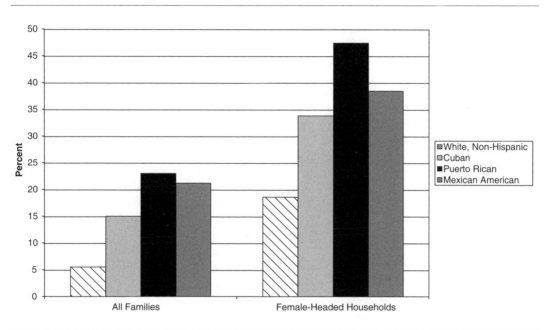

SOURCE: U.S. Bureau of the Census (2000p).

Exhibit 7.9 Income by Ethnicity and Sex, 1999 (Full-Time, Year-Round Workers)

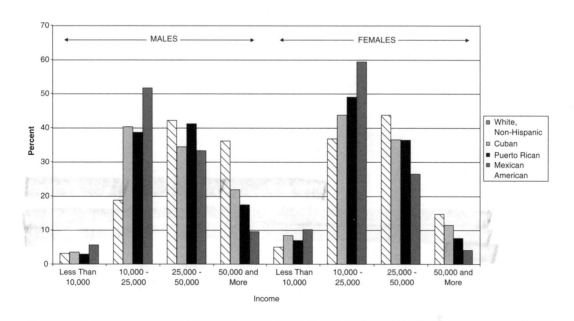

SOURCE: U.S. Bureau of the Census (2000p).

racial minority groups. Some studies report that contact is greater for the more affluent social classes, in the cities, and for the younger generations, who are presumably more Americanized (Fitzpatrick, 1976; Grebler et al., 1970, p. 397; Rodriguez, 1989, pp. 70–72).

Rates of intermarriage are higher for Latinos than for African Americans, but neither are a very high percentage of all marriages. Black and white interracial couples make up less than 1% of all marriages, and the comparable figure for Latinos is 3.5% of all marriages (U.S. Bureau of the Census, 2002, p. 47).

ASSIMILATION AND HISPANIC AMERICANS

As test cases for what we have called the traditional view of American assimilation, Latinos fare poorly. Mexican Americans continue to be concentrated in the low-wage sector of the labor market, a source of cheap labor for the dominant group's economy. Puerto Ricans, who are more recent arrivals, occupy a similar profile and position.

The fundamental reality faced by both groups, in their histories and in their present situations, is their colonized status in U.S. society. Both Mexican Americans and Puerto Ricans have struggled to rise from their subordinate positions in the United States, and some members have been successful. Yet the overall socioeconomic profiles of these groups continue to resemble those of other colonized minority groups, and they share many problems with other urban minority groups of color.

The traditional views of the nature of assimilation likewise fail to describe the experiences of Cuban Americans. They are more prosperous, on the average, than either Mexican Americans or Puerto Ricans, but they became successful by remaining separate.

There is no single Hispanic American experience or pattern of adjustment to the larger society. We have focused on just three of the many Latino groups in the United States, and the diversity of their experiences suggests the variety and complexity of what it means to be a minority group in this society. Their experiences also illustrate some of the fundamental forces that shape the experiences of minority groups: the split labor market and the U.S. appetite for cheap labor, the impact of industrialization, the dangers of a permanent urban underclass, the relationships between competition and levels of prejudice and rejection, and the persistence of race as a primary dividing line between people and groups.

MAIN POINTS

- Hispanic Americans are a diverse and growing part of U.S. society. There are many distinct groups, but the three largest are Mexican Americans, Puerto Ricans, and Cuban Americans. The various Hispanic groups do not think of themselves as a single entity.
- Hispanic Americans have some characteristics of colonized groups and some of immigrant groups. Similarly, these groups are racial minorities in some ways and ethnic minorities in others.
- Since the beginning of the 20th century, Mexican immigrants have served as a reserve labor force for the development of the U.S. economy. Immigrants from Mexico entered a social system in which the colonized status of the group was already established. Mexican Americans remain a colonized minority group despite the large numbers of immigrants in the group and they have been systematically excluded from opportunities for upward mobility by institutional discrimination and segregation.

- A Mexican American protest movement has been continuously seeking to improve the status of the group. In the 1960s, a more intense and militant movement emerged, guided by the ideology of Chicanismo.
- Puerto Ricans began to move to the mainland in large numbers only in recent decades. The group is concentrated in the urban Northeast and in the low-wage sector of the job market.
- Cubans began immigrating in large numbers after Castro's revolution in the late 1950s. They settled primarily in southern Florida, where they created an ethnic enclave.
- Immigration from Latin America and the Caribbean, especially Mexico, has been considerable since 1965 and has generated considerable controversy. Issues include competition for jobs, the primacy of the English language and Anglo-American culture, and whether immigrants are a tax and welfare burden.
- The overall levels of anti-Hispanic prejudice and discrimination seem to have declined along with the general decline in explicit, overt racism in American society. Recent high levels of immigration seem to have increased anti-Hispanic prejudice and discrimination, however, especially in areas with large numbers of immigrants.
- Levels of acculturation are highly variable from group to group and generation to generation. Acculturation increases with length of residence. The vitality of Latino cultures has been sustained by recent immigration.
- Secondary structural assimilation also varies from group to group. Poverty, unemployment, lower levels of educational attainment, and other forms of inequality continue to be major problems for Hispanic groups, even the relatively successful Cuban Americans. Primary structural assimilation with the dominant group is greater than for African Americans and Native Americans.

QUESTIONS FOR REVIEW AND STUDY

1. The text says that Hispanic Americans "combine elements of the polar extremes [immigrant and colonized] of Blauner's typology of minority groups" and that they are "partly an ethnic minority group and partly a racial minority group." Explain these statements in terms of the material presented in this chapter.
2. What important cultural differences between Mexican Americans and the dominant society shaped the relationships between the two groups?
3. How does the history of Mexican immigration demonstrate the usefulness of Noel's concepts of differentials in power and competition?
4. Compare and contrast the protest movements of Mexican Americans, Native Americans, and African Americans. What similarities and differences existed in Chicanismo, red power, and black power? How do the differences reflect the unique experiences of each group?
5. In what ways are the experiences of Puerto Ricans and Cuban Americans unique compared with those of other minority groups? How do these differences reflect other differences?
6. The Cuban American enclave has resulted in a variety of benefits for the group. Why don't other minority groups follow this strategy?
7. Sociologist Douglas Massey believes that contemporary immigrants will not assimilate in the same way as white ethnic groups whose ancestors arrived between the 1820s and the 1920s. Summarize his argument. What concepts does he use to analyze the situations of present-day immigrants? How does their situation reflect the structure of modern American society?
8. What images of Latinas are common in U.S. society? How do these images reflect the experiences of these groups?

9. Describe the situation of the major Hispanic American groups in terms of acculturation and integration. Which groups are closest to equality? What factors or experiences might account for the differences between groups? In what ways might the statement "Hispanic Americans are remaining pluralistic even while they assimilate" be true?

INTERNET RESEARCH PROJECT

The Mexican Migration Project was created to learn more about the complex process of Mexican migration to the United States. The project is binational and has been gathering data since 1982. A number of individual stories of Mexican migrants are available on-line at www.pop.upenn.edu/mexmig/expressions/prologue.htm. Read the prologue and then select several of the stories to read. Analyze each using the concepts developed in this chapter, especially the idea that Mexico serves as a reserve pool of cheap labor for the benefit of U.S. businesses.

FOR FURTHER READING

Acuna, Rodolfo. 1999. *Occupied America* (4th ed.). New York: Harper & Row.
The author reviews Mexican American history and argues that the experiences of this group resemble those of colonized groups.

Fitzpatrick, Joseph P. 1987. *Puerto Rican Americans: The Meaning of Migration to the Mainland* (2nd ed.). Englewood Cliffs, NJ: Prentice Hall.
A good overview of the history and present situation of Puerto Ricans.

García, María Cristina. 1996. *Havana USA: Cuban Exiles and Cuban Americans in South Florida, 1959–1994.* Berkeley: University of California Press.
A comprehensive history of the Cuban community in southern Florida.

Mirandé, Alfredo. 1985. *The Chicano Experience: An Alternative Perspective.* Notre Dame, IN: University of Notre Dame Press.
A passionate analysis of the Mexican American experience. Separate chapters on work, crime, education, the church, and family.

Portes, Alejandro, & Bach, Robert L. 1985. *Latin Journey: Cuban and Mexican Immigrants in the United States.* Berkeley: University of California Press.
A landmark analysis of Latino immigration, ethnic enclaves, U.S. society, and assimilation.

NOTES

1. The term *Latino* refers to the group as a whole or to male members. *Latina* is the female form.
2. The exact volume of illegal immigration is unknown but probably follows the general contours of Exhibit 7.2 and certainly has increased rapidly since the 1960s.

8

Asian Americans and Pacific Islanders

A "Model Minority"?

Asian American and Pacific Islander groups differ from each other in language, customs and culture, physical appearance and—most centrally for this text—in the ways in which they have entered American society. Some groups have experienced levels of discrimination and rejection that approach those endured by the colonized and conquered groups we covered in previous chapters. Others have developed strong enclave economies, and still others more closely resemble Blauner's immigrant minority group. Indeed, some groups have followed all three pathways or modes of incorporation. For example, the present situation of Chinese Americans is strongly shaped by high rates of immigration, but their history includes strong elements of colonization combined with an elaborate enclave community.

Asian Americans and Pacific Islanders are no more a single group than are Hispanic or Native Americans. They vary in their background characteristics as well as in their experiences in the United States, and like Hispanic Americans, they identify more with their national-origin group than with the broad, pan-ethnic category.

In this chapter, we will address the diversity of Asian Americans and Pacific Islanders and consider the causes and consequences of their varied modes of incorporation into U.S.

society. One of our major concerns will be exploring differences with groups we have covered in previous chapters and especially the perception that Asian Americans are "model minorities": successful, affluent, highly educated people who do not suffer from the problems usually associated with minority group status. How accurate is this view? Have Asian Americans forged a pathway to upward mobility that could be followed by other groups? Do the concepts and theories that have guided this text (particularly the Blauner and Noel hypotheses) apply? Does the success of these groups mean that the United States is truly an open, fair, and just society?

We begin with an overview of the population characteristics of the largest Asian American and Pacific Island groups and then briefly examine the traditions and customs that they bring with them to America. We then turn to the contact situation and experiences of Chinese Americans and Japanese Americans, the first Asian groups to immigrate to the United States in substantial numbers, as well as more recent immigrants. Finally, we use the concepts that we have developed in previous chapters to assess the present status of Asian Americans and Pacific Islanders and the view that they are a "success" story.

ASIAN AMERICANS AND PACIFIC ISLANDERS

Exhibit 8.1 lists the largest Asian American and Pacific Islander groups and further illustrates their diversity. The six largest groups are distinct from each other in terms of language and culture as well as in physical appearance, and each has had its own unique experience in America. The "other" groups further add to this diversity.

Several features of Exhibit 8.1 are worth noting. First, Asian Americans and Pacific Islanders are tiny fractions of the total U.S. population. Even when aggregated, they account for slightly less than 4% of the total population in 2000. In contrast, African Americans and Hispanic Americans are each about 12% of the total population (see Exhibit 1.1). Second, most Asian American

groups have grown dramatically in recent decades, largely because of high rates of immigration since the 1965 changes in U.S. immigration policy (Lee, 1998, p. 15). Each group listed in Exhibit 8.1 except Japanese Americans grew faster than the total population between 1980 and 2000. The Japanese American population grew at the slowest rate (largely because immigration from Japan has been low in recent decades), but the Vietnamese American population more than quadrupled in size, as did the number of Indian Americans. This rapid growth is projected to continue for decades to come, and the impact of Asian Americans on everyday life and American culture will increase accordingly. Today, fewer than 4 out of every 100 Americans are in this group, but this ratio will grow to nearly 10 out of every 100 by the year 2050. Finally, with the exception of Indian Americans, Asian Americans and Pacific Islanders are concentrated on the West Coast. West Coast cities have been the most common ports of entry for these groups since immigration began more than 150 years ago.

ORIGINS AND CULTURES

Asian Americans and Pacific Islanders have brought a wealth of traditions to the United States. They speak many different languages and practice diverse religions, including Buddhism, Confucianism, Islam, Hindu, and Christianity. Asian cultures predate the founding of the United States by centuries and even millennia. Although no two of these cultures are the same, some general similarities can be identified. These cultural traits have shaped the behavior of Asian Americans as well as the perceptions of members of the dominant group, and they compose part of the foundation on which Asian American experiences have been built.

Asian cultures tend to stress group membership over individual self-interest. For example, Confucianism, which was the dominant ethical and moral system in traditional China and had a powerful influence on many other Asian cultures, counsels people to see themselves as elements in larger social systems

Exhibit 8.1 Size and Recent Growth of Asian American and Pacific Island Groups

Group	1980	2000	Percentage of Total Population, 2000	Growth, 1980-2000 (Number of times as large)	Percentage Living in the West, 2000
Chinese	812,000	2,433,000	0.9	3.0	49
Filipino	782,000	1,850,000	0.7	2.4	68
Indian	387,000	1,679,000	0.6	4.3	23
Vietnamese	245,000	1,123,000	0.4	4.6	50
Korean	357,000	1,077,000	0.4	3.0	44
Japanese	716,000	797,000	0.3	1.1	73
Other Asian-American and Pacific Islander groups[a]	166,000	1,684,000[b]	0.6	10.2	51
Total for all Asian American and Pacific Islander groups	3,466,000	10,643,000	3.9	3.1	49
Total U.S. population	226,546,000	281,422,000	—	1.2	23

SOURCE: 1980: Lee (1998, p. 15); 2000: U.S. Bureau of the Census (2002).

a. Includes "other Asian" alone and people who claimed two or more Asian categories.
b. Includes Native Hawaiians, Cambodians, Laotians, Hmong, Thais, Pakistanis, Samoans, and many others.

and status hierarchies. Confucianism emphasizes loyalty to the group, conformity to societal expectations, and respect for one's superiors. In traditional China, as in other Asian societies, the business of everyday life was organized around kinship relations, and most interpersonal relations were with family members and other relatives (Lyman, 1974, p. 9). The family or the clan often owned the land on which all depended for survival, and kinship ties determined inheritance patterns. The clan also performed a number of crucial social functions, including arranging marriages, settling disputes between individuals, and organizing festivals and holidays.

Asian cultures stress sensitivity to the opinions and judgments of others and to the importance of avoiding public embarrassment and not giving offense. Especially when discussing Japanese culture, these cultural tendencies are often contrasted with Western practices in terms of "guilt versus shame" and the nature of personal morality (Benedict, 1946). In Western cultures, individuals are encouraged to develop and abide by a conscience, or an inner moral voice, and behavior is guided by one's personal sense of guilt. In contrast, Asian cultures stress the importance of maintaining the respect and good opinion of others and avoiding shame and public humiliation. Group harmony, or *wa* in Japanese, is a central concern, and displays of individualism are discouraged. These characteristics are reflected in a Japanese proverb: "The nail that sticks up must be hammered down" (Whiting, 1990, p. 70). Asian cultures emphasize proper behavior, conformity to convention and the judgments of others, and avoiding embarrassment and personal confrontations ("saving face").

Traditional Asian cultures were male dominated, and women were consigned to subordinate roles. A Chinese woman was expected to serve first her father, then her husband, and if widowed, her eldest son. Confucianism also decreed that women should observe the Four Virtues: chastity and obedience, shyness, a pleasing demeanor, and skill in the performance of domestic duties (Amott & Matthaei, 1991, p. 200). Women of high status in traditional China symbolized their subordination by binding their feet. This painful, crippling practice began early in life and required women to wrap their feet tightly to keep them artificially small. The bones in the arch were broken so that the toes could be bent under the foot, further decreasing the size of the foot. Bound feet were considered beautiful, but they also immobilized women and were intended to prevent them from "wandering away" from domestic and household duties (Jackson, 2000; Takaki, 1993, pp. 209–210).

The experiences of Asian Americans in the United States modified these patriarchal values and traditional traits. For the groups with longer histories in U.S. society such as Chinese Americans and Japanese Americans, the effects of these values on individual personality may be slight; for more newly arrived groups, the effects are more powerful. The cultural and religious differences among the Asian American groups also reflect the recent histories of each of the sending nations. For example, Vietnam was a colony of China for 1,000 years but for much of the past century was a colony of France. Although Vietnamese culture has been heavily influenced by China, many Vietnamese are Catholic, a result of the efforts of the French to convert them. The Philippines and India were also colonized by Western nations—the former by Spain and then by the United States, and the latter by England. As a result, many Filipinos are Catholic, and many Indian immigrants are familiar with English and with Anglo culture.

These examples are, of course, the merest suggestion of the diversity of these groups. In fact, Asian Americans and Pacific Islanders, who share little more than a slight physical resemblance and some broad cultural similarities, are much more diverse than Hispanic Americans, who are overwhelmingly Catholic

and share a common language and a historical connection with Spain (Min, 1995, p. 25).

CONTACT SITUATIONS AND THE DEVELOPMENT OF THE CHINESE AMERICAN AND JAPANESE AMERICAN COMMUNITIES

The earliest Asian groups to arrive in substantial numbers were from China and Japan. Their contact situations not only shaped their own histories but also affected the present situation of all Asian Americans and Pacific Islanders in many ways. As we will see, the contact situations for both Chinese Americans and Japanese Americans featured massive rejection and discrimination. Both groups adapted to the racism of the larger society by forming enclaves, a strategy that eventually produced some major benefits for their descendants.

Chinese Americans

Early Immigration and the Anti-Chinese Campaign

Immigrants from China to the United States began to arrive in the early 1800s and generally were motivated by the same kinds of social and economic forces that have inspired immigration everywhere for the past two centuries. Chinese immigrants were "pushed" to leave their homeland by the disruption of traditional social relations caused by the colonization of much of China by more industrialized European nations and by rapid population growth (Chan, 1990; Lyman, 1974; Tsai, 1986). At the same time, these immigrants were "pulled" to the West Coast of the United States by the Gold Rush of 1849 and by other opportunities created by the development of the West.

The Noel hypothesis (see Chapter 3) provides a useful way to analyze the contact situation that developed between Chinese and Anglo-Americans in the mid-19th century. As you recall, Noel argued that racial or ethnic stratification will result when a contact situation is characterized by three conditions:

ethnocentrism, competition, and a differential in power. Once all three conditions were met on the West Coast, a vigorous campaign against the Chinese began, and the group was pushed into a subordinate, disadvantaged position.

Ethnocentrism based on racial, cultural, and language differences was present from the beginning, but at first, competition for jobs between Chinese immigrants and native-born workers was muted by a robust, rapidly growing economy and an abundance of jobs. At first, in the 1840s, politicians, newspaper editorial writers, and business leaders praised the Chinese for their industriousness and tirelessness (Tsai, 1986, p. 17). Before long, however, the economic boom slowed, and the supply of jobs began to dry up. The Gold Rush petered out, and the transcontinental railroad, which thousands of Chinese workers had helped to build, was completed in 1869. The migration of Anglo-Americans from the East continued, and competition for jobs and other resources increased. An anti-Chinese campaign of harassment, discrimination, and violent attacks began. In 1871 in Los Angeles, a mob of "several hundred whites shot, hanged, and stabbed 19 Chinese to death" (Tsai, 1986, p. 67). Other attacks against the Chinese occurred in Denver, Seattle, Tacoma, and Rock Springs, Wyoming (Lyman, 1974, p. 77).

As the West Coast economy changed, the Chinese came to be seen as a threat, and elements of the dominant group tried to limit competition. The Chinese were a small group—there were only about 100,000 in the entire country in 1870—and by law, they were not permitted to become citizens. Hence, they controlled few power resources with which to withstand these attacks. During the 1870s, Chinese workers were forced out of most sectors of the mainstream economy, and in 1882, the anti-Chinese campaign experienced its ultimate triumph when the U.S. Congress passed the Chinese Exclusion Act, banning virtually all immigration from China. The act was one of the first restrictive immigration laws and was aimed solely at the Chinese. It established a "rigid competitive" relationship between the groups (see Chapter 4) and eliminated the threat presented by Chinese labor by excluding them from American society.

The primary antagonists of Chinese immigrants were native-born workers and organized labor. White owners of small businesses, feeling threatened by Chinese-owned businesses, also supported passage of the Chinese Exclusion Act (Boswell, 1986). Other social classes, like the capitalists who owned larger factories, might actually have benefited from the continued supply of cheaper labor created by immigration from China. Conflicts such as the anti-Chinese campaign can be especially intense because they confound racial and ethnic antagonisms with disputes between different social classes.

The ban on immigration from China remained in effect until World War II, when China was awarded a yearly quota of 105 immigrants in recognition of its wartime alliance with the United States. However, large-scale immigration from China did not resume until federal policy was revised in the 1960s.

Population Trends and the "Delayed" Second Generation

Following the Chinese Exclusion Act, the number of Chinese in the United States actually declined (see Exhibit 8.2) as some immigrants passed away or returned to China and were not replaced by newcomers. The huge majority of Chinese immigrants in the 19th century had been young adult male sojourners who intended to work hard, save money, and return to their homes in China (Chan, 1990, p. 66). After 1882, it was difficult for anyone from China, male or female, to immigrate, and the Chinese community in the United States remained overwhelmingly male for many decades. At the end of the 19th century, for example, males outnumbered females by more than 25 to 1, and the sex ratio did not approach parity for decades (Wong, 1995, p. 64; see also Ling, 2000). The scarcity of Chinese women in the United States delayed the second generation (the first born in the United States), and it wasn't until the 1920s, 80 years after immigration began, that as many as one third of all Chinese in the United States were native born (Wong, 1995, p. 64).

The delayed second generation may have reinforced the exclusion of the Chinese American community that began as a reaction to the overt discrimination of the dominant group (Chan, 1990, p. 66). The children of immigrants usually are much more acculturated, and their language facility and greater familiarity with the larger society often permit them to represent the group and speak for it more effectively. In the case of Chinese Americans (and other Asian groups), members of the second generation were citizens of the United States by birth, a status from which the immigrants were barred, and they had legal and political rights not available to their parents. Thus, the decades-long absence of a more Americanized, English-speaking generation increased the isolation of Chinese Americans.

The Ethnic Enclave

The Chinese became increasingly urbanized as the anti-Chinese campaign and rising racism took their toll. Forced out of towns and smaller cities, they settled in larger urban areas, such as San Francisco, which offered the safety of urban anonymity and ethnic neighborhoods where the old ways could be practiced and contact with the hostile larger society minimized. "Chinatowns" had existed since the start of immigration and now took on added significance as safe havens from the storm of anti-Chinese venom. The Chinese withdrew to these neighborhoods and became an "invisible minority" (Tsai, 1986, p. 67).

These early Chinatowns were ethnic enclaves like the more recently founded Cuban community in Miami, and a similar process formed them. The earliest urban Chinese included merchants and skilled artisans who, like the early waves of Cuban immigrants, were experienced in commerce (Chan, 1990, p. 44). They established businesses and retail stores that typically were small in scope and modest in profits. As the number of urban Chinese increased, the market for these enterprises became larger and more spatially

concentrated. New services were required, the size of the cheap labor pool available to Chinese merchants and entrepreneurs increased, and the Chinatowns became the economic, cultural, and social centers of the community.

Within the Chinatowns, an elaborate social structure developed that mirrored traditional China in many ways. The enforced segregation of the Chinese in America helped preserve much of the traditional food, dress, language, values, and religions of their homeland from the pressures of Americanization. The social structure was based on a variety of types of organizations, including family and clan groups and *huiguan,* or associations based on the region or district in China from which the immigrant had come.

These organizations performed various, often overlapping, social and welfare services, including settling disputes, aiding new arrivals from their regions, and facilitating the development of mutual aid networks (Lai, 1980, p. 221; Lyman, 1974, pp. 32–37, 116–118). Life was not always peaceful in Chinatown, and there were numerous disputes over control of resources and the organizational infrastructure. In particular, secret societies called *tongs* contested the control and leadership of the merchant-led *huiguan* and the clan associations. These sometimes bloody conflicts were sensationalized in the American press as "Tong wars," and they contributed to the popular stereotypes of Asians as exotic, mysterious, and dangerous (Lai, 1980, p. 222; Lyman, 1974, pp. 37–50).

Despite these internal conflicts, American Chinatowns evolved into highly organized, largely self-contained communities complete with their own leadership and decision-making structures. The internal "city government" of Chinatown was the Chinese Consolidated Benevolent Association (CCBA). Dominated by the larger *huiguan* and clans, the CCBA coordinated and supplemented the activities of the various organizations and represented the interests of the community to the larger society.

The local CCBAs, along with other organizations, also attempted to combat the anti-Chinese campaign, speaking out against racial discrimination and filing numerous

Exhibit 8.2   Population Growth for Chinese Americans and Japanese Americans

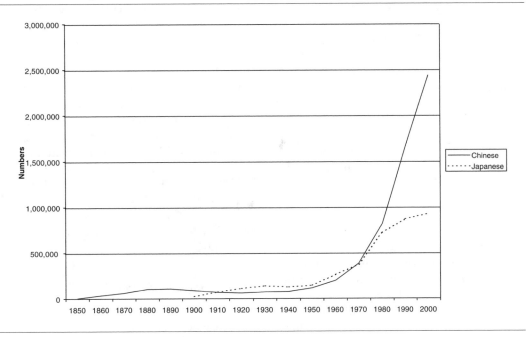

SOURCE: Kitano (1980, p. 562); Lee (1998, p. 15); U.S. Bureau of the Census (2002, p. 24).

lawsuits to contest racist legislation (Lai, 1980, p. 223). The effectiveness of the protest efforts was handicapped by the lack of resources in the Chinese community and by the fact that Chinese immigrants could not become citizens. Attempts were made to mobilize international pressure to protest the treatment of the Chinese in the United States. At the time, however, China was itself colonized and dominated by other nations (including the United States). China was further weakened by internal turmoil and could mount no effective assistance for its citizens in the United States (Chan, 1990, p. 62).

Survival and Development

The Chinese American community survived despite the widespread poverty, discrimination, and pressures created by the unbalanced sex ratio. Members of the group began to seek opportunities in other regions, and Chinatowns appeared and grew in New York, Boston, Chicago, Philadelphia, and many other cities.

The patterns of exclusion and discrimination that began during the 19th-century anti-Chinese campaign were common throughout the nation and continued well into the 20th century. Chinese Americans responded by finding economic opportunity in areas where dominant group competition for jobs was weak, continuing their tendency to be an "invisible" minority group. Very often, they started small businesses that served either other members of their own group (restaurants, for example) or that relied on the patronage of the general public (laundries, for example). The jobs provided by these small businesses were the economic lifeblood of the community but were limited in the amount of income and wealth they could generate. Until recent decades, for example, most restaurants served primarily other Chinese, especially single males. Because their primary clientele was poor, the profit potential of these businesses was sharply limited. Laundries served the more affluent dominant group, but the returns from this enterprise declined as washers and dryers became increasingly widespread in homes throughout the nation. The population of Chinatown generally was too small to sustain more than these two primary commercial enterprises (Zhou, 1992, pp. 92–94).

As the decades passed, the enclave economy and the complex subsociety of Chinatown evolved. However, discrimination combined with defensive self-segregation to ensure the continuation of poverty, limited job opportunities, and substandard housing. Relatively hidden from general view, Chinatown became the world in which the second generation grew to adulthood.

The Second Generation

Whereas the immigrant generation generally retained its native language and customs, the second generation was much more influenced by the larger culture. The institutional and organizational structures of Chinatown were created to serve the older, mostly male immigrant generation, but younger Chinese Americans tended to look beyond the enclave to fill their needs. They came in contact with the larger society through schools, churches, and voluntary organizations such as the YMCA and YWCA. They abandoned many traditional customs and were less loyal to and interested in the clan and regional associations that the immigrant generation had constructed. They founded organizations of their own that were more compatible with their Americanized lifestyles (Lai, 1980, p. 225).

As with other minority groups, World War II was an important watershed for Chinese Americans. During the war, job opportunities outside the enclave increased, and after the war, many of the 8,000 Chinese Americans who served in the armed forces were able to take advantage of the GI Bill to further their education (Lai, 1980, p. 226). In the 1940s and 1950s, many second-generation Chinese Americans moved out of the enclave and away from the traditional neighborhoods and pursued careers in the larger society. This group was mobile and Americanized, and with educational credentials comparable to those of the general population, they were prepared to seek success outside Chinatown.

In another departure from tradition, the women of the second generation also pursued education, and as early as 1960, median years of schooling for Chinese American women was slightly higher than for Chinese American men (Kitano & Daniels, 1995, p. 48). Chinese American women also became more diverse in their occupational profile as the century progressed. In 1900, three quarters of all employed Chinese American women worked in manufacturing (usually in garment industry sweatshops or in canning factories) or in domestic work. By 1960, less than 2% were in domestic work, 32% were in clerical occupations, and 18% held professional jobs, often as teachers (Amott & Matthaei, 1991, pp. 209–211).

An American Success Story?

The men and women of the second generation achieved considerable educational and occupational success and helped to establish the idea that Chinese Americans are a model minority. A closer examination reveals, however, that the old traditions of anti-Chinese discrimination and prejudice continued to limit the life chances of even the best-educated members of this generation. Second-generation Chinese Americans earned less on the average and had less favorable occupational profiles than comparably educated white Americans, a gap between qualifications and rewards that reflects persistent discrimination. Kitano and Daniels (1995, p. 50; see also Hirschman & Wong, 1984) concluded, for example, that although well-educated Chinese Americans could find good jobs in the mainstream economy, the highest, most lucrative positions—and those that required direct supervision of whites—were still closed to them.

Furthermore, many Chinese Americans, including many of those who stayed in the Chinatowns to operate the enclave economy and the immigrants who began arriving after 1965, do not fit the image of success at all. A large percentage of these Chinese Americans face the same problems as other colonized, excluded, exploited minority groups of color. They rely for survival on low-wage jobs in the garment industry, the service sector, and the small businesses of the enclave economy and are beset by poverty and powerlessness, much like the urban underclass segments of other groups.

Thus, Chinese Americans can be found at both ends of the spectrum of success and affluence, and the group is often said to be "bipolar" in its occupational structure (see Barringer, Takeuchi, & Levin, 1995; Takaki, 1993, pp. 415–416; Wong, 1995, pp. 77–78; Zhou & Logan, 1989). Although a high percentage are found in more desirable occupations—sustaining the idea of Asian success—others, less visible, are concentrated at the lowest levels of society. We consider the socioeconomic status of Chinese Americans and other Asian American groups as well as the accuracy of the image of success and affluence again later in this chapter.

Japanese Americans

Immigration from Japan began to increase shortly after the Chinese Exclusion Act of 1882 took effect, in part to fill the gap in the labor supply created by the restrictive legislation (Kitano, 1980). The 1880 census counted only a few hundred Japanese in the United States, but the group increased rapidly over the next few decades. By 1910, the Japanese in the United States outnumbered the Chinese and remained the larger of the two groups until large-scale immigration resumed in the 1960s (see Exhibit 8.2).

The Anti-Japanese Campaign

The contact situation for Japanese immigrants resembled that of the Chinese. They immigrated to the same West Coast regions as the Chinese, entered the labor force in a similar position, and were a small group with few power resources. Predictably, the feelings and emotions generated by the anti-Chinese campaign transferred to them. By the early 1900s, an anti-Japanese campaign to limit competition was in full swing. Efforts were being made to establish a rigid competitive system of group relations and to exclude Japanese

immigrants in the same way the Chinese had been barred (Kitano, 1980, p. 563; Kitano & Daniels, 1995, pp. 59–60; Petersen, 1971, pp. 30–55).

Japanese immigration was partly curtailed in 1907 when a "gentlemen's agreement" was signed between Japan and the United States limiting the number of laborers Japan would allow to emigrate (Kitano & Daniels, 1995, p. 59). This policy remained in effect until the United States changed its immigration policy in the 1920s and barred immigration from Japan completely. The end of Japanese immigration is largely responsible for the slow growth of the Japanese American population displayed in Exhibit 8.2.

Most Japanese immigrants, like the Chinese, were young male laborers who planned to return eventually to their homeland or to bring their wives after they were established in their new country (Duleep, 1988, p. 24). The gentlemen's agreement curtailed the immigration of men, but because of a loophole, females were able to continue to immigrate until the 1920s. Japanese Americans were thus able to maintain a relatively balanced sex ratio, marry, and begin families, and a second generation of Japanese Americans began to appear without much delay. Native-born Japanese numbered about half of the group by 1930 and were a majority of 63% on the eve of World War II (Kitano & Daniels, 1995, p. 59).

The anti-Japanese movement also attempted to dislodge the group from agriculture. Many Japanese immigrants were skilled agriculturists, and farming proved to be their most promising avenue for advancement (Kitano, 1980, p. 563). In 1910, between 30% and 40% of all Japanese in California were engaged in agriculture, and from 1900 to 1909, the number of independent Japanese farmers increased from fewer than 50 to about 6,000 (Jibou, 1988, p. 358).

Most of these immigrant farmers owned small plots of land, and they composed only a minuscule percentage of West Coast farmers (Jibou, 1988, pp. 357–358). Nonetheless, their presence and relative success did not go unnoticed and eventually stimulated discriminatory legislation, most notably the Alien Land Act, passed by the California legislature in 1913 (Kitano, 1980, p. 563). This bill declared aliens ineligible for citizenship (effectively meaning only immigrants from Asia) to be ineligible to own land as well. The bill did not achieve its goal of dislodging the Japanese from the rural economy. They were able to dodge the discriminatory legislation by various devices, mostly by putting the title of the land in the names of their American-born children, who were citizens by law (Jibou, 1988, p. 359).

The Alien Land Act was one part of a sustained campaign against the Japanese in the United States. In the early decades of the 20th century, the Japanese were politically disenfranchised and segregated from dominant group institutions in schools and residential areas. They were discriminated against in movie houses, swimming pools, and other public facilities (Kitano & Daniels, 1988, p. 56). The Japanese were excluded from the mainstream economy and confined to a limited range of poorly paid occupations (see Yamato, 1994). Thus, there were strong elements of systematic discrimination, exclusion, and colonization in their overall relationship with the larger society.

The Ethnic Enclave

Spurned and disparaged by the larger society, the Japanese, like the Chinese, constructed a separate subsociety. The immigrant generation, called the Issei (from the Japanese word *ichi*, meaning "one"), established an enclave in agriculture and related enterprises, a rural counterpart of the urban enclaves constructed by other groups we have examined.

By World War II, the Issei had come to dominate a narrow but important segment of agriculture on the West Coast, especially in California. Although they were never more than 2% of the total population of California, Japanese American–owned farms produced as much as 30% or 40% of various fruits and vegetables grown in that state. As late as 1940, more than 40% of Japanese Americans were involved directly in farming, and many more were dependent

on the economic activity stimulated by agriculture, including the marketing of their produce (Jibou, 1988, pp. 359–360). Other Issei lived in urban areas, where they were concentrated in a narrow range of businesses and services, such as domestic service and gardening, some of which catered to other Issei and some of which served the dominant group (Jibou, 1988, p. 362).

Japanese Americans in both the rural and urban sectors maximized their economic clout by doing business with other Japanese-owned firms as often as possible. Gardeners and farmers would purchase supplies at Japanese-owned firms, farmers would use other members of the group to haul their products to market, and businesspeople would rely on one another and mutual credit associations, rather than dominant group banks, for financial services. These networks helped the enclave economy to grow and also permitted the Japanese to avoid the hostility and racism of the larger society. However, these very same patterns helped sustain the stereotypes that depicted the Japanese as clannish and unassimilable. In the years before World War II, the Japanese American community was largely dependent for survival on their networks of cooperation and mutual assistance, not on Americanization and integration.

The Second Generation (Nisei)

In the 1920s and 1930s, anti-Asian feelings continued to run high, and Japanese Americans continued to experience exclusion and discrimination despite (or perhaps because of) their relative success. Unable to find acceptance in Anglo society, the second generation—called the Nisei—established clubs, athletic leagues, churches, and a multitude of other social and recreational organizations within their own communities (Kitano & Daniels, 1995, p. 63). These organizations reflected the high levels of Americanization of the Nisei and expressed values and interests quite compatible with those of the dominant culture. For example, the most influential Nisei organization was the Japanese American Citizens League, the creed of which expressed an ardent patriotism that was to be sorely tested: "I am proud that I am an American citizen . . . I believe in [American] institutions, ideas and traditions; I glory in her heritage; I boast of her history; I trust in her future" (Kitano & Daniels, 1995, p. 64).

Although the Nisei enjoyed high levels of success in school, the intense discrimination and racism of the 1930s prevented most of them from translating their educational achievements into better jobs and higher salaries. Many occupations in the mainstream economy were closed to even the best-educated Japanese Americans, and anti-Asian prejudice and discrimination did not diminish during the hard times and high unemployment of the Great Depression in the 1930s. Many Nisei were forced to remain within the enclave, and in many cases, jobs in the produce stands and retail shops of their parents were all they could find. Their demoralization and anger over their exclusion eventually were swamped by the larger events of World War II.

The Relocation Camps

On December 7, 1941, Japan attacked Pearl Harbor, killing almost 2,500 Americans. President Franklin D. Roosevelt asked Congress for a declaration of war the next day. The preparations for war stirred up a wide range of fears and anxieties among the American public, including concerns about the loyalty of Japanese Americans. Decades of exclusion and anti-Japanese prejudice had conditioned the dominant society to see Japanese Americans as sinister, clannish, cruel, unalterably foreign, and racially inferior. Fueled by the ferocity of the war itself and fears about a Japanese invasion of the mainland, the tradition of anti-Japanese racism laid the groundwork for a massive violation of civil rights.

Two months after the attack on Pearl Harbor, President Roosevelt signed Executive Order 9066, which led to the relocation of Japanese Americans living on the West Coast. By the late summer of 1942, more than 110,000 Japanese Americans, young and old, male and female—virtually the entire West Coast population—had been transported to relocation camps, where they were imprisoned behind barbed-wire fences patrolled by armed guards. Many of these people were American citizens, yet no attempt was made to distinguish between citizens and aliens. No trials were held, and no one was given the opportunity to refute the implicit charge of disloyalty.

The government gave families little notice to prepare for evacuation and secure their homes, businesses, and belongings. They were allowed to bring to the camps only what they could carry, and many possessions were simply abandoned. Businesspeople sold their establishments and farmers sold their land at panic-sale prices. Others locked up their stores and houses and walked away, hoping that the evacuation would be short-lived and their possessions undisturbed.

The internment lasted for nearly the entire war. At first, Japanese Americans were not permitted to serve in the armed forces, but eventually more than 25,000 escaped the camps by volunteering for military service. Nearly all of them served in segregated units or in intelligence work with combat units in the Pacific Ocean. Two all-Japanese combat units served in Europe and became the most decorated units in American military history (Kitano, 1980, p. 567). Other Japanese Americans were able to get out of the camps by means other than the military. Some, for example, agreed to move to militarily nonsensitive areas far away from the West Coast (and their former homes). Still, when the camps closed at the end of the war, about half of the original internees remained (Kitano & Daniels, 1988, p. 64).

The camps disrupted the traditional forms of family life, as people had to adapt to barracks living and mess hall dining. Conflicts flared between those who counseled caution and temperate reactions to the incarceration and those who wanted to protest in more vigorous ways. Many of those who advised moderation were Nisei intent on proving their loyalty and cooperating with the camp administration.

Despite the injustice and dislocations of the incarceration, the camps did reduce the extent to which women were relegated to a subordinate role. Like Chinese women, Japanese women were expected to devote themselves to the care of the males of their family. In Japan, for example, education for females was not intended to challenge their intellect so much as to make them better wives and mothers. In the camps, however, pay for the few jobs available was the same for both men and women, and the mess halls and small living quarters freed women from some of the burden of housework. Many took advantage of the free time to take classes to learn more English and other skills. The younger women were able to meet young men on their own, weakening the tradition of family-controlled, arranged marriages (Amott & Matthaei, 1991, pp. 225–229).

Some Japanese Americans protested the incarceration from the start and brought lawsuits to end the relocation program. Finally, in 1944, the Supreme Court ruled that detention was unconstitutional. As the camps closed, some Japanese American individuals and organizations began to seek compensation and redress for the economic losses the group had suffered. In 1948, Congress passed legislation to authorize compensation to Japanese Americans. Some 26,500 people filed claims under this act. These claims eventually were settled for a total of about $38 million—less than one tenth the amount of the actual economic losses. Demand for meaningful redress and compensation continued, and in 1988, Congress passed a bill granting reparations of about $20,000 in cash to each of the 60,000 remaining survivors of the camps. The law also acknowledged that the relocation program had been a grave injustice to Japanese Americans (Biskupic, 1989, p. 2879).

The World War II relocation devastated the Japanese American community and left it with few material resources. The emotional and psychological damage inflicted by this experience is incalculable. The fact that today, only six decades later, Japanese Americans are equal or superior to national averages on measures of educational achievement, occupational prestige, and income marks one of the more dramatic transformations in minority group history.

Japanese Americans After World War II

In 1945, Japanese Americans faced a world very different from the one they had left in 1942. To escape the camps, nearly half of the group had scattered throughout the country and lived everywhere but on the West Coast. As Japanese Americans attempted to move back to their former homes, they found their fields untended, their stores vandalized, their possessions lost or stolen, and their lives shattered. In some cases, there was simply no Japanese neighborhood to return to; the Little Tokyo area of San Francisco, for example, was now occupied by African Americans who had moved to the West Coast to take jobs in the defense industry (Amott & Matthaei, 1991, p. 231).

Japanese Americans themselves had changed as well. In the camps, the Issei had lost power to the Nisei. The English-speaking second generation had dealt with the camp administrators and held the leadership positions. Many Nisei had left the camps to serve in the armed forces or to find work in other areas of the country. For virtually every American minority group, the war brought new experiences and a broader sense of themselves, the nation, and the world. A similar transformation occurred for the Nisei. When the war ended, they were unwilling to rebuild the Japanese community as it had been before.

Like second-generation Chinese Americans, the Nisei had a strong record of success in school, and they also took advantage of the GI Bill to further their education. When anti-Asian prejudice began to decline in the 1950s and the job market began to open, the Nisei were educationally prepared to take advantage of the resultant opportunities (Kitano, 1980, p. 567).

The Issei-dominated enclave economy did not reappear after the war. One indicator of the shift away from an enclave economy was the fact that the percentage of Japanese American women in California who worked as unpaid family laborers (i.e., worked in family-run businesses for no salary) declined from 21% in 1940 to 7% in 1950 (Amott &

Matthaei, 1991, p. 231). In addition, between 1940 and 1990, the percentage of the group employed in agriculture declined from about 50% to 3%, and the percentage employed in personal services fell from 25% to 5% (Nishi, 1995, p. 116).

By 1960, Japanese Americans had an occupational profile very similar to that of whites, except that they were actually overrepresented among professionals. Many were employed in the primary economy, not in the ethnic enclave, but there was a tendency to choose "safe" careers (e.g., in engineering, optometry, pharmacy, accounting) that did not require extensive contact with the public or supervision of whites (Kitano & Daniels, 1988, p. 70).

Within these limitations, the Nisei, their children (Sansei), and their grandchildren (Yonsei) have enjoyed relatively high status, and their upward mobility and prosperity have contributed to the perception that Asian Americans are a model minority. An additional factor contributing to the high status of Japanese Americans (and to the disappearance of Little Tokyos) is that, unlike Chinese Americans, the number of immigrants from Japan has been quite small, and the community has not had to devote many resources to newcomers. Furthermore, recent immigrants from Japan tend to be highly educated professional people whose socioeconomic characteristics add to the perception of success and affluence.

The Sansei and Yonsei are highly integrated into the occupational structure of the larger society. In comparison with their parents, their connections with their ethnic past are more tenuous, and in their values, beliefs, and personal goals, they resemble dominant group members of similar age and social class (Kitano & Daniels, 1995, pp. 79–81; also see Spickard, 1996).

Comparing Minority Groups

What factors account for the differences in the development of Chinese Americans and Japanese Americans and other racial minority groups? First, unlike African Americans in the 1600s and Mexican Americans in the 1800s, the dominant group had no desire to control the labor of these groups. The contact situation featured economic competition (e.g., for jobs) during an era of rigid competition between groups (see Exhibit 4.3), and Chinese Americans and Japanese Americans were seen as a threat to security that needed to be eliminated, not as a labor pool that needed to be controlled.

Second, unlike Native Americans, Chinese Americans and Japanese Americans in the early 20th century presented no military danger to the larger society, so there was little concern with their activities once the economic threat had been eliminated. Third, Chinese Americans and Japanese Americans had the ingredients and experiences necessary to form enclaves. The groups were allowed to "disappear," but unlike other racial minority groups, the urban location of their enclaves left them with opportunities for schooling for later generations. As many scholars argue, the particular mode of incorporation developed by Chinese Americans and Japanese Americans is the key to understanding the present status of these groups.

COMPARATIVE FOCUS

JAPAN'S "INVISIBLE" MINORITY

One of the first things I did in this text was list the five characteristics that, together, define a minority group. The first and most important of these was disadvantage and inequality, and the second was visibility: Minority group members must be easily identifiable, either culturally (language, accent, dress) or physically (skin color, stature). These two traits work in tandem. Members of the dominant group must be able to determine a person's group membership quickly and easily, preferably at a glance, so that the systematic discrimination that is the hallmark of minority group status can be practiced.

Cultural and/or racial visibility is such an obvious precondition for discrimination that it almost seems unnecessary to state it. However, every generalization about human beings seems to have an exception, and there is at least one minority group, the Buraku of Japan, that has been victimized by discrimination and prejudice for hundreds of years but is virtually indistinguishable from the general population. That is, the Buraku people are a minority and fit all parts of the definition stated in Chapter 1 except that there is no physical, cultural, religious, or linguistic difference between them and other Japanese. How could such an "invisible" minority come into being? How could the disadvantaged status be maintained through time? If the Buraku can't be distinguished from other Japanese, why don't they simply integrate into the larger society and escape their disadvantaged status?

The Buraku were created centuries ago, during feudal times in Japan. At that time, the society was organized into a caste system (see Chapter 3) based on occupation, and the ancestors of today's Buraku people did work that brought them into contact with death (gravediggers, executioners) or required them to handle meat or meat products (leather workers, butchers). These occupations were regarded as very low in status, and their practitioners were seen as being "unclean" or polluted. In fact, an alternative name for the group, *eta*, means "extreme filth." The Buraku people were required to live in separate, segregated villages and to wear leather patches for purposes of identification (thus raising their social visibility). They were forbidden to marry outside their caste, and any member of the general population who touched a member of the Buraku

class had to be ritually purified or cleansed of pollution (Lamont-Brown, 1993, p. 137).

The caste system was officially abolished in the 19th century, at about the time that Japan began to industrialize. The Buraku today, however, continue to suffer from discrimination and rejection, even though most observers agree that the levels of discrimination today are lower than in the past and that the overall situation of the Buraku people is improving. For example, the Buraku have much lower levels of education than the general population, and the enrollment rate of the Buraku in higher education is about 60% of the national average (Buraku Liberation and Human Rights Research Institute, 2001). Lower levels of education in Japan, as in the United States, limit occupational mobility and lead to higher unemployment rates. The educational deficits also help to maintain gaps between the Buraku and the general population in income and poverty rates.

The Buraku are a small group, about 2% or 3% of Japan's population. About 1 million still live in the thousands of traditional Buraku areas that remain, and another 2 million or so live in non-Buraku areas, mostly in larger cities. They continue to be seen as "filthy" and not very bright or trustworthy—stereotypical traits that often are associated with minority groups mired in subordinate and unequal positions. Also, as is the case for many American minority groups, the Buraku have a vocal and passionate protest organization—the Buraku Liberation and Human Rights Research Institute (2001)—that is dedicated to improving the conditions of the group.

What forces maintain the disadvantaged status of this group? What keeps the Buraku attached to their group? In fact, it is relatively easy for those who choose to do so to "pass" into the mainstream, as attested by the fact that two thirds of the group no longer live in the traditional Buraku areas. Why doesn't the entire group follow this path?

One answer to this question, at least for some Buraku, is that they are committed to their group identity and proud of their heritage. They refuse to surrender to the dominant culture, insist on being accepted for who they are, and have no intention of trading their identity for acceptance or opportunity. For others, even those attempting to pass, the tie to the group and a subtle form of social visibility are maintained by the ancient system of residential segregation. The identity of the traditional Buraku villages and areas of residence are matters of public record, and it is this information—not race or culture—that establishes the boundaries of the group and forms the ultimate barrier to Buraku assimilation.

Japanese firms keep lists of local Buraku addresses and use the lists to screen out potential employees, even though this practice is now illegal. Also, the telltale information may be revealed when applying to rent an apartment (some landlords refuse to rent rooms to Buraku because of their alleged "filthiness") or purchase a home (banks may be reluctant to make loans to members of a group that is widely regarded as untrustworthy). A particularly strong line of resistance to the complete integration of the Buraku arises if they attempt to marry outside the group. It is common practice for Japanese parents to research the family history of their child's fiancé, and any secret Buraku connections are very likely to be unearthed by this process. Thus, members of the Buraku who pass undetected at work and in their neighborhood will be likely to be "outed" if they attempt to marry into the dominant group.

This link to the traditional Buraku residential areas means that this group is not really invisible. Although their social visibility is much lower than racial and ethnic minority groups, there is a way to determine group membership, a mark or sign of who belongs and who doesn't. Consistent with the definition presented in Chapter 1, this "birthmark" is the basis for a socially constructed boundary that differentiates "us" from "them" and allows for systematic discrimination, prejudice, inequality, and all the other disabilities and disadvantages associated with minority group status.

CONTEMPORARY IMMIGRATION FROM ASIA AND THE PACIFIC ISLANDS

Until recent years, Asian groups other than the Chinese and Japanese American have been quite small, but the immigration restrictions that kept these numbers low were abolished in 1965, after which immigration from Asia and the Pacific Islands increased in both number and diversity. In this section, we review the patterns of immigration and the modes of incorporation into the United States for these groups.

Rates and Causes

As shown in Exhibit 8.3, immigration from Asia and the Pacific Islands increased dramatically after 1965, as did immigration from Central and South America and the Caribbean (see Exhibit 7.3). The numbers rose sharply through the 1960s and 1970s and then fluctuated in the 1980s and 1990s, largely as a function of push and pull factors in both sending and receiving nations.

Exhibit 8.4 shows the numbers of immigrants from selected Asian nations since the 1960s and displays a variety of patterns. In three cases (Chinese, Filipinos, and Indians), the number of immigrants increases steadily, declines in the late 1990s, and then increases. The number of Korean immigrants increased through the 1970s, leveled off in the 1980s, declined in the 1990s, and then began to increase once again. In sharp contrast, the number of immigrants from Japan started low and stayed low. Japan has rarely

Exhibit 8.3   Immigration From Asia and the Pacific Islands, 1965–2000

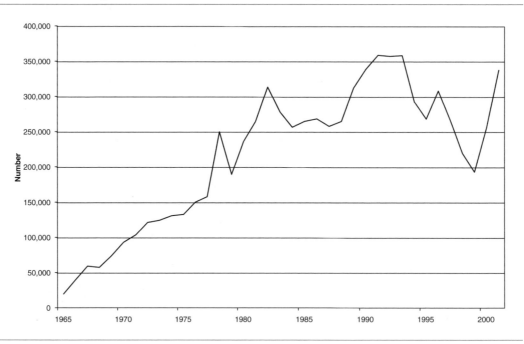

SOURCE: U.S. Immigration and Naturalization Service (1997, 2000).

contributed more than 1% or 2% to the total number of Asian immigrants to the United States since 1965.

How can these patterns be explained? Let's consider the "push" factors first. As we have seen every time we have considered immigration, joblessness and lack of opportunity in the sending countries almost always are a primary cause of the decision to move. To be sure, each immigrant is motivated by a unique set of circumstances, but when rates of population movement are high, economic survival is strongly implicated because immigration is primarily a labor flow from areas of low opportunity to areas of higher opportunity. For example, immigration from Korea has been primarily for economic reasons. The decline in immigration that began in the early 1990s was the result of an improved Korean economy and an expansion of opportunities for employment and advancement at home. In the same vein, the notable increases in immigration in 2001 for

four of the five nations included in the graph reflect a souring Asian economy.

In contrast, consider the fact that immigration from Japan has been low. The Japanese have not been compelled to seek opportunity in other lands because Japan is a highly developed, affluent nation with a low unemployment rate. The economies of other Asian nations are neither as strong nor as modern as Japan's, and economic push factors create pressures to immigrate. Many Filipino immigrants, for example, have relatively low levels of education and skills and are unable to find work in their homeland. Often, these immigrants compete for jobs in the United States with Latin American immigrants and with the urban underclass. Other immigrants from the Philippines, as well as those from India, are highly educated and are motivated by the desire to pursue a career or advance their skills. Although their credentials are more impressive, their motives are still to seek opportunities and jobs not available in their less developed homelands.

Exhibit 8.4   Immigration From Five Asian Nations

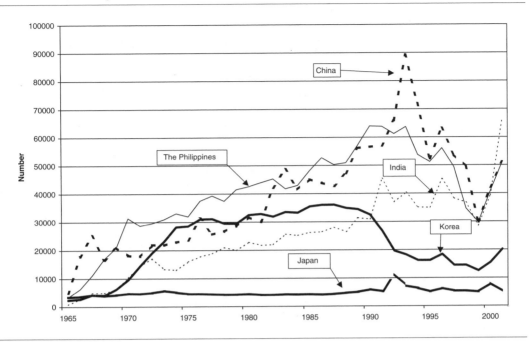

SOURCE: U.S. Immigration and Naturalization Service (2000).

NOTE: "China" includes Taiwan and Hong Kong as well as the People's Republic of China.

Asian immigration also is shaped by "pull" factors. The United States has maintained extensive military bases in South Korea, the Philippines, and Japan since the end of World War II, and many of the immigrants from these nations are the spouses of American soldiers. In addition, U.S. involvement in the war in Southeast Asia created interpersonal ties and governmental programs that drew refugees from Vietnam, Cambodia, and Laos.

Ports of Entry

Recent Asian and Pacific Islander immigrants use many of the same ports of entry as immigrants from Latin America, with the West Coast being the most common destination. For each year between 1984 and 2001, California received many more immigrants than any other state, with New York a distant second (U.S. Immigration and Naturalization Service, 1992, p. 63; 2000, p. 74; 2002, p. 68). In 2001, Los Angeles was the most

common destination for immigrants from Korea, the Philippines, and Taiwan; the second most popular for immigrants from the People's Republic of China; and the third most popular for those from Vietnam. Other major destinations for Asian immigrants have been New York, San Francisco, San Diego, Anaheim, and San Jose, all California cities except New York (U.S. Immigration and Naturalization Service, 2002, pp. 69–71).

Modes of Incorporation

The members of most Asian American groups are newcomers. Only the Chinese and Japanese had large communities in the mainland United States prior to the 1960s. Exhibit 8.5 shows the percentages of various Asian American groups that are foreign born. Only Japanese Americans are less than a majority foreign born, whereas about three quarters of Koreans and 80% of Vietnamese fall into this category. Thus, most Asian

Exhibit 8.5 Percentage of Foreign-Born Asian Americans and Pacific Islanders, 1990 and 1997

Group	Percentage Foreign-Born
All Asians and Pacific Islanders (1997)	61
All Asians and Pacific Islanders (1990)	66
Vietnamese	80
Indian	75
Korean	73
Chinese	69
Filipino	64
Other Asian[a]	62
Japanese	32

SOURCE: Lee (1998, p. 12).

a. Includes Cambodians, Laotians, Hmong, Pakistanis, Samoans, and many others.

immigrant groups are still in their first generations, and it will be years before the second and third generations grow to adulthood.

Although their destinations are similar, recent immigrants from Asia and Latin America have very different occupational and educational backgrounds. On average, Asian immigrants are more educated than immigrants from Central and South America and the Caribbean, and they are less likely to compete for jobs in the low-paid secondary sector of the economy. However, it is misleading to consider only the average differences between groups, and there is considerable variation in the occupational and educational backgrounds of recent Asian immigrants. Asian immigration is segmented (see Chapter 2), and individual immigrants enter U.S. society in three general ways: (a) through the primary or mainstream labor market in which jobs are well paid and relatively secure, (b) through the secondary labor market in which jobs are poorly paid and insecure, and (c) through ethnic enclaves.

Immigrants and the Primary Labor Market

The immigrants entering the primary labor market are highly educated, skilled professionals and businesspeople. Members of this group generally are fluent in English, and many were educated at U.S. universities. They are highly integrated into the global urban-industrial economy, and in many cases, they are employees of multinational corporations transferred here by their companies. These immigrants are affluent, urbane, and dramatically different from most of the immigrants we have considered up to this point. The Asian groups with the highest percentages of educated and skilled immigrants include those from Japan, the Philippines, China, and India.

The percentage of Asian immigrants with professional backgrounds has declined in recent years but is still quite high, at least compared to other groups. In 2001, between 14% and 32% of immigrants from Japan, the Philippines, and India were in the two highest occupational categories: professionals (medical doctors, college faculty) and administrators or managers. By contrast, fewer than 1% of Mexican immigrants in 1998 were in these occupational categories (U.S. Immigration and Naturalization Service, 2002, pp. 75, 77).

Because they tend to be affluent and enter a growing sector of the labor force, Asian immigrants with professional backgrounds tend to attract less notice and fewer racist reactions than their less skilled counterparts. Although they come closer to Blauner's pure immigrant group than most other minority groups we have considered, racism still complicates their assimilation. Anecdotal evidence of discrimination for these high-status immigrants is common. In a *New York Times* article about anti-Asian prejudice, Tun-Hsu McCoy, who immigrated more than 30 years ago and holds a PhD in physics, is quoted as saying: "Every Asian can tell you that we have all encountered subconscious discrimination. People don't equate an Asian face with being an American" (Polner, 1993, p. 1).

Immigrants and the Secondary Labor Market

A second mode of incorporation more closely follows the Latino immigration experience. Frequently ignored in the glitter of Asian success stories are sizable groups of uneducated and unskilled laborers. This group includes large numbers of undocumented aliens, the less skilled and less educated kinfolk of the higher-status immigrants, and a high percentage of the refugee groups from Southeast Asia. These immigrants compete for jobs in the secondary and service economy of the larger society.

Like several other Asian groups, the stream of Chinese immigrants—like the Chinese American community itself—is "bipolar" and includes unskilled laborers as well as professionals who enter the primary labor market. One study found that 60% of Chinese immigrants in New York City worked in just three areas, all in the low-pay, low-skill sector: 23% worked in the garment industry, another 23% in restaurants, and 14% in retail shops and services (Zhou & Logan, 1989, p. 812; see also Chin, 2000). The experiences of these less skilled immigrants are strongly affected by gender, with female immigrants often being more vulnerable and more exploited (see Espiritu, 1997). For example, immigrant Chinese women in New York City are heavily concentrated in the garment industry. Unlike their male counterparts, they experience no measurable benefit (specifically, no increase in income) from becoming Americanized. Chinese immigrant males who were more Americanized and had better job qualifications tended to receive greater rewards, a relationship consistent with traditional assimilation and human capital theory. In contrast, Chinese immigrant women who became citizens, had more education, or were fluent in English had about the same income as women who did not have these characteristics (Zhou & Logan, 1989, p. 817).

These differing income returns between the genders might be explained by the subordinate position of women in Chinese society and the triple role (wife, mother, worker) that Chinese immigrant women are expected (and expect themselves) to play. Women gravitate toward jobs that give them the flexibility they need to fill their domestic roles and support other family members. The

nature of work in the garment industry, for example, allows many women to balance the conflicts inherent in their multiple roles. The industry pays by the piece, not by the hour, and work can be scheduled around other obligations. Chinese women immigrants subordinate their work roles to their other roles, a pattern consistent with traditional Chinese male supremacy. This pattern also, however, reflects a family-oriented strategy for survival and mobility in the United States. The women do not generate income for themselves, but for the benefit of the family as a whole and especially for the younger family members (Zhou & Logan, 1989, p. 818).

Immigrants and Ethnic Enclaves

As we have seen, some Asian immigrants have established ethnic enclaves. Some members of these groups enter U.S. society as entrepreneurs, owners of small retail shops, and other businesses, while their less skilled and educated co-ethnics serve as a source of cheap labor to staff the ethnic enterprises. The enclave provides contacts, financial and other services, and social support for the new immigrants of all social classes. Koreans and Asian Indians have been particularly likely to follow this path.

Four Case Studies

In this section, we will cover four of the largest groups of Asian and Pacific Island immigrants and further illustrate their diversity in origins and modes of incorporation.

Filipino Americans

Today, Filipinos are the second largest Asian American group (see Exhibit 8.1), but their numbers became sizable only in the last few decades. There were fewer than 1,000 Filipinos in the United States in 1910, and by 1960, the group still numbered fewer than 200,000. Most of the recent growth has come from increased post-1965 immigration. By 2000, the group had increased to nearly 2.5 times its size in 1980.

Many of the earliest immigrants were agricultural workers recruited for the sugar plantations of Hawaii and the fields of the West Coast. The Philippines became a U.S. territory (along with Puerto Rico) as a result of the Spanish-American War of 1898, and Filipinos could enter the United States without regard to immigration quotas until 1935, when the nation became independent.

The most recent wave of immigrants is diversified, and like Chinese Americans, Filipino Americans are "bipolar" in their educational and occupational profiles. Many recent immigrants have entered under the family preference provisions of U.S. immigration policy. These immigrants are often poor and compete for jobs in the low-wage secondary labor market (Kitano & Daniels, 1995, p. 94). More than half of all Filipino immigrants since 1965, however, have been professionals, especially those in health and medical fields. Many female immigrants from the Philippines were nurses actively recruited by U.S. hospitals to fill gaps in the labor force (Amott & Matthaei, 1991, p. 245).

Thus, the Filipino American community is diverse, with some members in the higher-wage primary labor market and others competing for work in the low-wage secondary sector. Language differences and anti-Asian prejudice and discrimination limit the educational and occupational choices available to the group as a whole (Agbayani-Siewart & Revilla, 1995, pp. 134–168; Espiritu, 1996; Kitano & Daniels, 1995, pp. 83–94; Mangiafico, 1988; Posadas, 1999).

Korean Americans

Immigration from Korea to the United States began at the turn of the 20th century, when laborers were recruited to help fill the void in the job market left by the 1882 Chinese Exclusion Act. This group was extremely small until the 1950s, when the rate of immigration rose because of refugees and "war brides" after the Korean War. Immigration did not become substantial, however, until after 1965. The size of the group increased fivefold in the 1970s and tripled between 1980 and 2000 (see Exhibit 8.1).

Recent immigrants from Korea consist mostly of families and include many highly educated people. Although differences in culture, language, and race make Koreans visible targets of discrimination, the high percentage of Christians among them may help them appear more "acceptable" to the dominant group. Korean Americans have formed an enclave, and the group is heavily involved in small businesses and retail stores, particularly fruit and vegetable retail stores or green groceries. As is the case for other groups that have pursued this course, the enclave allows them to avoid the discrimination and racism of the larger society while surviving in an economic niche in which lack of English fluency is not a particular problem.

By many measures, Koreans have been successful in building their businesses and securing at least minimal economic returns. Data from the 2000 Census show that Koreans have the highest rate of business ownership among 11 different minority groups (U.S. Bureau of the Census, 2002). Korean Americans owned 126 businesses per 1,000 population, a rate higher than even other enclave minorities. For example, Japanese Americans had the second highest rate (108 businesses per 1,000 population), Chinese Americans were third (104 per 1,000 population), and Cuban Americans were fourth (101 per 1,000 population). In contrast, at the bottom of the rankings were racial minority groups with strong histories of colonization and exclusion: African Americans (24 businesses per 1,000 population) and Puerto Ricans (21 per 1,000 population). (See also Kim, Hurh, & Fernandez, 1989; Logan et al., 1994; Min, 1995, pp. 208–212; Pollard & O'Hare, 1999, p. 39).

The enclave has its perils and its costs, however. For one thing, the success of Korean enterprises depends heavily on the mutual assistance and financial support of other Koreans and the willingness of family members to work long hours for little or no pay. These resources would be weakened or destroyed by acculturation, integration, and the resultant decline in ethnic solidarity. Only by maintaining a distance from the dominant culture and its pervasive appeal can the infrastructure survive.

Furthermore, the economic niches in which mom-and-pop green groceries and other small businesses can survive often are in deteriorated neighborhoods populated largely by other minority groups. There has been a good deal of hostility and resentment expressed against Korean shop owners by African Americans, Puerto Ricans, and other urbanized minority groups. For example, anti-Korean sentiments were widely expressed in the 1992 Los Angeles riots that followed the acquittal of the police officers charged in the beating of Rodney King. Korean-owned businesses were some of the first to be looted and burned, and when asked why, one participant in the looting said simply, "Because we hate 'em. Everybody hates them" (Cho, 1993, p. 199). Thus, part of the price of survival for many Korean merchants is to place themselves in positions in which antagonism and conflict with other minority groups is common (Kitano & Daniels, 1995, pp. 112–129; Light & Bonacich, 1988; Min, 1995, pp. 199–231; see also Hurh, 1998).

Southeast Asians

A flow of refugees from Southeast Asia and particularly from Vietnam began in the 1960s as a result of the involvement of the United States in the region. The war began in Vietnam but expanded when the United States attacked communist forces in Cambodia and Laos. Social life was disrupted, and people were displaced throughout Southeast Asia. In 1975, when Saigon (the South Vietnamese capital) fell and the U.S. military withdrew, many Southeast Asians who had collaborated with the United States and its allies fled in fear for their lives. This group included high-ranking officials and members of the region's educational and occupational elite. Later groups of refugees tended to be less well educated and more impoverished. Many Vietnamese, Cambodians, and Laotians waited in refugee camps for months or years before being admitted to the United States, and they often arrived with few resources or social networks to ease their transition to the new society (Kitano & Daniels, 1995, pp. 151–152).

The Vietnamese are the largest of the Asian refugee groups, and contrary to Asian American success stories and notions of model minorities, they have incomes and educational levels comparable to colonized minority groups (Lee, 1998; Rumbaut, 1995, p. 248). One study measured the extent of residential segregation for a variety of minority groups, including African Americans and Latino Americans, and found that the Vietnamese were the "most segregated group in the society" (Massey & Denton, 1992, p. 170).

Indians

Immigration from India was low until the mid-1960s, and the group was quite small at that time. The size of the group more than quadrupled between 1980 and 2000 (see Exhibit 8.1), and Indians are the third largest Asian American group today. Unlike many other immigrant groups, Indian immigrants tend to be a select, highly educated, and skilled group. For example, in 1980, 11% of male Asian Indians in the United States were physicians, as were 8% of the females, compared with less than 1% of the total U.S. population (Kamen, 1992; U.S. Bureau of the Census, 1993, p. 118). Also, in 1990, the median income of immigrants from India was $18,000 above the national norm of $30,320 (Portes & Rumbaut, 1996, p. 19). These skilled immigrants from India are part of a worldwide movement of educated peoples from less developed countries to more developed countries. One need not ponder the differences in career opportunities, technology, and compensation for long to get some insight into the reasons for this movement. Other immigrants from India are more oriented to commerce and small business, and there is a sizable Indian ethnic enclave in many cities (Kitano & Daniels, 1995, pp. 96–111; Sheth, 1995).

Summary

Contrary to popular perceptions of Asian success, recent Asian immigrants are diverse in origin, characteristics, and impact on U.S. society. Each group has a unique contact situation, and the modes of incorporation into the larger society are diverse. Each trajectory has different implications for upward mobility, conflict with other groups, prejudice and discrimination, acculturation and integration, and a host of other variables. Although some of these contact situations reinforce and sustain the idea that Asian Americans are a "model minority," others raise the same questions and concerns as the wave of unskilled immigrant laborers from Latin America.

CONTEMPORARY RELATIONS

The diversity of Asian Americans and Pacific Islanders makes it difficult to characterize the group as a whole. Nonetheless, we once more use our guiding concepts to see what conclusions we can reach about these groups and their relationships with the larger society.

Prejudice and Discrimination

American prejudice against Asians first became prominent during the anti-Chinese movement of the 19th century. The Chinese were castigated as racially inferior, docile, and subservient, but also cruel and crafty, despotic, and threatening (Lai, 1980, p. 220; Lyman, 1974, pp. 55–58). The Chinese Exclusion Act of 1882 was justified by the idea that the Chinese were unassimilable and could never be a part of U.S. society. The Chinese were seen as a threat to the working class, to American democracy, and to other American institutions. Many of these stereotypes and fears transferred to the Japanese later in the 19th century and then to other groups as they, in turn, arrived in the United States.

The social distance scales presented in Exhibit 1.4 provide the only long-term record of anti-Asian prejudice in the society as a whole. In 1926, the five Asian groups included in the study were grouped in the bottom third of the scale, along with other racial and/or colonized minority groups. Twenty years later, in 1946, the Japanese had fallen to the bottom of the rankings, and the Chinese had risen seven positions, changes that reflect America's World War II conflict with Japan and alliance with China. This suggests that anti-Chinese prejudice may have softened during the war as distinctions were made between "good" and "bad" Asians. For example, an item published in a 1941 issue of *Time* magazine, "How to Tell Your Friends From the Japs," provided some tips for identifying "good" Asians: "The Chinese expression is likely to be more placid, kindly, open; the Japanese more positive, dogmatic, arrogant. . . . Japanese are nervous in conversation, laugh loudly at the wrong time" (p. 33).

In more recent decades, the average social distance scores of Asian groups have fallen even though the ranking of the groups remained relatively stable. In 1977 and 1993, the scores for the Asian groups were lower even though they were still clustered in the bottom third of the scale. The falling scores probably reflect the societywide increase in tolerance and/or the shift from blatant prejudice to modern racism that we first discussed in Chapter 5. However, the relative position of Asians in the American hierarchy of group preferences has remained remarkably consistent since the 1920s. This stability may reflect the cultural or traditional nature of much of American anti-Asian prejudice.

Although prejudice against Asian and Pacific Island groups may have weakened overall, there is considerable evidence that it remains a potent force in American life. The continuing force of anti-Asian prejudice is marked most dramatically, perhaps, by hate crimes against members of the group. Asian Americans and Pacific Islanders of all types—citizens, immigrants, tourists—have been attacked, beaten, and even murdered in recent years. For example, in 1996, an unemployed meat cutter named Robert Page murdered a randomly selected Chinese American male. Page said that he hated the Chinese because they "got all the good jobs" (Fong, 2002, p. 162). Incidents such as these suggest that the tradition of anti-Asian prejudice is close to the surface and could be activated under the right combination of competition and threat.

Asian Americans also have been the victims of "positive" stereotypes. The perception of Asian Americans as a model minority is exaggerated and, for some Asian American groups, simply false. This label has been applied to these groups by the media, politicians, and others. It is not an image that the Asian American groups themselves developed or particularly advocate. As you might suspect, people who apply these labels to Asian Americans have a variety of hidden moral and political agendas, and we explore these dynamics later in this chapter.

Assimilation and Pluralism

Acculturation

The extent of acculturation of Asian Americans is highly variable from group to group. Japanese Americans represent one extreme. They have been a part of American society for more than a century, and the current generations are highly acculturated. Immigration from Japan was low throughout the 20th century and has not revitalized the traditional culture or language. As a result, Japanese Americans probably are the most acculturated of the Asian American groups.

At the other extreme are groups such as Vietnamese Americans, who are often still in the first generation and scarcely have had time to learn American culture and the English language. In between are groups such as Chinese Americans, some of whom have roots in this country going back even further than Japanese Americans and some of whom are newcomers. The great variability both within and between Asian American groups makes it difficult to characterize their overall degree of acculturation.

Secondary Structural Assimilation

Let's cover this complex area in roughly the order followed in previous chapters.

Residence. Exhibit 8.6 shows the regional concentrations of Asian Americans. The tendency to reside on either coast and around Los Angeles, San Francisco, and New York stands out clearly. Note also the sizable concentrations in a variety of metropolitan areas including Chicago, Atlanta, Miami, Denver, and Houston.

Asian Americans are highly urbanized, a reflection of the entry conditions of recent immigrants as well as the appeal of ethnic neighborhoods, such as Chinatowns, with long histories and continuing vitality. The 2000 Census showed that more than 96% of the Asian American population lived in metropolitan areas (vs. about 80% of the total population) and about 48% lived in central city areas (U.S. Bureau of the Census, 2000k). As a group, Asian Americans are less concentrated in central city neighborhoods than blacks and Puerto Ricans but much more than Cuban Americans and non-Hispanic whites. The degree of residential segregation for Asian American groups varies by group and by region of the nation. One study found high levels of residential segregation for Southeast Asians in Los Angeles, one of the major ports of entry for Asian Americans, but lower levels for Indians and Filipinos. In part, this pattern reflects the importance of the enclave in helping some newcomers adjust to American society (Pollard & O'Hare, 1999, p. 29). A study based on results from the 2000 Census found that the extent of residential segregation for Asian Americans and Pacific Islanders generally increased between 1990 and 2000 (Iceland et al., 2002).

Asian Americans and Pacific Islanders are also moving away from their traditional neighborhoods and enclaves into the suburbs of metropolitan areas, most notably in the areas surrounding Los Angeles, San Francisco, New York, and other cities where the groups are highly concentrated. For example, Asian Americans have been moving in large numbers to the San Gabriel Valley, just east of downtown Los Angeles. Once a bastion of white, middle-class suburbanites, these areas have taken on a distinctly Asian flavor in recent years. Monterey Park in the

Exhibit 8.6   Number of People, 2000, One Race: Asian

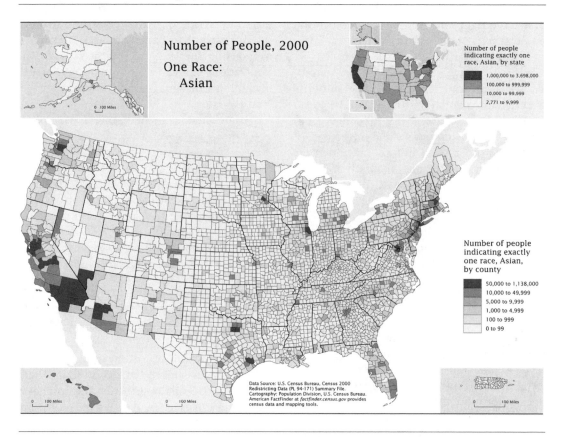

SOURCE: U.S. Bureau of the Census (2000h).

San Gabriel Ualley, once virtually all white, is now 62% Chinese and is often referred to as "America's first suburban Chinatown" or the "Chinese Beverly Hills" (Fong, 2002, p. 49).

Education. The pattern of schooling for these groups is very different from other U.S. racial minority groups. Asian Americans compare favorably with societywide standards for educational achievement, and they are above those standards on many measures. Exhibits 8.7a and 8.7b display three levels of educational attainment for male and female Asian Americans and Pacific Islanders and several other groups. The most dramatic feature of these figures is the much higher percentages, for both males and females, of Asian Americans and Pacific Islanders at the highest level of

educational attainment, a pattern that, once again, reinforces the label of "model minority."

However, when we look at the various groups separately, a more complex picture emerges. In 1990 (the most recent data available), for example, the males of four of the six groups covered in this chapter (Japanese, Korean, Filipino, and Indian American) ranked above national norms in percentage of high school graduates. Two groups (Chinese and Vietnamese Americans), however, ranked below the norm. Similarly, the males of five of the six Asian groups had much higher rates of college graduation. The exception was Vietnamese Americans, who as refugees tended to resemble black Americans—a colonized, racial minority group—more than white Americans.

Exhibit 8.7a   Educational Attainment for Asian Americans and Pacific Islanders and Selected Other Groups (Males)

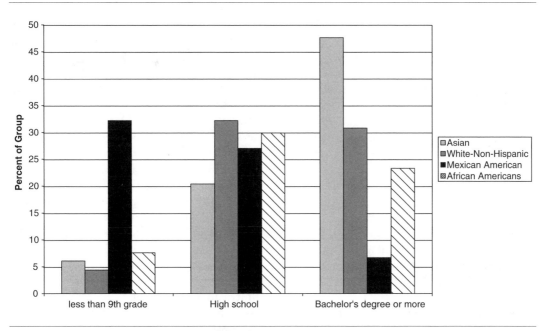

SOURCE: U.S. Bureau of the Census (2000c)

Exhibit 8.7b   Educational Attainment for Asian Americans and Pacific Islanders and Selected Other Groups (Females)

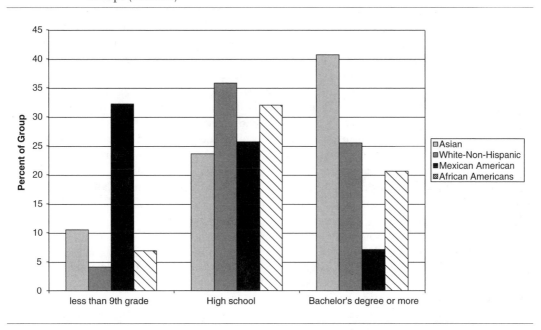

SOURCE: U.S. Bureau of the Census (2000c).

The picture for females is even more varied. Looking at high school graduation rates, only Japanese and Filipino women ranked above white women in 1990, but women of every Asian group except the Vietnamese have higher rates of college graduation than do white women.

This variation means that the image of the "model minority" needs to be balanced by the recognition that there is a full range of success and failure among Asian Americans and by the fact that average levels of achievement are "inflated" for some groups by recent immigrants who are highly educated, skilled professionals. Also, there is considerable variety in Asian educational performance by gender and group. Women generally do not fare as well as the men, and the pattern of high accomplishment and success does not describe some groups.

Jobs and Income. If we look at the occupations and income for Asian Americans as a single category, the picture of success and equality is sustained. Exhibits 8.8a and 8.8b show that both males and females are overrepresented in the highest occupational category, a reflection of the high levels of educational attainment for the group. In particular, Chinese, Japanese, and Indian Americans tend to be overrepresented at the highest levels of the workforce. Once again, however, a closer look reveals more diversity. For example, a high percentage of some Asian groups are concentrated in low-paying jobs in the service sector and in the unskilled labor force. Recall that Chinese Americans are often described as "bipolar" in their occupational profile and that the percentage of Vietnamese and other Southeast Asian groups in unskilled and semiskilled jobs is comparable to colonized racial minorities (Lee, 1998, p. 27).

Exhibit 8.9 shows that the percentage of Asian Americans and Pacific Islanders in the highest income bracket is virtually equal to non-Hispanic whites. This picture of economic success must again be qualified. There is considerable variation in average affluence from group to group. The 1990 Census, for example, showed that average incomes for Chinese and Japanese were well above national norms but that other groups, including the Southeast Asian groups, had low average incomes. Furthermore, the image of affluence must be tempered by several facts. First, Asian Americans generally reside in areas with higher-than average costs of living (e.g., San Francisco, Los Angeles, New York); thus, their higher incomes have relatively less purchasing power. Second, they are more likely than the general population to have multiple wage earners in each household. Thus, differences in per capita income are smaller than differences in median family income (Lee, 1998, p. 28).

In terms of poverty, Asian Americans as a whole rank between non-Hispanic whites and the racial and colonized minority groups. The 2000 Census, for example, showed that the percentage of Asian American families living in poverty was about half that of African American families but double that of non-Hispanic whites. Also, in a familiar pattern, the poverty rate is higher for female-headed-households, a reflection of the combined negative effects of racism and sexism.

As noted previously, Asian Americans in general tend to be "underrewarded" for their occupational positions and earn less than comparably educated whites. This differential benefit from education has been documented as far back as the 1950 census for Japanese Americans (Woodrum, 1979) and reflects lingering anti-Asian racism and discrimination. Using 1997 data, for example, Pollard and O'Hare found that a college education added an average of $19,000 to the yearly income of non-Hispanic whites but $18,700 to the yearly income of Asians. This income gap is the result of numerous factors, one of which is anti-Asian discrimination (Pollard & O'Hare, 1999, p. 37; see also Kitano & Daniels, 1995; Min, 1995).

Political Power. The ability of Asian Americans to pursue their group interests has been sharply limited by a number of factors, including their relatively small size, institutionalized discrimination, and the same kinds of racist practices that have limited the power resources of other minority groups of

Exhibit 8.8a Occupations of Asian Americans and Pacific Islanders and Non-Hispanic Whites (Males)

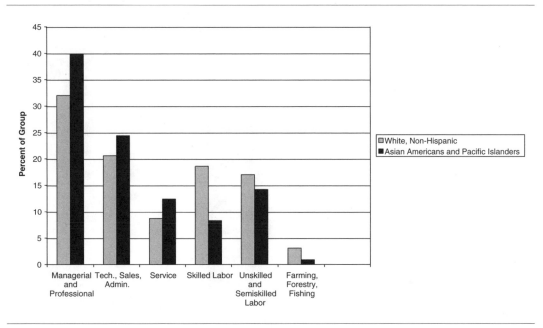

SOURCE: U.S. Bureau of the Census (2000e).

Exhibit 8.8b Occupations of Asian Americans and Pacific Islanders and Non-Hispanic Whites (Females)

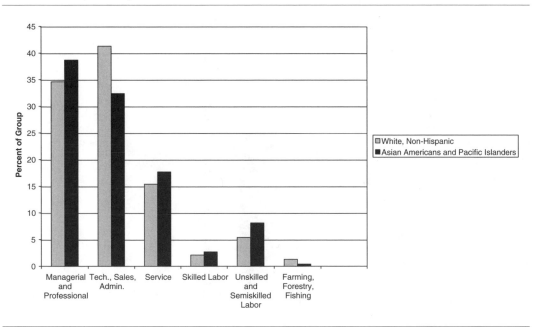

SOURCE: U.S. Bureau of the Census (2000e).

Exhibit 8.9   Income Distribution for Asian Americans and Pacific Islanders and Non-Hispanic Whites (All Families)

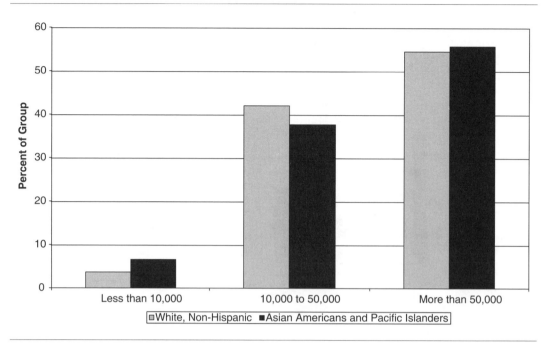

SOURCE: U.S. Bureau of the Census (2000x).

Exhibit 8.10   Poverty Rates for Asian Americans and Pacific Islanders, Non-Hispanic Whites, and African Americans by Type of Family

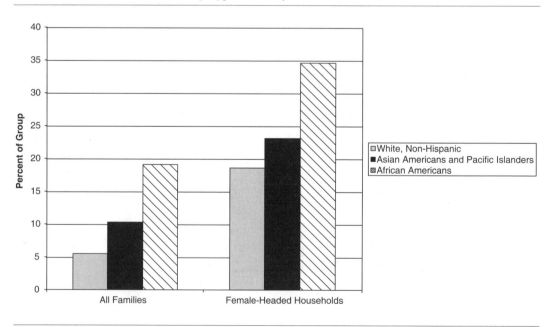

SOURCE: U.S. Bureau of the Census (2000p).

color. However, and contrary to the perception that Asian Americans are a "quiet" minority, the group has a long history of political action, including a Civil Rights movement in the 1960s and 1970s (Fong, 2002, pp. 273–281).

The political power of Asian Americans and Pacific Islanders today is also limited by their high percentage of foreign-born members (see Exhibit 8.5). Rates of political participation for the group (e.g., voting in presidential elections) are somewhat lower than national norms but may rise as more members Americanize, learn English, and become citizens (Lee, 1998, p. 30). Even today, there are signs of the growing power of the group, especially in the areas where they are most residentially concentrated. Of course, Asian Americans have been prominent in Hawaiian politics for decades, but they are increasingly involved in West Coast political life as well. For example, in 1996, the state of Washington elected Gary Locke as governor, the first Chinese American to hold this high office. Governor Locke was reelected in 2000.

Primary Structural Assimilation

Studies of integration at the primary level generally find high rates of interracial friendship choices and intermarriage. For example, using 1980 Census data, Lee and Yamanaka (1990) reported higher rates of intermarriage for Asian Americans than for other minority groups. They reported out-marriage rates at 2% for African Americans, 13% for Hispanic Americans, and from 15% to 34% for Asian Americans. They also found that native-born Asian Americans were much more likely to marry outside their group than the foreign born (see also Kitano & Daniels, 1995; Min, 1995; Sung, 1990). Some studies have found that the rate of intermarriage is decreasing in recent years in the nation as a whole and in California, a pattern that perhaps reflects the growing number of potential partners within Asian American groups (Lee & Fernandez, 1998; Shinagawa & Pang, 1996).

COMPARING MINORITY GROUPS: EXPLAINING ASIAN AMERICAN SUCCESS

To conclude this chapter, let's return to the questions raised in the opening pages: How can we explain the apparent success of Asian Americans? Relative affluence and high status are not characteristic of the other racial minority groups we have examined, and at least at first glance, there seems to be little in our theories and concepts to help us understand the situation of Asian Americans. Even after we recognize that the "success" label is simplistic and even misleading, the relatively high status of many Asian Americans begs a closer look. In this section, we will explore these issues by comparing the experiences of Asian Americans with those of European immigrant groups and colonized minority groups. What crucial factors differentiate the experiences of these groups? Can we understand these differences in terms of the framework provided by the Blauner and Noel hypotheses and the other concepts developed in this text?

The debate over the causes of Asian American success often breaks down into two different viewpoints. One view offers a *cultural* explanation, which accepts the evidence of Asian American success at face value and attributes it to the "good values" of traditional Asian cultures that we briefly explored at the beginning of this chapter. These values—including respect for elders and for authority figures, hard work and thriftiness, and conformity and politeness—are highly compatible with U.S. middle-class Protestant value systems and presumably helped Asian Americans gain acceptance and opportunities. The cultural explanation is consistent with traditional assimilation theory and human capital theory (for an example, see Kitano, 1980).

The other point of view stresses the ways in which these groups entered American society and the reactions of Asian Americans to the barriers of racism and exclusion they faced. This approach could be called a *structural* explanation, and it emphasize contact situations, modes of incorporation, enclave economies, group cohesion, position in the labor market, and institutionalized discrimination rather than cultural values. Also, this approach questions the whole notion that Asian Americans *are* successful and stresses the facts of Asian American poverty and the continuing patterns of racism and exclusion. The structural approach is more compatible with the theories and concepts used throughout this text and identifies several of the important pieces needed to solve the puzzle of Asian "success" and put it in perspective. This is not to suggest that the cultural approach is wrong or irrelevant, however. The issues we raise are complex and probably will require many approaches and perspectives before they are fully resolved.

Asian and European Immigrants

Chinese and Japanese immigrants arrived in America at about the same time as immigrants from Southern and Eastern Europe (see Chapter 9). Both groups consisted mainly of sojourning young men who were largely unskilled, from rural backgrounds, and not highly educated. European immigrants, like Asian immigrants, encountered massive discrimination and rejection and also were victims of restrictive legislation. Yet the barriers to upward mobility for European immigrants (or at least for their descendants) fell away more rapidly than the barriers for immigrants from Asia. Why?

Some important differences between the two immigrant experiences are clear, the most obvious being the greater racial visibility of the Asians and Pacific Islanders. Whereas the cultural and linguistic markers that identified eastern and southern Europeans faded with each passing generation, the racial characteristics of the Asian groups continued to separate them from the larger society. Thus, Asian and Pacific Island groups are not "pure immigrant" groups (see Blauner, 1972, p. 55). For most of the 20th century, Chinese Americans and Japanese Americans remained in a less favorable position than European immigrants and their descendants, excluded by their physical appearance from the mainstream economy until the decades following World War II.

Another important difference relates to position in the labor market. Immigrants from southern and eastern European entered the industrializing East Coast economy, where they took industrial and manufacturing jobs. Although such jobs were poorly paid and insecure, this location in the labor force gave European immigrants and their descendants the potential for upward mobility in the mainstream economy. At the very least, these urban industrial and manufacturing jobs put the children and grandchildren of European immigrants in positions from which skilled, well-paid, unionized jobs were reachable, as were managerial and professional careers.

In contrast, Chinese and Japanese immigrants on the West Coast were forced into ethnic enclaves and came to rely on jobs in the small business and service sector and, in the case of the Japanese, in the rural economy. By their nature, these jobs did not link Chinese and Japanese immigrants or their descendants to the industrial sector or to better-paid, more secure, unionized jobs. Furthermore, their exclusion from the mainstream economy was reinforced by overt discrimination based on race from both employers and labor unions (see Fong & Markham, 1991).

Asian Americans and Colonized Minority Groups

Comparisons between Asian Americans and African Americans, Native Americans, and Hispanic Americans have generated a level of controversy and a degree of passion that may be surprising at first. An examination of the issues and their implications, however, reveals that the debate involves some thinly disguised political and moral agendas and evokes sharply clashing views on the nature of U.S. society. What might appear on the surface to be merely an academic comparison of different minority groups turns out to be an argument about the quality of American justice and fairness and the very essence of the value system of U.S. society.

What is not in dispute in this debate is that some Asian groups (e.g., Chinese Americans and Japanese Americans) rank far above other racial minority groups on all the commonly used measures of secondary structural integration and equality. What is disputed is how to interpret these comparisons and assess their meanings. First, we need to recognize that gross comparisons between entire groups can be misleading. If we confine our attention to averages (mean levels of education or median income), the picture of Asian American success tends to be sustained. However, if we also observe the full range of differences within each group (e.g., the "bipolar" nature of occupations among Chinese Americans), we see that the images of success have been exaggerated and need to be placed in a proper context (Takaki, 1993). Even with these qualifications, however, discussion often slides on to more ideological ground, and political and moral issues begin to cloud the debate. Asian American success often is taken as proof that American society is truly the land of opportunity and that people who work hard and obey the rules will get ahead: In America, anyone can be anything they want as long as they work hard enough.

When we discussed modern racism in Chapter 5, we pointed out that a belief in the openness and fairness of the United States can be a way of blaming the victim and placing the responsibility for change on the minority groups rather than on the structure of society. Asian success has become a "proof" of the validity of this ideology. The none-too-subtle implication is that other groups (African Americans, Hispanic Americans, Native Americans) could achieve the same success as Asian Americans but for various reasons choose not to. Thus, the relative success of Chinese Americans and Japanese Americans has become a device for scolding other minority groups.

A more structural approach to investigating Asian success begins with a comparison of the history of the various racial minority groups and their modes of incorporation into the larger society. When Chinese Americans and Japanese Americans were building their enclave economies in the early part of the 20th century, African Americans and Mexican Americans were concentrated in unskilled agricultural occupations. Native Americans were isolated from the larger society on their reservations, and Puerto Ricans had not yet begun to arrive on the mainland. The social class differences between these groups today flow from their respective situations in the past.

Many of the occupational and financial advances made by Chinese Americans and Japanese Americans have been due to the high levels of education achieved by the second generations. Although education traditionally is valued in Asian cultures, the decision to invest limited resources in schooling also is quite consistent with the economic niche occupied by these immigrants. Education is one obvious, relatively low-cost strategy to upgrade the productivity and profit of a small business economy and improve the economic status of the group as a whole. An educated, English-speaking second generation could bring expertise and business acumen to the family enterprises and lead them to higher levels of performance. Education might also be the means by which the second generation could enter professional careers. This strategy may have been especially attractive to an immigrant generation that was itself relatively uneducated and barred from citizenship (Hirschman & Wong, 1986, p. 23; see also Bonacich & Modell, 1980, p. 152; Sanchirico, 1991).

The efforts to educate the next generation were largely successful. Chinese Americans and Japanese Americans achieved educational parity with the larger society as early as the 1920s. One study found that for men and women born after 1915, the median years of schooling completed actually was higher for Chinese Americans and Japanese Americans than for whites (Hirschman & Wong, 1986, p. 11). Before World War II, both Asian groups were barred from the mainstream economy and from better jobs. When anti-Asian prejudice and discrimination declined in the 1950s, however, the Chinese and Japanese second generations had the educational backgrounds necessary to take advantage of the increased opportunities.

Thus, there was a crucial divergence in the development of Chinese Americans and Japanese Americans and the colonized minority groups. At the time that native-born Chinese Americans and Japanese Americans reached educational parity with whites, the vast majority of African Americans, Native Americans, and Mexican Americans were still victimized by Jim Crow laws and legalized segregation and were excluded from opportunities for anything but a rudimentary education. The Supreme Court decision in *Brown v. Board of Education of Topeka* (1954) was decades in the future, and Native American schoolchildren were still being subjected to intense Americanization in the guise of a curriculum. Today, these other racial minority groups have not completely escaped from the disadvantages imposed by centuries of institutionalized discrimination. African Americans have approached educational parity with white Americans only in recent years (see Chapter 5), and Native Americans and Mexican Americans remain far below national averages (see Chapters 6 and 7).

The structural explanation argues that the recent upward mobility of Chinese Americans and Japanese Americans is the result of the methods by which they incorporated themselves into American society, not so much their values and traditions. The logic of their subeconomy led the immigrant generation to invest in the education of their children, who would be better prepared to develop the enclave businesses and seek opportunity in the larger society.

As a final point, note that the structural explanation is not consistent with traditional views of the assimilation process. The immigrant generation of Chinese Americans and Japanese Americans responded to the massive discrimination they faced by withdrawing, developing an ethnic enclave, and becoming "invisible" to the larger society. Like Cuban Americans, Chinese Americans and Japanese Americans used their traditional culture and patterns of social life to create and build their own subcommunities from which they launched the next generation. Contrary to traditional ideas about how assimilation is "supposed" to happen, we see again that integration can precede acculturation and that the smoothest route to integration may be the creation of a separate subsociety independent of the surrounding community.

MAIN POINTS

- Asian Americans and Pacific Islanders are diverse and have brought many different cultural and linguistic traditions to the United States. These groups are growing rapidly but are still only a tiny fraction of the total population.
- Chinese immigrants were the victims of a massive campaign of discrimination and exclusion and responded by constructing enclaves. Chinatowns became highly organized communities, largely run by the local CCBAs and other associations. The second generation faced many barriers to employment in the dominant society, although opportunities increased after World War II.
- Japanese immigration began in the 1890s and stimulated a campaign that attempted to oust the group from agriculture and curtail immigration from Japan. The Issei formed an enclave, but during World War II, Japanese Americans were forced into relocation camps, and this experience devastated the group economically and psychologically.
- Other Asian and Pacific Island groups come from the Philippines, Korea, Vietnam, and India, and many other societies. These groups are diverse in occupation, education, and degree of acculturation. Asian immigrants have entered the United States through the primary labor market, the secondary labor market, and the enclave economies.

- Overall levels of anti-Asian prejudice and discrimination probably have declined in recent years but remain widespread. Levels of acculturation and secondary structural assimilation are highly variable for these groups.
- The notion that Asian Americans are a model minority is exaggerated, but comparisons with European immigrants and colonized minority groups suggest some of the reasons for the relative "success" of these groups.

QUESTIONS FOR REVIEW AND STUDY

1. Describe the cultural characteristics of Asian American groups. How did these characteristics shape relationships with the larger society? Did they contribute to the perception of Asian Americans as "successful"? How?
2. Compare and contrast the contact situations for Chinese Americans, Japanese Americans, and Cuban Americans. What common characteristics led to the construction of ethnic enclaves for all three groups? How and why did these enclaves vary from each other?
3. In what sense was the second generation of Chinese Americans "delayed?" How did this affect the relationship of the group with the larger society?
4. Compare and contrast the campaigns that arose in opposition to the immigration of people from China and from Japan. Do the concepts of the Noel hypothesis help to explain the differences? Do you see any similarities with the changing federal policy toward Mexican immigrants across the 20th century? Explain.
5. Compare and contrast the Japanese relocation camps with Indian reservations in terms of paternalism and coerced acculturation. What economic impact did the internment experience have on Japanese Americans? How were Japanese Americans compensated for their losses? Does the compensation paid to Japanese Americans provide a precedent for similar payments (reparations) to African Americans for their losses under slavery? Why or why not?
6. How do the Buraku in Japan illustrate "visibility" as a defining characteristic of minority group status? How is the minority status of this group maintained?
7. Summarize the nature of contemporary immigrants from Asia in terms of their motivations for immigrating, their relationship to the U.S. job market, and their relationship to the communities and neighborhoods of their groups.
8. What gender differences characterize Asian American groups? What are some of the important ways in which the experiences of women and men vary?
9. Describe the situation of the major Asian American groups in terms of prejudice and discrimination, acculturation, and integration. Are these groups truly "success stories?" How? What factors or experiences might account for this "success?" Are all Asian American groups equally successful? Describe the important variations from group to group. Compare the integration and level of equality of these groups with other American racial minorities. How would you explain the differences? Are the concepts of the Noel and Blauner hypotheses helpful? Why or why not?

INTERNET RESEARCH PROJECT

A. *Updating the Chapter*

The "Asian Nation" Web site at www.asian-nation.org/index.html provides comprehensive coverage on a number of issues raised in this chapter. Update and expand the chapter by selecting one or two topics (e.g., the "model minority" image) and searching the Web site. Be sure to follow some of the links provided to see what additional information and perspectives you can uncover.

B. Learning More About Asian and Pacific Islander Americans

Select one of the Asian or Pacific Islander groups discussed in this chapter *other than* Japanese Americans and Chinese Americans and conduct an Internet search using the name of the group. Follow the links and see what information you can add to the profile provided in the chapter. You might focus your search by seeking answers to basic questions such as these: How large is the group? Where do the members live in the United States (region of the country, rural vs. urban)? How acculturated is the group in terms of language? How does the group compare with national norms in terms of education, occupational profile, and income? What are the major issues from the perspective of the group?

FOR FURTHER READING

Espiritu, Yen. 1997. *Asian American Women and Men.* Thousand Oaks, CA: Sage.
Analyzes the intersections of race, class, and gender among Asian Americans.

Kitano, Harry H. L. 1976. *Japanese Americans.* Englewood Cliffs, NJ: Prentice Hall.
Lyman, Stanford. 1974. *Chinese Americans.* New York: Random House.
Comprehensive case studies of the Asian American groups with the longest histories in the United States.

Kitano, Harry H. L., & Daniels, Roger. 1995. *Asian Americans: Emerging Minorities* (2nd ed.). Englewood Cliffs, NJ: Prentice Hall.
Min, Pyong Gap. 1995. *Asian Americans: Contemporary Trends and Issues.* Thousand Oaks, CA: Sage.
Good overviews of all the Asian American groups covered in this chapter.

Kwong, Peter. 1987. *The New Chinatown.* New York: Hill and Wang.
Zhou, Min. 1992. *Chinatown.* Philadelphia: Temple University Press.
Two excellent analyses of Chinatowns, with a behind-the-scenes look at the realities often hidden from outsiders.

9

White Ethnic Groups

*Assimilation and Identity—
The Twilight of Ethnicity?*

etween the 1820s and the 1920s, almost 40 million people journeyed from Europe to the United States. They came from every corner of the continent: Ireland, Greece, Germany, Italy, Poland, Portugal, Russia, and scores of other nations and provinces. They came as young men and women seeking jobs, as families fleeing religious persecution, as political radicals fleeing the police, as farmers seeking land and a fresh start, and as paupers barely able to scrape together the cost of the passage.

They were the first great waves of immigrants to strike these shores, and they shaped the United States in countless ways. When mass immigration from Europe began in the 1820s, the United States was not yet 50 years old, an agricultural nation clustered along

the East Coast. The nation was just coming into contact with Mexicans in the Southwest, immigration from China had not begun, slavery was flourishing in the South, and Native Americans had yet to be "removed" west of the Mississippi. When the period of mass immigration ended in the 1920s, the population of the United States had increased from less than 10 million to more than 100 million, and the society had industrialized, become a world power, and stretched from coast to coast with colonies in the Pacific and the Caribbean.

It was no coincidence that European immigration, American industrialization, and the rise to global prominence occurred simultaneously. These changes were intimately interlinked, the mutual causes and effects of each other. Industrialization fueled

Exhibit 9.1   Educational Attainment for Selected White Ethnic Groups, 1990

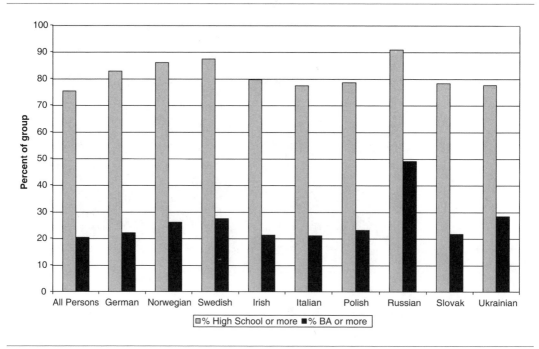

SOURCE: U.S. Bureau of the Census (1998a).

the growth of U.S. military and political power, and the industrial machinery of the nation depended heavily on the flow of labor from Europe. By World War I, for example, 25% of the nation's total labor force was foreign born, and more than half of the workforce in New York, Detroit, and Chicago consisted of immigrant men. Immigrants were the majority of the workers in many important sectors of the economy, including coal mining, steel manufacturing, the garment industry, and meatpacking (Martin & Midgley, 1999, p. 15; Steinberg, 1981, p. 36).

ASSIMILATION AND EQUALITY: SHOULD WHITE ETHNIC GROUPS BE CONSIDERED "MINORITY GROUPS"?

Perhaps the most important point about white ethnic groups (the descendants of the European immigrants) is that they are today on the verge of completing the assimilation process. Even the groups that were the most

despised and rejected in earlier years are acculturated, integrated, and thoroughly intermarried today. To illustrate this point, we will reverse our usual practice and consider matters of integration and equality at the start of this chapter.

To begin with secondary structural integration, Exhibits 9.1 through 9.3 display data collected during the 1990 Census for 9 of the more than 60 white ethnic groups that people mentioned when asked to define their ancestry.[1] The selected groups include the two largest white ethnic groups (German and Irish Americans) and seven chosen to represent a range of geographic regions of origin and times of immigration.[1] The graphs show that all nine of the groups selected are at or above national norms ("all persons") for all measures of equality. There is some variation among the groups, of course, but all exceed the national averages for both high school and college education and for median income. All nine groups also have dramatically lower poverty rates than the national

Exhibit 9.2 Median Household Income for Selected White Ethnic Groups, 1990

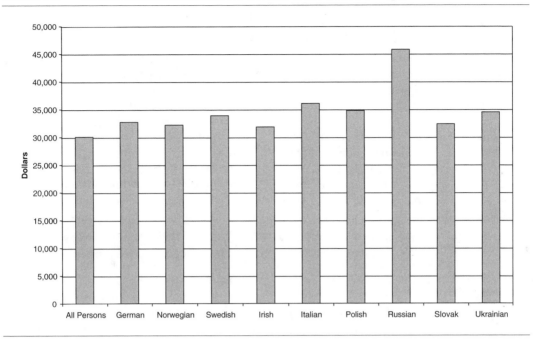

SOURCE: U.S. Bureau of the Census (1998b).

Exhibit 9.3 Percentage of Families Living in Poverty for Selected White Ethnic Groups, 1990

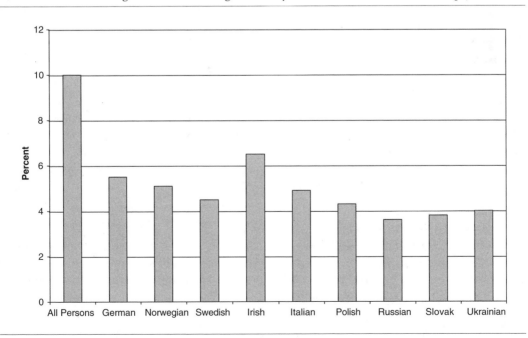

SOURCE: U.S. Bureau of the Census (1998b).

average, and for most, the poverty rate is less than half the national average.

In other areas, the evidence for assimilation and equality is also persuasive. The distinct ethnic neighborhoods that these groups created in American cities (Little Italy, Greektown, Little Warsaw, etc.) have faded away or been taken over by other groups, and the rate of intermarriage between members of different white ethnic groups is quite high. For example, based on data from the 1990 Census, about 56% of all married whites have spouses whose ethnic backgrounds do not match their own (Alba, 1995, pp. 13–14).

The evidence that white ethnic groups have achieved equality is so compelling that it raises a question: Should they be included in this series of case studies of minority groups, or should they be treated as part of the dominant group? In fact, there are a number of reasons for including them. First, although they no longer experience the systematic, widespread discrimination and inequality that is the major defining characteristic of a minority group, they have not completely vanished. Descendants of the European immigrants continue to identify themselves in ethnic terms and link themselves to the country from which their immigrant ancestors came. For example, when asked in a survey in the year 2000, "From what country or part of the world did your ancestors come?" about 85% of the white respondents named a European country, not the United States (National Opinion Research Council, 2000). Although this lingering ethnic identity is not very robust or deep (as we shall see at the end of the chapter), it is also not extinct (at least not yet). Furthermore, a few ethnic neighborhoods, like Irish Catholic South Boston, have survived the pressures of assimilation, and the political, religious, and gastronomical traditions of the European immigrant groups continue to manifest themselves, especially in the industrial cities of the Northeast and the Midwest. Ancestry and ethnicity still matter to millions of European Americans, even though they are no longer at the center of their lives. We will consider the strength of white ethnic identity in contemporary America in more detail at the end of this chapter.

A second, related reason for treating white ethnic groups as minority groups is that the traditional prejudices against them persist, even though in weakened form. Stereotypes of the various European groups (e.g., Jews as shrewd money handlers, Italians as quick-tempered and emotional, Irish as argumentative drunks, Poles as not very bright) along with a repertoire of insulting names (wop, mick, hunky, kike, kraut, frog, limey, Polack, and scores of others) remain a part of U.S. culture and national memory.

Third, each of the white ethnic groups had a unique assimilation history, and their varied experiences will add further depth and variety to our analysis. Some groups integrated by rising through the mainstream institutions and organizations of society, while others relied on separate ethnic enclave economies to propel their rise to equality. The white ethnic groups give us another comparison with and a sharper focus on the challenges and barriers facing today's racial and colonized minority groups.

Fourth, as we shall see, the actions of white ethnic groups also provide a partial explanation for the current situation of America's racial and colonized minority groups: The rise of the former was possible in part because of discrimination against the latter. European American immigrant groups protected their rising social class positions by helping to perpetuate the exclusion of African Americans, Hispanic Americans, and other minority groups of color.

Fifth, the experiences of the immigrants from Europe established a set of expectations and understandings about immigration and assimilation that shape our views of the post-1965 immigrants, the second great wave of humanity to strike these shores. As we have seen in the previous two chapters, these perceptions and ideas often are useful as starting points for analyzing contemporary immigration but have to be revised and updated to take account of the changing nature of the immigrant stream and the changing context of American society. Nonetheless, an understanding of both the "baseline" experiences of European immigrants a century ago and the popular notions and sociological theories that developed from those experiences can provide a useful and more informed perspective on the experiences of immigrants today.

Finally, we can use the experience of the immigrants from Europe to further test the theories and concepts we developed in previous chapters. We began this series of case studies by considering what Blauner (1972) calls colonized and conquered minority groups (African Americans and Native Americans) and then moved to mixed types (Hispanic Americans and Asian Americans). With European immigrants, we consider groups whose contact situation and conditions of entry most closely approximate "purely" immigrant groups, the end point of Blauner's typology. As we discussed in Chapter 5, Blauner hypothesized that minority groups created by immigration will experience less intense prejudice and discrimination and that they will be disadvantaged for a shorter time than groups created by colonization and conquest. In this chapter, we investigate the dynamics and consequences of this more favored status.

We begin this final case study by examining the immigration experiences and the history of the white ethnic groups in the 19th and 20th centuries. We identify and consider the implications of the various modes of incorporation into U.S. society that they followed. We close the chapter by considering the meaning of white ethnicity and white ethnic identity at the dawn of the 21st century.

INDUSTRIALIZATION AND IMMIGRATION

As you recall, one of the themes of this text is that dominant-minority relations reflect the economic and political characteristics of the larger society and change as those characteristics change (see Chapter 4). Thus, it will come as no surprise to learn that the immigration from Europe that created so many minority groups in the United States was, at base, motivated by a revolution in subsistence technology. The industrial revolution began in England in the mid-1700s, and it replaced the traditional, labor-intensive forms of work and production with capital-intensive forms. The new technology transformed social relations first in Europe and then throughout the world, forever altering everyday life and relations between groups as it proceeded.

At the dawn of the industrial revolution, most people in Europe lived in small, rural villages and survived by labor-intensive farming. Industrialization destroyed this traditional way of life as it spread across the continent from England to northern and western Europe and then to southern and eastern Europe. Agriculture was modernized, machines replaced both people and draft animals in the fields, and the need for human labor in rural areas declined. Farmland was consolidated into larger and larger tracts for the sake of efficiency, further decreasing the need for human laborers. At the same time, the rural population began to grow even as survival in the rapidly changing rural economy became more difficult.

In response, peasants began to leave their home villages and move toward urban areas. Factories were being built in or near the cities, opening up opportunities for employment. The urban population tended to increase faster than the job supply, however, and many migrants had to move on. Many of these former peasants responded to opportunities available in the New World, especially in the United States. As industrialization took hold in Europe, the population movement to the cities and then to North America eventually grew to become the largest in human history (so far).

The timing of immigration followed the timing of industrialization. The first waves of immigrants, often called the "old" immigrants, came from northern and western Europe beginning in the 1820s. A second wave, the "new" immigrants, began arriving from southern and eastern Europe in the 1880s. Exhibit 9.4 shows both waves. Also note that immigration was higher in the latter period and decreased dramatically in the late 1920s, the "hiatus" we discussed in Chapter 7.

Exhibit 9.4   Immigration to the United States, 1820–2001

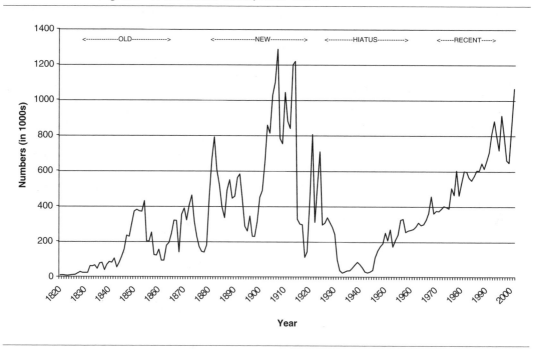

SOURCE: U.S. Immigration and Naturalization Service (2000).

NOTE: Does not include immigrants who legalized their status under the provisions of the Immigration Reform and Control Act (IRCA).

EUROPEAN ORIGINS, CONDITIONS OF ENTRY, AND THE CAMPAIGN AGAINST IMMIGRATION

European immigrants followed a variety of pathways into the United States, determined by their cultural and class characteristics, their country of origin, and the timing of their arrival. Some groups encountered much more resistance than others, and different groups played different roles in the industrialization and urbanization of America. To discuss these diverse patterns systematically, we can differentiate between three subgroups of European immigrants: Protestants from northern and western Europe, the largely Catholic immigrant laborers from Ireland and from southern and eastern Europe, and Jewish immigrants from eastern Europe. We look at these subgroups in roughly the order of their arrival.

Northern and Western Europeans

Northern and western European immigrants included Germans, Norwegians, Swedes (the first three groups listed in Exhibits 9.1 to 9.3), Welsh, French, Dutch, and Danes. These groups were similar to the dominant group in their racial and religious characteristics and also shared many cultural values with the host society, including the Protestant ethic—which stressed hard work, success, and individualism—and support for the principles of democratic government. These similarities eased their acceptance into a society that was highly intolerant of religious and racial differences until well into the 20th century, and these immigrant groups generally experienced a lower degree of ethnocentric rejection and racist disparagement than did the Irish and immigrants from southern and eastern Europe.

Northern and western European immigrants came from nations that were just as developed as the United States. Thus, these immigrants tended to be more skilled and educated than other immigrant groups, and they often brought money and other resources with which to secure a comfortable place for themselves in their new society. Many settled in the sparsely populated Midwest and in other frontier areas, where they farmed the fertile land that had become available after the conquest and removal of Native Americans and Mexican Americans. By dispersing throughout the mid-section of the country, they lowered their visibility and their degree of competition with dominant group members. Two brief case studies outline the experiences of these groups.

Immigrants From Norway

Norway had a small population base, and immigration from this Scandinavian nation was never sizable in absolute numbers. However, "America Fever" struck there as it did elsewhere in Europe, and on a per capita basis, Norway sent more immigrants to the United States before 1890 than any European nation except Ireland (Chan, 1990, p. 41).

The first Norwegian immigrants were moderately prosperous farmers searching for cheap land. They found abundant acreage in upper Midwest states such as Minnesota and Wisconsin, then found that the local labor supply was too small to effectively cultivate the available land. Many Norwegian immigrants turned to their homeland for assistance and used their relatives and friends to create networks and recruit a labor force. Thus, chains of communication and migration linking Norway to the northern plains were established, supplying immigrants to these areas for decades (Chan, 1990, p. 41). Today, a strong Scandinavian heritage is still evident in the farms, towns, and cities of the upper Midwest.

Immigrants From Germany

The stream of immigration from Germany was much larger than that from Norway, and German Americans left their mark on the economy, the political structure, and the cultural life of their new land. In the last half of the 19th century, at least 25% of the immigrants each year were German (Conzen, 1980, p. 406), and today more Americans trace their ancestry to Germany than to any other country except England (National Opinion Research Council, 2000).

The German immigrants who arrived earlier in the 1800s moved into the newly opened farmland and the rapidly growing cities of the Midwest, as had many Scandinavians. By 1850, large German communities could be found in Milwaukee, St. Louis, and other Midwestern cities (Conzen, 1980, p. 413). Some German immigrants followed the transatlantic route of the cotton trade between Europe and the southern United States and entered through the port of New Orleans, moving from there to the Midwest and Southwest.

German immigrants arriving later in the 19th century were more likely to settle in urban areas because fertile land was less available. Many of the city-bound German immigrants were skilled workers and artisans, and others found work as laborers in the rapidly expanding industrial sector. The double penetration of German immigrants into the rural economy and the higher sectors of the urban economy is reflected by the fact that by 1870, most employed German Americans were involved in skilled labor (37%) or farming (25%) (Conzen, 1980, p. 413).

German immigrants took relatively high occupational positions in the U.S. labor force, and their sons and daughters were able to translate that relative affluence into economic mobility. By the dawn of the 20th century, large numbers of second-generation German Americans were finding their way into white-collar and professional careers. Within a few generations, German Americans had achieved parity with national norms in education, income, and occupational prestige.

A Successful Assimilation

The process of acculturation and integration for Protestant immigrants from northern and western Europe was consistent with the traditional views of assimilation first stated in Chapter 2. Although members of these groups felt the sting of rejection, prejudice, and discrimination, their movement to integration and equality was relatively smooth, especially when compared with the experiences of racial minority groups who were created by conquest and colonization. Their relative success and high degree of assimilation are suggested in Exhibits 9.1 through 9.3.

Immigrant Laborers From Ireland and Southern and Eastern Europe

The relative ease of assimilation for northern and western Europeans contrasts sharply with the experiences of non-Protestant, less educated, and less skilled immigrants. These "immigrant laborers" came in two waves. The Irish were part of the "old" immigration that began in the 1820s, but the bulk of this group—Italians, Poles, Russians, Hungarians, Greeks, Serbs, Ukrainians, Slovaks, Bulgarians, and scores of other southern and eastern European nationalities—made up the "new" immigration that began in the 1880s. Most of the immigrants in these nationality groups were peasants or unskilled laborers with few resources other than their willingness to work. They came from rural, village-oriented cultures in which family and kin took precedence over individual needs or desires, not unlike the traditional Asian cultures we discussed in Chapter 8. Family life for them tended to be autocratic and male dominated, and children were expected to subordinate their personal desires and work for the good of the family as a whole. Arranged marriages were common. This cultural background was less consistent with the industrializing, capitalistic, individualistic, Protestant, Anglo-American culture and, as a result, these immigrant laborers experienced greater levels of rejection and discrimination than did the immigrants from northern and western Europe.

The immigrant laborers were much less likely to enter the rural economy than were the immigrants from northern and western Europe. Much of the better frontier land already had been claimed by the time most new immigrant groups began to arrive, and a large number of them had been permanently soured on farming by the oppressive and exploitative agrarian economies from which they had escaped. They settled in the cities of the industrializing Northeast and found work in plants, mills, mines, and factories. They supplied the armies of laborers needed to power the industrial revolution, although their view of this process generally was from the bottom looking up. They arrived during the decades in which the industrial and urban infrastructure of the United States was being constructed. They built roads, canals, and railroads, as well as the factories, plants, and mills that housed the machinery of industrialization. The first tunnels of the New York City subway system were dug, largely by hand, by laborers from Italy. Other immigrants found work in the coal fields of Pennsylvania and West Virginia and the steel mills of Pittsburgh, and they flocked by the millions to the factories of the Northeast.

Immigrant laborers took jobs in which strength and stamina were more important than literacy or skilled craftsmanship. In fact, the minimum level of skills required for employment actually declined as industrialization proceeded through its early phases. To keep wages low and take advantage of what seemed like an inexhaustible supply of cheap labor, industrialists and factory owners developed technologies and machines whose operation required few skills and little knowledge of English. As mechanization proceeded, unskilled workers replaced skilled workers in the workforce. Not infrequently, women and children replaced men because they could be hired for lower wages (Steinberg, 1981, p. 35).

Gender

The gender of the immigrants shaped their experiences in countless ways. When immigrant women entered the workforce, they generally found jobs as domestics (e.g., maids, cooks, and nannies in affluent, white, middle-class homes) or in factories, where they were assigned to the most menial, lowest-paid tasks. For example, many women from Bohemia had worked in cigar manufacturing in the old country and sought work in that industry in the United States. Although they were skilled and experienced, they were barred from the better, higher-paying jobs, which were reserved for U.S.-born men. The immigrant women were assigned to the hardest, least desirable jobs in the factory, such as stripping tobacco in dank, airless basements (Amott & Matthaei, 1991, p. 111).

Immigrant women often were sent to work by their families at young ages, as were many U.S.-born women of the working class. Women of these groups were expected to work until they married, after which time it was expected that their husbands would support them and their children. In many cases, however, immigrant men could not earn enough to support their families, and the earnings of wives and children were required to balance the family budget. Immigrant wives sometimes continued to work outside the home, but when they did not, they found other ways to make money. They took in boarders, did laundry or sewing, tended gardens, and were involved in myriad other activities that permitted them to contribute to the family budget while staying home and attending to family and child-rearing responsibilities. A 1911 report on southern and eastern European households found that about half kept lodgers and that the income from this activity amounted to about 25% of the husbands' wages. Children also contributed to the family income by taking after-school and summertime jobs (Morawska, 1990, pp. 211–212).

For European immigrant males, entry-level, unskilled jobs in the industrial sector were plentiful, but most of these jobs offered no possibility of upward mobility or promotion, and many were insecure and unsafe. Even salary raises were rare and given grudgingly, as there was a plentiful supply of immigrants just "off the boat" willing to work for less. Male immigrant laborers usually spent their entire working lives in jobs at the bottom of the occupational structure. The better-paid, more secure, and skilled or supervisory positions were reserved for U.S.-born Anglo-Americans

or for the descendants of northern and western European immigrants. The Irish and the southern and eastern European immigrants, and most of their descendants, remained a blue-collar, unskilled working class until well into the 20th century (Bodnar, 1985; Morawska, 1990).

Ethnic and Religious Prejudice

Today, it may be hard to conceive the bitterness and intensity of the prejudice that greeted the Irish, Italians, Poles, and other new immigrant groups. Even as they were becoming an indispensable segment of the American workforce, they were castigated, ridiculed, attacked, and disparaged. The Irish were the first immigrant laborers to arrive and thus the first to feel this intense prejudice and discrimination. Campaigns against immigration were waged, Irish neighborhoods were attacked by mobs, and Roman Catholic churches and convents were burned. Some employers blatantly refused to hire the Irish, often advertising their ethnic preferences with signs saying "No Irish Need Apply." Until later-arriving groups displaced them, the Irish were mired at the bottom of the job market. Indeed, at one time they were referred to as the "niggers of Boston" (Blessing, 1980; Potter, 1973; Shannon, 1964).

Other groups felt the same sting of rejection as they arrived. Italian immigrants were particularly likely to be the victims of violent attacks, one of the most vicious of which took place in New Orleans in 1891. The city's police chief was assassinated, and rumors of Italian involvement in the murder were rampant. Hundreds of Italians were arrested, and 9 were brought to trial. All were acquitted. Anti-Italian sentiment was running so high, however, that a mob lynched 11 Italians while police and city officials did nothing (Higham, 1963).

Much of the prejudice against the Irish and the new immigrants was expressed as anti-Catholicism. Prior to the mid-19th century, Anglo-American society had been almost exclusively Protestant. Catholicism, with its celibate clergy, Latin masses, and cloistered nuns, seemed alien, exotic, and threatening. The growth of Catholicism, especially because it was associated with non-Anglo immigrants, raised fears that the Protestant religions would lose status. There were even rumors that the Pope was planning to move the Vatican to America and organize a takeover of the U.S. government.

Although Catholics often were stereotyped as single groups, they varied along a number of dimensions. For example, the Catholic faith as practiced in Ireland was significantly different from that practiced in Italy, Poland, and other countries. Catholic immigrant groups often established their own parishes with priests who could speak the old language. These cultural and national differences often separated Catholic groups despite the common faith (Herberg, 1960). In Chapter 2, we discussed the concept of the "triple melting pot" and how religion and ethnicity often became fused for European immigrants and their descendants.

Upward Mobility

Eventually, as the generations passed, the prejudice, systematic discrimination, and other barriers to upward mobility for the immigrant laborer groups weakened, and their descendants began to rise out of the working class. Although the first and second generations of these groups were largely limited to jobs at the unskilled or semiskilled level, the third and later generations rose in the American social class system. As Exhibits 9.1 to 9.3 show, the descendants of the immigrant laborers achieved parity with national norms by the latter half of the 20th century.

Eastern European Jewish Immigrants and the Ethnic Enclave

Jewish immigrants from Russia and other parts of eastern Europe followed a third pathway into U.S. society. These immigrants were a part of the "new" immigration and began arriving in the 1880s. Unlike the immigrant laborer groups, who generally were economic refugees and included many young, single male sojourners, eastern European Jews were fleeing religious persecution and arrived as family units intending to settle permanently and become citizens. They settled in the urban areas of the Northeast and Midwest. New York City was the most common destination, and the Lower East Side became the best-known Jewish American neighborhood. By 1920, almost half of all Jewish Americans lived in New York City alone, with about 60% living in the urban areas between Boston and Philadelphia. Another 30% lived in the urban areas of the Midwest, particularly in Chicago (Goren, 1980, p. 581).

In Russia and other parts of eastern Europe, Jews had been barred from agrarian occupations and had come to rely on the urban economy for their livelihood. When they immigrated to the United States, they brought these urban skills and job experiences with them. For example, almost two thirds of the immigrant Jewish men had been tailors and other skilled laborers in eastern Europe (Goren, 1980, p. 581). In the rapidly industrializing U.S. economy of the early 20th century, they were able to use these skills to find work.

Other Jewish immigrants joined the urban working class and took manual labor, unskilled jobs in the industrial sector (Morawska, 1990, p. 202). The garment industry in particular became the lifeblood of the Jewish community and provided jobs to about one third of all eastern European Jews residing in the major cities (Goren, 1980, p. 582). Women as well as men were involved in the garment industry. Jewish women, like the women of the immigrant laborer groups and the Chinese women discussed in Chapter 8, found ways to combine their jobs and their domestic responsibilities. As young girls, they worked in factories and sweatshops, and after marriage, they did the same work at home, sewing precut garments together or doing other piecework such as wrapping cigars or making artificial flowers, often assisted by their children (Amott & Matthaei, 1991, p. 115).

The Enclave and Upward Mobility

Unlike the immigrant laborers, Jewish immigrants brought experience in commerce and marketing with them, and they often found ways to start their own businesses and become self-employed. The Jewish neighborhoods were densely populated and provided a ready market for services of all kinds. Some Jewish immigrants became street peddlers or started bakeries, butcher and candy shops, or any number of other retail enterprises. In a process that mirrored the activities of the Chinese and the Japanese on the West Coast at the same time, eastern European Jews constructed an enclave economy on the East Coast.

Capitalizing on their residential concentration and close proximity, Jewish immigrants created dense networks of commercial, financial, and social cooperation. Like the other ethnic enclaves we examined in previous chapters, the Jewish American enclave survived because of the cohesiveness of the group—the willingness of wives, children, and other relatives to work for little or no monetary compensation—and the commercial savvy of the early immigrants. In addition, a large pool of cheap labor and sources of credit and other financial services were available within the community. The Jewish American enclave grew and provided a livelihood for many of the children and grandchildren of the immigrants (Portes & Manning, 1986, pp. 51–52). As was also the case with other enclave groups, economic advancement preceded extensive acculturation, and Jewish Americans made significant strides toward economic equality before they became fluent in English or were otherwise Americanized.

As we discussed in Chapter 8, an obvious way in which an enclave immigrant group can improve its position is to develop an educated and acculturated second generation. The Americanized, English-speaking children of the immigrants used their greater familiarity with the dominant society and their language facility to help preserve and expand the family enterprise. Thus, the same logic that led Chinese Americans and Japanese Americans to invest in education for the next generation also applied to Jewish immigrants. Furthermore, as the second generation appeared, the public school system was expanding, and in New York City and other places, education through the college level was free or very cheap (Steinberg, 1981, pp. 128–138).

There was also a strong push for the second and third generations to enter professions, and as Jewish Americans excelled in school, resistance to and discrimination against them increased. By the 1920s, many elite colleges and universities such as Dartmouth had established quotas that limited the number of Jewish students they would admit (Dinnerstein, 1977, p. 228). These quotas were not abolished until after World War II.

The enclave economy and the Jewish neighborhoods established by the immigrants proved to be an effective base from which to integrate into American society. The descendants of the eastern European Jewish immigrants moved out of the ethnic neighborhoods years ago, and their positions in the economy—their pushcarts, stores, and jobs in the garment industry—have been taken over by more recent immigrants. When they left the enclave economy, many second- and third-generation eastern European Jews did not enter the mainstream occupational structure at the bottom, as the immigrant laborer groups tended to do. They used the resources generated by the entrepreneurship of the early generations to gain access to prestigious and advantaged social class positions (Portes & Manning, 1986, p. 53). Studies show that as a group, Jewish Americans today surpass national averages in income, levels of education, and occupational prestige (Sklare, 1971, pp. 60–69; see also Cohen, 1985; Massarik & Chenkin, 1973). The relatively higher status of Russian Americans shown in Exhibits 9.1 to 9.3 is due in part to the fact that many Jewish Americans are of Russian descent.

Anti-Semitism

One barrier that Jewish Americans were forced to overcome was prejudice and racism (or anti-Semitism). Biased sentiments against and negative stereotypes of Jews have been a part of Western tradition for centuries and, in fact, have been stronger and more vicious in Europe than in the United States. For nearly two millennia, European Jews have been chastised and persecuted as the killers of Christ and stereotyped as materialistic moneylenders and crafty businessmen. The stereotype that links Jews and moneylending has its origins in the fact that, in premodern Europe, Catholics were forbidden by the Church to engage in usury (charging interest for loans). Jews were under no such restriction and filled the gap thus created in the economy. The ultimate episode in the long history of European anti-Semitism was, of course, the Nazi Holocaust, in which about 6 million Jews died. European anti-Semitism did not end with the demise of the Nazi regime; it remains a prominent concern in Russia, Germany, and other nations.

Before the mass immigration of eastern European Jews began in the late 19th century, anti-Semitism in the United States was relatively mild, perhaps because the group was so small. As the immigration continued, anti-Jewish prejudice increased in intensity and viciousness, fostering the view of Jews as cunning but dishonest merchants. In the late 19th century, Jews began to be banned from social clubs and the boardrooms of businesses and other organizations. Summer resorts began posting notices such as "We prefer not to entertain Hebrews" (Goren, 1980, p. 585).

By the 1920s and 1930s, anti-Semitism had become quite prominent among American prejudices and was being preached by the Ku Klux Klan and other extreme racist groups. Because many of the political radicals and labor leaders of the time were Jewish immigrants, anti-Semitism became fused with a fear of Communism and other anticapitalist doctrines. Some prominent Americans espoused anti-Semitism, among them Henry Ford, the founder of Ford Motor Company; Charles Lindbergh, the aviator who was the first to fly solo across the Atlantic; and Father Charles Coughlin, a Catholic priest with a popular radio show (Selzer, 1972).

After reaching a peak before World War II, anti-Semitism has tapered off in recent decades, as illustrated in Exhibit 1.4 (see also Anti-Defamation League, 2000). Note that anti-Semitism persists, albeit in attenuated form. Stereotypes and prejudicial sentiments can become embedded in the culture and passed on from generation to generation through socialization. Anti-Semitism also has a prominent place in the ideologies of a variety of extremist groups that have emerged in recent years, including skinheads and various contemporary incarnations of the Ku Klux Klan. Some of this targeting of Jews seems to increase during economic recession and may be a type of scapegoating related to the stereotypical view of Jewish Americans as extremely prosperous and materialistic.

The Campaign Against Immigration

In Chapter 8, we discussed the campaign to end Chinese immigration that ended successfully with the passage of the Chinese Exclusion Act of 1882. Similar campaigns were waged against European immigration, the strength of which waxed and waned throughout the period of mass immigration from the 1820s to the 1920s. Organizations were formed to express opposition to immigration and to pressure the federal government to limit entry into the nation. Predictably, these organizations were particularly common during hard economic times and depressions.

The anti-Catholic, anti-Semitic, and anti-immigration forces ultimately triumphed with the passage of the National Origins Act in 1924. This act drastically reduced the overall number of immigrants who would be admitted each year. Furthermore, it established a quota system to determine the number of immigrants who would be accepted each year from each sending nation, a system that was openly racist. For example, the size of the quota for European nations was based on the proportional representation of each nationality in the United States as of 1890. This year was chosen because it predated the bulk of the new immigration and gave the most generous quotas to the more Anglo northern and western European nations. Immigration from the Western Hemisphere was not directly affected by this legislation, but immigration from non-European nations (i.e., China, Japan, and other Asian nations) was banned altogether. This quota system allocated nearly 70% of the available immigration slots to the nations of northern and western Europe, despite the fact that immigration from those areas had largely ended by the 1920s. The act had a marked and immediate effect on the volume of immigration (see Exhibit 9.4). By the time the Great Depression took hold of the American economy, immigration had dropped to the lowest levels in a century. The National Origins Act remained in effect until the mid-1960s.

COMPARATIVE FOCUS

IMMIGRATION AND ASSIMILATION IN CANADA

The United States was not the only destination for the immigrants who left Europe between the 1820s and the 1920s. Millions more went to Argentina and Brazil (mainly from Italy), Australia (mainly from Britain and Ireland), and to scores of other nations. The United States was the most popular destination, receiving about 60% of the immigrants (Daniels, 1990, p. 23), but the exodus out of Europe was a global phenomenon that deeply affected many other societies. Canada, for example, received more than 4 million immigrants during this time period. Did the immigrants to Canada follow patterns of settlement and adaptation similar to the groups that arrived in the United States?

Canada and the United States share history and culture along with their common border, and as you would expect, their immigration experiences are similar in many ways. The volume of immigration from Europe to both nations followed a similar rhythm, fluctuating according to social, economic, and political conditions in the Old and New Worlds. In both cases, rates of immigration peaked early in the 20th century, fell during World War I, rose again in the 1920s, and then plummeted during the Great Depression of the 1930s (a decline that in the United States was greatly abetted by the restrictive legislation passed in the 1920s).

On the other hand, the number of immigrants to Canada never approached the numbers coming to the United States. In fact, in many years prior to the 20th century, more people actually left Canada than arrived. For many European immigrants (particularly for the British and Irish), Canada was a cheaper or more convenient destination, but the greater economic opportunities available in the United States proved hard to resist. For example, during the famine years in Ireland, more than 2 million Irish left their homeland. Many went to Britain, Australia, and other places, but the bulk (nearly a million and a half) came directly to the United States. The second largest group, about a third of a million, went to Canada first and then drifted south, many reuniting with their countrymen in the urban Northeast (Daniels, 1990, p. 135).

Another important difference between the two nations is that Canadian immigrants have been much less diverse, and as a result, Canada has remained considerably more homogeneous than the United States. In the 18th and 19th centuries, immigrants to Canada were almost exclusively from the British Isles (including Ireland) and France, and in 1871 (the date of the first Canadian census), the Canadian population was more than 90% British or French. Other European groups did not begin to immigrate to Canada in substantial numbers until the completion of the national railroad system opened up the vast Canadian prairies in the late 1800s. Ukrainians were one such group. Fleeing political unrest and overpopulation, they settled in the rich farming country of the western provinces of Canada, where the soil and climate were similar to their homeland. Some 10,000 arrived by 1900, but this number swelled to more than 150,000 by the start of World War I in 1914 (Luciuk & Hryniuk, 1991).

The diversity of the Canadian immigrant stream continued to increase in the first half of the 20th century. The proportion of Canadians of European descent other than British and French rose from about 9% in 1901 to almost 20% in 1941. Parallel to the U.S. experience, the earlier immigrants were from northern and western Europe, and those arriving later were more likely to be of eastern and southern European origin (Fong & Wilkes, 1999). However, although gradually declining, the numerical predominance of the British and French ancestral groups held up throughout the 20th century. As late as the 1951 census, Canada was still nearly 50% British and more than 30% French, and the most recent census shows that these two "ancestral groups" still account for half the population.

What happened to the European immigrants who arrived in Canada in the 19th and 20th centuries? Briefly stated, they settled in patterns not too different from those of the immigrants who came to the United States, and today, their descendants are at or above national norms in terms of income, schooling, unemployment, and other measures of integration and acculturation. For example, Fong and Wilkes (1999) found that European immigrants and their descendants in Canada seemed to follow the predictions of what I have called traditional assimilation theory: Each generation rose in status relative to their parents and became increasingly assimilated.

Another study (Sweetman & Dicks, 1999) found substantial differences between white and nonwhite Canadian groups in terms of education and income but comparatively minor differences within the white ethnic Canadian groups. Stelcner (2000) used data from the 1991 Canadian census to compare income inequalities among groups and found that most white ethnic groups were close to the national norms, with Spanish, Polish, and Italian men slightly below and German, British, and Ukrainian men a little above. In both studies, the major exception to the pattern of rough equality for white ethnic groups were Jewish Canadians, who were far above the norms, a difference that reflects enclave experiences and higher levels of human capital, similar to Jewish Americans.

Today, the immigration experiences of the two nations continue to exhibit many parallels. Rates of immigration have risen in both cases, and recent immigrants are equally diverse, racially, culturally, and linguistically. The great majority of contemporary immigrants to both nations are coming from the same areas of Asia and Latin America, and Canada, like the United States, is becoming a more diverse and pluralistic society. For example, a half century ago, Canadians of Asian origin were less than 1% of the total population (Fong & Wilkes, 1999). Today, they are a little more than 7%.[2] Canadian immigration policy favors more skilled and educated applicants, and the government is officially committed to multiculturalism and a rejection of narrow Anglo-centered assimilation.

Still, as in the past, Canada and the United States will share many challenges (permanent immigration and segmented assimilation, for example) in their immigration experiences.

DEVELOPMENTS IN THE 20TH CENTURY: MOBILITY AND INTEGRATION

As the 20th century progressed, a number of factors in addition to their initial mode of incorporation affected the social class position and the rapidity of assimilation for white ethnic groups. The major factors included

- The degree of similarity between the immigrant group and the dominant group
- The processes of ethnic succession and secondary structural assimilation
- The broad structural changes in the American economy caused by industrialization

Degree of Similarity

When European immigration began, the dominant group consisted largely of Protestants with ethnic origins in northern and western Europe and especially in England. The degree of resistance, prejudice, and discrimination encountered by the different European immigrant groups varied in part by the degree to which they differed from these dominant group characteristics. The most significant differences related to religion, language, cultural values, and, for some groups, physical characteristics. Thus, Protestant immigrants from northern and western Europe experienced less resistance than the English-speaking but Catholic Irish, who in turn were accepted more readily than the new immigrants, who were both non-English-speaking and overwhelmingly non-Protestant.

These ethnocentric preferences of the dominant group correspond roughly to the arrival times of the immigrants. The most similar groups immigrated earliest, and the least similar tended to be the last to arrive. Because of this coincidence, resistance to any one group of immigrants tended to fade as new groups arrived. For example, anti-German prejudice and discrimination never became particularly vicious or widespread (except during the heat of the World Wars) because the Irish began arriving in large numbers at about the same time. Concerns about the German immigrants were swamped by the fear that the Catholic Irish could never be assimilated. Then, as the 19th century drew to a close, immigrants from southern and eastern Europe—even more different from the dominant group—began to arrive and made concern about the Irish seem trivial.

In addition, the "new" immigration was far more voluminous than the "old" immigration (see Exhibit 9.4). Southern and eastern Europeans arrived in record numbers in the early 20th century, and the sheer volume of the immigration raised fears that American cities and institutions would be swamped by hordes of racially inferior, unassimilable immigrants (another fear that is echoed in the present).

Thus, a preference hierarchy was formed among the European American ethnic groups by religion and region of origin. The hierarchy is illustrated by the social distance scale results presented in Exhibit 1.4. These rankings reflect more than the degree of dominant group ethnocentrism; they also reflect the ease with which the groups have been integrated. The sequence of mobility is captured by the concept of ethnic succession, the topic of the next section.

Ethnic Succession

The process of *ethnic succession* refers to the myriad ways in which European ethnic groups unintentionally affected one another's position in the social class structure of the larger society. The overall pattern was that each European immigrant group tended to be pushed to higher social class levels and more favorable economic situations by the groups that arrived after them.

As more experienced groups became upwardly mobile and began to move out of the neighborhoods that served as their "ports of entry," they often were replaced by a new group of immigrants who would begin the process all over again. Some neighborhoods in the cities of the Northeast served as *the* ethnic neighborhood—the first safe haven in the new society—for a variety of successive groups. Some neighborhoods continue to fill this role today.

Secondary Structural Assimilation

This section traces the general pattern of ethnic succession and integration into the larger society. We focus on the Irish, the first immigrant laborers to arrive in large numbers, but the patterns generally apply to all white ethnic groups.

The Irish tended to follow the northern and western Europeans up in the job market and social class structure and were in turn followed by the wave of new immigrants. In many urban areas of the Northeast, the Irish moved into the neighborhoods and took jobs left behind by German laborers. After a period of adjustment, the Irish began to create their own connections with the mainstream society and improve their economic and social position. They were replaced in their neighborhoods and at the bottom of the occupational structure by Italians, Poles, and other immigrant groups arriving after them.

Local Politics. As the years passed and as the Irish gained more experience, they began to forge links to the larger society through several institutions, with politics being perhaps the most important connection. The Irish allied themselves with the Democratic Party and helped to construct the political machines that came to dominate many city governments in the 19th and early 20th centuries.

Machine politicians were corrupt and even criminal, regularly subverting the election process, bribing city and state officials, using city budgets to line their own pockets, and passing out public jobs as payoffs for favors and faithful service. Although not exactly models of good government, the political machines performed a number of valuable social services for their constituents and loyal followers. Machine politicians, such as Boss Tweed of Tammany Hall in New York City, could find jobs, provide food and clothing for the destitute, aid victims of fires and other calamities, or intervene in the criminal and civil courts.

Much of the power of the urban political machines derived from their control of the city payroll. The leaders of the machines used municipal jobs and the city budget as part of a "spoils" system (as in "to the victor go the spoils") and as rewards to their supporters and allies. The faithful Irish party worker might be rewarded for service to the machine with a job in the police department (thus, the stereotypical Irish cop) or some other agency. Private businessmen might be rewarded with lucrative contracts to supply services or perform other city business.

The political machines served as engines of economic opportunity and linked Irish Americans to a central and important institution of the dominant society. Using the resources controlled by local government as a power base, the Irish (and other immigrant groups after them) began to integrate themselves into the larger society and carve out a place in the mainstream structures of American society.

Labor Unions. The labor movement provided a second link between the Irish, other European immigrant groups, and the larger society. Although virtually all white ethnic groups had a hand in the creation and eventual success of the movement, many of the founders and early leaders were Irish. For example, Terence Powderly, an Irish Catholic, founded one of the first U.S. labor unions, and in the early years of the 20th century, about one third of union leaders were Irish and more than 50 national unions had Irish presidents (Bodnar, 1985, p. 111; Brody, 1980, p. 615).

As the labor movement grew in strength and gradually acquired legitimacy, the leaders of the movement also gained status, power, and other resources, while the rank-and-file membership gained job security, increased wages, and better fringe benefits. The labor movement provided another channel through which resources, power, status, and jobs flowed to the white ethnic groups.

Because of the way in which jobs were organized in industrializing America, union work typically required communication and cooperation across ethnic lines. The American workforce at the turn of the 20th century was multiethnic and multilingual, and union leaders had to coordinate and mobilize the efforts of many different language and cultural groups in order to represent the interest of the workers as a social class. Thus, labor union leaders became important intermediaries between the larger society and European immigrant groups.

Women also were heavily involved in the labor movement. Immigrant women were among the most exploited segments of the labor force, and they were involved in some of the most significant events in American labor history. For example, one of the first victories of the union movement occurred in New York City in 1909. The Uprising of the 20,000 was a massive strike of mostly Jewish and Italian women (many in their teens) against the garment industry. The strike lasted 4 months despite attacks by thugs hired by the bosses and abuses by the police and the courts. The strikers eventually won recognition of the union from many employers, a reversal of a wage decrease, and a reduction in the 56- to 59-hour week they were expected to work (Goren, 1980, p. 584).

One of the great tragedies in the history of labor relations in the United States also involved European immigrant women. In 1911, a fire swept through the Triangle Shirtwaist Company, a garment industry shop located on the 10th floor of a building in New York City. The fire spread rapidly, and the few escape routes were quickly cut off. About 140 young immigrant girls died, many of them choosing to leap to their deaths rather than be consumed by the flames. The disaster outraged the public, and the funerals of the victims were attended by more than a quarter of a million people. The incident fueled a drive for reform and improvement of work conditions and safety regulations (Amott & Matthaei, 1991, pp. 114–116; see also Schoener, 1967).

European immigrant women also filled leadership roles in the labor movement and served as presidents and in other offices, although usually in female-dominated unions. Female union activists often faced opposition from men as well as from employers. The major unions were not only racially discriminatory but also hostile to organizing women. For example, female laundry workers in San Francisco at the turn of the century were required to live in dormitories and work from 6 a.m. until midnight. When they applied to the international laundry workers union for a charter, the male members blocked them. They eventually went on strike and won the right to an 8-hour workday in 1912 (Amott & Matthaei, 1991, p. 117).

The Catholic Church. A third avenue of mobility for the Irish and other white ethnic groups was provided by the religious institution. The Irish were the first large group of Catholic immigrants and were thus in a favorable position to eventually dominate the church's administrative structure. The Catholic priesthood became largely Irish, and as they were promoted through the hierarchy, these priests became bishops and cardinals.

The Catholic faith was practiced in different ways in different nations. As other Catholic immigrant groups began to arrive, conflict within the Irish-dominated church increased. Both Italian and Polish Catholic immigrants demanded their own parishes in which they could speak their own languages and celebrate their own customs and festivals. Dissatisfaction was so intense that some Polish Catholics broke with Rome and formed a separate Polish National Catholic Church (Lopata, 1976, p. 49).

The other Catholic immigrant groups eventually began to supply priests and other religious functionaries and to occupy leadership positions within the church. Although the church continued to be disproportionately influenced by the Irish, other white ethnic groups also used the Catholic Church as parts of their power bases for gaining acceptance and integration into the larger society.

Other Pathways of Mobility. Besides party politics, the union movement, and religion, European immigrant groups forged other not-so-legitimate pathways of upward mobility. One alternative to legitimate success was offered by crime, a pathway that has been used by every ethnic group to some extent. Crime became particularly lucrative and attractive when Prohibition, the attempt to eliminate all alcohol use in the United States, went into effect in the 1920s. The criminalization of liquor failed to lower the demand, and Prohibition created a golden economic opportunity for those willing to take the risks involved in manufacturing and supplying alcohol to the American public.

Italian Americans headed many of the criminal organizations that took advantage of Prohibition. Criminal leaders and organizations with roots in Sicily, a region with a long history of secret antiestablishment societies, were especially important (Alba, 1985, pp. 62–64). The connection between organized crime, Prohibition, and Italian Americans is well known, but it is not so widely recognized that ethnic succession operated in organized crime as it did in the legitimate opportunity structures. The Irish and Germans had been involved in organized crime for decades before the 1920s, and the Italians competed with these established gangsters and with Jewish crime syndicates for control of bootlegging and other criminal enterprises. The pattern of ethnic succession

continued after the repeal of Prohibition, and members of groups newer to urban areas, including African Americans, Jamaicans, and Hispanic Americans, recently have challenged the Italian-dominated criminal "families."

Ethnic succession also can be observed in the institution of sports. Since the beginning of the 20th century, sports have offered a pathway to success and affluence that has attracted countless millions of young men. Success in sports requires little in the way of formal credentials, education, or English fluency, and sports have been particularly appealing to the young men in minority groups that have few resources or opportunities.

For example, at the turn of the century, the Irish dominated the sport of boxing, but boxers from the Italian American community and other new immigrant groups eventually replaced them. Each successive wave of boxers reflected the concentration of a particular ethnic group at the bottom of the class structure. The succession of minority groups continues to this day, with boxing now dominated by African American and Latino fighters (Rader, 1983, pp. 87–106). A similar progression, or "layering," of ethnic and racial groups can be observed in other sports and in the entertainment industry.

The institutions of American society, legitimate and illegal alike, reflect the relative positions of minority groups at a particular moment in time. Just a few generations ago, European immigrant groups dominated both crime and sports because they were blocked from legitimate opportunities. Now, the colonized racial minority groups that are still excluded from the mainstream job market and mired in the urban underclass are supplying disproportionate numbers of young people to these alternative opportunity structures.

Continuing Industrialization and Structural Mobility

Changes in the American economy and occupational structure also shaped the social class position and speed of integration of the European immigrants and their descendants. Industrialization is a continuous process, and as it proceeded, the nature of work in America evolved and changed, creating opportunities for upward mobility for white ethnic groups. One important form of upward mobility throughout the 20th century, called *structural mobility,* resulted more from changes in the structure of the economy and the labor market than from any individual effort or desire to "get ahead."

Structural mobility is the result of the continuing mechanization and automation of the workplace. As machines replaced people in the workforce, the supply of manual, blue-collar jobs that had provided employment for so many first- and second-generation European immigrant laborers dwindled. At the same time, the supply of other types of jobs increased. We saw in Chapter 4 (see Exhibit 4.2) that job growth in recent decades has been in the service sector and in white-collar jobs and that access to the better jobs in these areas depends heavily on educational credentials. For white ethnic groups, a high school education became much more available in the 1930s, and college and university programs began to expand rapidly in the late 1940s, spurred in large part by the educational benefits made available to World War II veterans. Members of each generation of white ethnics, especially those born after 1925, were significantly more educated than their parents, and many were able to translate that increased human capital into upward mobility in the mainstream job market (Morawska, 1990, pp. 212–213).

Thus, the descendants of European immigrants became upwardly mobile not only because of their values or ambition but also because of the changing location of jobs and the progressively greater opportunities for education available to them. Of course, the pace and timing of this upward movement were highly variable from group to group and place to place. Ethnic succession continued to operate, and the descendants of the more recent immigrants from Europe tended to be the last to benefit from the general upgrading in education and the job market. Still, structural mobility is one of the keys to the eventual successful integration that is

documented in Exhibits 9.1 to 9.3. At the same time, the racial and colonized minority groups, with the notable exceptions of the enclave-oriented Chinese Americans and Japanese Americans, generally were excluded from the dominant group's educational system and from the opportunity to compete for better jobs.

COMPARING EUROPEAN IMMIGRANTS AND COLONIZED MINORITY GROUPS

Could other groups have followed the pathways to integration and mobility forged by European immigrants and their descendants? How relevant are these experiences for today's racial minority groups? Let's address this question by comparing the relative positions of the groups at the start of the 20th century.

A century ago, when European immigrants were forging their links to the larger society, most African Americans still resided in the South, where Jim Crow segregation excluded them from better jobs and from political power. Mexican Americans also were victimized by systematic segregation and exclusion, and Native Americans were dealing with military defeat, threats to the integrity of their culture, and the isolation and enforced dependency of the reservation. The Chinese, and later the Japanese, had been banned from immigration and were responding to the campaigns of rejection and discrimination by withdrawing to ethnic enclaves.

Clearly, white ethnic groups were in a better position to pursue integration and equality. Their relative advantage was the result of many factors, not the least of which was that they entered the United States through the industrializing, urbanizing sectors of the economy, whereas other minority groups, especially the colonized racial minority groups, remained geographically and socially distant from opportunities for inclusion.

European immigrants were not immune from racism and rejection, as we have seen. In an urban industrial economy based on wage labor, however, there was no need to control the European immigrant groups in the same way that black sharecroppers in the South or Mexican farm workers in the Southwest were controlled. It was impractical and unnecessary to construct repressive systems of group relations like de jure segregation in the urban, industrial environment occupied by white ethnic groups, especially because no obvious physical or "racial" difference separated them from the dominant group. As pointed out in the Blauner hypothesis, if such attempts had been made to control and repress European immigrants, they could have selected a different destination or not immigrated at all.

Their status as (relatively) free immigrants gave white ethnic groups a control of their fate that, although minimal in many ways, was superior to the decision-making power available to members of the colonized minority groups. At a time when the racial minority groups faced nearly complete exclusion and massive discrimination, the European immigrants, their children, and their grandchildren were finding pathways into the dominant society.

Why didn't the racial minority groups follow the same pathways? While the European immigrant groups were "pushing" one another up in the mainstream economy during the first half of the 20th century, the racial and colonized minority groups, particularly African Americans in the rural South, began to move to the cities and seek places in the industrial workforce (see Chapter 4). Often, African American migrants moved into the very neighborhoods abandoned by the upwardly mobile European American ethnic groups and began to compete with them and with elements of the dominant group for jobs and other resources.

In their efforts to penetrate the urban industrial labor market, members of racial minority groups often found themselves caught between the labor unions, which excluded them, and the factory owners, employers, and other capitalists, who wanted to exploit them. African Americans and other racial minorities often were used as strikebreakers or scabs. Because they were barred from membership by the unions, the racial minority groups had little to lose by crossing the picket lines (Brody, 1980, p. 615).

As the labor movement gradually succeeded, more and more workplaces became closed shops in which all workers were required to become members of a certain union. When that union practiced racial discrimination, all the jobs it controlled were closed to nonunion members (i.e., nonwhites). Thus, the discriminatory labor unions made it more difficult for minority groups of color to follow the path that European American ethnic groups had carved out.

In addition, discrimination against African Americans and Hispanic Americans by employers was widespread and when combined with the discrimination by the unions, resulted in the general exclusion of racial minority groups from the better-paying, more secure jobs. This made it extremely difficult to emulate white ethnic groups and penetrate the mainstream industrial occupational structure (Geschwender, 1978, p. 184). As the white ethnic groups rose in the social class structure, they tended to close the doors behind them.

The job prospects of the colonized minority groups were further limited by the continuing mechanization of the economy, the same process that tended to benefit white ethnic groups. By the time the nonwhite groups arrived in the manufacturing and industrial sectors of the economy, the unskilled, manual labor jobs that had sustained generations of white ethnic groups already were disappearing. The escalator to comfortable middle-class prosperity ceased to function just as minority groups of color began arriving in the industrial urban areas. The process of ethnic succession—one group pushing up earlier arrivals—tended to grind to a halt as the urban working class became non-Caucasian.

As European American ethnic groups have integrated and attained equality, the opportunities for upward mobility in the mainstream economy for racial minorities have dwindled. Thus, instead of following the white ethnic groups out of the old ethnic neighborhoods, ghettoes, and slums, racial minority groups (and some new immigrant groups) have disproportionately become part of an impoverished, powerless urban underclass.

WILL WHITE ETHNICITY SURVIVE?

By the 1950s and 1960s, the assimilation documented in Exhibits 9.1 to 9.3 was well under way. The great majority of the descendants of the European immigrants had left the old ethnic neighborhoods for better housing more in keeping with their relative prosperity. These grandchildren and great-grandchildren of immigrants grew up in a non-ethnic world, and as adults, they were virtually indistinguishable in their values, voting patterns, and personal lives from others of their social class and educational background.

As the groups dispersed into middle-class suburbia, the white ethnic community networks—political, religious, and economic—lost strength and performed fewer and fewer functions. Inevitably, as the old ethnic community infrastructure faded away, the personal sense of ethnicity and common peoplehood faded as well. People might continue to think of themselves in ethnic, "hyphenated" terms (as Irish-American, Italian-American, Polish-American, etc.), but such labels have become increasingly tangential to their self-images and increasingly minor in their effects on everyday life.

Ethnic Revivals

Absorption into the American mainstream was neither linear nor continuous, however. White ethnic identity sporadically reasserted itself in many ways, two of which are especially notable. First, there was a tendency for later generations to be more interested in their ancestry and ethnicity than were earlier generations. Marcus Hansen (1952) captured this phenomenon in his *principle of third-generation interest:* "What the second generation tries to forget, the third generation tries to remember" (pp. 493). Hansen observed that the children of the immigrants tended to minimize or de-emphasize ("forget") their ethnicity to avoid the prejudice and

intolerance of the larger society and compete on more favorable terms for jobs and other opportunities. As they became adults and started families of their own, the second generation tended to raise their children in non-ethnic settings with English as their first and only language.

By the time the third generation reached adulthood, especially for the "new" immigrant groups that arrived last, the larger society had become more tolerant of ethnicity and diversity. Having little to risk, the third generation tried to reconnect with their grandparents and their roots. They wanted to remember their ethnic heritage and understand it as part of their personal identities, their sense of who they were and where they belonged in the larger society. Thus, interest in the "old ways" and the strength of the identification with the ancestral group often was stronger in the more Americanized third generation than in the more ethnic second. Ironically, of course, the grandchildren of the immigrants could not recover much of the richness and detail of their heritage because their parents had spent their lives trying to forget it. Nonetheless, the desire of the third generation to reconnect with their ancestry and recover their ethnicity shows, once again, that assimilation is not a simple, unidimensional, or linear process.

In addition to this generational pattern, the strength of white ethnic identity also responded to the changing context of American society and the activities of other groups. For example, in the late 1960s and early 1970s, there was a notable increase in the visibility of and interest in white ethnic heritage, an upsurge often referred to as the *ethnic revival.* The revival manifested itself in a variety of ways. Some people became more interested in their families' genealogical roots, while others increased their participation in ethnic festivals, traditions, and organizations. The "white ethnic vote" became a factor in local, state, and national politics, and appearances at the churches, meeting halls, and neighborhoods associated with white ethnic groups became almost mandatory for candidates for office. Demonstrations and festivals celebrating white ethnic heritages were organized, and buttons and bumper stickers proclaiming the ancestry of everyone from Irish to Italian were widely displayed. The revival also was endorsed by politicians, editorialists, and intellectuals (e.g., see Novak, 1973), reinforcing the movement and giving it additional legitimacy.

The ethnic revival may have been partly fueled, à la Hansen's principle, by the desire to reconnect with ancestral roots, even though most groups were well beyond their third generation by the 1960s. More likely, the revival was a reaction to the increase in pluralistic sentiment in the society in general and by the pluralistic, even separatist assertions of other groups that marked the decade. Virtually every minority group generated a protest movement (Black Power, Red Power, Chicanismo, etc.) and proclaimed a recommitment to its own heritage and to the authenticity of its own culture and experience. The visibility of these movements for cultural pluralism among racial minority groups helped make it more acceptable for European Americans to express their own ethnicity and heritage.

Besides the general tenor of the times, the resurgence of white ethnicity had some political and economic dimensions that bring us back to issues of inequality, competition, and control of resources. In the 1960s, a white ethnic urban working class, largely Irish and southern and eastern European in makeup, still remained in the neighborhoods of the industrial Northeast and Midwest and still continued to breathe life into the old networks and traditions. At the same time that cultural pluralism was coming to be seen as more legitimate, this ethnic working class was feeling increasingly threatened by minority groups of color. In the industrial cities, it was not unusual for white ethnic neighborhoods to adjoin black and Hispanic neighborhoods, putting these groups in direct competition for housing, jobs, and other resources. Many members of the white ethnic working class saw racial minority groups as inferior and perceived the advances being made by these groups as unfair, unjust, and threatening. They also reacted to what they saw as special treatment and attention being accorded on the basis of race, such as school busing and affirmative action. They had problems of their own (the declining number of good, unionized jobs; inadequate schooling; and deteriorating city services) and felt that their problems were being given lower priority and less legitimacy because they were white.

The revived sense of ethnicity in the urban working class neighborhoods was in large part a way of resisting racial reform and expressing resentment for the racial minority groups. Thus, among its many other causes and forms, the revival of white ethnicity that began in the 1960s was fueled by competition for resources and opportunities. As we have seen throughout our analysis, such competition commonly leads to increased prejudice and a heightened sense of cohesion among group members.

White Ethnicity in the 21st Century

As the conflicts of the 1960s faded and white ethnic groups continued to leave the old neighborhoods and rise in the class structure, the strength of white ethnic identity resumed its slow demise. Today, generations removed from the tumultuous 1960s, white ethnic identity has become increasingly nebulous and largely voluntary. Today, white ethnic identity often is described as *symbolic ethnicity*. The descendants of the European immigrants feel only vaguely connected (if that) to their ancestors and to the "old country," and this part of their identity does not affect their lifestyles, circles of friends and neighbors, job prospects, eating habits, or other everyday routines (Gans, 1979; Lieberson & Waters, 1988). For today's descendants of European immigrants, ethnicity is an increasingly minor part of their identities, which is expressed only occasionally or sporadically. For example, they might join in ethnic or religious festivals (e.g., St. Patrick's Day for Irish Americans), but these activities are seasonal or otherwise peripheral to their lives and self-images. The descendants of the European immigrants have choices. In stark contrast with their ancestors and with members of racial minority groups, they can stress their ethnicity, ignore it completely, or maintain any degree of ethnic identity they choose. Many people have ancestors in more than one ethnic group and may change their sense of affiliation over time, sometimes emphasizing one group's traditions and sometimes another's (Waters, 1990).

In fact, white ethnic identity has become so ephemeral that it may be on the verge of disappearing altogether. For example, based on a series of in-depth interviews with white Americans from various regions of the nation, Gallagher (2001) found a sense of ethnicity so weak that it didn't even rise to the level of "symbolic." His respondents were the products of ancestral lines so thoroughly intermixed and intermarried that any trace of a unique heritage from a particular group was completely lost. They had virtually no knowledge of the experiences of their immigrant ancestors or of the life and culture of the ethnic communities they had inhabited. For many, their ethnic ancestry was no more meaningful to them than their state of birth. Their lack of interest in and information about their ethnic heritage was so complete that it led Gallagher to propose an addendum to Hansen's principle: "What the grandson wished to remember, the great-granddaughter has never been told."

As the more specific white ethnic identities are disappearing, new shapes and forms also are evolving. In the view of many analysts, a new identity is developing that merges the various white ethnic identities into a single, generalized "European American" identity based on race and a common history of immigration and assimilation. This new identity reinforces the racial lines of separation that run through contemporary society, but it does more than simply mark group boundaries. Embedded in this emerging identity is an understanding, often deeply flawed, of how the white immigrant groups succeeded and assimilated in the past and a view, often deeply ideological, of how the racial minority groups should behave in the present.

These understandings are encapsulated in "immigrant tales" or family legends that stress heroic individual effort and grim determination as the key ingredients that led to success in the old days. These tales feature impoverished, victimized immigrant ancestors who survived and made a place for themselves and their children by working hard, saving their money, and otherwise exemplifying the virtues of the Protestant ethic and American individualism. They stress the idea that past generations became successful despite the brutal hostility of the dominant group and with no government intervention, and they equate the historical difficulties faced by immigrants from Europe with those suffered by colonized and conquered minority groups (slavery, segregation, attempted genocide, etc.). They strongly imply—and sometimes blatantly assert—that the latter groups could succeed in America by simply following the example set by the former (Alba, 1990; Gallagher, 2001).

These accounts echo some of the debate over Asian Americans as "model minorities" and mix versions of human capital theory and traditional views of assimilation with modern racism. Without denying or trivializing the resolve and fortitude of European immigrants, equating their experiences and levels of disadvantage with those of African Americans, Native Americans, and Mexican Americans is a comparison so far off the mark that it should not require further comment at this point in the text. These views support an attitude of disdain and lack of sympathy for the multiple dilemmas faced today by the racial minority groups and by many contemporary immigrants. They permit the subtle expression of prejudice and racism and allow whites to use these highly distorted views of their immigrant ancestors as a rhetorical device to express a host of race-based grievances without appearing racist (Gallagher, 2001). As Alba (1990) concludes:

> The thrust of the [emerging] European American identity is to defend the individualistic view of the American system, because it portrays the system as open to those who are willing to work hard and pull themselves out of poverty and discrimination. Recent research suggests that it is precisely this individualism that prevents many whites from sympathizing with the need

for African Americans and other minorities to receive affirmative action in order to overcome institutional barriers to their advancement. (p. 317)

COMPARING MINORITY GROUPS: IMMIGRATION VS. COLONIZATION

Among all the groups covered in this text, white ethnic groups are the closest to achieving assimilation and equality, an outcome that is quite consistent with the Blauner hypothesis. These groups succeeded because they entered the U.S. society through the dynamic, urban industrial sector (often at the bottom, in the most miserable and least desirable jobs). Their rise to success took generations and was made possible not only by their own efforts but also by structural mobility and the expanding educational opportunities provided

by the larger society. Not least among the ingredients in their recipe for success was their race and their consequent ability to blend into the mainstream and, when necessary, lose their ethnic identity completely.

Can their experiences serve as a model for today's racial minority groups or for the immigrants who have arrived since the mid-1960s? How relevant are the "immigrant tales" of determination and hard work? As we have seen repeatedly, the United States today no longer bears much resemblance to the society in which the white immigrant ancestors lived, worked, and died. The postindustrial economy provides few opportunities for less educated manual laborers, and the promise of mobility for future generations has a distinctly hollow ring in the impoverished, inner-city neighborhoods inhabited by so many American minority groups.

MAIN POINTS

- Mass immigration from Europe to the United States lasted for a century and supplied much of the labor force needed to fuel the American industrial revolution. In turn, the economic strength of the United States helped it become a world power.
- The descendants of the immigrants are assimilated today, but there are many reasons to include them in a review of American minority groups.
- European immigrant groups were highly diversified and accommodated to U.S. society through a variety of modes of incorporation.
- Social class position and the speed of assimilation were affected by the degree of similarity between European immigrants and white Anglo-Saxon Protestants. In the process of ethnic succession, European immigrant groups pushed one another up in the social class structure of the dominant society. The upward mobility of European American ethnic groups was abetted by structural mobility, the changing nature of the occupational structure, and the increasing availability of education.
- The pathways to integration followed by the European American ethnic groups in the past generally are not available to racial minority groups today.
- European American ethnicity generally has faded away as part of the process of assimilation. However, white ethnic identity tended to reassert itself in the third generation and especially in the 1960s. Today, white ethnic identity is largely symbolic and in the process of fading away. It may be replaced by a new, race-based identity that incorporates an ideology of modern racism.

QUESTIONS FOR REVIEW AND STUDY

1. Compared to the colonized and conquered groups we have considered in previous chapters, how does the history of white ethnic groups illustrate the Blauner hypothesis? Are these groups acculturated and integrated? How? Have they completed the stages of assimilation as described by Gordon? Provide evidence from the chapter for your answer.

2. Review the definition of "minority group" presented in Chapter 1. Do contemporary white ethnic groups meet the criteria stated in the definition? Why or why not? How would your answer to this question change if you were considering the ancestors of today's groups that lived in the early decades of the 20th century?

3. In arguing that white ethnic groups can still be considered minorities, the text states that traditional prejudices and stereotypes against these groups persist. Is this convincing in terms of your own personal experience? Are you personally familiar with these attitudes and images? If you are, how do you think you acquired these ideas? If not, was there something about your socialization experience that might have insulated you from this type of prejudice?

4. Explain the importance of the industrial revolution both in motivating the immigration from Europe that led to the creation of white ethnic minority groups and in shaping the assimilation of the descendants of the immigrants.

5. Describe the immigration from Europe in terms of timing and the national origins of groups. What were the important social, cultural, and economic differences between the old and new immigration?

6. How did gender, religion, and social class shape the experiences of the immigrants and their descendants?

7. Compare the experiences of Jewish immigrants with Chinese, Japanese, and Cuban immigrants. What differences and similarities can you cite in their enclave experiences? What kept other European immigrant groups from also forming enclaves?

8. What effect did the National Origins Act of 1924 have on immigration from Europe? In what ways was that legislation based on racism and prejudice? What effects did the act have on the assimilation of white ethnic groups (see Massey's argument in Chapter 7)?

9. Compare and contrast immigration and assimilation in Canada and the United States. What important similarities and differences can you identify in the two national experiences?

10. What factors shaped the assimilation of white ethnic groups? What is "ethnic succession," and how did it affect white ethnic groups? How did it affect the racial minority groups that followed white ethnic groups? What institutions and organizations of the larger society were involved in this assimilation process? How? What is "structural mobility," and why is the concept important for understanding the experiences of these groups?

11. Will white ethnicity survive? In what form? What is "symbolic ethnicity?" Is white ethnic identity becoming increasingly racial? Why?

INTERNET RESEARCH PROJECT

A. Comparing Anti-Immigration Movements

The text describes the campaign against immigration that began in the 19th century and culminated in the passage of the National Origins Act in 1924. Keeping in mind relevant information from Chapters 7 and 8, compare and contrast the campaign against immigration then with the contemporary movement. To get started, here are the addresses of two anti-immigrant sites:

The Federation for Immigration Reform (FAIR): www.fairus.org/

Vdare: www.vdare.com/

What specific arguments against immigration are cited in the contemporary campaign? To what extent are the arguments based on data, objective sources, and logical reasoning? To what extent does the argument rely on emotional appeals and subtle prejudice? To develop a more balanced picture, search for counterarguments on the Internet and summarize and analyze these arguments as well.

B. Immigration From Europe

Expand the information in this chapter about the experience of immigration from Europe between the 1820s and the 1920s by picking a group and doing an Internet search with the group's name (e.g., "Italian American" or "Polish American") and the keyword "immigration." Sort through the list of sites and links to find information and stories to supplement the material in this chapter. For the group you select, you might focus on such questions as these: When did immigration begin and end? What were the primary motives for leaving? What resources did the immigrants typically bring with them? Where did they go in the United States? How did the dominant group (or other groups) respond to their arrival? What kind of work did they do? Other questions will occur to you from your reading of the chapter or during the process of your Internet search, but it is unlikely that you will find answers to all your questions on-line.

FOR FURTHER READING

Alba, Richard. 1985. *Italian Americans: Into the Twilight of Ethnicity*. Englewood Cliffs, NJ: Prentice Hall.

Fallows, Marjorie R. 1979. *Irish Americans: Identity and Assimilation*. Englewood Cliffs, NJ: Prentice Hall.

Goldstein, Sidney, & Goldscheider, Calvin. 1968. *Jewish Americans: Three Generations in a Jewish Community*. Englewood Cliffs, NJ: Prentice Hall.

Lopata, Helena Znaniecki. 1976. *Polish Americans*. Englewood Cliffs, NJ: Prentice Hall.

Sklare, Marshall. 1971. *America's Jews*. New York: Random House.
   Concise, readable accounts of some of the most prominent European American ethnic groups.

Cohen, Adam, & Taylor, Elizabeth. 2000. *American Pharaoh: Mayor Richard J. Daley: His Battle for Chicago and the Nation*. New York: Little, Brown.
   An impressive analysis of one of the most powerful urban political machines and its connections with ethnicity, religion, and race.

Higham, John. 1963. *Strangers in the Land: Patterns of American Nativism, 1860–1925*. New York: Atheneum.
   The classic historical account of the efforts to restrict immigration and other movements of opposition to immigrants.

Schoener, Allon. 1967. *Portal to America: The Lower East Side, 1870–1925*. New York: Holt, Rinehart & Winston.
   An outstanding collection of photographs of a famous New York City ethnic neighborhood at the turn of the century. Moving, revealing, humorous, and informative. Includes a narrative regarding the nature of everyday life.

NOTES

1. For further information on the groups, see www.census.gov/population/socdemo/ancestry.

2. See "Statistics Canada: 1996 Census" at www.statcan.ca/english/Pgdb/People/Population/dem028a.htm.

Part IV

A Global View,
Some Conclusions,
and a Look to the Future

In this part, the analytical framework developed in this text is applied to a variety of dominant-minority relations around the globe. The objective is to test the universality of these ideas and to identify the common dynamics that shape intergroup relations everywhere. Issues of assimilation and pluralism are not peculiar to the United States, and colonization and conquest are common causes of the most explosive and longest-lasting group conflicts. Racism, prejudice, discrimination, and inequality also are common and important aspects of group relations. However, not all societies that incorporate more than one group are characterized by conflict and rancor, and we will take a look at some societies that are widely regarded as having relatively harmonious group relations.

Chapter 11 summarizes the major themes of this text, brings the analysis to a close, and speculates about the future of American race and ethnic relations.

10

Dominant-Minority Relations in Cross-National Perspective

Early in this text, a set of concepts and hypotheses was developed to help us analyze and understand dominant-minority relations. In Chapters 5 through 9, our analytical framework was further elaborated and applied to the creation and present-day realities of minority group status in the United States. Although our concepts have proven their usefulness, it is important to recognize that they have been tested against the experiences of just a single nation. Just as you would not accept an interview with a single person as an adequate test of a psychological theory, you should not accept the experiences of a single nation as proof for the sociological perspective developed in this text. If our ideas apply to dominant-minority situations in other societies, we will have some assurance that

the dynamics of intergroup relations in the United States are not unique and that our conclusions have some general applicability.

In this chapter, we will first briefly review the ideas that have guided our analysis and then apply them to various societies from around the globe. Because it is not possible to investigate every society in the world, I will focus on "trouble spots" or societies with dominant-minority group conflicts that have been widely publicized and are therefore familiar to most people. For purposes of comparison, I also have included several societies in which group relations are thought to be generally peaceful.

You should be very clear about the limits of this "test." The sample of societies is small and is not representative of human societies in general, and therefore it will not permit a final or definitive test of theory. Before final conclusions can be reached, we need much more research on a broad array of societies drawn from a variety of time periods, regions, levels of development, and cultural backgrounds. Just as important, information about many of our most crucial concepts (for example, the degree and nature of prejudice or discrimination) simply is not available for many societies. Without precise, trustworthy information, our tests will necessarily be informal and impressionistic. At any rate, you may rest assured that the conclusions reached in this chapter will not be the final word on the subject.

A BRIEF REVIEW OF
MAJOR ANALYTICAL THEMES

Before commencing our cross-national tour, it will be useful to review the major analytical themes developed in this text. These ideas were summarized as seven themes in the introduction to Part III and have been used extensively throughout the text. Thus, a brief review will be sufficient.

One theme that has been stressed constantly is the importance of the initial *contact situation* between groups. The characteristics of the initial meeting (particularly the nature and intensity of the competition and the balance of power between the groups) can shape relations for centuries. We also have found that the fates of minority groups created by colonization and conquest are very different from the fates of those created by immigration. As we have seen repeatedly in U.S. history, colonized or conquered minority groups are subjected to greater rejection, discrimination, and inequality and become more completely mired in their minority status. Positive change is more difficult to accomplish for conquered or colonized groups, especially when the group is racially or physically different from the dominant group.

As we examine the most difficult and explosive group conflicts from around the globe in this chapter, you will notice that their origins often lie in contact situations in which the colonizers were white Europeans and the eventual minority groups were peoples of color. This pattern of dominance and subordination reflects the conditions under which the present world system of societies was created. By the 1400s, the nations of Europe were the most technologically advanced in the world, and they used their superiority to explore, conquer, and sometimes destroy much of the rest of the globe. The scores of conflicts between whites and nonwhites strewn around the globe today are one legacy of this enormous burst of European power and energy.

Of course, the pattern of white dominance is also in part an accident of history. Nations have been conquering, enslaving, persecuting, and oppressing their neighbors for millennia. When the neighbors differed from each other in some visible way, prejudice, racism, and systems of inequality based on group membership often followed the military conquests. The unique contribution of Europeans to this ancient pattern was that their era of conquest and colonization coincided with breakthroughs in shipbuilding, navigation, and other technologies that enabled them to spread their influence far wider and more permanently than colonizers of the past. The nations of Europe (and the British in particular) ruled much of the world until very recent decades, and many of the present ethnic and racial conflicts were born during the era of European colonialism (see Wallace, 1997).

A second important theme is that dominant-minority relationships tend to change most rapidly and dramatically when the level of development or the basic subsistence technology of the larger society changes. For example, industrialization not only revolutionized technology and modes of production but also transformed group relationships in Europe, in the United States, and, eventually, around the globe. In Europe, the new subsistence technology motivated massive waves of immigration beginning in the 1820s, and the new technology helped European nations to dominate the world system of societies in the 19th and much of the 20th centuries. In the

United States, the industrial revolution led to a transition from paternalistic to rigid competitive group relations starting in the 19th century and, in the latter half of the 20th century, continuing modernization resulted in the emergence of fluid competitive relations between groups. The blatant racism and overt discrimination of the past have moderated into milder, more ambiguous forms that are more difficult to identify and measure, and this evolution to less repressive forms of group relations has been propelled by the protest activities of minority group members and their allies.

We have seen the importance of these ideas and themes for U.S. group relations. To what extent are they applicable to group relations around the world? We begin our tour with Canada, our neighbor to the north, and then continue to the east, spanning the globe and returning to the Western Hemisphere with Brazil.

A GLOBAL TOUR

Canada

Citizens of the United States often see Canada as simply a colder version of their home society, a perception that is sustained by the enormous impact the United States has had on everyday social, economic, and political life in Canada. In fact, dominant-minority situations in the two societies share many similarities, both historically and at present. But the two societies are also quite different. For example, although black Africans were enslaved in colonial Canada, the institution never took on the economic, political, or social significance it assumed in the United States.

Perhaps the most obvious difference between the two nations is that the major minority issues in Canada have been cultural and linguistic, not racial. For more than two centuries, Canadian society has been divided into two major language groups, French speaking and English speaking. French speakers (or Francophones) are the minority group and are concentrated in the province of Quebec. Nationally, French speakers are about 25% of the population, but in Quebec they constitute about 80% of the population.

In our terms, issues of assimilation and pluralism separate these two linguistic and cultural groups. French Canadians have preserved their language and culture in the face of domination by English speakers for more than 200 years, and they continue to maintain their traditions today. Although French Canadians are largely pluralistic, they are not unanimous about the type of relationship that they would like to have with the larger society. At the extreme, some Francophones want complete separation between Quebec and English-speaking Canada: Their goal is to make Quebec an independent nation. Others would be satisfied with guarantees of more autonomy for Quebec and national recognition of the right of the French-speaking residents of Quebec to maintain their language and culture.

English-speaking Canadians have shown little support for separation or pluralism. In a series of referenda over the past several decades, the national electorate has defeated several different proposals to grant more autonomy to Quebec. In 1992, for example, Canadians voted down a proposal to grant special status and more self-governance to Quebec. Interestingly, the proposal was also defeated in Quebec, but for different reasons. Whereas Canadians outside Quebec felt the 1992 proposal went too far in granting special status to Quebec, residents of Quebec rejected the proposal because it didn't go far enough. Nationalist sentiment remains strong in Quebec, and the intertwined issues of bilingualism, cultural separation, and political autonomy remain unresolved as Canada, like the United States, searches for ways to deal with its diversity (see Exhibit 10.1).

What caused the conflict between French- and English-speaking Canadians? Not surprisingly, the answer begins with the contact situation between the English and the French in Canada. Throughout the 1600s and 1700s, France and England (and other European nations) fought for control

Exhibit 10.1   Canada

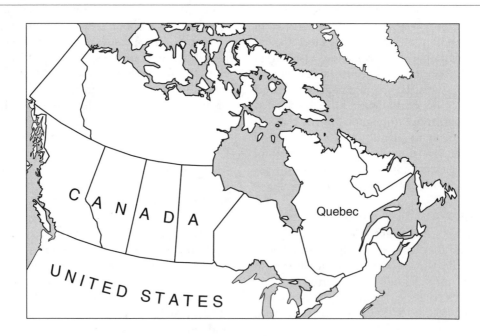

of North America. The French were eliminated as a colonial power when, in 1759 and 1760, the British captured Quebec City and Montreal and ended the French and Indian War, as it is called in the United States. The French who remained after the war were largely concentrated in what is now Quebec, and they became the ancestral community of today's pluralistic movement. The French community was organized around farming, and the victorious British took control of the economic and political institutions of the region.

The present pluralistic movement began in the 1960s. At that time, about 200 years after France ceased to be a colonial power in North America, French-speaking residents of Quebec were still a minority group. English-speaking Canadians remained in control of the central institutions of Quebec, and there were marked differences in wealth, education, occupational profile, and political power between French- and English speakers in the province. Since the 1960s, the status of Quebec's French-speaking residents has risen, and they have gained more economic

and political power, but issues of control of resources and wealth continue to animate the struggle.

While Quebec attempts to work out its relationship with the rest of the nation, Canada faces a number of other minority group issues, most of which would be familiar to citizens of the United States. For example, after years of maintaining a restrictive immigration policy that favored Caucasians, Canada reformed its laws in the 1960s. Since that time, there has been a steady and large influx of newcomers from the same areas that supply immigrants to the United States: Latin America, the Caribbean, and Asia. In addition, the native peoples of Canada share many problems and inequities with Native Americans in the United States. Many live on remote reservations (called "reserves"), which have high levels of poverty and unemployment and low levels of health care and educational opportunities.

In conclusion, Canada's problems of group relations can be analyzed in familiar terms. Some Canadian minority groups (French speakers and Indians) originated in conquest and colonization and have been victimized by discrimination and rejection for centuries. Especially since the 1960s, members of these groups have actively protested their situations, and some reforms and improvements have been made. Other groups consist of recent immigrants who have much in common with similar groups in the United States. In fact, despite the clear and important differences that exist between the nations, Canada faces many of the same issues that confront U.S. society: questions of unity and diversity, fairness and equality, and assimilation and pluralism.

Northern Ireland

Other nations face issues similar to those faced by Canada but with different levels of intensity, urgency, and lethality. In Northern Ireland, the bitter, violent conflict between Protestants and Catholics has some parallels with Canadian and U.S. group relations and has been closely watched and widely reported. Thousands of people have lost their lives during the struggles, many of them victims of terrorist attacks.

The roots of this conflict lie in armed hostilities between England and Ireland that began centuries ago. By the 1600s, England had colonized much of Ireland and had encouraged Protestants from Scotland and England to move to what is now Northern Ireland to help pacify and control the Catholic Irish. The newcomers, assisted by the English invaders, came to own much of the land and control the economy and the governing structure. Over the centuries, the Protestants in Northern Ireland have consolidated their position and power and separated themselves from the native Catholic population in the school system, in residential areas, and in most other areas of society. Law and strong custom reinforced the subordinate position of Catholics, and the system, at its height, came to resemble Jim Crow segregation. That is, it was a system of rigid competitive relations in which the Protestants sought to limit the ability of Catholics to compete for jobs, political power, housing, wealth, and other resources.

The British never succeeded in completely subordinating the Irish, who periodically attempted to achieve their independence through violent rebellions. These efforts came to partial fruition in the 1920s when an uprising that began with the Easter Rebellion in 1916 led to the creation of an independent Republic of Ireland. The new nation encompassed most of the island, but the largely Protestant northern counties, traditionally known as the province of Ulster, remained part of Great Britain (see Exhibit 10.2).

The partition of the island into an overwhelmingly Catholic Republic and a Protestant Northern Ireland set the stage for the troubles that continue to the present. The Catholics of Northern Ireland began a civil rights movement in the late 1960s, seeking amelioration for their minority status. Protestants, fearing loss of privilege and control, resisted attempts at reform, and the confrontation escalated into terrorism and violence. In 1998, lengthy and difficult negotiations—made possible in large part by the involvement and support of Great Britain, the Republic of Ireland, and the United States—resulted in the "Good Friday Agreement." This accord established a new power-sharing arrangement for the governance of Northern Ireland in which both Protestant and Catholic parties will participate. The new governmental arrangement has not gone smoothly but has survived several difficult crises, including a terrorist attack on a shopping area in Omagh, Northern Ireland, in August 1998 that left almost 30 people dead. Although fragile and tenuous, the Good Friday Agreement is overwhelmingly supported by the electorate and may eventually lead to a peaceful resolution to this ancient rivalry.

Note that in this case, as in the case of relations between Quebec and the rest of Canada, the dominant and the minority group are of the same race. The deep divisions that separate groups are mainly ethnic (English speaking vs. non-English speaking) and religious (Protestant vs. Catholic). In both nations, these divisions do not exist in a

Exhibit 10.2   Great Britain, Northern Ireland, and the Republic of Ireland

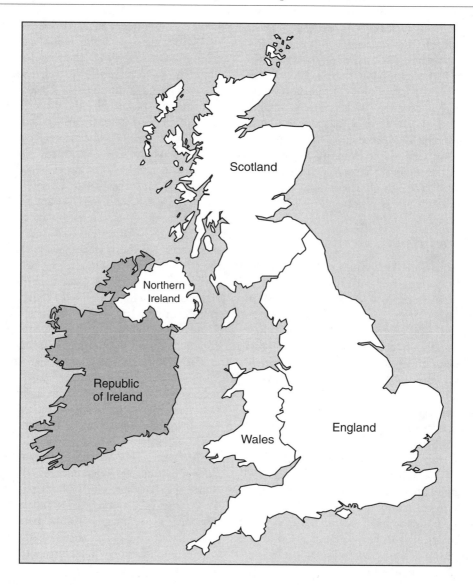

vacuum; they are highly correlated with social class position, access to education and jobs, and political power. That is, Catholics in Northern Ireland—like the French-speaking residents of Quebec—are a minority group that has been victimized by intense, systematic, and persistent discrimination and prejudice. What is at stake is not simply a question of cultural survival or religion. These clashes are so bitter, so deadly, and so intractable because they also concern the distribution of real resources and questions about who gets what and how much.

Germany

In the annals of intergroup relations, Germany is infamous as the site of the greatest minority group atrocities in history. In the 1930s and 1940s, the Nazi leadership of the nation attempted to eradicate the Jewish community (and several other groups) and

Exhibit 10.3   Germany, Switzerland, and Former Yugoslavia

nearly succeeded. Six million Jews died in the concentration camps.

Since the end of World War II, modern Germany (see Exhibit 10.3) has broken from its racist past, democratized, industrialized, and modernized. It is a global leader politically and economically and has one of the world's best-trained and best-educated workforces. Germany has worked hard to atone for its Nazi past, but it now faces new dominant-minority group challenges. Like the United States, Canada, and other nations of Western Europe, Germany has become a highly desirable destination for immigrants who come to satisfy the demand for both unskilled, cheap labor and "high-tech"

professionals. Besides the demand in various parts of the job market, immigrants are also pulled to Germany (and many other European nations) by the low rate of population growth. Birth rates are low throughout Western Europe, and Germany in particular is projected to actually lose population in the next several decades (Rinaldi, 1999, pp. 23–25).

Germany has responded to the threat of population loss by instituting a new immigration policy that recognizes that the society needs immigrant workers to fill the gaps in the labor force and continue to prosper. At any rate, the experience of Germany (along with that of Canada and the United States) confirms the idea that immigration is in large measure a flow of labor from areas of lower opportunity (less developed nations) to areas of higher opportunity.

Based on the patterns we have documented in the United States, we would predict that high rates of immigration would be accompanied by episodes of racist violence. Unfortunately, it is easy to find hate crimes and violent attacks against immigrants and other minority group members in Germany (and other European nations) in recent years. These attacks include bombings, killings, beatings, and myriad other forms of violence and brutality. Skinheads, neo-Nazis, and other hate groups are active and well-publicized elements of German life. These phenomena are, of course, a part of everyday life in other European nations and the United States and seem to have similar causes: high rates of immigration combined with economic uncertainty for working-class, less educated males and strong traditions of racism and intolerance. Still, the memory of the Holocaust gives special resonance to attacks on minority groups in Germany.

Switzerland

Although our focus is on the ethnic and racial trouble spots around the globe, it is also important to consider societies in which group relations are generally peaceful and conflict is comparatively minimal. One such society is Switzerland (see Exhibit 10.3). Swiss society incorporates three major and distinct language and cultural groups: French speakers, German speakers, and Italian speakers. Each language group resides in a particular region of the country and enjoys considerable control of its local affairs. In our terms, Switzerland is a pluralistic society in which the groups are separate both culturally and structurally. That is, at the local level, the groups have neither acculturated nor integrated. Each group maintains its unique cultural and linguistic heritage and its separate institutional and organizational structures.

At the national level, political power and economic resources are shared in proportion to the size of each group. The leaders of the different groups are careful to cooperate in national affairs and maintain the sense of proportional sharing and fundamental fairness. With the combination of cooperation at the national level and autonomy at the local level, Switzerland is able to function effectively as a multicultural, multilingual society.

Perhaps the key to the success of the Swiss in combining diversity and unity is that none of the three major groups was forced to join the nation by military conquest or coercion. The groups joined together voluntarily and created this pluralistic nation for mutual advantage. Thus, for the three major groups that make up Swiss society, there is no history of conquest or subordination, and there are no patterns of structured inequality, prejudice, and resentment.

Former Yugoslavia

The case of Switzerland indicates that peaceful and prosperous pluralistic societies *can* be created, but it is not typical of multigroup societies. Conquest and coercion are more common than voluntary cooperation, and the potential for rancor, conflict, and violence is high. The case of the former nation of Yugoslavia is an example (see Exhibit 10.3).

Eastern Europe is a region of immense ethnic, linguistic, and religious diversity. Travel, trade, and warfare have mixed and scattered groups and, over the centuries, nations and empires have come and gone. The former nation of Yugoslavia exemplifies both the diversity of the region and the complex history of intergroup conflict and cooperation.

The history of the modern nation of Yugoslavia is both short and complex. When it was created in 1918, at the end of World War I, the nation encompassed a variety of ethnic groups, each with its own language, religion, history, and memories of grievances against other groups. The larger groups include Croats (who are mainly Roman Catholic), Serbs (primarily Eastern Orthodox), and Bosnians (roughly half Muslim and half Christian). Each of these groups had a home territory in which it was the numerical majority. For example, in 1992, Croatia was 78% Croatian, and Serbia was 85% Serbian. Bosnia was the most diverse of the former republics of Yugoslavia. In 1992, about 44% of the population of Bosnia was Muslim, 39% were Serbs, and 17% were Croats (Remington, 1997, p. 275).

Yugoslavia was one of the bloody battlegrounds of World War II. German forces invaded the region and created a puppet government in Croatia. The Croatian allies of the Nazis participated not only in the persecution of Jews but also in a campaign against the Serbs residing within their reach. Concentration camps were constructed, and mass executions were carried out. By the end of the war, the fascist Croatian government had murdered hundreds of thousands of Serbs. The Croats, however, were not alone in their atrocities. Their campaign against Serbs provoked anti-Croatian violence in Serbia; hostility and resentment between the two groups had grown to new heights by the end of the war.

World War II also saw the emergence of Josip Broz Tito as a leader of anti-Nazi guerrilla forces. After the war, Tito became the chief architect of the modern nation of Yugoslavia. Tito's design incorporated many of the same elements that make Switzerland a successful pluralistic society. Postwar Yugoslavia comprised several different subnations, or republics, each of which was associated with a particular ethnic group. Power at the national level was allocated proportionately, and each region had considerable autonomy in the conduct its affairs.

A major difference between Yugoslavia and Switzerland, however, lies in the contact situation. Whereas the latter nation was formed on a voluntary basis, Yugoslavia was created by post–World War I diplomatic negotiations and then re-created at the end of World War II by the authoritarian regime of Tito. The nation was held together largely by the forcefulness of Tito's leadership. After his death in 1980, little remained to preserve the integrity of the Yugoslavian experiment

in nation building. The memories of past hostilities and World War II atrocities were strong, and the separate republics began to secede from the Yugoslav federation in the 1990s.

Self-serving political and military leaders in Serbia and in the other former Yugoslavian states inflamed prejudices and antipathies. Vicious conflicts broke out throughout the region, with the worst violence occurring in Bosnia. Bosnia's attempt to establish its independence was opposed by Serbia and by the Serbian and Croatian residents of Bosnia, both of whom formed armed militias. Bosnia became a killing field as these different contingents confronted each other. The Serbs began a campaign of "ethnic cleansing" in Bosnia in 1992 and committed the worst excesses. In the areas of Bosnia where Serbs could establish control, non-Serbs were the victims of a concerted campaign to eliminate them by forced relocation or, if necessary, by wholesale massacre. Concentration camps appeared, houses were torched, former neighbors became blood enemies, women were raped, and children were killed along with their parents.

The Serbs were not alone in resorting to the tactics of mass terror and murder. Croats used the same tactics against Bosnian Muslims, and Bosnians retaliated in kind against Serbs. By the time relative peace was established in Bosnia in 1995, more than 200,000 people had died in the murderous ethnic conflict. Many of the patterns of vicious brutality reappeared in the conflict between Serbia and Kosovo that began in 1999 and was ended by the armed intervention of the United States and its NATO allies. The disintegration of the former Yugoslavia into savage ethnic violence is one of the nightmarish episodes of the 20th century. Unfortunately, it is not unique.

Rwanda

In the spring of 1994, the tiny African nation of Rwanda (see Exhibit 10.4) sprang into international headlines. Rwanda's two ethnic groups, Hutus and Tutsis, had a long

Exhibit 10.4   Rwanda and South Africa

history of mutual enmity and hatred, but the attacks that began in 1994 reached new heights of brutality. An estimated 800,000 people—perhaps many more—were murdered, and millions fled to neighboring nations (Gourevitch, 1999, p. 133).

Accounts by witnesses and survivors told of massacres with rifles, machetes, rocks, and fists. No one was spared in the killing frenzy. Old people, pregnant women, and small children were executed along with men in what became one of the most horrific,

unimaginable episodes of intergroup violence in world history.

What caused this outburst? As seems to be the case whenever intense ethnic violence is found, colonization and conquest are part of the explanation for the brutal confrontation between the Hutus and Tutsis. European nations began colonizing Africa in the 1400s, and the area that became Rwanda did not escape domination. Germany established control over the region in the late 1800s, but following its defeat in World War I,

Germany lost its overseas possessions and Belgium became the dominant power in the region. Both European powers valued Rwanda for its mild climate and fertile soil. The native population was harnessed to the task of producing agricultural products, especially tea and coffee, for export.

The European colonizers attempted to ease the difficulty of administering and controlling Rwanda by capitalizing on the long-standing enmity between Tutsis and Hutus. In a classic case of divide and rule, Germany placed the Tutsis in position to govern the Hutus, a move that perpetuated and intensified hostilities between the tribes. The Belgians continued the tradition and maintained the political and economic differentials between the tribes.

Throughout the colonial era, mutual tribal hostilities were punctuated by periodic armed clashes, some of which rose to the level of massacre. In the early 1960s, the era of direct European political colonialism ended, and two nations were created in the region. Rwanda was dominated by the Hutus and neighboring Burundi by the Tutsis. Hostilities did not stop at this point, however, and the short histories of these two new nations are filled with conflicts with each other. What portion of these conflicts are international and what portion are domestic is difficult to determine because a substantial number of Tutsis continued to reside in Rwanda and many residents of Burundi were Hutus. In other words, the borders between the two nations were drawn arbitrarily and do not reflect local traditions or tribal realities.

In the early 1990s, a rebel force led by exiled Tutsis invaded Rwanda with the intention of overthrowing the Hutu-dominated government. The conflict continued until the spring of 1994, when the plane carrying the Hutu president of Rwanda was shot down, killing all aboard. It was this incident that set off the massacres, with Hutus seeking revenge for the death of their president and attempting to eliminate their Tutsi rivals. In another of the great nightmarish episodes of the 20th century, perhaps as many as half of the Tutsis in Rwanda died in the confrontation and millions more fled for their lives. Although surely not a complete explanation for these horrors, the history of intertribal enmity and competition for power and control, enhanced and magnified by European colonialism, is part of the background for understanding these horrors—if such a thing is possible.

South Africa

Not all stories are nightmares, however, and the dreary litany of hatred, conflict, and violence occasionally takes a surprising twist. As recently as the late 1980s, the Republic of South Africa (see Exhibit 10.4) was one of the most racist and discriminatory societies in the world. A small minority of whites (about 30%) dominated the black African population and enjoyed a level of race-based privilege rarely equaled in the history of the world. Today, although enormous problems of inequality and racism remain, South Africa has officially dismantled the machinery of racial oppression, has enfranchised nonwhites, and has elected two black presidents. Even in a world in which rapid, unanticipated change is commonplace, the end of state-supported racism and race privilege in South Africa is one of the more stunning surprises of recent times.

Some background will illuminate the magnitude of the change. Europeans first came into contact in the 1600s with the area that became the nation of South Africa, at about the time the British were establishing colonies in North America. First to arrive were the Dutch, who established ports on the coast to resupply merchant ships for the journey between Asia and Europe. Some of the Dutch began moving into the interior to establish farms and sheep and cattle ranches. The "trekkers," as they were called, regularly fought with indigenous black Africans and with tribes moving into the area from the north. These interracial conflicts were extremely bloody and resulted in enslavement for some black Africans, genocide for others, and a gradual push of the remaining black Africans into the interior. In some ways, this contact period resembled that between European Americans and Native Americans, and in other ways, it resembled the early days of the establishment of black slavery in North America.

In the 1800s, South Africa became a British colony, and the new governing group attempted to grant more privileges to blacks. These efforts stopped far short of equality, however, and South Africa continued to evolve into the 20th century as a racially divided, white-dominated society. The white community continued to be split along ethnic lines, and hostilities erupted into violence on a number of occasions. In 1899, British and Dutch factions fought each other in the Boer War, a bitter and intense struggle that widened and solidified the divisions between the two white communities. Generally, the descendants of the Dutch have been more opposed to racial change than have the descendants of the British.

In 1948, the National Party, the primary political vehicle of the Afrikaans, or Dutch, segment of the white community, came into control of the state. As the society modernized and industrialized, there was growing concern about controlling the majority black population, and under the leadership of the National Party, the system of *apartheid* was constructed to firmly establish white superiority. In Afrikaans, apartheid means "separate" or "apart." The basic logic of the system was to separate whites and blacks in every area of life: schools, neighborhoods, jobs, buses, churches, and so forth. Apartheid resembled the Jim Crow system of segregation in the United States but was even more repressive, elaborate, and unequal.

Although the official government propaganda claimed that apartheid would permit blacks and whites to develop separately and equally, the system clearly was intended to solidify white privilege and black powerlessness. By keeping blacks poor and powerless, white South Africans created a pool of workers who were both cheap and docile. Whites of even modest means could afford the luxuries of personal servants, and employers could minimize their payrolls and their

overhead. Of the dominant-minority situations considered in this text, perhaps only American slavery rivals apartheid for its naked, unabashed subjugation of one group for the benefit of another.

Note that the coming of apartheid reverses the relationship between modernization and control of minority groups we observed in the United States. As the United States industrialized and modernized, group relations evolved from paternalistic to rigid competitive to fluid competitive forms, each stage representing a looser form of control over the minority group. In South Africa after 1948, group relations became *more* rigid, and the structures of control became stronger and more oppressive. Why the difference?

Just as U.S. Southerners attempted to defend their privileged status and resist the end of de jure segregation in the 1950s and 1960s, white South Africans were committed to retaining their status and the benefits it created. Although South Africans of British descent tended to be more liberal in matters of race than those of Dutch descent, both groups were firmly committed to white supremacy. Thus, unlike the U.S. situation at the end of Jim Crow segregation, in which white liberals and non-Southerners put considerable pressure on the racist South, there was little internal opposition among South African whites to the creation of apartheid.

Furthermore, South African blacks in the late 1940s were comparatively more powerless than blacks in the United States in the 1950s and 1960s. Although South African black protest organizations existed, they were illegal and had to operate underground or from exile and under conditions of extreme repression. In the United States, in contrast, blacks living outside the South were able to organize and pool their resources to assist in the campaign against Jim Crow, and these activities were protected (more or less) by the national commitment to civil liberties and political freedom.

A final difference between the two situations has to do with numbers. Whereas in the United States, blacks are a numerical minority, they were the great majority of the population in South Africa. Part of the impetus for establishing the rigid system of apartheid was the fear of whites that they would be "swamped" by the numerical majority unless black powerlessness was perpetuated. The difference in group size helped to contribute to what has been described as a "fortress" mentality among some white South Africans: the feeling that they were defending a small (but luxurious) outpost surrounded and besieged by savage hordes who threatened their immediate and total destruction. This strong sense of threat among whites and the need to be vigilant and constantly resist the least hint of racial change is part of what made the events of the 1990s so remarkable and unexpected.

The system of racial privilege called apartheid lasted about 40 years. Through the 1970s and 1980s, changes within South Africa and in the world in general built up pressure against the system. Internally, protests against apartheid by blacks began in the 1960s and continued to build in intensity. The South African government responded to these protests with violent repression, and thousands died in confrontations with police and the army. Nonetheless, anti-apartheid activism continued to attack the system from below.

Apartheid also suffered from internal weaknesses and contradictions. For example, jobs were strictly segregated, along with all other aspects of South African society. In a modern, industrial economy, however, new types of jobs are continually being created, and old jobs are continually lost to mechanization and automation, making it difficult to maintain simple, caste-like rules about who can do what kinds of work. In addition, many of the newer jobs required higher levels of education and special skills, and the number of white South Africans was too small to fill the demand. Thus, some black South Africans were slowly rising to positions of greater affluence and personal freedom even as the system attempted to coerce and repress the group as a whole.

Internationally, pressure on South Africa to end apartheid was significant. Other nations established trade embargoes and organized boycotts of South African goods. South Africa was officially banned from the Olympics and other international competitions. Although many of these efforts were more symbolic than real and had only minor impacts on everyday social life, they sustained an outcast status for South Africa and helped create an atmosphere of uncertainty among its economic and political elite.

In the late 1980s, these various pressures made it impossible to ignore the need for reform any longer. In 1990, F. W. de Klerk, the leader of the National Party and the prime minister of the nation, began a series of changes that eventually ended apartheid. He lifted the ban on many outlawed black African protest organizations, and perhaps most significantly, he released Nelson Mandela from prison. Mandela was the leader of the African National Congress (ANC), one of the oldest and most important black organizations, and he had served a 27-year prison term for actively protesting apartheid. Together, de Klerk and Mandela helped to ease South Africa through a period of rapid racial change that saw the franchise being extended to blacks, the first open election in South African history, and, in 1994, Mandela's election to a 5-year term as president. In 1999, Mandela was replaced by Thabo M. Mbeke, another black South African.

The future of South Africa remains unclear. Although the majority black population now has considerable political power, much of the wealth of the nation remains in white hands. Furthermore, the school system did little to prepare blacks for positions of leadership and for jobs demanding specialized skills or technical expertise. Thus, most of the crucial jobs in business and government continue to be held by whites. Tribal affiliations, language differences, and political loyalties split black South Africans, and unified action often is problematical for the minority group. This experiment in racial reform might still fail, and South Africa could still become the site of a devastating race war, but this dramatic transition away from massive racism and institutionalized

Exhibit 10.5   The Middle East

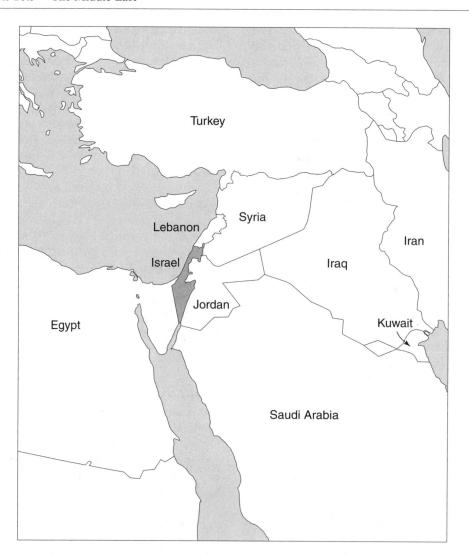

discrimination could also provide a model of change for other racially divided societies.

The Middle East

The tense, often violent relations between Israel and its Arab neighbors are yet another of the complex, long-lasting conflicts that seem to defy the most concerted, best-intentioned efforts at conciliation. Hatred, terrorism, and pledges to fight to the death are common in the Middle East (see Exhibit 10.5), as they are in other situations around the globe. The conflict has roots deep in history but took on its modern form with the founding of the nation of Israel in 1948.

As with many of the situations considered in this chapter, the present-day Middle East conflict between Jews and Arabs has its origins in military conquest. Following World War II and the horrors of the Holocaust, European Jews began to push for the establishment of a Jewish state in their traditional homeland. This cause was strongly supported by the United Nations and by the United States, and the modern state of Israel was founded in 1948. Unfortunately, the Jewish homeland was established by taking land that was occupied by Arabs (Palestinians) who also regarded it as their rightful homeland. Thus began the dominant (Israelis)–minority (Palestinians) situation that continues today.

A major difference between this and other intergroup struggles is the scale of time involved. Although the modern state of Israel encompasses the traditional Jewish homeland, few Jews have lived in this area in recent times. Jews had been exiled from the region and resettled in parts of Europe, Africa, and Asia, and the Middle East has been Arab land for most of the past thousand years. When Jews began to immigrate to the area after World War II, they found a well-entrenched Arab society and more than one million Palestinian Arabs on what they considered to be "their" land.

After its establishment, Israel found itself surrounded by hostile Arab nations. Warfare began almost immediately, and violent confrontations of one sort or another have been nearly continuous. Full-scale wars were fought in 1948, 1967 (the famous Six-Day War), and again in 1973. Israel was victorious in all three instances, and it claimed additional territory from its Arab neighbors to reduce the threat and provide a buffer zone. The wars also created a large group of refugees in the Arab countries neighboring Israel. The Arabs who remained in Israel tended to be a subordinate group, although some eventually became Israeli citizens.

Today, the number of Palestinian Arabs exceeds six million, many of whom continue to live as displaced people in refugee camps, longing for a return to their former homes or, increasingly as time wears on, to the homes of their parents or grandparents. Part of the complexity and the intensity of this situation stems from the fact that the groups involved are separated along so many different lines: religion, language, ethnicity, history, and social class. In addition, because of the huge oil reserves in the region, the Israeli-Arab conflict has political and international dimensions that directly involve the rest of

the world. For example, the Gulf War of 1991 brought troops from the United States and other industrial nations to expel Iraq from oil-rich Kuwait. Furthermore, the September 11, 2001, attacks on the United States; the subsequent war on terrorism in Afghanistan; and the second invasion of Iraq, in 2003, are directly and indirectly spin-offs of this long-standing conflict.

There are some indications that a solution to these enmities is not impossible. In 1979, Egypt, formerly committed to the destruction of the Jewish state, signed a peace accord with Israel. More recently, Israel and the Palestinians have been negotiating a peace settlement that would permit a Palestinian state. These negotiations have been extremely difficult and constantly threatened by violence, suicide bombings, attacks, and counterattacks. As of this writing, there is little indication that the negotiations will lead to peace in the region.

Hawaii

Like Switzerland, Hawaii often is identified as a society that maintains peaceful group relations in the face of great diversity. This reputation justifies the inclusion of the islands in this global survey despite the fact that Hawaii is a state, not a separate, autonomous nation.

The diversity of Hawaiian society is suggested by its racial and ethnic makeup. First of all, the population of Hawaii is much more racially mixed than the general population of the United States. In the 2000 Census, for example, 21.4% of Hawaiians chose more than one category to describe their race, compared with less than 3% of the U.S. population as a whole. The racial breakdown of the state, including both people who chose only one racial or ethnic category and people who chose more than one, is shown in Exhibit 10.6.

Americans of Asian descent were the largest group, and within that group, Japanese and Filipino Americans were the largest categories. Whites were a numerical minority, and only about 7% of the population identified

Exhibit 10.6   Racial and Ethnic Makeup of Hawaii, 2000

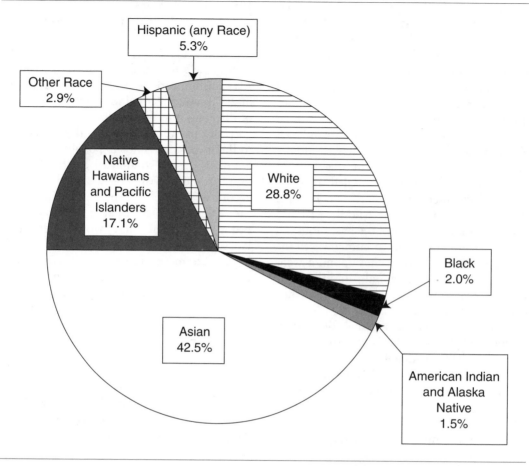

SOURCE: U.S. Bureau of the Census (2000n).

themselves as "pure-bred" Native Hawaiians (that is, chose only Native Hawaiian as their race). The population also includes a large number of people of Chinese, Korean, and Samoan descent, along with Hispanic Americans and African Americans. The cultures and traditions of all these groups are evident in the mix of Hawaiian society and the rhythm of everyday life. The relatively low levels of prejudice, discrimination, and group conflict in the midst of this diversity are the bases for the sometimes glowing (and, many would argue, overstated) depictions of Hawaii as a racial paradise.

The comparatively high levels of tolerance seem unusual in a world that often features just the opposite. A brief review of the history of the islands provides some insight into the development of these peaceful relations as well as the suggestion that the peaceful facade hides a grimmer reality.

Hawaii first came into contact with Europeans in 1788, but conquest and colonization did not follow the initial contact. Early relations between the islanders and Europeans were organized around trade and commerce—not agriculture, as was the case in the United States, South Africa, Northern Ireland, Quebec, and so many other places. Thus, the contact situation did not lead to competition over the control of land or labor. In addition, Hawaiian society was

Exhibit 10.7   The Hawaiian Islands

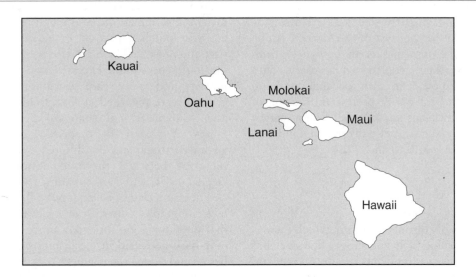

highly developed and had sufficient military strength to protect itself from the relatively few Europeans who came to the islands in these early days. Although initial contact with Europeans did not result in conquest or military dominance, it did bring other consequences, including smallpox and other diseases to which native Hawaiians had no immunity. Death rates began to rise, and the population of native Hawaiians, which numbered about 300,000 in 1788, fell to less than 60,000 a century later (Kitano & Daniels, 1995, p. 137).

As relations between the island and Europeans developed, the land gradually began to be turned to commercial agriculture. By the mid-1800s, white planters had established sugar plantations, an enterprise that is extremely labor intensive and that often has been associated with systems of enforced labor and slavery (Curtin, 1990). By that time, however, there were not enough native Hawaiians to fill the demand for labor, and the planters began to recruit abroad, mostly from China, Portugal, Japan, Korea, Puerto Rico, and the Philippines. Thus, the original immigrants of the Asian American groups we discussed in Chapter 8 often came first to the Hawaiian Islands, not to the U.S. mainland.

The white plantation owners came to dominate the island economy and political structure. Other groups, however, were not excluded from secondary structural assimilation. Laws banning entire groups from public institutions or practices, such as school segregation, are unknown in Hawaiian history. Americans of Japanese ancestry, for example, are very powerful in politics and have produced many of the leading Hawaiian politicians. (In contrast to events on the mainland, Japanese Americans in Hawaii were not interned during World War II.) Most other groups have taken advantage of the relative openness of Hawaiian society and have carved out niches for themselves in the institutional structure.

In the area of primary structural assimilation, rates of intermarriage among the various groups are much higher than on the mainland, reflecting an openness to intimacy across group lines that has characterized Hawaii since first contact. In particular, native Hawaiians have intermarried freely with other groups (Kitano & Daniels, 1995, pp. 138–139).

Hawaii has no history of the most blatant and oppressive forms of group domination, racism, and legalized discrimination. Yet all is not perfect in the reputed racial paradise, and there is evidence of ethnic and racial stratification as well as prejudice and discrimination. In particular, native Hawaiians tend to be the poorest of the various ethnic and racial groups, and recent immigrants from Asia, like their mainland counterparts, tend to be "bipolar" in their occupational and economic profiles. A protest movement of native Hawaiians stressing self-determination and the return of illegally taken land has existed since at least the 1960s.

Brazil

Imagine a contact situation involving three racially distinct groups in which there is a struggle for land and labor. Imagine that the victorious (dominant) group is white and that harsh treatment and disease devastate one of the defeated groups. Imagine that the other defeated (minority) group is used for slave labor on plantations owned by the whites. What predictions would you make about the future of race relations in such a society? Would you expect the society to be highly stratified by race? Would you predict intense prejudice and widespread institutional discrimination? These predictions would be logical and well supported by the evidence we have reviewed in this text, at least for the case of the United States. In the case of Brazil, however, they would be overstated and, in some ways, wrong.

Brazil is the largest nation in South America. Its territory stretches from the Atlantic Ocean deep into the interior, and almost across the continent (see Exhibit 10.8). Its population of 172 million, about 62% of the U.S. population, is racially and ethnically diverse. Several hundred thousand Indians survive, down from perhaps five million at first contact. Brazil was a colony of Portugal until 1822, and Portuguese remains its primary language. The colonial history of Brazil began almost a century before Jamestown was established in colonial America. In fact, the African slave trade on which the British colonies became so dependent in the 1600s and 1700s was created to provide labor for colonial Brazil in the 1500s (Curtin, 1990).

The racial histories of Brazil and the United States run parallel in many ways, and racism, discrimination, and racial inequality are very much a part of Brazilian society, past and present. There are also some important differences in the experiences of the two nations, and today, race relations in Brazil generally are regarded as less problematical and confrontational than in the United States. A variety of theories have been advanced to explain the difference in group relations between the two nations (see Degler, 1971, and Tannenbaum, 1947).

The issues cannot be explored fully in these few paragraphs, but we can make the point that the foundation for today's race relations may have been laid in the distant past, both before and during the contact situation. At the time Brazil was established, Portugal, unlike England, had had a long acquaintance with African cultures and peoples. In fact, Moors from North Africa ruled Portugal for a time. Thus, darker skin and other African "racial" features were familiar to the Portuguese and not, in and of themselves, regarded as a stigma or an indication of inferiority.

The relative absence of skin-color prejudice also may be reflected in the high rates of intermarriage between Portuguese, Africans, and natives. The Brazilian colonists were mostly males, unlike their British counterparts who were much more likely to immigrate in family groups, and they took brides from other groups. These intermarriages produced a large class of mulattos or people of mixed race. Today, whites are a bare majority of the Brazilian population (54%) and blacks are only a little more than 5%. The remainder of the population (almost 40%) consists of *pardos,* or people of mixed-race ancestry (Instituto Brasileiro de Geografia e Estatística 1999).

Brazilian slavery tended to be more open than the North American variety. Brazilian slaves were freed at a much higher rate than British American slaves were, and there was a large class of free blacks and mulattos filling virtually every job and position available in society. Compared with the U.S. experience, slavery lasted longer in Brazil (until

Exhibit 10.8   South America

1888) but ended more gradually and with less opposition.

In Brazil, slavery was not so thoroughly equated with race as it was in North America. Although slave status certainly was regarded as undesirable and unfortunate, it did not carry the presumption of racial inferiority. In North America, in contrast, anti-black prejudice and racism came into being as a way of rationalizing and supporting the system (see Chapter 5); slavery, blackness, and inferiority were tightly linked in the dominant ideology, an equation with powerful echoes in the present.

The results of the higher rates of racial intermarriage, large population of mulattos, and lower levels of racial prejudice in Brazil are manifold. First, they helped to sustain a way of thinking about race that is sharply different from North American practices. In Brazil and other parts of South and Central America, race is seen as a series of categories that have ambiguous, indeterminate boundaries. Black, white, and other colors shade into each other in an infinite variety of ways, and no hard or sharp borders mark the end of one group and the start of another.

In the United States, in contrast, race is seen as a set of sharply delimited categories with clear, definite boundaries. One's race is determined by the social group one belongs to, regardless of appearance or actual ancestry, and everyone belongs to one and *only* one race. Thus, people who are raised in and identify with the black community—including people who "look white"—are black.

Second, after the end of slavery, Brazil did not go through a period of legalized racial segregation like the Jim Crow system or apartheid. Such a system would be difficult to construct or enforce when race is seen as a set of open-ended categories that gradually fade into one another. Racial segregation requires a simple racial classification system in which everyone is classified unambiguously into one, and only one, category. The more nuanced and subtle perception of race in Brazil is not conducive to a strict system of racial inequality.

It should be stressed that Brazil has not solved its dominant-minority problems. The legacy of slavery is still strong, and there is a very high correlation between skin color and social status. For example, mortality rates for black children are nearly double those for whites, and life expectancy is 6 years shorter. Black Brazilians have much higher illiteracy, unemployment, and poverty rates and are much less likely to have access to a university education (Kuperman, 2001, p. 25). Whites dominate the more prestigious and lucrative occupations and the leadership positions in the economy and in politics, whereas blacks are concentrated at the bottom of the class system, with mixed-race people in between.

Brazil is not a racial utopia, as is sometimes claimed. Racial discrimination and inequality are massive problems there, as they are in the United States. Still, the comparison between the two nations is instructive. Differences in the contact period and in the development of race relations over time have resulted in a notably different and somewhat milder form of group relations today.

ANALYZING GROUP RELATIONS

Our tour of group relations around the globe has been brief and highly selective in the stops we made. Nonetheless, some conclusions are possible.

1. Problems of dominant-minority relations are extremely common. It seems that the only nations that lack such problems are the relatively few (such as Sweden) that are homogeneous in their racial, cultural, religious, and linguistic makeup.

2. Dominant-minority problems are highly variable in their form and their intensity. They range from genocide in former Yugoslavia and Rwanda to hate crimes motivated by race, religion, or ethnicity in Germany and many other locales to universal complaints of racism, unfairness, and injustice. Some long-standing minority grievances remain unresolved (e.g., Catholics in Northern Ireland), and new problem areas appear on a regular basis. There is little indication that these various problems of group relations will be settled or otherwise fade away at any point in the near future.

3. As we have noted on a number of occasions, the most intense, violent, and seemingly intractable problems of group relations almost always have their origin in contact situations in which one group is conquered or colonized by another. Blauner's hypothesis seems well supported by this examination of dominant-minority relations around the globe.

4. The impact of modernization and industrialization on racial and ethnic relations is variable. Whereas these forces led to less rigid group relations in the United States, they had the opposite effect in South Africa until the 1990s. Furthermore, around the globe, ethnic and racial groups that were thought to have been submerged in the hustle and bustle of modern society have been reappearing with surprising regularity. The former Yugoslavia supplies some of the most dramatic examples of the seeming imperviousness of a sense of ethnicity to industrialization and modernization, but others can be found in Great Britain, Belgium, Spain, the former U.S.S.R., Mexico, China, Nigeria, Iraq, and scores of other nations. In each of these cases, pluralistic or separatist movements based on ethnic and racial groups are present and, in some cases, thriving.

5. It seems unlikely that even the most sophisticated and modern of nations will outgrow the power of ethnic loyalties at any point in the near future. In virtually all the cases discussed, whatever tendencies modernization creates to set prejudice aside and judge others rationally are offset by memories of past injustices; unresolved grievances; a simple yearning for revenge; and continuing struggles over control of land, labor, and other resources. Ethnic and racial lines continue to reflect inequalities of wealth and power, and as long as minority group status is correlated with inequality, ethnic and racial loyalties will remain powerful motivations for conflict.

6. As suggested in the previous point, ethnic and racial group conflicts are especially intense when they coincide with class divisions and patterns of inequality. For example, minority group members in Canada, South Africa, and Northern Ireland command lower shares of wealth and political power and have worse jobs, poorer housing, and lower levels of education. When a conflict arises in these societies, whether the issue is one of economics, politics, or a dominant-minority issue, the same groups face each other across the lines of division. The greater the extent to which issues and lines of fracture coincide and reinforce each other, the greater the threat to society as a whole, and the more difficult it will be to manage the conflict and avoid escalation to the extremes.

7. With respect to the intensity and nature of dominant-minority problems, the United States is hardly in a unique or unusual position. Many nations are dealing with problems of assimilation and pluralism and diversity and unity, and some of these issues seem far more difficult and complex than those facing our society. Societies such as Switzerland and Hawaii help sustain the idea that peaceful, just, and equal group relations are possible even for very diverse nations. Our tour of the globe also shows that there are no racial paradises; even the multigroup societies with the most glowing reputations for tolerance are not immune from conflict, inequality, discrimination, and racism.

MAIN POINTS

- This chapter applies the ideas developed in this text to a variety of societies around the globe. Although examinations of various societies are not a complete or definitive test of theory, confidence in our ideas will increase to the extent that they are found to be applicable to dominant-minority situations in other societies.
- Dominant-minority conflicts, inequality, and discrimination were found in Canada, Northern Ireland, Germany, the former Yugoslavia, Rwanda, South Africa, and the Middle East. With the exception of immigrant workers in Germany, all these conflicts are decades or centuries old and began in a contact period that featured competition and conquest. The exact issues at the core of the conflicts are highly variable but commonly rotate around

questions of assimilation and pluralism, inequality and access to resources and opportunities, prejudice and racism, and diversity and unity.

- Hawaii, Switzerland, and Brazil have reputations for relatively peaceful intergroup relations and high levels of tolerance. Although none (particularly Brazil) is a racial paradise, two of these three societies lack the history of colonization and conquest that characterize the societies with more hostile group relations.

QUESTIONS FOR REVIEW AND STUDY

1. Apply the major concepts of this text to the case studies examined in this chapter. How do the case studies illustrate the importance of the contact situation and subsistence technology? How do modernization and industrialization shape group relations?

2. For each case study in this chapter (except Switzerland and Hawaii), list the racial and cultural characteristics of the dominant and minority groups, the nature of the contact situation, and the type of competition that motivated the construction of minority status. Look for common patterns in your list and describe what you see in terms of the concepts presented in this text.

3. Switzerland and Hawaii are often cited as examples of multigroup societies that are relatively harmonious. What characteristics of their contact situations might help account for this?

4. Compare the development of dominant-minority relations in Brazil with the United States. What important differences and similarities can you identify? How do these historical differences affect contemporary group relations?

5. What does this chapter suggest about the prevalence and persistence of minority inequality, prejudice, and racism? Will there ever be a time when the nations of the world will be free of these problems?

INTERNET RESEARCH PROJECT

Select one or more of the dominant-minority situations covered in this chapter and update the information. What events have transpired since this text was published? You might search for information using the home pages of major newspapers or conduct an Internet search using the group or country names as keywords. Your search for information could cite the issue (e.g., language diversity in Canada) as a keyword phrase. Note that a more refined search using multiple keywords is likely to produce the most relevant information.

FOR FURTHER READING

The first four sources below deal with more than one society. All others are basically case studies.

Curtin, Philip. 1990. *The Rise and Fall of the Plantation Complex: Essays in Atlantic History.* New York: Cambridge University Press.

Degler, Carl. 1971. *Neither Black nor White: Slavery and Race Relations in Brazil and the United States.* New York: Macmillan.

van den Berghe, Pierre L. 1967. *Race and Racism: A Comparative Perspective.* New York: Wiley.

Wilson, William J. 1973. *Power, Racism, and Privilege: Race Relations in Theoretical and Sociohistorical Perspectives.* New York: Free Press.

Beinart, William. 1994. *Twentieth-Century South Africa.* New York: Oxford University Press.

Fontaine, Pierre-Michel. 1986. *Race, Class, and Power in Brazil.* Los Angeles: UCLA Center for Afro-American Studies.

Fraser, Morris. 1973. *Children in Conflict: Growing Up in Northern Ireland.* New York: Basic Books.

Gourevitch, Philip. 1999. *We Wish to Inform You That Tomorrow We Will Be Killed With Our Families: Stories from Rwanda*. New York: Picador.

Li, Peter. 1990. *Race and Ethnic Relations in Canada*. Toronto: Oxford University Press.

McFarlane, Bruce. 1988. *Yugoslavia: Politics, Economics and Society*. London: Pinter.

McRoberts, Kenneth. 1988. *Quebec: Social Change and Political Crisis*. Toronto: McClelland and Stewart.

Smith, David, & Chambers, Gerald. 1991. *Inequality in Northern Ireland*. Oxford: Clarendon.

11

Minority Groups and U.S. Society
Themes, Patterns, and the Future

Over the past 10 chapters, we have analyzed ideas and theories about dominant-minority relations, examined the historical and contemporary situations of minority groups in U.S. society, and surveyed group relations around the globe. Now it is time to reexamine our major themes and concepts and determine what conclusions can be derived from our analysis. In this final chapter, I restate the general themes of this text and raise some questions about the future. As we look backward to the past and forward to the future, it seems appropriate to quote the words of historian Oscar Handlin (1951): "Once I thought to write a history of minority groups in America. Then, I discovered that the minority groups *were* American history" (p. 3).

THE IMPORTANCE OF SUBSISTENCE TECHNOLOGY

Perhaps the most important sociological idea we have developed is that dominant-minority relations are shaped by large social, political, and economic forces and that those relations change as these broad characteristics change. To understand the evolution of America's minority groups is to understand the history of the United States, from the earliest colonial settlement to the modern megalopolis. As we saw in Chapter 10, these same broad forces have left their imprint on many societies around the globe.

Subsistence technology is the most basic force shaping a society and the relationships between dominant and minority groups in that society. In the colonial United States, minority relations were bent to the demands of a land-hungry, labor-intensive agrarian technology, and the early relationships between Africans, Europeans, and Native Americans flowed from the colonists' desire to control both land and labor. By the mid-1800s, two centuries after Jamestown was founded, the same dynamics that had enslaved African Americans and nearly annihilated Native Americans made a minority group out of Mexican Americans.

The agrarian era came to an end in the 19th century as the new technologies of the industrial revolution increased the productivity of the economy and eventually changed every aspect of life in the United States. The paternalistic, oppressive systems used to control the labor of minority groups in the agrarian system were abolished and replaced by competitive systems of group relations. These newer systems evolved from more rigid forms to more fluid forms as industrialization and urbanization progressed.

As the United States grew and developed, new minority groups were created, and old minority groups were transformed. Rapid industrialization combined with the opportunities available on the frontier made the United States an attractive destination for immigrants from Europe, Asia, Latin America, and other parts of the world. Immigrants helped to farm the Great Plains, mine the riches of the West, and, above all, supply the armies of labor required by industrialization.

The descendants of the immigrants from Europe benefited from the continuing industrialization of the economy, rising in the social class structure as the economy grew and matured. Immigrants from Asia and Latin America were not so fortunate. Chinese Americans and Japanese Americans survived in ethnic enclaves on the fringes of the mainstream society, while Mexican Americans and Puerto Ricans supplied low-paid manual labor for both the rural and the urban economy. Both Asian Americans and Hispanic Americans were barred from access to dominant group institutions and higher-paid jobs.

The racial minority groups, particularly African Americans, Mexican Americans, and Puerto Ricans, began to enter the urban working class after European American ethnic groups had started to move up in the occupational structure, at a time when the supply of manual, unskilled jobs was dwindling. Thus, the processes that allowed upward mobility for European Americans failed to work for the racial minority groups, who confronted urban poverty and bankrupt cities in addition to the continuing barriers of racial prejudice and institutional discrimination.

We can only speculate about what the future holds, but the emerging information-based, high-tech society is unlikely to offer many opportunities for people with lower levels of education and fewer occupational skills. It seems fairly certain that members of the racial and colonized minority groups will be participating in the mainstream economy of the future at lower levels than the dominant group and the descendants of European and Asian immigrants. Upgraded urban educational systems, job training programs, and other community development programs might alter the grim scenario of continued exclusion, but current public opinion about matters of race and discrimination makes it unlikely that such programs will be created.

Inaction and perpetuation of the status quo will bar a large percentage of the population from the emerging mainstream economy. Those segments of the African American, Hispanic American, and Asian American communities currently mired in the urban underclass will continue to compete with the newer immigrants for jobs in the low-wage, secondary labor market or in alternative opportunity structures, including crime.

THE IMPORTANCE OF THE CONTACT SITUATION, GROUP COMPETITION, AND POWER

We have stressed the importance of the contact situation—the conditions under which the minority group and dominant group first come into contact with each other—throughout this text. Blauner's distinction between immigrant and colonized minority groups is fundamental, a distinction so basic that it helps to clarify minority group situations centuries after the initial contact period. In Chapters 5–9, we used Blauner's distinction as an organizing principle and covered American minority groups in approximate order from "most colonized" to "most immigrant." The groups covered first (African Americans and Native Americans) are clearly at a greater disadvantage in contemporary society than the groups covered last (Asian Americans and white ethnic groups). For example, prejudice, racism, and discrimination against African Americans remain formidable forces in contemporary America even though they may have softened into more subtle forms. In contrast, prejudice and discrimination against European American groups such as Irish Americans, Italian Americans, and Polish Americans have nearly disappeared today even though they were quite formidable just a few generations ago. Note, however, that American anti-Semitism persists, a pattern that may be related to the fact that eastern European Jews established an enclave and followed a mode of incorporation different from those of other European immigrant groups (see Chapter 9).

Noel's hypothesis states that if three conditions are present in the contact situation—ethnocentrism, competition, and the differential in power—ethnic or racial stratification will result. The relevance of ethnocentrism is limited largely to the actual contact situation, but the other two concepts help to clarify the changes occurring after initial contact.

We have examined numerous instances in which group competition—or even the threat of competition—increased prejudice and led to greater discrimination and more repression. Recall, for example, the opposition of the labor movement (dominated by European American ethnic groups) to Chinese immigrants. The anti-Chinese campaign led to the Chinese Exclusion Act of 1882, the first significant restriction on immigration to the United States. There are parallels between campaigns for exclusion in the past and current ideas about ending or curtailing immigration. Clearly, some part of the current opposition to immigration is motivated by a sense of threat and the fear that immigrants are a danger not only to jobs and to the economy but also to the cultural integrity of U.S. society.

Noel's third variable, the differential in power, determines the outcome of the initial contact situation and which group becomes dominant and which becomes minority. Following the initial contact, the superior power of the dominant group helps it to sustain the inferior position of the minority group. Minority groups by definition have fewer power resources, but they characteristically use what they have in an attempt to improve their situation. The improvements in the situations of American minority groups since the middle of the 20th century have been due in large part to the fact that they (especially African Americans, who typically led the way in protest and demands for change) finally acquired some power resources of their own. For example, one important source of power for the Civil Rights movement in the South during the 1950s and 1960s was the growth of African American voting strength in the North. After World War II, the African American electorate became too sizable to ignore, and its political power helped pressure the federal government to take action and pass the legislation that ended the Jim Crow era.

Minority status being what it is, however, each of the groups we have discussed (with the exception of the white ethnic groups) still controls relatively few power resources and is limited in its ability to pursue its own self-interest. Many of these limitations are economic and related to social class; many minority groups simply lack the monetary resources to finance campaigns for reform or to exert significant pressure on the political institution. Other limitations include small group size (e.g., Asian American groups), language barriers (e.g., many Hispanic groups), and divided loyalties within the group (e.g., Native Americans separated by tribal allegiances).

At any rate, the relative powerlessness of minority groups today is a legacy of the contact situations that created the groups in the first place. In general, colonized groups are at a greater power disadvantage than immigrant groups. Contact situations set agendas for group relations that have impacts centuries after the initial meeting.

Given all that we have examined in this text, it is obvious that competition and differences in power resources will continue to shape intergroup relations (including relations between minority groups themselves) well into the future. Because they are so basic and consequential, jobs will continue to be primary objects of competition, but there will be plenty of other issues to divide the nation. Included on this divisive list will be debates about crime and the criminal justice system, welfare reform, national health care policy, school busing, bilingual education, immigration policy, and multicultural curricula in schools.

These and other public issues will continue to separate us along ethnic and racial lines because those lines have become so deeply embedded in the economy, in politics, in our schools and neighborhoods, and in virtually every nook and cranny of U.S. society. These deep divisions reflect fundamental realities about who gets what in the United States, and they will continue to reflect the distribution of power and stimulate competition along group lines for generations to come.

DIVERSITY WITHIN MINORITY GROUPS

All too often, and this text is probably no exception, minority groups are seen as unitary and undifferentiated. Although overgeneralizations are sometimes difficult to avoid, I want to stress again the diversity within each of the groups we have examined. Minority group members vary from each other by age, sex, region of residence, levels of education, urban versus rural residence, political ideology, and many other variables. The experience of one segment of the group (college-educated, fourth-generation, native-born Chinese American females) may bear little resemblance to the experience of another (illegal Chinese male immigrants with less than a high school education), and the problems of some members may not be the problems of others.

I have tried to highlight the importance of this diversity by exploring gender differentiation within each minority group. Study of minority groups by U.S. social scientists has focused predominantly on males, and the experiences of minority women have been described in much less depth. All the cultures examined in this text have strong patriarchal traditions. Women of the dominant group as well as minority women have had much less access to leadership roles and higher-status positions, and they generally have occupied a subordinate status, even in their own groups. The experiences of minority group women and the extent of their differences from minority group males and dominant group women are only now being fully explored.

One clear conclusion we can make about gender is that minority group females are doubly oppressed and disempowered. Limited by both their minority status and their gender roles, they are among the most vulnerable and exploited segments of the society. At one time or another, the women of every minority group have taken the least-desirable, lowest-status positions available in the economy, often while trying to raise children and attend to other family needs. They have been expected to provide support for other members of their families, kinship groups, and communities, often sacrificing their own self-interest to the welfare of others.

In their roles outside the family, minority women have encountered discrimination based on their minority group membership compounded with discrimination based on their gender. The result is, predictably, an economic and social status at the bottom of the social structure. For example, average incomes of African American females today are lower than those of white males, white females, and black males (see Exhibit 5.2).

The same pattern holds for Hispanic American women (see Exhibit 7.9). Minority women are highly concentrated in the low-paid secondary labor market and often are employed in jobs that provide services to members of more privileged groups.

The inequality confronted by minority women extends beyond matters of economics and jobs: Women of color have higher rates of infant mortality, births out of wedlock, and a host of other health-related, quality-of-life problems. In short, there is ample evidence to document a pervasive pattern of gender inequality within America's minority groups. Much of this gender inequality is deeply intertwined with rising rates of poverty and female-headed households, teenage pregnancy, and unemployment for minority males in the inner city.

Gender differentiation cuts through minority groups in a variety of ways. Specific issues might unite minority women with women of the dominant group (e.g., sexual harassment in schools and the workplace), and others might unite them with the men of their minority group (e.g., the enforcement of civil rights legislation). Solving the problems faced by minority groups will not resolve the problems faced by minority women, and neither will resolving the problems of gender inequality alone. Women of color are embedded in structures of inequality and discrimination that limit them in two independent but simultaneous ways. Articulating and addressing these difficulties requires the recognition of the complex interactions between gender and minority group status.

ASSIMILATION AND PLURALISM

It seems fair to conclude that the diversity and complexity of minority group experiences in the United States are not well characterized by the traditional or "melting pot" views of assimilation. For example, the idea that assimilation is a linear, inevitable process has little support. Immigrants from Europe probably fit that model better than other groups, but as the ethnic revival of the

1960s demonstrated, assimilation and ethnic identity can take surprising turns.

Also without support is the notion that there is always a simple, ordered relationship between the various stages of assimilation: acculturation, integration into public institutions, integration into the private sector, and so forth. We have seen that some groups integrated *before* they acculturated, others have become *more* committed to their ethnic and/or racial identity over the generations, and still others have been acculturated for generations but are no closer to full integration. New expressions of ethnicity come and go, and minority groups emerge, combine, and recombine in unexpected and seemingly unpredictable ways. The 1960s saw a reassertion of ethnicity and loyalty to old identities among some groups, even while other groups developed new coalitions and invented new ethnic identities (for example, pan-tribalism among Native Americans). No simple or linear view of assimilation can begin to make sense of the array of minority group experiences.

Indeed, the very desirability of assimilation has been subject to debate. Since the 1960s, many minority spokespersons have questioned the wisdom of becoming a part of a sociocultural structure that was constructed by the systematic exploitation of minority groups. Pluralistic themes increased in prominence as the commitment of the larger society to racial equality faltered. Virtually every minority group proclaimed the authenticity of its own experiences, its own culture, and its own version of history, separate from but as valid as that of the dominant groups. From what might have seemed like a nation approaching integration in the 1950s, America evolved into what might have seemed like a Tower of Babel in the 1960s. The consensus that assimilation was the best solution and the most sensible goal for all of America's minority groups was shattered (if it ever really existed at all).

By way of summary, let's review the state of acculturation and integration in the United States on a group-by-group basis. African Americans are highly acculturated.

Despite the many unique cultural traits forged in America and those that survive from Africa, black Americans share language, values and beliefs, and most other aspects of culture with white Americans of similar class and educational background.

In terms of integration, in contrast, African Americans present a mixed picture. For middle-class, more educated members of the group, American society offers more opportunities for upward mobility and success than ever before. Without denying the prejudice, discrimination, and racism that remain, this segment of the group is in a favorable position to achieve higher levels of affluence and power for their children and grandchildren. At the same time, a large percentage of African Americans remain mired in urban poverty, and for them, affluence, security, and power are just as distant (perhaps more so) than a generation ago. African Americans as a group remain highly segregated in their residential and school attendance patterns, and their political power, although rising, is not proportional to their size. Unemployment, lower average incomes, and poverty in general remain serious problems, and may be more serious than they were a generation ago.

Native Americans are less acculturated than African Americans, and there is evidence that Native American culture and language may be increasing in strength and vitality. On measures of integration, there is some indication of improvement, but by and large, Native Americans remain the most isolated and impoverished minority group in the United States. One possible bright spot for some reservations lies in the further development of the gambling industry and the investment of profits in the tribal infrastructure to upgrade schools, health clinics, job-training centers, and so forth.

Hispanic Americans also are generally less acculturated than African Americans. Hispanic traditions and the Spanish language have been sustained by the exclusion and isolation of these groups within the United States and have been continually renewed and revitalized by immigration. Cubans have moved closer to equality than other Hispanic groups but did so by resisting assimilation and building an ethnic enclave economy. Mexican Americans, Puerto Ricans, and many recent immigrants share many of the problems of urban poverty that confront African Americans and are far below national norms on measures of equality and integration.

As with Hispanic Americans, the extent of assimilation among Asian Americans is highly variable. Some groups (for example, third- and fourth-generation native-born Japanese Americans and Chinese Americans) have virtually completed the assimilation process and are remarkably successful. Other Asian American groups consist largely of newer immigrants with occupational and educational profiles that resemble those of colonized minority groups. Still other Asian American groups have used their cohesiveness and solidarity to construct ethnic enclaves in which, like Cubans, they have achieved relative economic equality by resisting acculturation.

Only European American ethnic groups seem to approximate the traditional model of assimilation. The development of these groups, however, has taken unexpected twists and turns, and the pluralism of the 1960s and 1970s suggests that ethnic traditions and ethnic identity, in some form, may withstand the pressures of assimilation for generations to come. Culturally and racially, these groups are the closest to the dominant group. If they still retain a sense of ethnicity, even if merely symbolic, after generations of acculturation and integration, what is the likelihood that the sense of group membership will fade in the racially stigmatized minority groups?

Assimilation is far from accomplished. The group divisions that remain are real and consequential; they cannot be willed away by pretending we are all "just American." Group membership continues to be important because it continues to be linked to fundamental patterns of exclusion and inequality. The realities of pluralism, inequality, and ethnic and racial identity continue to persist to the extent that the American promise of a truly open opportunity structure continues to fail. The group divisions forged in the past and perpetuated over the decades by racism and discrimination will remain to the extent that racial and ethnic group membership continues to be correlated with inequality and position in the social class structure.

Besides economic and political pressures, other forces help to sustain the pluralistic group divisions. Many people find their own ancestry to be a matter of great interest and work hard to preserve the traditions of their ancestors. Some (perhaps most) of the impetus behind this preservation of ethnic and racial identity may be a result of the most vicious and destructive intergroup competition. In other ways, though, these group identities can be positive forces that help people locate themselves in time and space and understand their position in the contemporary world. For many Americans, their group membership remains an important aspect of their self-identity and pride, and it seems unlikely that this sense of a personal link to one's ethnic and racial heritage will soon disappear.

Can we survive as a pluralistic, culturally and linguistically fragmented, racially and ethnically unequal society? What will save us from balkanization, fractionalization, and nightmares such as those that occurred in the former Yugoslavia or Rwanda? Given our history of colonization and racism, can U.S. society move closer to the relatively harmonious models of race relations found in Switzerland and Hawaii? As we deal with these questions, we need to remember that in and of itself, diversity is no more "bad" than unity is "good." Our society has grown to a position of global preeminence despite, or perhaps because of, our diversity. In fact, many have argued that our diversity is a fundamental and essential characteristic of U.S. society and a great strength to be cherished and encouraged.

The question for our future might not be so much "Unity or diversity?" as "What *blend* of pluralistic and assimilationist

policies will serve us best in the 21st century?" Are there ways in which society can prosper without repressing diversity? How can we increase the degree of openness, fairness, and justice without threatening group loyalties? The one-way, Anglo-conformity mode of assimilation of the past is too narrow and destructive to be a blueprint for the future, but the more extreme forms of minority group pluralism and separatism might be equally dangerous.

How much unity do we need? How much diversity can we tolerate? These are questions you must answer for yourself, and they are questions you will face in a thousand different ways over the course of your life. Let me illustrate by citing some pertinent issues.

• Is it desirable to separate college dormitories by racial or ethnic group? Is this destructive self-segregation or a positive strategy for group empowerment? Will such practices increase prejudice, or will they work like ethnic enclaves and strengthen minority group cohesion and solidarity and permit the groups to deal with the larger society from a stronger position? For the campus as a whole, what good could come from residential separation? In what ways would minority students benefit? Is there a "correct" balance between separation and unity in this situation? Who gets to define what the balance is?

• How much attention should be devoted to minority group experiences in elementary and high school texts and curricula? Who should write and control these curricula? What should they say? How critical should they be of America's often dismal past? How should such topics as slavery, genocide, and the racist exclusion of certain immigrant groups be presented in elementary school texts? In high school texts? Will educating children about the experiences of U.S. minority groups be an effective antidote to prejudice? Should classrooms be used to build respect for the traditions of other groups and an appreciation of their experiences?

- What are the limits of free speech with respect to minority relations? When does an ethnic joke become offensive? When are racial and ethnic epithets protected by the First Amendment? As long as lines of ethnicity and race divide the nation and as long as people feel passionately about these lines, the language of dominant-minority relationships will continue to have harsh, crude, and intentionally insulting components. Under what conditions, if any, should a civil society tolerate disparagement of other groups? Should the racial and ethnic epithets uttered by minority group members be treated any differently from those of dominant group members?

- What should the national policy on immigration be? How many immigrants should be admitted each year? How should immigrants be screened? What qualifications should be demanded? Should immigration policy favor the family and close relatives of citizens and permanent residents? What should be done about illegal immigrants? Should illegal immigrants or their children receive health care and schooling? If so, who should pay for these services?

I do not pretend that the ideas presented in this text can fully resolve these issues or others that will arise in the future. As long as immigrants and minority groups are a part of the United States, and as long as prejudice and discrimination persist, the debates will continue, and new issues will arise as old ones are resolved.

As U.S. society attempts to deal with new immigrants and unresolved minority grievances, we should recognize that it is not diversity per se that threatens stability but the realities of split labor markets, racial and ethnic stratification, urban poverty, and institutionalized discrimination. We need to focus on the issues that confront us with an honest recognition of the past and the economic, political, and social forces that have shaped us. As the United States continues to remake itself, an informed sense of where we have been will help us decide where we

should go. Clearly, the simplistic, one-way, Anglo-conformity model of assimilation of the past does not provide a basis for dealing with these problems realistically and should not be the blueprint for the future of U.S. society.

We also should remember that our understandings are always limited by who we are, where we come from, and what we have experienced. If we are to understand the forces that have created racial and ethnic minority groups in the United States and around the globe, we must find ways to surpass the limitations of our personal experiences and honestly confront the often ugly realities of the past and present. I believe that the ideas, concepts, and information presented in this text can help us liberate ourselves from the narrow confines of our own experiences and perspectives, but our ability to imagine the realities faced by others is never perfect, and what we can see of the world depends very much on where we stand.

MINORITY GROUP PROGRESS AND THE IDEOLOGY OF AMERICAN INDIVIDUALISM

There is so much sadness, misery, and unfairness in the history of minority groups that evidence of progress sometimes goes unnoticed. Lest we be guilty of ignoring the good news in favor of the bad, let us note some ways in which the situations of American minority groups are better today than they were in the past. Evidence of progress is easy to find for every minority group, and in some cases (European American ethnic groups and some Asian American groups) the movement toward economic, educational, and income equality has been truly impressive. Over the past five decades, the United States has become more tolerant and open, and minority group members now can be found at the highest levels of success, affluence, and prestige.

One of the most obvious signs of progress is the decline of traditional racism and prejudice. As we discussed in Chapter 5, the strong racial and ethnic sentiments and stereotypes of the past are no longer the primary vocabulary for discussing race relations among dominant group members, at least not in public. Although the prejudices unquestionably still exist, Americans have become more circumspect and discreet in their public utterances.

The demise of blatant bigotry in polite company is, without doubt, a positive change. However, it seems that negative intergroup feelings and stereotypes have not so much disappeared as changed their form. Modern or symbolic racism holds that the routes of upward mobility in American society are now open freely and equally to all. This individualistic view of social mobility is consistent with the human capital perspective and the traditional, melting-pot view of assimilation. Taken together, these ideologies present a powerful and widely shared perspective on the nature of minority group problems in modern American society. Proponents of these views tend to be unsympathetic to the plight of minorities and to programs, such as school busing and affirmative action, that are intended to ameliorate these problems. The overt bigotry of the past has been replaced by an indifference more difficult to define and harder to measure than "old-fashioned" racism, yet still unsympathetic to racial change.

This text has argued that the most serious problems facing contemporary minority groups, however, are structural and institutional, not individual or personal. For example, the paucity of jobs and high rates of unemployment in the inner cities are the result of economic and political forces beyond the control not only of the minority communities but also of local and state governments. The marginalization of the minority group labor force reflects the essence of modern American capitalism. The mainstream, higher-paying blue-collar jobs available to people with modest educational credentials are controlled by national and multinational corporations, which maximize profits by automating their production processes and moving the jobs that remain to areas, often outside the United States, with abundant supplies of cheaper labor.

We also have seen that some of the more effective strategies for pursuing equality require strong in-group cohesion and networks of cooperation, not heroic individual effort. Immigration to this country is and always has been a group process that involved extensive, long-lasting networks of communication and chains of population movement, usually built around family ties and larger kinship groups. Group networks continue to operate in America and assist individual immigrants with early adjustments and later opportunities for jobs and upward mobility. A variation on this theme is the ethnic enclave found among so many different groups.

Survival and success in America for all minority groups has had more to do with group processes than with individual will or motivation. The concerted, coordinated actions of the minority community provided support during hard times and, when possible, provided the means to climb higher in the social structure during good times. Far from being a hymn to individualism, the story of U.S. minority groups is profoundly sociological.

A FINAL WORD

U.S. society and its minority groups are linked in fractious unity. They are part of the same structures but are separated by lines of color and culture and by long histories (and clear memories) of exploitation and unfairness. This society owes its prosperity and position of prominence in the world no less to the labor of minority groups than to that of the dominant group. By harnessing the labor and energy of these minority groups, the nation has grown prosperous and powerful, but the benefits have flowed disproportionately to the dominant group.

Since the middle of the 20th century, minority groups have demanded greater openness, fairness, equality, respect for their traditions, and justice. Increasingly, the demands have been made on the terms of the minority groups, not on those of the dominant group. Some of these demands have been met, at least verbally, and the society as a whole has rejected the oppressive racism of the past. Minority group progress has stalled well short of equality, however, and the patterns of poverty, discrimination, marginality, hopelessness, and despair continue to limit the lives of millions.

As we begin the 21st century, the dilemmas of America's minority groups remain perhaps the primary unresolved domestic issue facing the nation. The answers of the past—the faith in assimilation and the belief that success in America is open to all who simply try hard enough—have proved inadequate, even destructive and dangerous, because they help to sustain the belief that the barriers to equality no longer exist and that any remaining inequalities are the problems of the minority groups, not the larger society.

These problems of equality and access will not solve themselves or simply fade away. They will continue to manifest themselves in myriad ways; through protest activities, rancorous debates, diffused rage, and pervasive violence. The solutions and policies that will carry us through these coming travails are not clear. Only by asking the proper questions, realistically and honestly, can we hope to find the answers that will help our society fulfill its promises to the millions who are currently excluded from achieving the American Dream.

As we saw in Chapter 10, the United States is one of many nations in the world today that are ethnically and racially diverse. As the globe continues to shrink and networks of communication, immigration, trade, and transportation continue to link all peoples into a single global entity, the problems of diversity will become more international in their scope and implications. Ties will grow between African Americans and the nations of Africa, agreements between the United States and the nations of Latin America will have direct impacts on immigration patterns, Asian Americans will be affected by international developments on the Pacific Rim, and so forth. Domestic and international group relations will blend into a single reality. In many ways, the patterns of dominant-minority relations discussed in this text already have been reproduced on the global stage. The mostly Anglo industrialized nations of the Northern Hemisphere have continuously exploited the labor and resources of the mostly nonwhite, undeveloped nations of the Southern Hemisphere. Thus, the tensions and resentments we have observed in U.S. society are mirrored in the global system of societies.

The United States is neither the most nor the least diverse society in the world. Likewise, our nation is neither the most nor the least successful in confronting the problems of prejudice, discrimination, and racism. However, the multigroup nature of our society, along with the present influx of immigrants from around the globe, does present an opportunity to improve on our record and make a lasting contribution. A society that finds a way to deal fairly and humanely with the problems of diversity and difference, prejudice and inequality, and racism and discrimination can provide a sorely needed model for other nations and, indeed, for the world.

QUESTIONS FOR REVIEW AND STUDY

1. "To understand the evolution of America's minority groups is to understand the history of the United States, from the earliest colonial settlement to the modern megalopolis." Explain this statement in terms of the importance of subsistence technology in shaping intergroup relationships. Cite examples from throughout the text and from across the globe.
2. Summarize the Noel and Blauner hypotheses and apply them to the case studies of minority groups covered in this text. Are these hypotheses supported by the facts? Why or why not?

3. How have the experiences of minority groups been shaped by gender? Within each group covered in this text, how and why have the experiences of men and women differed? How have the experiences of minority women varied from those of dominant group women? How are they the same? Is it valid to conclude that minority women are "doubly oppressed and disempowered?" Why or why not?

4. How useful are the concepts of assimilation and pluralism for understanding the experiences of American minority groups? What forms of assimilation seem most applicable to the American experience? Why?

5. "More diversity" or "more unity?": Which would you select as a direction for the development of U.S. society? Why? How might your answer change if you were a member of some other racial or ethnic group?

6. What is "American individualism," and how does it affect perceptions of dominant-minority relations? What is the relationship between an individualistic perspective, human capital theory, and traditional views of assimilation? How accurate are these ideas? How do they compare with the version of sociology presented in this text? Can you say that any of these ideas are right or wrong? Can any be rejected and discarded? Why?

References

Abrahamson, Harold. 1980. "Assimilation and Pluralism." In Stephan Thernstrom (Ed.), *Harvard Encyclopedia of American Ethnic Groups* (pp. 150–160). Cambridge, MA: Harvard University Press.

Acuna, Rodolfo. 1999. *Occupied America* (4th ed.). New York: Harper & Row.

_____. 1988. *Occupied America* (3rd ed.). New York: Harper & Row.

Adarand Constructors Inc. v. Pena, 515 U.S. 200 (1995).

Agbayani-Siewert, Pauline, & Revilla, Linda. 1995. "Filipino Americans." In Pyong Gap Min (Ed.), *Asian Americans: Contemporary Issues and Trends*. Thousand Oaks, CA: Sage.

Alba, Richard. 1995. "Assimilation's Quiet Tide." *The Public Interest,* 119:3–19.

_____. 1990. *Ethnic Identity: The Transformation of White America*. New Haven, CT: Yale University Press.

_____. 1985. *Italian Americans: Into the Twilight of Ethnicity*. Englewood Cliffs, NJ: Prentice Hall.

Alba, Richard, & Nee, Victor. 1997. "Rethinking Assimilation Theory for a New Era of Immigration." *International Migration Review,* 31:826–875.

Allport, Gordon. 1954. *The Nature of Prejudice*. Reading, MA: Addison-Wesley.

Almquist, Elizabeth M. 1979. "Black Women and the Pursuit of Equality." In Jo Freeman (Ed.), *Women: A Feminist Perspective* (pp. 430–450). Palo Alto, CA: Mayfield.

Alvarez, Rodolfo. 1973. "The Psycho-Historical and Socioeconomic Development of the Chicano Community in the United States." *Social Science Quarterly,* 53:920–942.

Amott, Teresa, & Matthaei, Julie. 1991. *Race, Gender, and Work: A Multicultural History of Women in the United States*. Boston: South End.

Andersen, Margaret L. 1993. *Thinking About Women: Sociological Perspectives on Sex and Gender* (3rd ed.). New York: Macmillan.

Anti-Defamation League. 2000. "Anti-Semitism in the United States." Retrieved from the World Wide Web on July 12, 2002, at www.adl.org/backgrounders/Anti_Semitism_us.asp.

Ashmore, Richard, & DelBoca, Frances. 1976. "Psychological Approaches to Understanding Group Conflict." In Phyllis Katz (Ed.), *Towards the Elimination of Racism* (pp. 73–123). New York: Pergamon.

Australian Bureau of Statistics. 2002. *Australian Social Trends 2002: Population—National Summary Tables*. Retrieved from the World Wide Web on July 5, 2002, at www.abs.gov.au.

Australian Human Rights and Equal Opportunity Commission. 1997. *Bringing Them Home: Report of the National Inquiry into the Separation of Aboriginal and Torres Strait Islander Children from Their Families*. Retrieved from the World Wide Web on July 5, 2002, at www.austlii.edu.au/au/special/rsjproject/rsjlibrary/hreoc/stolen/.

Barringer, Herbert, Takeuchi, David, & Levin, Michael. 1995. *Asians and Pacific Islanders in the United States*. New York: Russell Sage.

Barringer, Herbert, Takeuchi, David, & Xenos, Peter. 1990. "Education, Occupational Prestige, and Income of Asian Americans." *Sociology of Education,* 63:27–43.

Becerra, Rosina. 1988. "The Mexican American Family." In Charles H. Mindel, Robert W. Habenstein, & Roosevelt Wright (Eds.), *Ethnic Families in America: Patterns and Variations* (3rd ed., pp. 141–159). New York: Elsevier.

Beinart, William. 1994. *Twentieth-Century South Africa*. New York: Oxford University Press.

Bell, Daniel. 1973. *The Coming of Post-Industrial Society*. New York: Basic Books.

Bell, Derrick. 1992. *Race, Racism, and American Law* (3rd ed.). Boston: Little, Brown.

Benedict, Ruth. 1946. *The Chrysanthemum and the Sword: Patterns of Japanese Culture*. Boston: Houghton Mifflin.

Bird, Elizabeth. 1999. "Gendered Construction of the American Indian in Popular Media." *Journal of Communication,* 49:60–83.

Biskupic, Joan. 1989. "House Approves Entitlement for Japanese-Americans." *Congressional Quarterly Weekly Report,* October 28, p. 2879.

Black-Gutman, D., & Hickson, F. 1996. "The Relationship Between Racial Attitudes and Social-Cognitive Development in Children: An Australian Study." *Developmental Psychology,* 32:448–457.

Blassingame, John W. 1972. *The Slave Community: Plantation Life in the Antebellum South.* New York: Oxford University Press.

Blau, Peter M., & Duncan, Otis Dudley. 1967. *The American Occupational Structure.* New York: Wiley.

Blauner, Robert. 1972. *Racial Oppression in America.* New York: Harper & Row.

Blessing, Patrick. 1980. "Irish." In Stephen Thornstrom (Ed.), *Harvard Encyclopedia of Ethnic Groups* (pp. 524–545). Cambridge, MA: Harvard University Press.

Bluestone, Barry, & Harrison, Bennett. 1982. *The Deindustrialization of America.* New York: Basic Books.

Blumer, Herbert. 1965. "Industrialization and Race Relations." In Guy Hunter (Ed.), *Industrialization and Race Relations: A Symposium* (pp. 200–253). London: Oxford University Press.

Bobo, Lawrence. 2001. "Racial Attitudes and Relations at the Close of the Twentieth Century." In Neil J. Smelser, William Julius Wilson, & Faith Mitchell (Eds.), *America Becoming: Racial Trends and Their Consequences* (Vol. 1, pp. 264–301). Washington, DC: National Academy Press.

———. 1988. "Group Conflict, Prejudice, and the Paradox of Contemporary Racial Attitudes." In Phyllis Katz & Dalmar Taylor (Eds.), *Eliminating Racism: Profiles in Controversy* (pp. 85–114). New York: Plenum.

Bodnar, John. 1985. *The Transplanted.* Bloomington: Indiana University Press.

Bogardus, Emory. 1933. "A Social Distance Scale." *Sociology and Social Research,* 17:265–271.

Bonacich, Edna, & Modell, John. 1980. *The Economic Basis of Ethnic Solidarity: Small Business in the Japanese American Community.* Berkeley: University of California Press.

Bordewich, Fergus. 1996. *Killing the White Man's Indian.* New York: Doubleday.

Boswell, Terry. 1986. "A Split Labor Market Analysis of Discrimination Against Chinese Immigrants, 1850–1882." *American Sociological Review,* 51:352–371.

Bouvier, Leon F., & Gardner, Robert W. 1986. "Immigration to the U.S.: The Unfinished Story." *Population Bulletin* (Vol. 41, No. 4). Washington, DC: Population Reference Bureau.

Brace, Matthew. 2001. "A Nation Divided." *Geographical,* 73:14–20.

Brody, David. 1980. "Labor." In Stephen Thornstrom (Ed.), *Harvard Encyclopedia of Ethnic Groups* (pp. 609–618). Cambridge, MA: Harvard University Press.

Brown, Dee. 1970. *Bury My Heart at Wounded Knee.* New York: Holt, Rinehart & Winston.

Brown, Rupert. 1995. *Prejudice: Its Social Psychology.* Cambridge, MA: Blackwell.

Brown v. Board of Educ., 247 U.S. 483 (1954)

Buraku Liberation and Human Rights Research Institute. 2001. *Discrimination Against Buraku People.* Retrieved from the World Wide Web on July 10, 2002, at www.blhrri.org/ index_e.htm.

Buriel, Raymond. 1993. "Acculturation, Respect for Cultural Differences, and Biculturalism Among Three Generations of Mexican American and Euro-American School Children." *Journal of Genetic Psychology,* 154:531–544.

Camarillo, Albert, & Bonilla, Frank. 2001. "Hispanics in a Multicultural Society: A New American Dilemma?" In Neil J. Smelser, William Julius Wilson, & Faith Mitchell (Eds.), *America Becoming: Racial Trends and Their Consequences* (Vol. 2, pp. 103–134). Washington, DC: National Academy Press.

Cancio, S., Evans, T., & Maume, D. 1996. "Reconsidering the Declining Significance of Race: Racial Differences in Early Career Wages." *American Sociological Review,* 61:541–556.

Central Intelligence Agency. 2001. *The World Factbook 2002.* Retrieved from the World Wide Web on April 8, 2003, at www.odci.gov/ cia/publications/factbook.

Chan, Sucheng. 1990. "European and Asian Immigrants into the United States in Comparative Perspective, 1820s to 1920s." In Virginia Yans-McLaughlin (Ed.), *Immigration Reconsidered: History, Sociology, and Politics* (pp. 37–75). New York: Oxford University Press.

Chin, Ko-lin. 2000. *Smuggled Chinese: Clandestine Immigration to the United States.* Philadelphia: Temple University Press.

Chirot, Daniel. 1994. *How Societies Change.* Thousand Oaks, CA: Pine Forge Press.

Cho, Sumi. 1993. "Korean Americans vs. African Americans: Conflict and Construction." In Robert Gooding-Williams (Ed.), *Reading Rodney King, Reading Urban Uprising* (pp. 196–211). New York: Routledge and Kegan Paul.

Churchill, Ward. 1985. "Resisting Relocation: Dine and Hopis Fight to Keep Their Land." *Dollars and Sense,* December, pp. 112–115.

Civil Rights Act of 1964, Pub. L. 88–352 § 42 U.S.C. 2000 (1964)

Cofer, Judith Ortiz. 1995. "The Myth of the Latin Woman: I Just Met a Girl Named Maria." In *The*

Latin Deli: Prose and Poetry (pp. 148–154). Athens, GA: University of Georgia Press.

Cohen, Adam, & Taylor, Elizabeth. 2000. *American Pharaoh: Mayor Richard J. Daley: His Battle for Chicago and the Nation.* New York: Little, Brown.

Cohen, Steven M. 1985. *The 1984 National Survey of American Jews: Political and Social Outlooks.* New York: American Jewish Committee.

Cohn, D'Vera. 2001. "Illegal Immigrant Total Is Raised." *Washington Post,* October 25, A24.

Coltrane, Scott, & Messineo, Melinda. 2000. "The Perpetuation of Subtle Prejudice: Race and Gender Imagery in 1990s Television Advertising." *Sex Roles: A Journal of Research,* 42:363–389.

Conot, Robert. 1967. *Rivers of Blood, Years of Darkness.* New York: Bantam.

Conzen, Kathleen N. 1980. "Germans." In Stephen Thornstrom (Ed.), *Harvard Encyclopedia of Ethnic Groups* (pp. 405–425). Cambridge, MA: Harvard University Press.

Cornell, Stephen. 1990. "Land, Labor, and Group Formation: Blacks and Indians in the United States." *Ethnic and Racial Studies,* 13:368–388.

_____. 1988. *The Return of the Native: American Indian Political Resurgence.* New York: Oxford University Press.

_____. 1987. "American Indians, American Dreams, and the Meaning of Success." *American Indian Culture and Research Journal,* 11:59–71.

Cornell, Stephen, & Kalt, Joseph. 2000. "Where's the Glue? Institutional and Cultural Foundations of American Indian Economic Development." *Journal of Socio-Economics,* 29:443–470.

Cornell, Stephen, Kalt, Joseph, Krepps, Mathew, & Taylor, Johnathon. 1998. *American Indian Gaming Policy and Its Socio-Economic Effects: A Report to the National Impact Gambling Study Commission.* Cambridge, MA: Economics Resource Group.

Cortes, Carlos. 1980. "Mexicans." In Stephen Thornstrom (Ed.), *Harvard Encyclopedia of Ethnic Groups* (pp. 697–719). Cambridge, MA: Harvard University Press.

Cose, Ellis. 1993. *The Rage of a Privileged Class.* New York: HarperCollins.

Curtin, Philip. 1990. *The Rise and Fall of the Plantation Complex.* New York: Cambridge University Press.

D'Angelo, Raymond. 2001. *The American Civil Rights Movement: Readings and Interpretations.* New York: McGraw-Hill.

Daniels, Roger. 1990. *Coming to America.* New York: HarperCollins.

Debo, Angie. 1970. *A History of the Indians of the United States.* Norman: University of Oklahoma Press.

Degler, Carl. 1971. *Neither Black nor White: Slavery and Race Relations in Brazil and the United States.* New York: Macmillan.

de la Garza, Rodolfo O., DeSipio, Louis, García, F. Chris, García, John, & Falcon, Angelo. 1992. *Latino Voices: Mexican, Puerto Rican, and Cuban Perspectives on American Politics.* Boulder, CO: Westview.

de la Garza, Rodolfo, Falcon, Angelo, & García, F. Chris. 1996. "Will the Real Americans Please Stand Up: Anglo and Mexican-American Support of Core American Political Values." *American Journal of Political Science,* 40:335–351.

Deloria, Vine. 1995. *Red Earth, White Lies.* New York: Scribner's.

_____. 1970. *We Talk, You Listen.* New York: Macmillan.

_____. 1969. *Custer Died for Your Sins.* New York: Macmillan.

del Pinal, Jorge, & Singer, Audrey. 1997. "Generations of Diversity: Latinos in the United States." *Population Bulletin* (Vol. 52, No. 3). Washington, DC: Population Reference Bureau.

Dinnerstein, Leonard. 1977. "The East European Jewish Immigration." In Leonard Dinnerstein & Frederic C. Jaher (Eds.), *Uncertain Americans* (pp. 216–231). New York: Oxford University Press.

D'Orso, Michael. 1996. *Like Judgement Day: The Ruin and Redemption of a Town Called Rosewood.* New York: Putnam.

Doyle, Anna Beth, & Aboud, Frances E. 1995. "A Longitudinal Study of White Children's Racial Prejudice as a Socio-Cognitive Development." *Merrill-Palmer Quarterly,* 41:209–228.

Du Bois, W. E. B. 1961. *The Souls of Black Folk.* Greenwich, CT: Fawcett.

Duleep, Harriet O. 1988. *Economic Status of Americans of Asian Descent.* Washington, DC: U.S. Commission on Civil Rights.

Eichenwald, Kurt. 1996. "Texaco to Make Record Payment in Bias Lawsuit." *The New York Times,* November 16, p. 1.

Elkins, Stanley. 1959. *Slavery: A Problem in American Institutional and Intellectual Life.* New York: Universal Library.

Ellsworth, Scott. 1982. *Death in a Promised Land: The Tulsa Race Riot of 1921.* Baton Rouge: Louisiana State University Press.

Espinosa, Kristin, & Massey, Douglas. 1997. "Determinants of English Proficiency Among Mexican Migrants to the United States." *International Migration Review,* 31:28–51.

Espiritu, Yen. 1997. *Asian American Women and Men.* Thousand Oaks, CA: Sage.

_____. 1996. "Colonial Oppression, Labour Importation, and Group Formation: Filipinos in the United States." *Ethnic and Racial Studies,* 19:29–49.

Essien-Udom, E. U. 1962. *Black Nationalism.* Chicago: University of Chicago Press.

Evans, Sara M. 1989. *Born for Liberty: A History of Women in America.* New York: Free Press.

———. 1979. *Personal Politics.* New York: Knopf.

Fallows, Marjorie R. 1979. *Irish Americans: Identity and Assimilation.* Englewood Cliffs, NJ: Prentice Hall.

Farley, John. 1995. *Majority-Minority Relations* (3rd ed.) Englewood Cliffs, NJ: Prentice Hall.

———. 2000. *Majority-Minority Relations* (4th ed.). Englewood Cliffs, NJ: Prentice Hall.

Farley, Reynolds. 1996. *The New American Reality.* New York: Russell Sage.

Feagin, Joe. 2001. *Racist America: Roots, Current Realities, and Future Reparations.* New York: Routledge.

Feagin, Joe R., & Feagin, Clairece Booher. 1986. *Discrimination American Style: Institutional Racism and Sexism.* Malabar, FL: Robert E. Krieger.

Fernandez-Kelly, M. Patricia, & Schauffler, Richard. 1994. "Divided Fates: Immigrant Children in a Restructured U.S. Economy." *International Immigration Review,* 28:662–689.

Firefighters Local Union No. 1784 v. Stotts, 467 U.S. 561 (1984).

Fitzpatrick, Joseph P. 1987. *Puerto Rican Americans: The Meaning of Migration to the Mainland* (2nd ed.). Englewood Cliffs, NJ: Prentice Hall.

———. 1980. "Puerto Ricans." In Stephen Thornstrom (Ed.), *Harvard Encyclopedia of Ethnic Groups* (pp. 858–867). Cambridge, MA: Harvard University Press.

———. 1976. "The Puerto Rican Family." In Charles H. Mindel & Robert W. Habenstein (Eds.), *Ethnic Families in America* (pp. 173–195). New York: Elsevier.

Fong, Eric, & Markham, William. 1991. "Immigration, Ethnicity, and Conflict: The California Chinese, 1849–1882." *Sociological Inquiry,* 61:471–490.

Fong, Eric, & Wilkes, Rima. 1999. "The Spatial Assimilation Model Reexamined: An Assessment by Canadian Data." *International Migration Review,* 33:594–615.

Fong, Timothy. 2002. *The Contemporary Asian American Experience* (2nd ed.). Upper Saddle River, NJ: Prentice Hall.

Fontaine, Pierre-Michel. 1986. *Race, Class, and Power in Brazil.* Los Angeles: UCLA Center for Afro-American Studies.

Franklin, John Hope. 1967. *From Slavery to Freedom* (3rd ed.). New York: Knopf.

Franklin, John Hope, & Moss, Alfred. 1994. *From Slavery to Freedom* (7th ed.). New York: McGraw-Hill.

Fraser, Morris. 1973. *Children in Conflict: Growing Up in Northern Ireland.* New York: Basic Books.

Frazier, E. Franklin. 1957. *Black Bourgeoisie: The Rise of a New Middle Class.* New York: Free Press.

Gallagher, Charles. 2001. "Playing the Ethnic Card: How Ethnic Narratives Maintain Racial Privilege." Paper presented at the Annual Meeting of the Southern Sociological Society, April 4–7, Atlanta, GA.

Gallup Organization. 2000. "What Americans Think: Black or White?" *Spectrum,* 73:7.

Gans, Herbert. 1979. "Symbolic Ethnicity: The Future of Ethnic Groups and Cultures in America." *Ethnic and Racial Studies,* 2:1–20.

García, María Cristina. 1996. *Havana USA: Cuban Exiles and Cuban Americans in South Florida, 1959–1994.* Berkeley: University of California Press.

Garvey, Marcus. 1977. *Philosophy and Opinions of Marcus Garvey* (Vol. 3). Amy Jacques Garvey & E. U. Essien-Udom (Eds.). London: Frank Cass.

———. 1969. *Philosophy and Opinions of Marcus Garvey* (Vols. 1–2). Amy Jacques Garvey (Ed.). New York: Atheneum.

Genovese, Eugene D. 1974. *Roll, Jordan, Roll: The World the Slaves Made.* New York: Pantheon.

Gerth, Hans, & Mills, C. Wright (Eds.). 1946. *From Max Weber: Essays in Sociology.* New York: Oxford University Press.

Geschwender, James A. 1978. *Racial Stratification in America.* Dubuque, IA: William C. Brown.

Giago, T. 1992. "I Hope the Redskins Lose." *Newsweek,* January 27, p. 8.

Glazer, Nathan, & Moynihan, Daniel. 1970. *Beyond the Melting Pot* (2nd ed.). Cambridge: MIT Press.

Gleason, Philip. 1980. "American Identity and Americanization." In Stephen Thornstrom (Ed.), *Harvard Encyclopedia of Ethnic Groups* (pp. 31–57). Cambridge, MA: Harvard University Press.

Godstein, Amy, & Suro, Robert. 2000. "A Journey on Stages: Assimilation's Pull is Still Strong But Its Pace Varies." *Washington Post,* January 16, A1.

Goldberg, Steven. 1999. "The Logic of Patriarchy." *Gender Issues,* 17:53–62.

Goldstein, Sidney, & Goldscheider, Calvin. 1968. *Jewish Americans: Three Generations in a Jewish Community.* Englewood Cliffs, NJ: Prentice Hall.

Gooding-Williams, Robert. 1993. *Reading Rodney King, Reading Urban Uprising.* New York: Routledge and Kegan Paul.

———. 1964. *Assimilation in American Life.* New York: Oxford University Press.

Gordon, Milton. 1964. *Assimilation in American Life.* New York: Oxford University Press.

Goren, Arthur. 1980. "Jews." In Stephen Thornstrom (Ed.), *Harvard Encyclopedia of Ethnic Groups* (pp. 571–598). Cambridge, MA: Harvard University Press.

Gourevitch, Philip. 1999. *We Wish to Inform You That Tomorrow We Will Be Killed With Our Families: Stories from Rwanda.* New York: Picador.

Grebler, Leo, Moore, Joan W., & Guzman, Ralph C. 1970. *The Mexican American People.* New York: Free Press.

Greeley, Andrew M. 1974. *Ethnicity in the United States: A Preliminary Reconnaissance.* New York: Wiley.

Green, Donald. 1999. "Native Americans." In Anthony Dworkin & Rosalind Dworkin (Eds.), *The Minority Report* (pp. 255–277). Orlando, FL: Harcourt-Brace.

Gutman, Herbert G. 1976. *The Black Family in Slavery and Freedom, 1750–1925.* New York: Vintage.

Hacker, Andrew. 1992. *Two Nations: Black and White, Separate, Hostile, Unequal.* New York: Scribner's.

Haley, Alex. 1976. *Roots.* Garden City, NY: Doubleday.

Hamer, Fannie Lou. 1967. *To Praise Our Bridges: An Autobiography of Fannie Lou Hamer.* Jackson, MI: KIPCO.

Handlin, Oscar. 1951. *The Uprooted.* New York: Grosset & Dunlap.

Hansen, Marcus Lee. 1952. "The Third Generation in America." *Commentary,* 14:493–500.

Hanson, Jeffery, & Rouse, Linda. 1987. "Dimensions of Native American Stereotyping." *American Indian Culture and Research Journal,* 11:33–58.

Harjo, Suzan. 1996. "Now and Then: Native Peoples in the United States." *Dissent,* 43:58–60.

Harris, Marvin. 1988. *Culture, People, Nature.* New York: Harper & Row.

Hawkins, Hugh. 1962. *Booker T. Washington and His Critics: The Problem of Negro Leadership.* Boston: D. C. Heath.

Heer, David M. 1996. *Immigration in America's Future.* Boulder, CO: Westview.

Herberg, Will. 1960. *Protestant-Catholic-Jew: An Essay in American Religious Sociology.* New York: Anchor.

Higham, John. 1963. *Strangers in the Land: Patterns of American Nativism, 1860–1925.* New York: Atheneum.

Hill-Collins, Patricia. 1991. *Black Feminist Thought.* New York: Routledge.

Hirschman, Charles. 1983. "America's Melting Pot Reconsidered." *Annual Review of Sociology,* 9:397–423.

Hirschman, Charles, & Wong, Morrison. 1986. "The Extraordinary Educational Attainment of Asian-Americans: A Search for Historical Evidence and Explanations." *Social Forces,* 65:1–27.

_____. 1984. "Socioeconomic Gains of Asian Americans, Blacks, and Hispanics: 1960–1976." *American Journal of Sociology,* 90:584–607.

Hostetler, John. 1980. *Amish Society.* Baltimore Johns Hopkins University Press.

"How to Tell Your Friends From the Japs." 1941. *Time,* October–December, p. 33.

Hoxie, Frederick. 1984. *A Final Promise: The Campaign to Assimilate the Indian, 1880–1920.* Lincoln: University of Nebraska Press.

Hraba, Joseph. 1994. *American Ethnicity.* (2nd ed.). Itasca. Ill.: F.E. Peacock.

Hughes, Michael, & Thomas, Melvin. 1998. "The Continuing Significance of Race Revisited: A Study of Race, Class and Quality of Life in America, 1972 to 1996." *American Sociological Review,* 63:785–803.

Hurh, Won Moo. 1998. *The Korean Americans.* Westport, CT: Greenwood.

Hyman, Herbert, & Sheatsley, Paul. 1964. "Attitudes Toward Desegregation." *Scientific American,* 211:16–23.

Iceland, John, Weinberg, Daniel, & Steinmetz, Erika. 2002. *Racial and Ethnic Segregation in the United States: 1980–2000.* Washington, DC: Government Printing Office.

Instituto Brasileiro de Geografia e Estatística. 1999. *Distribution of the Resident Population, by Major Regions, Urban or Rural Situation, Sex, Skin Color or Race.* Retrieved from the World Wide Web on July 17, 2002, at www.ibge.gov.br/english/ estatistica/populacao/trabalhoerendimento/pnad99/ sintese/tab1_2_b_1999.shtm.

Jackson, Beverly. 2000. *Splendid Slippers: A Thousand Years of an Erotic Tradition.* Berkeley, CA: Ten Speed.

Jibou, Robert M. 1988. "Ethnic Hegemony and the Japanese of California." *American Sociological Review,* 53:353–367.

Joe, Jennie, & Miller, Dorothy. 1994. "Cultural Survival and Contemporary American Indian Women in the City." In Maxine Zinn & Bonnie T. Dill (Eds.), *Women of Color in U.S. Society.* Philadelphia: Temple University Press.

Jones, Jeffrey. 2001. "Racial or Ethnic Labels Make Little Difference to Blacks, Hispanics." Retrieved from the World Wide Web on July 5, 2002, at www.gallup.com/poll/releases/pr010911.asp.

Jordan, Winthrop. 1968. *White Over Black: American Attitudes Towards the Negro: 1550–1812.* Chapel Hill: University of North Carolina Press.

Josephy, Alvin M. 1968. *The Indian Heritage of America.* New York: Knopf.

Kallen, Horace M. 1915a. "Democracy Versus the Melting Pot." *The Nation,* February 18, pp. 190–194.

_____. 1915b. "Democracy Versus the Melting Pot." *The Nation,* February 25, pp. 217–222.

Kamen, Al. 1992. "After Immigration, An Unexpected Fear: New Jersey's Indian Community Is Terrorized by Racial Violence." *Washington Post,* November 16, A1.

Kasarda, John D. 1989. "Urban Industrial Transition and the Underclass." *Annals of the American Academy of Political and Social Sciences,* 501:26–47.

Katz, Phyllis. 1976. "The Acquisition of Racial Attitudes in Children." In Phyllis Katz (Ed.), *Towards the Elimination of Racism* (pp. 125–154). New York: Pergamon.

Kennedy, Randall. 2001. "Racial Trends in the Administration of Criminal Justice." In Neil J. Smelser, William Julius Wilson, & Faith Mitchell (Eds.), *America Becoming: Racial Trends and Their Consequences* (Vol. 2, pp. 1–20). Washington, DC: National Academy Press.

Kennedy, Ruby Jo. 1952. "Single or Triple Melting Pot: Intermarriage Trends in New Haven, 1870–1950." *American Journal of Sociology,* 58:56–59.

_____. 1944. "Single or Triple Melting Pot: Intermarriage Trends in New Haven, 1870–1940." *American Journal of Sociology,* 49:331–339.

Kephart, William, & Zellner, William. 1994. *Extraordinary Groups.* New York: St. Martin's.

Killian, Lewis. 1975. *The Impossible Revolution, Phase 2: Black Power and the American Dream.* New York: Random House.

Kim, Kwang Chung, Hurh, Won Moo, & Fernandez, Marilyn. 1989. "Intra-group Differences in Business Participation: Three Asian Immigrant Groups." *International Migration Review,* 23:73–95.

Kinder, Donald R., & Sears, David O. 1981. "Prejudice and Politics: Symbolic Racism Versus Racial Threats to the Good Life." *Journal of Personality and Social Psychology,* 40:414–431.

Kinder, Donald, & Winter, Nicholas. 2001. "Exploring the Racial Divide: Blacks, Whites, and Opinion on National Policy." *American Journal of Political Science,* 45:439–453.

King, Martin Luther Jr. 1968. *Where Do We Go from Here: Chaos or Community?* New York: Harper & Row.

_____. 1963. *Why We Can't Wait.* New York: Mentor.

_____. 1958. *Stride Toward Freedom: The Montgomery Story.* New York: Harper & Row.

Kitano, Harry H. L. 1980. "Japanese." In Stephen Thornstrom (Ed.), *Harvard Encyclopedia of Ethnic Groups* (pp. 561–571). Cambridge, MA: Harvard University Press.

_____. 1976. *Japanese Americans.* Englewood Cliffs, NJ: Prentice Hall.

Kitano, Harry, & Daniels, Roger. 2001. *Asian Americans: Emerging Minorities* (3rd ed.). Upper Saddle River, NJ: Prentice Hall.

_____. 1995. *Asian Americans: Emerging Minorities* (2nd ed.). Englewood Cliffs, NJ: Prentice Hall.

_____. 1988. *Asian Americans: Emerging Minorities.* Englewood Cliffs, NJ: Prentice Hall.

Kleg, Milton, & Yamamoto, Kaoru. 1998. "As the World Turns: Ethno-Racial Distances After 70 Years." *The Social Science Journal,* 35:183–190.

Kluegel, James R., & Smith, Eliot R. 1982. "Whites' Beliefs About Blacks' Opportunities." *American Sociological Review,* 47:518–532.

Kraybill, Donald B., & Bowman, Carl F. 2001. *On the Backroad to Heaven: Old Order Hutterites, Mennonites, Amish, and Brethren.* Baltimore: Johns Hopkins University Press.

Kuperman, Diane. 2001. "Stuck at the Gates of Paradise." *Unesco Courier,* September, pp. 24–26.

Kwong, Peter. 1987. *The New Chinatown.* New York: Hill and Wang.

Labaton, Stephen. 1994. "Denny's Restaurants to Pay $54 Million in Race Bias Suits." *The New York Times,* May 25, p. A1.

Lach, Jennifer. 2000. "Interracial Friendships." *American Demographics,* January (p. n.a.).

Lacy, Dan. 1972. *The White Use of Blacks in America.* New York: McGraw-Hill.

Lai, H. M. 1980. "Chinese." In Stephen Thornstrom (Ed.), *Harvard Encyclopedia of Ethnic Groups* (pp. 217–234). Cambridge, MA: Harvard University Press.

Lamont-Brown, Raymond. 1993. "The Burakumin: Japan's Underclass." *Contemporary Review,* 263:136–140.

Landale, Nancy, & Oropesa, R. S. 2002. "White, Black, or Puerto Rican? Racial Self-Identification Among Mainland and Island Puerto Ricans." *Social Forces,* 81:231–254.

LaPiere, Robert. 1934. "Attitudes vs. Actions." *Social Forces,* 13:230–237.

Lee, Sharon. 1998. "Asian Americans: Diverse and Growing." *Population Bulletin* (Vol. 53, No. 2). Washington, DC: Population Reference Bureau.

Lee, Sharon, & Fernandez, Marilyn. 1998. "Trends in Asian American Racial/Ethnic Intermarriage: A

Comparison of 1980 and 1990 Census Data." *Sociological Perspectives,* 41:323–343.

Lee, Sharon M., & Yamanaka, Keiko. 1990. "Patterns of Asian American Intermarriage and Marital Assimilation." *Journal of Comparative Family Studies,* 21:287–305.

Lenski, Gerhard, Nolan, Patrick, & Lenski, Jean. 1995. *Human Societies: An Introduction to Macrosociology* (7th ed.). New York: McGraw-Hill.

Levine, Lawrence. 1977. *Black Culture and Black Consciousness.* New York: Oxford University Press.

Levy, Jacques. 1975. *Cesar Chavez: Autobiography of La Causa.* New York: Norton.

Lewis, Mark. 2003. "Bush Faults Preferences (Opposes Affirmative Action on College Admissions)." *The New York Times,* January 19, pp. WK2(N)–WK2(L).

Lewis, Oscar. 1966. "The Culture of Poverty." *Scientific American,* October, pp. 19–25.

———. 1965. *La Vida: A Puerto Rican Family in the Culture of Poverty.* New York: Random House.

———. 1959. *Five Families: Mexican Case Studies in the Culture of Poverty.* New York: Basic Books.

Li, Peter. 1990. *Race and Ethnic Relations in Canada.* Toronto: Oxford University Press.

Lieberson, Stanley. 1980. *A Piece of the Pie: Blacks and White Immigrants Since 1880.* Berkeley: University of California Press.

Lieberson, Stanley, & Waters, Mary C. 1988. *From Many Strands.* New York: Russell Sage.

Light, Ivan, & Bonacich, Edna. 1988. *Immigrant Entrepreneurs: Koreans in Los Angeles, 1965–1982.* Berkeley: University of California Press.

Lincoln, C. Eric. 1961. *The Black Muslims in America.* Boston: Beacon.

Ling, Huping. 2000. "Family and Marriage of Late-Nineteenth and Early-Twentieth Century Chinese Immigrant Women." *Journal of American Ethnic History,* 9:43–65.

Locust, Carol. 1990. "Wounding the Spirit: Discrimination and Traditional American Indian Belief Systems." In Gail Thomas (Ed.), *U.S. Race Relations in the 1980s and 1990s: Challenges and Alternatives* (pp. 219–232). New York: Hemisphere.

Logan, John, Alba, Richard, & McNulty, Thomas. 1994. "Ethnic Economies in Metropolitan Regions: Miami and Beyond." *Social Forces,* 72:691–724.

A Long-Overdue Scalping: Justice for Indians. 2002. *The Economist,* March 23 (p. n. a). Retrieved from the World Wide Web on April 8, 2003, at http://www.uwec.edu/geography/Ivogeler/w188/Indians/lawsuit.htm.

Lopata, Helena Znaniecki. 1976. *Polish Americans.* Englewood Cliffs, NJ: Prentice Hall.

Luciuk, Lubomyr, & Hryniuk, Stelkla (Eds.). 1991. *Canada's Ukrainians Negotiating an Identity.* Toronto: University of Toronto Press.

Lurie, Nancy Oestrich. 1982. "The American Indian: Historical Background." In Norman Yetman & C. Hoy Steele (Eds.), *Majority and Minority* (3rd ed., pp. 131–144). Boston: Allyn & Bacon.

Lyman, Stanford. 1974. *Chinese Americans.* New York: Random House.

Malcolm X. 1964. *The Autobiography of Malcolm X.* New York: Grove.

Mangiafico, Luciano. 1988. *Contemporary American Immigrants.* New York: Praeger.

Mannix, Daniel P. 1962. *Black Cargoes: A History of the Atlantic Slave Trade.* New York: Viking.

Marcelli, Enrico, & Heer, David. 1998. "The Unauthorized Mexican Immigrant Population and Welfare in Los Angeles County: A Comparative Statistical Analysis." *Sociological Perspectives,* 41:279–303.

Margolis, Richard. 1989. "If We Won, Why Aren't We Smiling?" In Charles Willie (Ed.), *Round Two of the Willie/Wilson Debate* (2nd ed., pp. 95–100). Dix Hills, NY: General Hall.

Martin, Philip, & Midgley, Elizabeth. 1999. "Immigration to the United States." *Population Bulletin* (Vol. 54, No. 2). Washington, DC: Population Reference Bureau.

Marx, Karl, & Engels, Friedrich. 1967. *The Communist Manifesto.* Baltimore: Penguin. (Original work published 1848)

Massarik, Fred, & Chenkin, Alvin. 1973. "United States National Jewish Population Study: A First Report." In American Jewish Committee, *American Jewish Year Book, 1973* (pp. 264–306). New York: American Jewish Committee.

Massey, Douglas. 2000. "Housing Discrimination 101." *Population Today,* 28:1, 4.

———. 1995. "The New Immigration and Ethnicity in the United States." *Population and Development Review,* 21:631–652.

Massey, Douglas, & Denton, Nancy. 1993. *American Apartheid.* Cambridge, MA: Harvard University Press.

———. 1992. "Residential Segregation of Asian Origin Groups in U.S. Metropolitan Areas." *Sociology and Social Research,* 76:170–177.

Massey, Douglas, & Singer, Audrey. 1995. "New Estimates of Undocumented Mexican Migration to the United States and the Probability of Apprehension." *Demography,* 32:203–213.

Mauer, Marc, & Huling, Tracy. 2000. "Young Black Americans and the Criminal Justice System." In

Jerome Skolnick & Elliot Currie (Eds.), *Crisis in American Institutions* (11th ed., pp. 417–424). New York: Allyn & Bacon.

McConahy, John B. 1986. "Modern Racism, Ambivalence, and the Modern Racism Scale." In John F. Dovidio & Samuel Gartner (Eds.), *Prejudice, Discrimination and Racism* (pp. 91–125). Orlando, FL: Academic Press.

McFarlane, Bruce. 1988. *Yugoslavia: Politics, Economics and Society.* London: Pinter.

McLemore, S. Dale. 1973. "The Origins of Mexican American Subordination in Texas." *Social Science Quarterly,* 53:656–679.

McNickle, D'Arcy. 1973. *Native American Tribalism: Indian Survivals and Renewals.* New York: Oxford University Press.

McRoberts, Kenneth. 1988. *Quebec: Social Change and Political Crisis.* Toronto: McClelland and Stewart.

McWilliams, Carey. 1961. *North from Mexico: The Spanish Speaking People of the United States.* New York: Monthly Review Press.

Min, Pyong Gap. 1995. *Asian Americans: Contemporary Trends and Issues.* Thousand Oaks, CA: Sage.

Mirandé, Alfredo. 1985. *The Chicano Experience: An Alternative Perspective.* Notre Dame, IN: University of Notre Dame Press.

Mirandé, Alfredo, & Enríquez, Evangelica. 1979. *La Chicana: The Mexican-American Woman.* Chicago: University of Chicago Press.

Moore, Joan W. 1970. *Mexican Americans.* Englewood Cliffs, NJ: Prentice Hall.

Moore, Joan W., & Pachon, Harry. 1985. *Hispanics in the United States.* Englewood Cliffs, NJ: Prentice Hall.

Moore, Joan, & Pinderhughes, Raquel. 1993. *In the Barrios: Latinos and the Underclass Debate.* New York: Russell Sage.

Moquin, Wayne and Van Doren, Charles (Eds.) 1971. *A Documentary History of Mexican Americans.* New York: Bantam.

Morawska, Ewa. 1990. "The Sociology and Historiography of Immigration." In Virginia Yans-McLaughlin (Ed.), *Immigration Reconsidered: History, Sociology, and Politics* (pp. 187–328). New York: Oxford University Press.

Morgan, Edmund. 1975. *American Slavery, American Freedom.* New York: Norton.

Morin, Richard, & Cottman, Michael. 2001. "Discrimination's Lingering Sting." *Washington Post,* June 22, A1.

Morris, Aldon D. 1984. *The Origins of the Civil Rights Movement.* New York: Free Press.

Moynihan, Daniel. 1965. *The Negro Family: The Case for National Action.* Washington, DC: U.S. Department of Labor.

Myrdal, Gunnar. 1962. *An American Dilemma: The Negro Problem and Modern Democracy.* New York: Harper & Row. (Original work published 1944)

Nabakov, Peter (Ed.). 1999. *Native American Testimony.* (Rev. ed.). New York: Penguin.

National Advisory Commission. 1968. *Report of the National Advisory Commission on Civil Disorders.* New York: New York Times.

National Opinion Research Council (NORC). 1972–2000. *General Social Survey.* Chicago: Author.

National Origins Act, Pub. L. 139, Chapter 190, § 43 Stat. 153 (1924).

Nelli, Humbert S. 1980. "Italians." In Stephen Thornstrom (Ed.), *Harvard Encyclopedia of Ethnic Groups* (pp. 545–560). Cambridge, MA: Harvard University Press.

Nishi, Setsuko. 1995. "Japanese Americans." In Pyong Gap Min (Ed.), *Asian Americans: Contemporary Trends and Issues* (pp. 95-133). Thousand Oaks, CA: Sage.

Noel, Donald. 1968. "A Theory of the Origin of Ethnic Stratification." *Social Problems,* 16:157–172.

Nolan, Patrick, & Lenski, Gerhard. 1999. *Human Societies: An Introduction to Macrosociology* (8th ed.). New York: McGraw-Hill.

Novak, Michael. 1973. *The Rise of the Unmeltable Ethnics: Politics and Culture in the 1970s.* New York: Collier.

O'Hare, William P. 1992. "America's Minorities: The Demographics of Diversity." *Population Bulletin* (Vol. 47, No. 4). Washington, DC: Population Reference Bureau.

O'Hare, William, Pollard, Kelvin, Mann, Taynia, & Kent, Mary. 1991. *African Americans in the 1990s.* Washington, DC: Population Reference Bureau.

O'Hare, William P., & Usdansky, Margaret. 1992. "What the 1990 Census Tells Us About Segregation in 25 Large Metros." *Population Today* (Vol. 20, No. 9). Washington, DC: Population Reference Bureau.

Oliver, Melvin, & Shapiro, Thomas. 2001. "Wealth and Racial Stratification." In Neil J. Smelser, William Julius Wilson, & Faith Mitchell (Eds.), *America Becoming: Racial Trends and Their Consequences* (Vol. 1, pp. 222–251.). Washington, DC: National Academy Press.

———. 1995. *Black Wealth, White Wealth.* New York: Routledge.

Olson, James, & Wilson, Raymond. 1984. *Native Americans in the Twentieth Century.* Provo, UT: Brigham Young University Press.

Omi, Michael, & Winant, Howard. 1986. *Racial Formation in the United States From the 1960s to the 1980s.* New York: Routledge and Kegan Paul.

Orfield, Gary. 2001. *Schools More Separate: Consequences of a Decade of Resegregation.* Cambridge, MA: Harvard University, The Civil Rights Project. Retrieved from the World Wide Web on April 10, 2003, at www.civilrightsproject. harvard.edu/research/deseg/separate_schools01. php.

Orreniou, Pia. 2001. "Illegal Immigration and Enforcement Along the U.S.-Mexico Border: An Overview." *Economic & Financial Review,* 2002:2–11.

Oswalt, Wendell, & Neely, Sharlotte. 1996. *This Land Was Theirs.* Mountain View, CA: Mayfield.

Parish, Peter J. 1989. *Slavery: History and Historians.* New York: Harper & Row.

Park, Robert E., & Burgess, Ernest W. 1924. *Introduction to the Science of Society.* Chicago: University of Chicago Press.

Parke, Ross, & Buriel, Raymond. 2002. "Socialization Concerns in African American, American Indian, Asian American, and Latino Families." In Nijole Benokraitis (Ed.), *Contemporary Ethnic Families in the United States* (pp. 18–29). Upper Saddle River, NJ: Prentice Hall.

Parrado, Emilio, & Zenteno, Rene. 2001. "Economic Restructuring, Financial Crises, and Women's Work in Mexico." *Social Problems,* 48:456–477.

Pego, David. 1998. "To Educate a Nation: Native American Tribe Hopes to Bring Higher Education to an Arizona Reservation." *Black Issues in Higher Education,* 15:60–63.

Perez, Lisandro. 1980. "Cubans." In Stephen Thornstrom (Ed.), *Harvard Encyclopedia of Ethnic Groups* (pp. 256–261). Cambridge, MA: Harvard University Press.

Petersen, Williams. 1971. *Japanese Americans.* New York: Random House.

Peterson, Mark. 1995. "Leading Cuban-American Entrepreneurs: The Process of Developing Motives, Abilities, and Resources." *Human Relations,* 48:1193–1216.

Pettigrew, Thomas. 1971. *Racially Separate or Together?* New York: McGraw-Hill.

_____. 1958. "Personality and Sociocultural Factors in Intergroup Attitudes: A Cross-National Comparison." *Journal of Conflict Resolution,* 2:29–42.

Phillips, Ulrich B. 1918. *American Negro Slavery.* New York: Appleton and Company.

Pilger, John. 2000. "Australia Is the Only Developed Country Whose Government Has Been Condemned as Racist by the United Nations." *New Statesman,* 129:17.

Pitt, Leonard. 1970. *The Decline of the Californios: A Social History of the Spanish-Speaking Californians, 1846–1890.* Berkeley: University of California Press.

Plessy v. Ferguson, 163 U.S. 537 (1896).

Pollard, Kelvin, & O'Hare, William. 1999. "America's Racial and Ethnic Minorities." *Population Bulletin* (Vol. 52, No. 3). Washington, DC: Population Reference Bureau.

Polner, Murray. 1993. "Asian Americans Say They Are Treated Like Foreigners." *The New York Times,* March 7, p. 1.

Portes, Alejandro. 1990. "From South of the Border: Hispanic Minorities in the United States." In Virginia Yans-McLaughlin (Ed.), *Immigration Reconsidered* (pp. 160–184). New York: Oxford University Press.

Portes, Alejandro, & Bach, Robert L. 1985. *Latin Journey: Cuban and Mexican Immigrants in the United States.* Berkeley: University of California Press.

Portes, Alejandro, & Manning, Robert. 1986. "The Immigrant Enclave: Theory and Empirical Examples." In Susan Olzak & Joane Nagel (Eds.), *Competitive Ethnic Relations* (pp. 47–68). New York: Academic Press.

Portes, Alejandro, & Rumbaut, Rubén G. 2001. *Legacies: The Story of the Immigrant Second Generation.* Berkeley: University of California Press.

_____. 1996. *Immigrant America: A Portrait* (2nd ed.). Berkeley: University of California Press.

Portes, Alejandro, & Zhou, Min. 1993. "The New Second Generation: Segmented Assimilation and Its Variants." In *Annals of the American Academy of Political and Social Sciences,* 530:74–96.

Posadas, Barbara. 1999. *The Filipino Americans.* Westport, CT: Greenwood.

Potter, George. 1973. *To the Golden Door: The Story of the Irish in Ireland and America.* Westport, CT: Greenwood.

Powlishta, K., Serbin, L., Doyle, A., & White, D. 1994. "Gender, Ethnic, and Body-Type Biases: The Generality of Prejudice in Childhood." *Developmental Psychology,* 30:526–537.

Proctor, Bernadette, & Dalakar, Joseph. 2002. *Poverty in the United States, 2001* (Current Population Reports P60-219). Washington, DC: Government Printing Office.

Rader, Benjamin G. 1983. *American Sports: From the Age of Folk Games to the Age of Spectators.* Englewood Cliffs, NJ: Prentice Hall.

Rawick, George P. 1972. *From Sundown to Sunup: The Making of the Black Community.* Westport, CT: Greenwood.

Raymer, Patricia. 1974. "Wisconsin's Menominees: Indians on a Seesaw." *National Geographic,* August, pp. 228–251.

Remington, Robin. 1997. "Ethnonationalism and the Disintegration of Yugoslavia. In Winston Van Horne (Ed.), *Global Convulsions: Race, Ethnicity, and Nationalism at the End of the Twentieth Century* (pp. 261-279). Albany: State University of New York Press.

Rifkin, Jeremy. 1996. *The End of Work: The Decline of the Global Labor Force and the Dawn of the Post-Market Era.* New York: Putnam.

Rinaldi, Alfred. 1999. "No Turks, Please, We're German." *New Statesman,* 128:23–25.

Roberts, Johnnie. 2002. "The Race to the Top." *Newsweek,* January 28, pp. 44–49.

Robertson, Claire. 1996. "Africa and the Americas? Slavery and Women, the Family, and the Gender Division of Labor." In David Gaspar & Darlene Hine (Eds.), *More Than Chattel: Black Women and Slavery in the Americas* (pp. 4–40). Bloomington: Indiana University Press.

Rodriguez, Clara. 1989. *Puerto Ricans: Born in the USA.* Boston: Unwin Hyman.

Rodriguez, Clara, & Cordero-Guzman, Hector. 1992. "Placing Race in Context." *Ethnic and Racial Studies,* 15:523–542.

Rouse, Linda, & Hanson, Jeffery. 1991. "American Indian Stereotyping, Resource Competition, and Status-Based Prejudice." *American Indian Culture and Research Journal,* 15:1–17.

Royster, Deirdre A. In press. *Race and the "Invisible Hand": The Power of Segregated Networks in the Blue Collar Trades.* Berkeley: University of California Press.

Rumbaut, Rubén. 1995. "Vietnamese, Laotian, and Cambodian Americans." In Pyong Gap Min (Ed.), *Asian Americans: Contemporary Issues and Trends* (pp. 232–270). Thousand Oaks, CA: Sage.

_____. 1991. "Passage to America: Perspectives on the New Immigration." In Alan Wolfe (Ed.), *America at Century's End* (pp. 208–244). Berkeley: University of California Press.

Russell, James W. 1994. *After the Fifth Sun: Class and Race in North America.* Englewood Cliffs, NJ: Prentice Hall.

Saenz, Rogelio. 1999. "Mexican Americans." In Anthony Dworkin & Rosalind Dworkin (Eds.), *The Minority Report* (pp. 209–229). Orlando, FL: Harcourt Brace.

Sanchirico, Andrew. 1991. "The Importance of Small Business Ownership in Chinese American Educational Achievement." *Sociology of Education,* 64:293–304.

Schlesinger, Arthur M. Jr. 1992. *The Disuniting of America: Reflections on a Multicultural Society.* New York: Norton.

Schmitt, Eric. 2001. "New Census Shows Hispanics Are Even With Blacks in U.S. *The New York Times,* March 8, p. A1.

Schoener, Allon. 1967. *Portal to America: The Lower East Side, 1870–1925.* New York: Holt, Rinehart & Winston.

Sears, David. 1988. "Symbolic Racism." In Phyllis Katz & Dalmas Taylor (Eds.), *Eliminating Racism: Profiles in Controversy* (pp. 53–84). New York: Plenum.

See, Katherine O'Sullivan, & Wilson, William J. 1988. "Race and Ethnicity." In Neil Smelser (Ed.), *Handbook of Sociology* (pp. 223–242). Newbury Park, CA: Sage.

Seller, Maxine S. 1987. "Beyond the Stereotype: A New Look at the Immigrant Woman." In Ronald Takaki (Ed.), *From Different Shores: Perspectives on Race and Ethnicity in America* (pp. 197–203). New York: Oxford University Press.

Selzer, Michael. 1972. *"Kike": Anti-Semitism in America.* New York: Meridian.

Shannon, William V. 1964. *The American Irish.* New York: Macmillan.

Sheet Metal Workers v. EEOC, 478 U.S. 421 (1986).

Shelton, Beth Anne, & John, Daphne. 1996. "The Division of Household Labor." *Annual Review of Sociology,* 22:299–322.

Sherif, Muzafer, Harvey, O. J., White, B. Jack, Hood, William, & Sherif, Carolyn. 1961. *Intergroup Conflict and Cooperation: The Robber's Cave Experiment.* Norman, OK: University Book Exchange.

Sheth, Manju. 1995. "Asian Indian Americans." In Pyong Gap Min (Ed.), *Asian Americans: Contemporary Issues and Trends* (pp. 169–198). Thousand Oaks, CA: Sage.

Shinagawa, Larry, & Pang, Gin Yong. 1996. "Asian American Panethnicity and Intermarriage." *Amerasia Journal,* 22:127–153.

Simon, Julian. 1989. *The Economic Consequences of Immigration.* Cambridge, MA: Blackwell.

Simpson, George, & Yinger, Milton. 1985. *Racial and Cultural Minorities: An Analysis of Prejudice and Discrimination.* New York: Plenum.

Sklare, Marshall. 1971. *America's Jews.* New York: Random House.

Smedley, Audrey. 1999. *Race in North America: Origin and Evolution of a Worldview* (2nd ed.). Boulder, CO: Westview.

Smith, David, & Chambers, Gerald. 1991. *Inequality in Northern Ireland.* Oxford: Clarendon.

Smith, James, & Edmonston, Barry (Eds.). 1997. *The New Americans: Economic, Demographic, and*

Fiscal Effects of Immigration. Washington, DC: National Academy Press.

Smith, Tom, & Dempsey, Glenn. 1983. "The Polls: Ethnic Social Distance and Prejudice." *Public Opinion Quarterly,* 47:584–600.

Snipp, C. Matthew. 1996. "The First Americans: American Indians." In Silvia Pedraza & Ruben Rumbaut (Eds.), *Origins and Destinies: Immigration, Race, and Ethnicity in America* (pp. 390–403). Belmont, CA: Wadsworth.

_____. 1992. "Sociological Perspectives on American Indians." *Annual Review of Sociology,* 18:351–371.

_____. 1989. *American Indians: The First of This Land.* New York: Russell Sage.

"A Sorry Tale." 2000. *The Economist,* 356:12.

Spicer, Edward H. 1980. "American Indians." In Stephan Thernstrom (Ed.), *Harvard Encyclopedia of Ethnic Groups* (pp. 58–122). Cambridge, MA: Harvard University Press.

Spickard, Paul. 1996. *Japanese Americans: The Formation and Transformations of an Ethnic Group.* New York: Twayne.

Spilde, Kate. 2001. "The Economic Development Journey of Indian Nations." Retrieved from the World Wide Web on July 5, 2002, at indiangaming. org/library/newsletters/index.html.

Stampp, Kenneth. 1956. *The Peculiar Institution: Slavery in the Ante-Bellum South.* New York: Random House.

Staples, Robert. 1988. "The Black American Family." In Charles Mindel, Robert Habenstein, & Roosevelt Wright (Eds.), *Ethnic Families in America* (3rd ed., pp. 303–324). New York: Elsevier.

Steinberg, Stephen. 1981. *The Ethnic Myth: Race, Ethnicity, and Class in America.* New York: Atheneum.

Stelcner, Morton. 2000. "Earnings Differentials Among Ethnic Groups in Canada: A Review of the Research." *Review of Social Economy,* 58: 295–317.

Stoddard, Ellwyn. 1973. *Mexican Americans.* New York: Random House.

Stuckey, Sterling. 1987. *Slave Culture: Nationalist Theory and the Foundations of Black America.* New York: Harper & Row.

Sung, Betty Lee. 1990. "Chinese American Intermarriage." *Journal of Comparative Family Studies,* 21:337–352.

Sweetman, Arthur, & Dicks, Gordon. 1999. "Education and Ethnicity in Canada." *Journal of Human Resources,* 34: 668–690.

Takaki, Ronald. 1993. *A Different Mirror: A History of Multicultural America.* Boston: Little, Brown.

Tannenbaum, Frank. 1947. *Slave and Citizen: The Negro in the Americas.* New York: Knopf.

Taylor, Jared, & Whitney, Glayde. 1999. "Crime and Racial Profiling by U.S. Police: Is There an Empirical Basis?" *Journal of Social, Political and Economic Studies,* 24:485–516.

Thernstrom, Stephan, & Thernstrom, Abigail. 1997. *America in Black and White.* New York: Simon & Schuster.

Thomas, Melvin. 1993. "Race, Class, and Personal Income: An Empirical Test of the Declining Significance of Race Thesis, 1968–1988." *Social Problems,* 40:328–342.

Thornton, Russell. 2001. "Trends Among American Indians in the United States." In Neil J. Smelser, William Julius Wilson, & Faith Mitchell (Eds.), *America Becoming: Racial Trends and Their Consequences* (Vol. 1, pp. 135–169). Washington, DC: National Academy Press.

Tilly, Charles. 1990. "Transplanted Networks." In Virginia Yans-McLaughlin (Ed.), *Immigration Reconsidered: History, Sociology, and Politics* (pp. 79–95). New York: Oxford University Press.

Tsai, Shih-Shan Henry. 1986. *The Chinese Experience in America.* Bloomington: Indiana University Press.

Udry, Richard. 2000. "Biological Limits of Gender Construction." *American Sociological Review,* 65:443–457.

United Nations. 2000. "United Nations Releases Most Recent Statistics on World's Women." Retrieved from the World Wide Web on June 27, 2002, at unstats.un.org/unsd/demographic/ww2000/ww2 000pr.htm.

United Steelworkers of America, AFL-CIO-CLC v. Weber, 443 U.S. 193 (1979).

U.S. Bureau of Indian Affairs. 1997. "1997 Labor Market Information on the Indian Labor Force." Retrieved from the World Wide Web on May 17, 2002, at www.doi.gov/bia/Labor/97LFR CovFinal. pdf.

_____. 1991. *American Indians Today: Answers to Your Questions.* Washington, DC: U.S. Department of the Interior.

U.S. Bureau of the Census. 2000. *Total Money Income in 1999 of Families by Type, and Race and Hispanic Origin of the Householder.* Retrieved from the World Wide Web on July 11, 2002, at: http://www.census.gov/population/socdemo/race/ api/ppl-146/tab15.txt

_____2003a. *The Black Population of the United States, March 2002.* Retrieved from the World Wide Web on April 25, 2003, at www.census.gov/ prod/2003pubs/p20-541.pdf.

_____. 2003b. *Race and Hispanic Origin of People by Median Income and Sex: 1948-2001.* Retrieved from the World Wide Web on April 24, 2003, at www.census.gov/hhes/income/histinc/p02.html.

U.S. Bureau of the Census. 2003c. *Statistical Abstract of the United States, 2002* (122nd ed.). Washington, DC: Government Printing Office.

———. 2002. *Statistical Abstract of the United States, 2001* (121st ed.). Washington, DC: Government Printing Office.

———. 2001a. *Overview of Race and Hispanic Origin*. Retrieved from the World Wide Web on June 17, 2002, at blue.census.gov/prod/2001 pubs/c2kbr01–1.pdf.

———. 2001b. *Profiles of General Demographic Characteristics, 2000*. Retrieved from the World Wide Web on July 5, 2002, at www.census.gov/prod/cen2000/dp1/2kh00.pdf.

———. 2000a. *Earnings of Full-Time, Year-Round Workers 15 Years and Over in 1999 by Sex, Hispanic Origin, and Race*. Retrieved from the World Wide Web on July 8, 2002, at http://www.census.gov/population/socdemo/hispanic/p20–535/tab11–2.txt and www.census.gov/population/socdemo/hispanic/p20–535/tab11–3.txt.

———. 2000b. *Educational Attainment of the Population 25 Years and Over by Sex, Hispanic Origin, and Race*. Retrieved from the World Wide Web on July 8, 2002, at www.census.gov/population/socdemo/hispanic/p20–535/tab07–2.txt.

———. 2000c. *Educational Attainment of the Population 25 Years and Over by Sex, and Race and Hispanic Origin*. Retrieved from the World Wide Web on July 11, 2002, at http://www.census.gov/population/socdemo/race/api/ppl-146/tab07.txt.

———. 2000d. *Historical Income Tables-Families*. Retrieved from the World Wide Web on July 2, 2002, at www.census.gov/hhes/income/histinc/f05.html.

———. 2000e. *Major Occupation Group of the Employed Civilian Population 16 Years and Over by Sex, and Race and Hispanic Origin*. Retrieved from the World Wide Web on July 11, 2002, at www.census.gov/population/socdemo/race/api/ppl-146/tab11.txt.

———. 2000f. *Number of People, 2000. Hispanic or Latino Origin, All Races*. Retrieved from the World Wide Web on July 8, 2002, at www.census.gov/population/cen2000/atlas/censr01–111.pdf. (See map referenced in thumbnail #5)

———. 2000g. *Number of People, 2000. One Race: American Indian and Alaska Native*. Retrieved from the World Wide Web on July 2, 2002, at www.census.gov/population/cen2000/atlas/censr01–107.pdf. (See map referenced in thumbnail #6)

———. 2000h. *Number of People, 2000. One Race: Asian*. Retrieved from the World Wide Web on July 10, 2002, at www.census.gov/population/cen2000/atlas/censr01–108.pdf. (See map referenced in thumbnail #6)

———. 2000i. *Number of People, 2000. One Race: Black or African American*. Retrieved from the World Wide Web on July 2, 2002, at www.census.gov/population/cen2000/atlas/censr01–106.pdf. (See map referenced in thumbnail #6)

———. 2000j. *Occupation of the Employed Civilian Population 16 Years and Over by Sex, Hispanic Origin, and Race*. Retrieved from the World Wide Web on July 8, 2002, at www.census.gov/population/socdemo/hispanic/p20–535/tab10–2.txt.

———. 2000k. *Population by Metropolitan-Nonmetropolitan Residence, Sex, Hispanic Origin, and Race, With Percent Distribution by Hispanic Origin and Race*. Retrieved from the World Wide Web on July 8, 2002, at www.census.gov/population/socdemo/hispanic/p20–535/tab21–1.txt.

———. 2000l. *Population by Metropolitan and Nonmetropolitan Residence, Sex, and Race and Hispanic Origin*. Retrieved from the World Wide Web on July 11, 2002, at www.census.gov/population/socdemo/race/api/ppl-146/tab21.pdf.

———. 2000m. *Population by Region, Sex, Hispanic Origin, and Race, With Percentage Distribution by Hispanic Origin and Race: March 2000*. Retrieved from the World Wide Web on July 8, 2002, at www.census.gov/population/socdemo/hispanic/p20–535/tab19–1.txt.

———. 2000n. *Population, Race, Hispanic or Latino. Hawaii*. Retrieved from the World Wide Web on July 12, 2002, at factfinder.census.gov/bf/_lang=en_vt_name=DEC_2000_PL_U_QTPL_geo_id=04000US15.html.

———. 2000o. *Poverty Status of Families in 1999 by Family Type, and by Hispanic Origin and Race of Householder*. Retrieved from the World Wide Web on July 8, 2002, at www.census.gov/population/socdemo/hispanic/p20–535/tab15–1.txt.

———. 2000p. *Poverty Status of Families in 1999 by Type, and Race and Hispanic Origin of the Householder*. Retrieved from the World Wide Web on July 11, 2002, at www.census.gov/population/socdemo/race/api/ppl-146/tab17.txt.

———. 2000q. *Profiles of General Demographic Characteristics, 2000*. Retrieved from the World Wide Web on July 2, 2002, at www.census.gov/prod/cen2000/dp1/2khus.pdf.

———. 2000r. *Profiles of General Demographic Characteristics, 2000* (Table DP-1). Retrieved from the World Wide Web on July 5, 2002, at www.census.gov/prod/cen2000/dp1/2khus.pdf.

_____. 2000s. *Profiles of General Demographic Characteristics, 2000*. Retrieved from the World Wide Web on July 8, 2002, at www2.census.gov/census_2000/datasets/demographic_profile/Florida/2kh12.pdf.

_____. 2000t. *Quarterly Estimates of the United States Foreign-Born and Native Resident Populations*. Retrieved from the World Wide Web on July 8, 2002, at eire.censusgov/popest/archives/national/us_nativity/fbtab001.txt.

_____. 2000u. *Race and Hispanic Origin of People by Median Income and Sex: 1947 to 2000*. Retrieved from the World Wide Web on July 2, 2002, at www.census.gov/hhes/income/histinc/p02.html.

_____. 2000v. *Statistical Abstract of the United States, 2000* (120th ed.). Retrieved from the World Wide Web on April 10, 2003 at www.census.gov/prod/2003pubs/02statab/pop.pdf.

_____. 2000w. *Total Money Income in 1999 of Families by Type, and Race and Hispanic Origin of the Householder*. Retrieved from the World Wide Web on July 11, 2002, at www.census.gov/population/socdemo/race/api/ppl-146/ tab15.txt.

_____. 1999. *Statistical Abstract of the United States, 1999* (119th ed.). Washington, DC: Government Printing Office.

_____. 1998a. *Educational Attainment for Selected Ancestry Groups*. Retrieved from the World Wide Web on July 11, 2002, at www.census.gov/population/socdemo/ancestry/table_01.txt.

_____. 1998b. "Income and Poverty for Selected Ancestry Groups." Retrieved from the World Wide Web on July 11, 2002, at www.census.gov/population/socdemo/ancestry/table_04.txt.

_____. 1997. *Statistical Abstract of the United States: 1996* (116th ed.). Washington, DC: Government Printing Office.

_____. 1995. *Selected Social and Economic Characteristics for the 25 Largest American Indian Tribes: 1990*. Retrieved from the World Wide Web on July 5, 2002, at www.census.gov/population/socdemo/race/indian/ailang2.txt.

_____. 1993. *Statistical Abstract of the United States: 1993* (113th ed.). Washington, DC: Government Printing Office.

_____. 1992. *Statistical Abstract of the United States: 1992* (112th ed.). Washington, DC: Government Printing Office.

_____. 1990. *Summary Population and Housing Characteristics: United States*. Washington, DC: Government Printing Office.

_____. 1988. *Statistical Abstract of the United States: 1988* (108th ed.) Washington, DC: Government Printing Office.

_____. 1979. *Current Population Survey*. Washington, DC: Government Printing Office.

_____. 1977. *Statistical Abstract of the United States: 1977* (98th ed.). Washington, DC: Government Printing Office.

U.S. Commission on Civil Rights. 1976. *Puerto Ricans in the Continental United States: An Uncertain Future*. Washington, DC: Government Printing Office.

U.S. Immigration and Naturalization Service. 2002. *Statistical Yearbook of the Immigration and Naturalization Service, 2001*. Washington, DC: Government Printing Office.

_____. 2000. *Statistical Yearbook of the Immigration and Naturalization Service, 1998*. Washington, DC: Government Printing Office.

_____. 1997. *Statistical Yearbook of the Immigration and Naturalization Service, 1995*. Washington, DC: Government Printing Office.

_____. 1993. *Statistical Yearbook of the Immigration and Naturalization Service, 1992*. Washington, DC: Government Printing Office.

_____. 1992. *Statistical Yearbook of the Immigration and Naturalization Service, 1991*. Washington, DC: Government Printing Office.

Valentine, Sean, & Mosley, Gordon. 2000. "Acculturation and Sex-Role Attitudes Among Mexican Americans: A Longitudinal Analysis." *Hispanic Journal of Behavioral Sciences*, 22:104–204.

van den Berghe, Pierre L. 1967. *Race and Racism: A Comparative Perspective*. New York: Wiley.

Vigilant, Linda. 1997. "Race and Biology." In Winston Van Horne (Ed.), *Global Convulsions: Race, Ethnicity, and Nationalism at the End of the Twentieth Century* (pp. 49–62). Albany: State University of New York Press.

Vincent, Theodore G. 1976. *Black Power and the Garvey Movement*. San Francisco: Ramparts.

Vinje, David. 1996. "Native American Economic Development on Selected Reservations: A Comparative Analysis." *American Journal of Economics and Sociology*, 55:427–442.

Voting Rights Act, 42 U.S.C. § 1971 (1965)

Wagley, Charles, & Harris, Marvin. 1958. *Minorities in the New World: Six Case Studies*. New York: Columbia University Press.

Wallace, Walter. 1997. *The Future of Ethnicity, Race, and Nationality*. Westport, CT: Praeger.

Washington, Booker T. 1965. *Up from Slavery*. New York: Dell.

Waters, Mary. 1990. *Ethnic Options*. Berkeley: University of California Press.

Wax, Murray. 1971. *Indian Americans: Unity and Diversity*. Englewood Cliffs, NJ: Prentice Hall.

Weeks, Philip. 1988. *The American Indian Experience*. Arlington Heights, IL: Forum Press.

Wertheimer, Barbara M. 1979. "'Union Is Power': Sketches From Women's Labor History." In Jo Freeman (Ed.), *Women: A Feminist Perspective* (pp. 339–358). Palo Alto, CA: Mayfield.

Whitaker, M. 1995. "Whites v. Blacks." *Newsweek,* October 16, pp. 28–35.

White, Deborah Gray. 1985. *Ar'n't I a Woman? Female Slaves in the Plantation South.* New York: Norton.

White, Jack. 2000. "The Real Winners: Black Voters." *Time,* November 27, p. 60.

Whiting, Robert. 1990. *You Gotta Have Wa.* New York: Macmillan.

Wickham, DeWayne. 2000. "Gore Topped Bush in Appeal to Broader Segment of Americans." *USA Today,* November 27, 2000. Retrieved from the World Wide Web on April 8, 2003, at www.usatoday.com/news/opinion/columnists/wickham/wick165.htm.

Wilkens, Roger. 1992. "L.A.: Images in the Flames—Looking Back in Anger: 27 Years After Watts, Our Nation Remains Divided by Racism." *Washington Post,* May 3, C1.

Williams, Juan. 1987. *Eyes on the Prize: America's Civil Rights Years, 1954–1965.* New York: Penguin.

Willie, Charles (Ed.). 1989. *Round Two of the Willie/Wilson Debate* (2nd ed.). Dix Hills, NY: General Hall.

Wilson, William J. 1996. *When Work Disappears.* New York: Knopf.

———. 1987. *The Truly Disadvantaged: The Inner City, the Underclass, and Public Policy.* Chicago: University of Chicago Press.

———. 1980. *The Declining Significance of Race* (2nd ed.). Chicago: University of Chicago Press.

———. 1978. *The Declining Significance of Race* (1st ed.). Chicago: University of Chicago Press.

———. 1973. *Power, Racism, and Privilege: Race Relations in Theoretical and Sociohistorical Perspectives.* New York: Free Press.

Wilson, William J. (Ed.). 1992. *The Ghetto Underclass.* Newbury Park, CA: Sage.

Wirth, Louis. 1945. "The Problem of Minority Groups." In Ralph Linton (Ed.), *The Science of Man in the World* (pp. 347–372). New York: Columbia University Press.

Wolfenstein, Eugene V. 1993. *The Victims of Democracy: Malcolm X.* New York: Guilford.

Women's International Network. 1998. "Philippines: Women Bearing the Cross of Globalization." *WIN News,* 24:62–64.

Wong, Morrison. 1995. "Chinese Americans." In Pyong Gap Min (Ed.), *Asian Americans: Contemporary Trends and Issues* (pp. 58–94). Thousand Oaks, CA: Sage.

Woodrum, Eric. 1979. "Japanese Americans: A Test of the Assimilation Success Story." Paper presented at the Annual Meeting of the Southern Sociological Society, April, Atlanta, GA.

Woodward, C. Vann. 1974. *The Strange Career of Jim Crow* (3rd rev. ed.). New York: Oxford University Press.

Worsnop, Richard. 1992. "Native Americans." *CQ Researcher,* May 8, pp. 387–407.

Wyman, Mark. 1993. *Round Trip to America.* Ithaca, NY: Cornell University Press.

Yamato, Alexander. 1994. "Racial Antagonism and the Formation of Segmented Labor Markets: Japanese Americans and Their Exclusion from the Work Force." *Humboldt Journal of Social Relations,* 20:31–63.

Yinger, J. Milton. 1985. "Ethnicity." *Annual Review of Sociology,* 11:151–180.

Zhou, Min. 1992. *Chinatown.* Philadelphia: Temple University Press.

Zhou, Min, & Bankston, Carl. 1998. *Growing Up American: How Vietnamese Children Adapt to Life in the United States.* New York: Russell Sage.

Zhou, Min, & Logan, John R. 1989. "Returns on Human Capital in Ethnic Enclaves: New York City's Chinatown." *American Sociological Review,* 54:809–820.

Zinn, Maxine Baca, & Dill, Bonnie Thornton. (Eds.). 1994. *Women of Color in U.S. Society.* Philadelphia: Temple University Press.

Zinn, Maxine Baca, & Eitzen, D. Stanley. 1990. *Diversity in Families.* New York: Harper Collins.

Index